REFLECTING BLACK

MAR 1996

AMERICAN CULTURE

Cutting across traditional boundaries between the human and social sciences, volumes in the American Culture series study the multiplicity of cultural practices from theoretical, historical, and ethnographic perspectives by examining culture's production, circulation, and consumption.

Edited by Stanley Aronowitz, Nancy Fraser, and George Lipsitz

9. Michael Eric Dyson, *Reflecting Black: African-American Cultural Criticism*
8. Paul Smith, *Clint Eastwood: A Cultural Production*
7. Maria Damon, *The Dark End of the Street: Margins in American Vanguard Poetry*
6. Virginia Carmichael, *Framing History: The Rosenberg Story and the Cold War*
5. Elayne Rapping, *The Movie of the Week: Private Stories/ Public Events*
4. George Lipsitz, *Time Passages: Collective Memory and American Popular Culture*
3. Alice Echols, *Daring to Be Bad: Radical Feminism in America, 1965–1975*
2. Nancy Walker, *A Very Serious Thing: Women's Humor and American Culture*
1. Henry Giroux, *Schooling and the Struggle for Private Life*

AMERICAN CULTURE · VOLUME NINE

MICHAEL ERIC DYSON

REFLECTING B·L·A·C·K

AFRICAN-AMERICAN CULTURAL CRITICISM

UNIVERSITY OF MINNESOTA PRESS
MINNEAPOLIS
LONDON

305.786
D

Copyright 1993 by the Regents of the University of Minnesota

For copyright information see pages 345–46.

All rights reserved. No part of this publication may be reproduced, stored in a retrieval system, or transmitted, in any form or by any means, electronic, mechanical, photocopying, recording, or otherwise, without the prior written permission of the publisher.

Published by the University of Minnesota Press
2037 University Avenue Southeast, Minneapolis, MN 55455-3092
Printed in the United States of America on acid-free paper

Third printing, 1994

Library of Congress Cataloging-in-Publication Data

Dyson, Michael Eric.
Reflecting Black / African-American cultural criticism / Michael Eric Dyson.
p. cm. — (American culture : 9)
Includes bibliographical references and index.
ISBN 0-8166-2141-1 (hc. : acid-free)
ISBN 0-8166-2143-8 (pb. : acid-free)
1. Afro-Americans—Intellectual life. 2. Afro-American arts.
3. Afro-Americans—Social conditions—1975- 4. United States—Popular culture. 5. United States—Race relations. I. Title. II. Series: American culture (Minneapolis, Minn.) ; 9.
E185.86.D95 1993
973′.0496073—dc20 92-47395
CIP

The University of Minnesota is an
equal-opportunity educator and employer.

To my parents
Everett Dyson, Sr. (1915–81), and Addie Dyson
Bearers of many talents

To Dr. Frederick George Sampson, Jr.
Pastor of Tabernacle Missionary Baptist Church, Detroit
Pastor, mentor, and father

To my wife, Marcia Louise Dyson
Companion, counselor, and friend

Contents

Part II

Beyond the Mantra: Reflections on Race, Gender, and Class

Part III

This Far by Faith: Black Religion

Acknowledgments

I would like first to thank series editors Stanley Aronowitz, George Lipsitz, and Nancy Fraser (who conceived this collection and brought it to the attention of the University of Minnesota Press; thanks very much, Nancy!) for their support and belief in my work.

I also want to thank the people at the University of Minnesota Press who have been instrumental in the production of this book, especially Biodun Iginla, who gave expert help in realizing the book; Kerry Sarnoski, who gave untiring attention to all the details; Anne Running, who gave critical editorial help; and Mary Byers, Lorrie Oswald, and the rest of the production department. My thanks in advance as well to the entire support staff of the press who market and publicize the book.

The following persons have contributed to my life or thought in some way that bears significantly on this book. I express my profound gratitude to them all: Mrs. James, my fifth-grade teacher from Wingert Elementary School, Detroit, who boldly and unceasingly taught us all the importance of knowledge of and pride in our heritage; Mr. Otis Burdette, my seventh-grade English teacher at Webber Junior High School, Detroit, who early discerned and encouraged my oratorical ability and who, along with the Detroit Optimist Club, helped me greatly; the late Mrs. Bennett, my next-door neighbor, whose gift to me as a young teen of her late husband's Harvard Classics opened a vast world of learning; Dr. Frederick Sampson (and Freda and Frederick III), and the people at Tab, thanks for the love, support, and inspiration; the late Ms. Mary Stewart, my English professor at Knoxville College, whose brilliant mind and tough demands made me a better writer; my friends William and Ruth Booth, and the Mt. Zion Baptist Church of Knoxville, Tennessee, who believed in me and gave me an opportunity to preach and minister; Brenda Joyce Dyson, whose untiring devotion to this work through blood, sweat, and tears made its appearance possible; Charles Johnson and Greg Helton, two precious friends whose commitment has proved that the bonds of friendship transcend race; Khary, Maya, and Ruth J. Simmons, whose brilliance, friendship, loyalty, and love have sustained me in hard times; Barrie and Dominique Royce, whose friendship only grows stronger with the years; Robert Bright and Joanne Mitchell, two beautiful oaks who stand strong and weather well, thanks for your love and encouragement; Shanti Singham and Daniel Goodwin, thanks for the wonderful support and sharp criticism throughout the years; Derrick and Sheila Scott, my inventive and supportive friends, thanks for your inspiration, support, love, and, most of all, "two tickets"; Louis and Barbara Williams, whose affection, love, and support are a precious jewel, thanks for all your kind words; Kenneth and Gladys Smith, friends whose wisdom, insight, and compassion are rarely met, thank you for believing in and standing with me; my wonderful children Mwata and Maisha Dyson, your future is bright and unlimited, embrace it with zeal and freedom; and my inimitable son, Michael Eric Dyson II, my love for you is boundless, my hope for your great future is unperishable, my pride in you unmatched.

And for Marcia Louise Dyson, to whom this book is dedicated, I have gratitude beyond words for what your love and life have meant to me—they have been balm to my mind and heart. Your sacrifices on behalf of everything these essays symbolize have been exceedingly great, and this book is a small offering of thanks for your patience, love, and support.

Introduction

Beyond Essentialism: Expanding African-American Cultural Criticism

Contemporary African-American culture is radically complex and diverse, marked by an intriguing variety of intellectual reflections, artistic creations, and social practices. Its vibrant diversity cautions against portraying the constitutive experiences of African-American culture in monolithic terms. And yet, there exists an unfailing precedent to cast black culture in a distorted light and to view it through the prisms of racist stereotype or racial essentialism. The former is the attempt to apply inferior science to undisciplined social observation, fueled by the effort to foist overdrawn generalizations about individual character onto entire racial groups. The latter often occurs as black intellectuals oppose the strangling of black culture by caricature, offering instead cultural standards to help define racial authenticity.

Ironically, the crude half-light that escapes through stereotype and the well-meaning but illusory absolutes generated by essentialism share similar traits: both ignore black culture's relentless evolutions and metamorphoses. Any substantial investigation of the protean meanings of African-American culture must take these factors into account.

Of course, any book that seeks to contribute to African-American cultural criticism must reckon decisively with the vulgar effects associated with a certain species of criticism long dishonored in black communities. Although critical consciousness has traced the resilient circumference of black culture, deep suspicions about criticism's worth and function roil incessantly beneath the cultural surface. This is a direct consequence of the thinly veiled malevolence that characterized much of what passed for criticism of black culture from outside its precincts early on in our national history.

Most early criticism of black culture was vicious and unjust, reflecting the self-validating sciolism of cultural imperials whose prejudice clouded their reason. Most white public figures and men of letters habitually castigated black culture, viewing blacks as ugly and savage. And when conveniently vexed by pangs of charitable guilt, white intellectuals believed blacks to be captives of racial infantilism. In many early forms, then, criticism of black culture was indistinguishable from racist assumptions about black intelligence, beauty, and humanity that are deeply premised in American life. In this light, black skepticism about criticism, itself involving an implicit critical judgment, is understandable and even healthy.

A damaging consequence of racist judgments about black culture being passed off as "objective" cultural criticism is their success in portraying black culture as inferior to white society. In the wake of such claims, black cultural creativity often acquired a protective ideological function, shielding African-American culture from the lambasting of its detractors. Phillis Wheatley's poetry, Alexander Crummell's lectures, Frederick Douglass's orations, and Ida B. Wells's journalism were never *merely* artistic creations of sharp and resourceful intelligences. Rather, they provided models of cultural excellence in an ethos of white disbelief in black humanity, and in other instances, they served to thaw the frozen regions of white indifference to black life.

African-American cultural expression often served propagandistic and practical intellectual ends as well, demonstrating the political dimensions of cultural expression. Black cultural expression continually reinforced the idea that culture must be understood within the environment of its material production and in relation to forces like political change, economic evolution, and religious transformation. African-American culture has taken shape in the defining interplay of historical contingency and the pursuit of a humane racial identity that have been the heart of black culture's growth.

Unfortunately, the ideological function that attached to black cultural expression fed off of the energies of an evolutionary cultural trait that long ago exhausted its founding logic and many of its redemptive uses: the demand of racial unity. Conceived in the mid-nineteenth century as manumitted and fugitive slaves acquired literacy and public voice, racial unity was a socially useful way of speaking about the need of consolidated cultural resources to offset slavery's divisive effects on black culture. To this day, the narrative of racial unity has survived mainly as a rhetorical strategy of black intellectuals, artists, and leaders to impose provisional order on the perplexing and chaotic politics of racial identity.

Strands of that narrative have usefully recounted how tactics of white racial tyranny, employed by slave masters and political demagogues alike, undermined black racial solidarity and molded the unavoidable dependence of blacks on the diffuse forms of white culture. Still other fragments of the racial unity narrative recount how unity was complicated by diversities in tongue among slaves in the earliest stages of slavery, and was made still more difficult by the differences in culture, region, and nation these linguistic dissimilarities embodied. Eventually, however, the commonalities of black racial experience, which were fashioned under the rigorous and, in some instances, almost immediate decline of African identity in slavery, precipitated the emergence of a distinct racial identity in American culture. The dynamics of this burgeoning racial identity prompted many blacks to lament a lack of intraracial regard, intimacy, and cooperation, qualities that are prized and encouraged within the symbolic universe of racial unity.

The quest for racial unity has largely represented the desperate effort to replace a cultural uprooting that should never have occurred with a racial unanimity that actually never existed. While clan, community, and nation were central to African societies, only a cultural catastrophe the magnitude of chattel slavery could impose upon blacks an artificial and single racial identity. Blacks responded by asserting their racial identity in defense of their humanity and against the claims of worthlessness advanced by racist intellectuals. Once on American soil, the intricate interactions and forced symbiosis of African and American cultures produced a hybrid worldview whose cultural and social dimensions continue to be vividly explored.

Under the rhetoric of racial unity, the undeniable commonalities of racial experience have been recast in mythic and homogeneous terms, a project fueled by the utopic and romanticizing visions of race most notably espoused by black nationalists. But the difficulties of racial unity—the weight of its narrow understanding of racial cooperation and its ignoble infelicities in defining "in" and "out," "friend" and "enemy," and "us" and "them"—were overlooked in the desperate search for an enabling explanation of the evils of racial extirpation and debasement. It was not long, though, before the lacerating contradictions of racial history and memory undercut the overarching impulses of racial unity, making it increasingly apparent that homogeneous racial images are an untenable source of African-American identity.

The peculiar complexions of racial identity, which inherit their distinctive hues from the specific and cumulative conditions of black life from plantation to suburb, mean that black folk do have a history and memory in common. The incalculable grief and titanic inhumanities of chattel slavery; the unsayable trauma brought on by the erosion of embryonic liberties after Reconstruction; the sometimes acoustic, sometimes muted pain borne in response to the chafing indignities imposed by Jim Crow law; the stunning affirmation of race and culture that accompanied the transformation of social relations in the civil rights movement; and the inviolable courage and unshakable hope that ripple from religious faith all form, in part, the content of common racial history and memory from which black culture is fashioned.

But black culture is not static or one-dimensional. Neither is it drawn forward by a single historical end. While historical memory permits the identification of characteristics of black culture that make it singular and unto itself, historical experience—which is generated and shaped by cultural renewal and decay, and the ongoing encounter by black culture with new social and cultural forces that impact its future—provides a basis to resist essentialist modes of expression. An essence is an immutable, history-transcending characteristic of, for instance, art objects, religions, and cultures. It does not reflect the historical, social, and cultural forces that produce black culture and that continue to inflect the tenor of contemporary black cultural practices from painting to basketball. While one may cherish black cultural norms, values, and ideals—or even wish to protect them from rejection, irrelevance, or extinction—such desires must not be realized through appeals to an unvarying racial or cultural essence that remains unaffected by vicissitude or chance.

Hence, the desire to promote love, friendship, and mutual cooperation among black folk is a laudable cultural goal, especially in light of the vicious and paralyzing forms of self-hatred and mutual contempt that have riddled black culture from its fragile origins in slavery through present postindustrial urban conditions. One might even describe such an aspiration as the quest for an enabling solidarity. And how is an enabling solidarity to be distinguished from most varieties of black unity? It will only appeal to the richly varied meanings of cultural practices, the diversity of authentic roles one may express within the repertoire of black cultural identities, and the ever-expanding context of historical experience in supporting its vision of racial cooperation.

An enabling solidarity should not appeal to truncated understandings of authentic racial identity or place an ideological noose of loyalty around the necks of critical dissenters from received ideas about racial unity. The proponents of racial unity have often operated on the assumption that black people have one overriding vision, purpose, and destiny. While it is true that our common history of slavery and racial oppression signifies a common goal of freedom from oppression for black people, broadened horizons of racial experience and more sophisticated conceptions of racial identity make the articulation of a single, unitary racial goal highly problematic.

Black culture is not simply formed in the response to forces of oppression. Its purposes do not easily reduce to resisting racism. Although black cultural creativity and agency are profoundly influenced by racist oppression, their rich range of expressions are not exhausted by preoccupation with such oppression. And even when due consideration is paid to the oppressive forces that constrain black life, we must transcend the gaze of race and look to a more ecumenical constellation of forces—age, gender, and class among them—that crisscross the landscape of cultural identity and that affect the shape of life and the racial destinies of black

Americans. Most versions of racial unity have failed to engage these issues in liberating or illuminating fashion.

Complicating matters more, the rhetorics of race loyalty and racial authenticity are almost naturally clustered around the rhetoric of racial unity. Taken together, these rhetorics compose the moral center of a politics of racial propriety, used by some black intellectuals to determine what is legitimate and acceptable for a widening body of black cultural expression. Loyalty to race has been historically construed as primary and unquestioning allegiance to the racial quest for freedom and the refusal to betray that quest to personal benefit or the diverting pursuit of lesser goals. Those who detour from the prescribed path are labeled "sell-outs," "traitors," or "Uncle Toms."

At various times in African-American history, race loyalty has meant refusing to reveal slave plans to revolt or escape; empathy for emigrationist movements back to Africa in the Conventionist Era; support for various strategies of mass civil disobedience and other tactics of racial rebellion and protest developed during the civil rights and Black Power movements; holding radical class-based interrogations of racial politics at arm's length; repudiating neoconservative criticism of black culture, especially attacks on black liberal or nationalist race ideology; refraining from public criticism of black leaders, especially elected officials; and chastising black women writers for "betraying" black men with "negative" literary portraits.

The rhetoric of racial authenticity has been employed to reveal the ostensibly authentic bases of black intellectual and artistic expression. Those who deviate from familiar forms of racial identity and cultural expression are termed "oreos" or "incognegroes." Debates about racial authenticity have questioned whether black cultural icons like Michael Jackson and Whitney Houston have rejected enabling expressions of blackness in their art; whether black politicians like Douglas Wilder, David Dinkins, and Wilson Goode have abandoned the goals of historic black politics in their bid for the political mainstream; whether a black literary critical theory should enlarge upon a black aesthetic that is grounded in a black or Afrocentric worldview or traffic in avant-garde theories rife with French prefixes and German suffixes.

It is in the crossfire between unprincipled assaults upon black culture's raison d'être from outside its ranks, the debilitating decline in intellectual acuity in American culture at large, and the romantic and myth-producing impulses of African-American culture that black critical consciousness has been fatefully caught. Because black critical consciousness has been unable to find its best voice at the center of black culture, it has found fruitful exile on black culture's creative margins, inspiring varying degrees of support within academic and literary circles, ecclesiastical organizations, and vernacular cultural traditions.

But the peripheral position of criticism means that it is often expressed in disenabling forms as well. The deflection of the critical impulse into destructive expressions is poignantly symbolized in the legendary crab-barrel metaphor of intraracial strife. This familiar black cultural metaphor compares the plight of African-Americans to crabs in a barrel that, instead of pooling their resources to help free each other, prevent the successful escape of any member through the self-defeating activity of mutual clawing. More specifically the comparison captures the untamed envy on the part of some blacks for another black's social mobility, economic well-being, or educational accomplishment, assuming the form of hostile hints of personal defect or outright character assassination. A deflected critical reaction is transparent as well in the elliptic criticism that is expressed in signifying speech and in the often humorous but sometimes lethal linguistic put-down of the "dozens."

Aside from criticism's disenabling expressions, veiled criticism is also employed by persons who suffer exclusion from official authority or by those who fear that explicit criticism is likely to incur penalty or scorn. Such concealed criticism is manifest, for example, in church gossip that slows or interrupts the harmful effects that antidemocratic leadership may have on ecclesiastical life. This variety of criticism is especially directed at pastors who view even gentle criticism as disloyalty or at boards of deacons or trustees who view the legitimation of any voice other than their own as institutional treason.

The cultural realities I have discussed reinforce the need of a mature and oppositional criticism of black culture. Such criticism revels in black culture's virtues, takes pleasure in its achievements, laments its failed opportunities, and interrogates its weaknesses. An oppositional African-American cultural criticism is engaged in resisting the labored seductions of all narrow views of black life, whether they be racist, essentialist, or otherwise uncritically disposed toward African-American culture.

Moreover, an oppositional African-American cultural criticism is open in its search for truth about black culture wherever it may be found. It views black folk not merely as victims of history, but in limited manner as agents of their own jubilation and pain and as creators of worlds of meaning through art, thought, and sport that fend off the prospects of personal and social absurdity. An oppositional African-American cultural criticism roots critical reflection in a racial maturity that acknowledges the differentiation of black life. The expansion of criticism upon the basis of such racial maturity appeals to criticism's best history and works toward the most progressive possibilities for its richest future. Three principles guide my understanding of an oppositional African-American cultural criticism.

Such a criticism must be antiessentialist about black racial and cultural identity. Racial essences have been promoted through literary critical theories that attempt to mine the conceptual riches of blackness as sign and symbol; through philosophical arguments intent on rebutting the denial of humanity to Africans and African-Americans by tracing racial identity to a unitary cultural source in Africa; through everyday criticism of crossover music; and through black films that aspire to an archetypal representation of black life.

An oppositional African-American cultural criticism holds that identity is socially and culturally constructed from the raw materials of the individual and social, the private and public, and the domestic and civic. Racial identity is not exhausted by genetic inheritance. The processes by which the meanings of race are shattered and reconstituted over time and place in American culture convincingly make the case against a narrow understanding of racial identity.

Although it is undeniably rooted in pigment and physiology, racial identity transcends their boundaries. It is created and remade in a network of conflicting and converging social relations, political options, civil limits, gender politics, economic crises, religious narratives, and moral choices. Given the variety of elements and the complexity of means by which racial identity is constructed, there can be no essential black identity, because racial identity is relentlessly reshaped. Also, the intellectual, empirical, and material strata of black culture—from which racial identity can be usefully excavated—challenge the politics of essentialism. The differences that geography, sexual preference, gender, and class position generate within black culture cannot be captured by essentialist thought.

Of course, I don't mean that there are not distinct black cultural characteristics that persist over space and time, but these features of black life are the products of the historical and social construction of racial identity. For instance, we may point to patterns of verbal and artistic invention, identified as call and response, that are threaded through various dimensions of black culture. Evidences of call and response can be glimpsed in the rhetorical improvisations of ministers in the black pulpit. Black preachers refine their craft in sacred settings where their verbal performances are shaped by a responsive audience that employs either ecstatic vocal support or silent rejection of the preacher's declared truth. Call and response may also be viewed in concerts where vocal artists' performances evoke affirmative applause or signs of disruptive disapproval, responsive elements that are often creatively woven into the fabric of the live and electric performed moment.

But call and response and countless other characteristics of black life, as well, are socially created, culturally improvised, and historically transmitted. These distinct features of black life nuance and shape black cultural expression, from the preaching of Martin Luther King to the singing of Gladys Knight. They do not, however, form the basis of a black racial or cultural essence. Nor do they indicate that *the* meaning of blackness will be expressed in a quality or characteristic without which a person, act, or practice no longer qualifies as black. Rigid racial essentialism must be opposed.

Oppositional African-American cultural criticism must also acknowledge the broad range of American experiences that influence its makeup, shape its expression, and challenge its existence. Although it must always keep track of the effects of racism, an oppositional criticism also describes how class and gender affect African-American culture, while creating strategies to reveal their importance as categories of social theory, criticism, and struggle. For instance, as intellectuals have charted the gargantuan forces that circumscribe African-American life, class politics have been largely ignored. Of course, exceptions prevail. Du Bois, Robeson, and Cox, among others, argued for the prominence of class politics in an earlier day, while Fields, Marable, West, and Wilson have made more contemporary claims. Class politics and conflicts constitute a crucial ideological juncture in African-American intellectual history, proving that a methodological loyalty to race-*only* analysis—versus a race-*specific* analysis—fails to fully illumine our current cultural crises.

Given the renaissance of black nationalist discourse, and a concomitant revival of explicit race hatred on college campuses and in ethnic communities across America, the difficulty of pushing past narrow understandings of our condition becomes more complicated but no less urgent. Class differentiation complicates simple and reductive cultural versions of unified racial action. Many significant differences between blacks follow the axis of class and are shaped by its unyielding persistence. Although, for example, Bill Cosby's and a black shoeshiner's lives are intertwined by race, their perceptions of the world are also bounded by differences of class location and economic stability.

Gender, too, has been similarly neglected as a useful category for organizing social resistance or for comprehending vital aspects of black culture. The presumed primacy of eliminating racism as a black cultural goal—a crucial ideological pillar in both integrationist and nationalist racial politics—has obscured the distinctive voices of black women who suffer the cruel jeopardies of multiple oppression and who have had to skillfully criticize the constitutive elements of black feminist identities. Sojourner Truth, Ida Wells Barnett, Harriet Tubman, Harriet Jacobs, Anna Cooper, Alice Walker, Michele Wallace, Audre Lorde, and bell hooks have mapped the enormously difficult route to full voice for black women. Gender figures prominently in a healthy African-American cultural criticism that in the past has mostly failed to oppose an ironic black patriarchy, on the one hand a faded reflection of white patriarchy in regard to black men wielding institutional power, and on the other hand a faithful imitation of white patriarchy's worst effects, felt most severely in domestic violence by black men aimed at women and children.

An oppositional African-American cultural criticism is also public and receptive to the best critical insights available from all responsible and reasonable quarters. It does not observe a tedious etiquette of racial manners that maintains that negative, controversial, or critical news about black folk, especially if its source is other blacks, must be handled in secrecy away from the omniscient gaze of white society. We may term this protective response to the harmful white surveillance of black culture the "dirty-laundry theory" of racial politics.

Of course, it made sense for slaves to handle their business in their own domain, not exposing their differences to the threat of exploitation by white masters. But even in slavery, the conditions for successful privacy—an intimate geographical environment where information flow could be controlled, with all relevant parties having access to conversation in a relatively democratic space—were barely available. Moreover, slaves held conflicting views on how best to cope with their condition: some wanted to revolt (Turner, Vesey); some advocated escape (Tubman); some preferred subtler forms of subversion (hymns, spirituals); some believed remaining under white rule was a greener pasture than the wilderness of black escape (so-called "Toms"); and many advocated enduring slavery while rebelling in small but significant symbolic rituals of resistance (for example, mixing in unsavory elements during food preparation).

Under contemporary conditions of African-American diaspora, migration, dispersion, exile, and differentiation, attempting to emulate such racial privacy and secrecy is clearly detrimental. When it is secret and closed, cultural criticism threatens to become elitist and antidemocratic. Making criticism public encourages the widest possible participation of a diverse audience of potential interlocutors. The dirty-laundry theory of racial politics has recently surfaced at three cultural sites: the controversy surrounding Spike Lee's production of his second film *School Daze,* the political controversy occasioned by former Washington mayor Marion Barry's drug case, and the tragic racial fiasco involving New York's Tawana Brawley.

Spike Lee's *School Daze,* a morality play about black intraracial conflict, was roundly criticized in many quarters as a harsh and punitive peek into ugly black racial identity politics; such gestures, many believed, were better left to the black pulpit, beauty salon, or classroom. Lee's film, a minor succès de scandale, was staged during a homecoming weekend celebration at a historically black college, and revealed the lethal confrontations black folk have over hair texture, skin complexion, class status, and educational attainment. During the course of filming, Lee was forced off the campus of his alma mater, Morehouse College. The move was allegedly due to crossed signals regarding the availability of dorm space for filming, but a more likely explanation may be retaliation by Morehouse's administration against Lee's critical look at the rituals of black self-hate dramatized in full color and sketched on a film canvas that the entire public was invited to view. Such narrowness of racial vision, as embodied in Morehouse's response, and the racial insecurity that feeds it, must be addressed and opposed.

The alleged rape of Tawana Brawley by a gang of white men illustrated the pernicious consequences of the dirty-laundry theory of racial politics. After it became likely that Brawley was ominously entangled in a web of deceit, most segments of the black (leadership) community were largely unable to offer public criticism of Brawley or her handlers, Alton Maddox, C. Vernon Mason, and Al Sharpton. Most tragically, the likely reason for Brawley's desperate public disregard for truth—the fear of domestic violence by her mother's male companion as reprisal for Tawana's disobedience—was obscured in the scattered and weak black public criticism of the Brawley case. The confused black response contributed once again to the silencing of the black female voice about a significant source of its repression and helped divert attention from the sometimes brutal consequences of the sexism and patriarchy that are deeply entrenched in black culture.

The case of Barry is more complex, but nonetheless exemplary. Barry was videotaped smoking crack cocaine, and answered for his behavior in a highly publicized criminal trial. Remarkably, with few exceptions, there was little black public criticism of Barry's behavior or of his flagrant abuse of his black supporters' stringent and sometimes colorful loyalty. Of course, this silence was achieved in part because of the wide black cultural perception of the general attack on prominent black political leadership by federal, state, and local government officials.

Unfailingly, many black leaders are denigrated for alleged political, moral, or legal indiscretions, a pattern of attack that began in recent times with the varied personal and political troubles of Adam Clayton Powell. Thus, Barry became the highly charged symbol of black political power under assault, which exacerbated the public resentment of black citizens across America. Interestingly, there was not a commensurate public criticism of Barry motivated by the evidence of his political decline prior to his public downfall. Undoubtedly, many believed that silence about Barry's foibles was the most eloquent emblem of racial solidarity. But given the corruption of contemporary American politics and the political hustling from which black political leadership is not exempt, such forces must be energetically opposed.

In broad compass, an oppositional African-American cultural criticism is concerned to examine the redemptive and unattractive features of African American culture, to pass fair but critical judgment on a variety of cultural expressions and historic figures, from popular music to preaching, from black nationalist politics to the political economy of crack, from Jesse Jackson to Michael Jordan. It promotes the preservation of black culture's best features, the amelioration of its weakest parts, and the eradication of its worst traits.

Before I explain the makeup of this book, perhaps a brief note of autobiography might help clarify how I have come to where I am. I was born in 1958, the second oldest of five sons (in an extended family that also included four step-siblings), in Detroit, a city of remarkable cultural vitality, especially with the dynamic musical presence of Motown Records. Detroit was also at that time a city of immense industrial prowess, fueled by the booming automobile industry whose mammoth factories dotted the city's landscape. The automobile industry served as a faithful barometer of the economic health of the city; as its fate went, so went Detroit's. My father labored in a wheelbrake and drum factory for thirty-three years, and later worked as a drugstore and church maintenance man before his death in 1981. My parents raised five boys in Detroit's inner city, no mean task, with my mother working as a paraprofessional for the Detroit Board of Education from the time of my early youth.

At eight, I witnessed the 1967 riot in Detroit. I vividly recall the ominous, dirty clouds that hovered over our troubled city and the gleeful looters who reigned over this bizarre carnival of urban decay, much as the participants in L.A.'s rebellion did after the Rodney King verdict. I also felt the reprimand and fear of the word that regulated our lives during that painful period and that signified the sharp division of safe and unsafe social time: curfew. At nine, the death of Martin Luther King was one of the most traumatic but also most meaningful events to occur in my young life. In a sense, it heralded the end of my youthful innocence, an end that was fatefully foreshadowed in the rioting of the previous summer. For months, I was afraid to stand in front of a window or door at night, thinking someone would assassinate me: if it had happened to Martin Luther King, who neither intended nor inflicted harm on anyone, then it could happen to me.

King's death was my initial plunge into the tortuous meanings of racial politics, and I began to believe that the world was largely predicated upon color, its vain and violent ubiquity becoming increasingly apparent to my newly opened eyes. For me, King became the most resonant metaphor for the persistent conundrum of racial hatred, but he also served as a startlingly resilient symbol of the possibility of achieving meaningful life beyond the ruinous reach of racism.

When he was assassinated, however, I had never heard of King, and when the television newsman announced that he had been shot the evening of April 4, 1968, I fretfully beseeched my mother to point him out during a brief film clip. As I listened to his last speech, I was immediately converted beyond the realm of will into a passionate identification with this soldier of love. Because of his example, and the example of Dr. Frederick Sampson, who would later pastor our church, I wanted to be able to move crowds with the stirring oratory and powerful words he artfully deployed in portraying his vision for America.

From the age of twelve, I worked with my father, who supplemented his factory job by hauling sod, plants, and dirt for Morton's Nursery. After my father was laid off from the factory after thirty-three years of service, he started "Dyson and Sons Grass-cutting and Sodding," our name neatly painted across our family station wagon, which doubled as our work vehicle. Every day after school during the spring and summer months, we laid sod for customers throughout the Detroit area. We also ferreted through countless Detroit alleys in search of discarded iron and steel that fetched a modest return from the junkyard's cashier.

At sixteen, I won a scholarship to the prestigious boarding school, Cranbrook, in Bloomfield Hills, Michigan, only thirty miles down Woodward Avenue, which divides Detroit into East and West. That short distance had divided me from a world I had never known as a poor black inner-city youth: white wealth, power, and privilege. I had never gone to school with white kids before, much less wealthy white kids, many the sons and daughters of famous parents, a banking magnate here, a film giant there. I immediately experienced a Hitchcockian vertigo about the place, its seductive grandeur, warming grace, and old world elegance not enough to conceal the absurdity of racism that lurked beneath its breathtaking exterior. I left Cranbrook near the end of my second year, returning to Detroit and obtaining my diploma in night school, and taking a succession of jobs in the fast-food industry, in maintenance work, and in construction. I finally became an employee at my father's alma mater, the Kelsey-Hayes Wheelbrake and Drum company, becoming an arc-welder and later unloading trains brimming with brake drums. I was married in 1977 and became the father of a son, Michael, in 1978.

In 1979, I headed south to Knoxville, Tennessee, to attend Knoxville College, a historically black college, pastoring three churches along the way. When I transferred to Carson-Newman College, a small Southern Baptist school, it was to gain greater exposure to my declared field of study, philosophy. While attending Carson-Newman and receiving a good education in the history of philosophy and the philosophy of religion, I worked at Robertshaw Factory as a cleaner and degreaser of heavy machinery on the 3:00-to-11:00-P.M. shift. I never received a penny of scholarship money from Carson-Newman, a predominantly white college, despite graduating magna cum laude and receiving an award as the Outstanding Graduate in Philosophy.

It was at Carson-Newman College that I met my first philosophy teacher, Don Olive, who had written a good book on the German religious philosopher Pannenberg and who possessed a clean grasp of analytic moral and religious philosophy. It was at Carson-Newman that I began to indulge my intellectual curiosity in a variety of academic disciplines, including religious studies, contemporary literary and critical theory, and contemporary history and political theory. I also began looking beyond the pale of Kant, Austin, Alston, and Frankena to read Sartre, Pascal, and Du Bois again, and to read Hegel, Schleiermacher, Heidegger, Wittgenstein, Dewey, Ricoeur, Marcel, and a whole host of Continental and American philosophers. I also read in the history of African-American intellectual traditions, including Douglass, Washington, Johnson, Barnett, Hurston, Baldwin, Ellison, Blassingame, Gates, Morrison, Wilson, hooks, and Wallace, among many others.

It was during this period that I also met James Washington and Cornel West, both professors at Union Theological Seminary in New York, who encouraged me to maintain my strong interest in the life of the mind. My further education in religious history was benefited by Washington's enormous erudition, and my expansive explorations within contemporary philosophy were inspired by West's brilliant conversations, lectures, and writings. It was because of him that I began to read his mentor, Richard Rorty, whose writings opened up new vistas in my philosophical education.

After graduation, I went to Princeton University's Department of Religion, where I studied with Jeffrey Stout and with Albert Raboteau, John Gager, and Victor Preller. At Princeton I explored a range of questions concerning moral philosophy, cultural and social criticism, and religious ethics that I continued to entertain as a teacher at Hartford Theological Seminary and as a teacher of ethics, philosophy, and cultural criticism at Chicago Theological Seminary. As a teacher of Afro-American Studies and American Civilization at Brown University, I remain interested in broad cultural criticism that appeals to a variety of disciplines in addressing our society's sexism, racism, and classism, as well as an array of other forces that have not been adequately named or described.

As a scholar commited to many progressive issues, the tensions created by membership in multiple kinship groups force me to think ecumenically about a formidable range of cultural and intellectual issues, placing me in deep personal and intellectual identification with the named and unnamed victims of postmodern life. There is one victim, however, whose malady I partially understand and with whose condition I intimately identify: my brother Everett Dyson, Jr., who is presently incarcerated as prisoner number 212687 at a state prison in Muskegon, Michigan, staring down the barrel of a second-degree murder conviction and facing life in prison. He is innocent, and his defense has cost much, monetarily and emotionally, but we continue to work, hope, and even pray for his release.

The essays that compose this book are divided into three sections, each division representing a fertile sphere within which black cultural creativity has been concentrated and expanded. In each section, I include longer essays that are often followed by a brief book review, personal essay, interview, or editorial response that bears in some way on the themes taken up in the longer piece. These are termed "improvisations."

The first section, "What's Going On?: Black Popular Culture," explores the varied meanings and expressions of African-American popular culture, which have wielded a sizable influence on the wider American culture. I begin this section with a long essay and an interview, in which I trace the emergence, development, and relentless redefinition of the culture of hip-hop, which has spawned a whole "B-boy" (and, increasingly, B-girl) rhetoric and cultural worldview and which has influenced diverse forms of popular culture, ranging from the late-night discourse of the phenomenally popular "Arsenio Hall Show" to countless television commercials and, more important, to the educational styles of millions of black youth.

In my essay on Spike Lee, I probe the significance of his cinematic quest to represent the richness, humor, and conflicts of black culture on screen. I attempt to map the ways in which his neonationalist racial essentialism shapes the contours of his artistic vision, sets the boundaries of expression for his cinematic characters, and informs the aesthetic sensibilities he employs to convey his lessons about black culture and history. I include after the Lee essay a short review of *Talk That Talk*, a collection of short stories, raps, fables, and other genres of expression within a resonant black oral tradition.

I continue this section with an essay on Michael Jackson. My interpretation of Jackson's significance as a cultural icon is wedded to his embodiment of black religious themes that find powerful, if idiosyncratic, expression in his visual and musical artistry. Jackson's videos, song lyrics, and live performances mediate a religious worldview that is sometimes difficult to discern because of his peculiar postmodern cultural expression of religious sensibilities, moral outlooks, and spiritual themes. I argue, as my essay title suggests, that Jackson represents a postmodern African-American secular spirituality. I include a short piece on a live concert performed by Luther Vandross and Anita Baker, two of the most gifted bearers of the contemporary rhythm-and-blues tradition.

I tackle here also the easy but problematic confluence of black cultural motifs of flight and mobility, the cultural and personal agency achieved through athletic competition, and the commercial uses of the black body, through an examination of the career of Michael Jordan. Jordan provides convenient and persuasive points of departure for a discussion of the culture of consumption that has been constructed around American athletics, and the paradoxical possibility of presenting at once a "safe," and potentially oppositional, model of black male activity in an American sports tradition where Jordan's athletic exploits are reverenced and emulated. I include as well a short review of four books that explore the impact of the media, especially as it relates to the construction of desire and other social values, on contemporary culture.

I also attempt to gauge the cultural and televisual achievement of Bill Cosby, an iconic figure possessing a charmed and mythic grandeur in American popular culture. While Cosby's pioneering significance is undeniable, the specter of his success raises questions about the possibility of the televisual medium to convey progressive understandings about race, class, and gender, and the extent to which his show both resists and reproduces wider cultural understandings of such issues. I include here also a short review of a book by a modern renaissance man—author, photographer, filmmaker, musician, and painter Gordon Parks's masterly autobiography, which is an instant classic in black letters.

I conclude this section with an essay that takes up the complex issues of urban despair, and the possibilities of black male agency within the modern city, that are focused in John Singleton's important film, *Boyz N the Hood*. Singleton's film marked a real turning point in the portrayal of black communal choice as it is linked to the social limits and life options of black inner-city residents. It is a film that will generate commentary for a while to come. I include as well a review of the sound track to the Damon Wayans film, *Mo' Money*. The sound track is a cornucopia of black musical styles and illustrates the integral part music plays in the recent slew of black films.

In the second section, "Beyond the Mantra: Reflections on Race, Gender, and Class," I examine the complex and sometimes contradictory meanings that collect around race, gender, and class in American society. I begin this section with a review essay of the major books, and the interpretive tendencies they embody, that address the life and thought of Malcolm X, the towering presence and the most popular figure and ideological icon of black nationalism. Malcolm X's breadth of influence, scope of vision, and fiery intelligence make him supremely important to American society, especially to young blacks, for whom he represents the last best hope of a compelling model of social rebellion and personal integrity. I include here a response to Georgetown law professor Gary Peller regarding the current status of black nationalist thought.

In two long essays and two shorter pieces, I explore the limits and contents of liberal and progressive race theory, reflecting upon how they fashion analytic frameworks to explain the intricate racial relations and immense racial catastrophes that have developed, particularly in the twentieth century. In an article on Leonard Jeffries, I try to move beyond mere repudiation or romanticization of a controversial cultural figure by examining the content of his major beliefs and the way they function either to enable or prevent productive discussion of the issues of Afrocentrism and multiculturalism. I also include a short critical piece on Columbus in the five hundredth anniversary of his discovery-as-conquest of the "new world."

I include an essay on the functions of sex, race, and class in two recent events: the Central Park jogger case and the rap group 2 Live Crew's misogynist lyrics, highlighted during a much-publicized landmark obscenity trial. Both cases foreground the rampant sexism of minority communities and the underdeveloped state of gender analysis, linked to sensitive and subtle understandings of class and age, in a good deal of contemporary racial and social theory. I continue with a short review of Toni Morrison's book on the relationship between race and the formation of an American national literature, *Playing in the Dark*.

In my essay on black men and a short piece on Emmett Till, I attempt to understand and illumine the difficult dimensions of an enduring problem: the often shortened, crime-ridden, poverty-filled lives of black males, who have been controversially termed "an endangered species." I also examine the economic, social, moral, and political bases of the black male predicament, interrogating the culture of crime, the political economy of crack, and the shift from manufacturing to service industries as primary causes of black male misery. My review of Mitchell Duneier's *Slim's Table*, which appears after the essay on black grass-roots leaders, is an attempt to highlight the neglected social achievements of black working-poor and working-class men who often provide moral leadership to inner-city communities. In the chapter on black grass-roots leaders and an essay on the 1988 presidential election, I explore the forms of progressive black political leadership that can best aid America, especially black communities, in the development of a politics that has the chance of ameliorating the lives of black and progressive peoples. I conclude this section with a short review of Barbara Ehrenreich's collection of essays, *The Worst Years of Our Lives*.

In the final section, "This Far By Faith: Black Religion," I examine the still profound engagement in black culture with religious symbols and institutions as major ways of grounding intellectual quests for meaning, shaping individual and social behavior, and exercising political and moral agency. In a long essay and in a short personal piece, I investigate various interpretations of the King holiday for American moral life, suggesting ways in which the King celebration might aid the ongoing interpretive struggle progressives must wage in illumining the difficult moral lessons contained in King's rich legacy, probing manners in which we might expand and extend King's heroic legacy to address our particular cultural situation more than twenty years after his death. In a review essay of James Cone's book *Martin & Malcolm & America*, I examine Cone's treatment of the two central figures of contemporary black American culture, probing his understanding of how they embody ideological and religious options open to African-Americans in search of enabling models of social resistance and prophetic and public moral criticism. I also include a short review of Taylor Branch's tome, *Parting the Waters*.

I include a sermon on the importance of memory within African-American culture and a short piece on Riverside Church senior minister James Forbes, the first African-American to head this prestigious religious institution. In an essay on rap music and the church, I explore how rap embodies the visions of life of many young blacks and how American churches are presented with ample opportunity to carry on important discussions about crucial social and personal issues. I include as well a short review of Cornel West's collection of essays, *Prophetic Fragments*. In my essay on American society and Christian faith, I make an extended critical reply to the recent work of leading Christian ethicist Stanley Hauerwas, highlighting the contributions of the black church to the religion-politics debate. I include as well a short essay on political correctness and its function on seminary campuses. Finally, in an article on contemporary gospel music, I explore the tensions between traditional forms of the music and its more recent expressions, which have intentionally played to a secular audience in an attempt to spread the message of the church. I conclude with a short review of Michael Bryan's *Chapter and Verse*, an informal observer-participant study of a Southern Baptist church school.

Part I

What's Going On? Black Popular Culture

1

The Culture of Hip-Hop

From the very beginning of its recent history, hip-hop music—or rap, as it has come to be known—has faced various obstacles. Initially, rap was deemed a passing fad, a playful and ephemeral black cultural form that steamed off the musical energies of urban black teens. As it became obvious that rap was here to stay, a permanent fixture in black ghetto youths' musical landscape, the reactions changed from dismissal to denigration, and rap music came under attack from both black and white quarters. Is rap really as dangerous as many critics argue? Or are there redeeming characteristics to rap music that warrant our critical attention? I will attempt to answer these and other questions as I explore the culture of hip-hop.

Trying to pinpoint the exact origin of rap is a tricky process that depends on when one acknowledges a particular cultural expression or product as rap. Rap can be traced back to the revolutionary verse of Gil Scott-Heron and the Last Poets, to Pigmeat Markham's "Here Come de Judge," and even to Bessie Smith's rapping to a beat in some of her blues. We can also cite ancient African oral traditions as the antecedents to various contemporary African-American cultural practices. In any case, the modern history of rap probably begins in 1979 with the rap song "Rapper's Delight," by the Sugarhill Gang. Although there were other (mostly underground) examples of rap, this record is regarded as the signal barrier breaker, birthing hip-hop and consolidating the infant art form's popularity. This first stage in rap record production was characterized by rappers placing their rhythmic, repetitive speech over well-known (mostly R & B) black music hits. "Rapper's Delight" was rapped over the music to a song made by the popular seventies R & B group Chic, titled "Good Times." Although rap would later enhance its technical virtuosity through instrumentation, drum machines, and "sampling" existing records—thus making it creatively symbiotic—the first stage was benignly parasitic upon existing black music.

As rap grew, it was still limited to mostly inner-city neighborhoods and particularly its place of origin, New York City. Rap artists like Funky 4 Plus 1, Kool Moe Dee, Busy Bee, Afrika Bambaata, Cold Rush Brothers, Kurtis Blow, DJ Kool Hurk, and Grandmaster Melle Mel were experimenting with this developing musical genre. As it evolved, rap began to describe and analyze the social, economic, and political factors that led to its emergence and development: drug addiction, police brutality, teen pregnancy, and various forms of material deprivation. This new development was both expressed and precipitated by Kurtis Blow's "Those Are the Breaks" and by the most influential and important rap song to emerge in rap's early history, "The Message," by Grandmaster Flash and The Furious Five. The picture this song painted of inner-city life for black Americans—the hues of dark social misery and stains of profound urban catastrophe—screeched against the canvas of most suburban sensibilities:

> You'll grow up in the ghetto living second rate / And your eyes will sing a song of deep hate / The places you play and where you stay, / Looks like one great big alleyway / You'll admire all the number book takers / Thugs, pimps, and pushers, and the big money makers / Drivin' big cars, spendin' twenties and tens, And you want to grow up to be just like them / . . . It's like a jungle sometimes / It makes me wonder how I keep from goin' under.

"The Message," along with Flash's "New York, New York," pioneered the social awakening of rap into a form combining social protest, musical creation, and cultural expression.

As its fortunes slowly grew, rap was still viewed by the music industry as an epiphenomenal cultural activity that would cease as black youth became bored and moved on to another diversion, as they did with break-dancing and graffiti art. But the successes of the rap group Run-D.M.C. moved rap into a different sphere of artistic expression that signaled its increasing control of its own destiny. Run-D.M.C. is widely recognized as the progenitor of modern rap's creative integration of social commentary, diverse musical elements, and uncompromising cultural identification—an integration that pushed the music into the mainstream and secured its future as an American musical genre with an identifiable tradition. Run-D.M.C.'s stunning commercial and critical success almost single-handedly landed rap in the homes of many black and nonblack youths across America by producing the first rap album to be certified gold (five hundred thousand copies sold), the first rap song to be featured on the twenty-four-hour music video channel MTV, and the first rap album (1987's *Raising Hell*) to go triple platinum (3 million copies sold).

On *Raising Hell*, Run-D.M.C. showcased the sophisticated technical virtuosity of its DJ Jam Master Jay—the raw shrieks, scratches, glitches, and language of the street, plus the innovative and ingenious appropriation of hard-rock guitar riffs. In doing this, Run-D.M.C. symbolically and substantively wedded two traditions—the waning subversion of rock music and the rising, incendiary aesthetic of hip-hop music—to produce a provocative musical hybrid of fiery lyricism and potent critique. *Raising Hell* ended with the rap anthem, "Proud to Be Black," intoning its unabashed racial pride:

> Ya know I'm proud to be black ya'll, And that's a fact ya'll / . . . Now Harriet Tubman was born a slave, She was a tiny black woman when she was raised / She was livin' to be givin', There's a lot that she gave / There's not a slave in this day and age, I'm proud to be black.

At the same time, rap, propelled by Run-D.M.C.'s epochal success, found an arena in which to concentrate its subversive cultural didacticism aimed at addressing racism, classism, social neglect, and urban pain: the rap concert, where rappers are allowed to engage in ritualistic refusals of censored speech. The rap concert also creates space for cultural resistance and personal agency, loosing the strictures of the tyrannizing surveillance and demoralizing condemnation of mainstream society and encouraging relatively autonomous, often enabling, forms of self-expression and cultural creativity.

However, Run-D.M.C.'s success, which greatly increased the visibility and commercial appeal of rap music through record sales and rap concerts, brought along another charge that has had a negative impact on rap's perception by the general public: the claim that rap expresses and causes violence. Tipper Gore has repeatedly said that rap music appeals to "angry, disillusioned, unloved kids" and that it tells them it is "okay to beat people up." Violent incidents at rap concerts in Los Angeles, Pittsburgh, Cleveland, Atlanta, Cincinnati, and New York City have only reinforced the popular perception that rap is intimately linked to violent social behavior by mostly black and Latino inner-city youth. Countless black parents, too, have had negative reactions to rap, and the black radio and media establishment, although not as vocal as Gore, have voted on her side with their allocation of much less airplay and print coverage to rap than is warranted by its impressive record sales.

Such reactions betray a shallow understanding of rap, which in many cases results from people's unwillingness to listen to rap lyrics, many of which counsel antiviolent and antidrug behavior among the youths who are their avid audience. Many rappers have spoken directly against violence, such as KRS-One in his "Stop the Violence." Another rap record produced by KRS-One in 1989, the top-selling *Self Destruction*, insists that violence predates rap and speaks against escalating black-on-black crime, which erodes the social and communal fabric of already debased black inner cities across America:

> Well, today's topic is self-destruction, It really ain't the rap audience that's buggin' / It's one or two suckers, ignorant brothers, Tryin' to rob and steal from one another / . . . 'Cause the way we live is positive. We don't kill our relatives / . . . Back in the sixties our brothers and sisters were hanged. How could you gang-bang? / I never, ever ran from the Ku Klux Klan, and I shouldn't have to run from a black man, 'Cause that's / Self-destruction, ya headed for self-destruction.

Despite such potent messages, many mainstream blacks and whites persist in categorically negative appraisals of rap, refusing to distinguish between enabling, productive rap messages and the social violence that exists in many inner-city communities and that is often reflected in rap songs. Of course, it is difficult for a culture that is serious about the maintenance of social arrangements, economic conditions, and political choices that create and reproduce poverty, racism, sexism, classism, and violence to display a significant appreciation for musical expressions that contest the existence of such problems in black and Latino communities. Also disappointing is the continued complicity of black radio stations in denying rap its rightful place of prominence on their playlists. The conspiracy of silence and invisibility has affected the black print media, as well. Although rapper M. C. Shan believes that most antirap bias arises from outside the black community, he faults black radio for depriving rap of adequate airplay and laments the fact that "if a white rock 'n' roll magazine like *Rolling Stone* or *Spin* can put a rapper on the cover and *Ebony* and *Jet* won't, that means there's really something wrong."

In this regard, rap music is emblematic of the glacial shift in aesthetic sensibilities between blacks of different generations, and it draws attention to the severe economic barriers that increasingly divide ghetto poor blacks from middle- and upper-middle-class blacks. Rap reflects the intraracial class division that has plagued African-American communities for the last thirty years. The increasing social isolation, economic hardship, political demoralization, and cultural exploitation endured by most ghetto poor communities in the past few decades have given rise to a form of musical expression that captures the terms of ghetto poor existence. I am not suggesting that rap has been limited to the ghetto poor, but only that its major themes and styles continue to be drawn from the conflicts and contradictions of black urban life. One of the later trends in rap music is the development of "pop" rap by groups like JJ Fad, The Fat Boys, DJ Jazzy Jeff and The Fresh Prince, and Tone Loc. DJ Jazzy Jeff and The Fresh Prince, for example, are two suburbanites from South West Philadelphia and Winfield. (For that matter, members of the most radical rap group, Public Enemy, are suburbanites from Long Island.) DJ Jazzy Jeff and The Fresh Prince's album, *He's the DJ, I'm the Rapper*, sold over 3 million copies, boosted by the enormously successful single "Parents Just Don't Understand." This record, which rapped humorously about various crises associated with being a teen, struck a chord with teenagers across the racial and class spectra, signaling the exploration of rap's populist terrain. The Fresh Prince's present success as the star of his own Quincy Jones–produced television series is further testimony to his popular appeal.

Tone Loc's success also expresses rap's division between "hardcore" (social consciousness and racial pride backed by driving rhythms) and "pop" (exploration of common territory between races and classes, usually devoid of social message). This division, while expressing the commercial expansion of rap, also means that companies and willing radio executives have increasingly chosen pop rap as more acceptable than its more realistic, politically conscious counterpart. (This bias is also evident in the selection of award recipients in the newly created rap category at the annual Grammy Awards.) Tone Loc is an L.A. rapper whose first single, "Wild Thing," sold over 2 million copies, topping *Billboard*'s "Hot Singles Chart," the first rap song to achieve this height. Tone Loc's success was sparked by his video's placement in heavy rotation on MTV, which devotes an hour on Saturdays to "Yo! MTV Raps," a show that became so popular that a daily hour segment was added.

The success of such artists as Tone Loc and DJ Jazzy Jeff and The Fresh Prince inevitably raises the specter of mainstream dilution, the threat to every emergent form of cultural production in American society, particularly the fecund musical tradition that comes from black America. For many, this means the sanitizing of rap's expression of urban realities, resulting in sterile hip-hop that, devoid of its original fire, will offend no one. This scenario, of course, is a familiar denouement to the story of most formerly subversive musical genres. Also, MTV's avid acceptance of rap and the staging of rap concerts run by white promoters willing to take a chance on rap artists add further commentary to the sad state of cultural affairs in many black communities: the continued refusal to acknowledge authentic (not to mention desirable) forms of rap artistry ensures rap's existence on the margins of many black communities.

Perhaps the example of another neglected and devalued black musical tradition, the blues, can be helpful for understanding what is occurring among rap, segments of the black community, and mainstream American society. The blues now has a mostly young white audience. Blacks do not largely support the blues through concert patronage or record buying, thus neglecting a musical genre that was once closely identified with devalued and despised people: poor southern agrarian blacks and the northern urban black poor, the first stratum of the developing underclass. The blues functioned for another generation of blacks much as rap functions for young blacks today: as a source of racial identity, permitting forms of boasting and asserting machismo for devalued black men suffering from social degradation, allowing commentary on social and personal conditions in uncensored language, and fostering the ability to transform hurt and anguish into art and commerce. Even in its heyday, however, the blues existed as a secular musical genre over against the religious traditions that saw the blues as "devil's music" and the conservative black cultural perspectives of the blues as barbaric. These feelings, along with the direction of southern agrarian musical energies into a more accessible and populist soul music, ensured the contraction of the economic and cultural basis for expressing life experience in the blues idiom.

Robert Cray's recent success in mainstreaming the blues perhaps completes the cycle of survival for devalued forms of black music: it originates in a context of anguish and pain and joy and happiness, it expresses those emotions and ideas in a musical language and idiom peculiar to its view of life, it is altered as a result of cultural sensibilities and economic factors, and it undergoes distribution, packaging, and consumption for leisurely or cathartic pleasure through concert attendance or record buying. Also, in the process, artists are sometimes removed from the immediate context and original site of their artistic production. Moreover, besides the everyday ways in which the music is used for a variety of entertainment functions, it may occasionally be employed in contexts that undermine its critique of the status quo, and it may be used to legitimize a cultural or social setting that, in negative ways, has partially given rise to its expression. A recent example of this is the late Lee Atwater's positioning of himself as a privileged patron of the blues and soul music traditions in the 1989 Bush inauguration festivities, which was preceded by his racist use of the Willie Horton case. Atwater's use of Willie Horton viciously played on the very prejudice against black men that has often led blues musicians to express the psychic, personal, and social pain occasioned by racism in American (political) culture. Rap's visibility may alter this pattern as it continues to grow, but its self-defined and continuing challenge is to maintain its aesthetic, cultural, and political proximity to its site of original expression: the ghetto poor.

Interestingly, a new wave of rap artists may be accomplishing this goal, but with foreboding consequences. For example, N.W.A. (Niggaz With Attitudes) reflects the brutal circumstances that define the boundaries within which most ghetto poor black youth in Los Angeles must live. For the most part they—unlike their socially conscientious counterparts Public Enemy, Boogie Down Productions, and Stetsasonic—have no ethical remove from the violence, gang-bangin', and drugs in L.A.'s inner city. In their song "—— Tha Police," N.W.A. gives a sample of their reality:

> Fuck the police, comin' straight from the underground. A young nigger got it bad 'cause I'm brown / And not the other color, so police think, / They have the authority to kill a minority / . . . Searchin' my car looking for the product, / Thinkin' every nigger is sellin' narcotic / . . . But don't let it be a black and a white one, / 'Cause they'll slam ya down to the street top, / Black police showin' out for the white cop.

Such expressions of violence certainly reflect the actual life circumstances of many black and Latino youth caught in the desperate cycle of drugs and gangs involved in L.A. ghetto living. N.W.A. celebrates a lethal mix of civil terrorism and personal cynicism. Their attitude is both one answer to, and the logical outcome of, the violence, racism, and oppression in American culture. On the other hand, their vision must be criticized, for the stakes are too high for the luxury of moral neutrality. Having at least partially lived the life they rap about, N.W.A. understands the viciousness of police brutality. However, they must also be challenged to develop an ethical perspective on the drug gangs that duplicate police violence in black-on-black crime. While rappers like N.W.A. perform an invaluable service by rapping in poignant and realistic terms about urban underclass existence, they must be challenged to expand their moral vocabulary and be more sophisticated in their understanding that description alone is insufficient to address the crises of black urban life. Groups like N.W.A. should be critically aware that blacks are victims of the violence of both state repression *and* gang violence, that one form of violence is often the response to the other, and that blacks continue to be held captive to disenabling lifestyles (gang-bangin', drug dealing) that cripple the life of black communities.

Also problematic is the sexist sentiment that pervades so much of rap music. It is a rampant sexism that continues to mediate the relations within the younger black generation with lamentable intensity. While it is true that rap's sexism is indeed a barometer of the general tenor and mood that mediates black male-female relations, it is not the role of women alone to challenge it. Reproach must flow from women *and* men who are sensitive to the ongoing sexist attitudes and behavior that dominate black male-female relationships. Because women by and large do not run record companies, or even head independent labels that have their records distributed by larger corporations, it is naive to assume that protest by women alone will arrest the spread of sexism in rap. Female rappers are certainly a potential resource for challenging existing sexist attitudes, but given the sexist barriers that patrol rap's borders, male rappers must be challenged by antisexist men, especially male rappers who contest the portrayal of women in most rap music. The constant reference to women as "skeezers," "bitches," and "ho's" only reinforces the perverted expression of male dominance and patriarchy and reasserts the stereotyping of women as sexual objects intended exclusively for male pleasure.

Fortunately, many of the problems related to rap—particularly with black radio, media, and community acceptance—have only fostered a sense of camaraderie that transcends in crucial ways the fierce competitive streak in rap (which, at its best moments, urges rappers on to creative musical heights). While the "dis" rap (which humorously musicalizes "the dozens") is alive and well, the overall feeling among rap artists that rap must flourish outside the sanctions of traditional means of garnering high visibility or securing record sales has directed a communal energy into the production of their music. The current state of affairs has also precipitated cooperative entrepreneurial activity among young black persons. The rap industry has spawned a number of independent labels, providing young blacks (mostly men) with experience as heads of their own businesses and with exposure as managers of talent, positions that might otherwise be unavailable to them. Until recently, rap flourished, for the most part, outside of the tight artistic and economic constraints imposed by major music corporations. Although many independent companies have struck distribution deals with major labels—such as Atlantic, MCA, Columbia, and Warner Brothers—it has usually been the case, until the late 1980s, that the inexperience of major labels with rap, coupled with their relatively conservative musical tastes, has enabled the independent labels to control their destinies by teaching the major music corporations invaluable lessons about street sales, the necessity of having a fast rate of delivery from the production of a record to its date of distribution, and remaining close to the sensibilities of the street, while experimenting with their marketing approach in ways that reflect the diversification of styles in rap.

Rap expresses the ongoing preoccupation with literacy and orality that has characterized African-American communities since the inception of legally coerced illiteracy during slavery. Rap artists explore grammatical creativity, verbal wizardry, and linguistic innovation in refining the art of oral communication. The rap artist, as Cornel West has indicated, is a bridge figure who combines the two potent traditions in black culture: preaching and music. The rap artist appeals to the rhetorical practices eloquently honed in African-American religious experiences and the cultural potency of black singing/musical traditions to produce an engaging hybrid. They are truly urban griots dispensing social and cultural critique, verbal shamans exorcising the demons of cultural amnesia. The culture of hip-hop has generated a lexicon of life that expresses rap's B-boy/B-girl worldview, a perspective that takes delight in undermining "correct" English usage while celebrating the culturally encoded phrases that communicate in rap's idiom.

Rap has also retrieved historic black ideas, movements, and figures in combating the racial amnesia that threatens to relegate the achievements of the black past to the ash heap of dismemory. Such actions have brought a renewed sense of historical pride to young black minds that provides a solid base for racial self-esteem. Rap music has also focused renewed attention on black nationalist and black radical thought. This revival has been best symbolized by the rap group Public Enemy. Public Enemy announced its black nationalism in embryonic form on their first album, *Yo! Bum Rush the Show*, but their vision sprang forward full-blown in their important *It Takes a Nation of Millions to Hold Us Back*. The album's explicit black nationalist language and cultural sensibilities were joined with a powerful mix of music, beats, screams, noise, and rhythms from the streets. Its message is provocative, even jarring, a précis of the contained chaos and channeled rage that informs the most politically astute rappers. On the cut "Bring the Noise," they intone:

> We got to demonstrate, come on now, they're gonna have to wait / Till we get it right / Radio stations I question their blackness / They call themselves black, but we'll see if they'll play this / Turn it up! Bring the noise!

Public Enemy also speaks of the criminality of prison conditions and how dope dealers fail the black community. Their historical revivalism is noteworthy, for instance, as they rap on "Party for Your Right to Fight":

> Power Equality / And we're out to get it / I know some of you ain't wit' it / This party started right in '66 / With a pro-Black radical mix / Then at the hour of twelve / . . . J. Edgar Hoover, and he coulda' proved to 'ya / He had King and X set up / Also the party with Newton, Cleaver, and Seale / . . . Word from the honorable Elijah Muhummad / Know who you are to be Black / . . . the original Black Asiatic man.

Public Enemy troubled even more sociocultural waters with their Nation of Islam views, saying in "Don't Believe the Hype":

> The follower of Farrakhan / Don't tell me that you understand / Until you hear the man.

Such rap displays the power and pitfalls associated with the revival of earlier forms of black radicalism, nationalism, and cultural expression. The salutary aspect of the historical revival is that it raises consciousness about important figures, movements, and ideas, prompting rappers to express their visions of life in American culture. This renewed historicism permits young blacks to discern links between the past and their own present circumstances, using the past as a fertile source of social reflection, cultural creation, and political resistance.

On the other hand, it has also led to perspectives that do not provide *critical* reflection on the past. Rather, many rappers attempt to duplicate the past without challenging or expanding it. Thus, their historical insight fails to illumine our current cultural problems as powerfully as it might, and the present generation of black youth fails to benefit as fully from the lessons that it so powerfully revives. This is an unfortunate result of the lack of understanding and communication among various segments of the black community, particularly along generational and class lines, problems symbolized in the black community's response to rap. Historical revival cries out for contexts that render the past understandable and usable. This cannot occur if large segments of the black community continue to be segregated from one of the most exciting cultural transformations occurring in contemporary American life: the artistic expression, cultural exploration, political activity, and historical revival of hip-hop artists.

An issue in rap that is closely related to the acknowledgment of history and sources is sampling, or the grafting of music, voices, and beats from another sonic source onto a rap record. The practice of sampling expresses the impulse to collage that characterizes the best of black musical traditions, particularly jazz and gospel. Sampling is also postmodernist activity that merges disparate musical and cultural forms to communicate an artistic message. Sampling is a transgressive activity because rappers employ it to interrupt the narrative flow and musical stability of other musical texts, producing a new and often radically different creation. But rap may potentially take back in its technical appropriation what it has given in its substantive, lyrical achievements: a recognition of history. While sampling permits a rap creator to reconfigure voices and rhythms in creating an alternate code of cultural exchange, the practice may also deprive other artists of recognition or even financial remuneration. The classic case in point is James Brown, who, along with George Clinton, is the most sampled man in rap and the primal progenitor of the beats and rhythms in hip-hop music. Although his voice, rhythms, and beats are often easily identifiable and rap's debt to him is obvious, Brown's benefit has been limited. Recent legal woes connected to the status of rap's practice of creative borrowing may hasten rap's codification of appropriate acknowledgment, particularly in an economic practice similar to the royalty that distinguishes between small bites of music and significant borrowing and quotation.

Rap is a form of profound musical, cultural, and social creativity. It expresses the desire of young black people to reclaim their history, reactivate forms of black radicalism, and contest the powers of despair and economic depression that presently besiege the black community. Besides being the most powerful form of black musical expression today, rap projects a style of self into the world that generates forms of cultural resistance and transforms the ugly terrain of ghetto existence into a searing portrait of life as it must be lived by millions of voiceless people. For that reason alone, rap deserves attention and should be taken seriously; and for its productive and healthy moments, it should be promoted as a worthy form of artistic expression and cultural projection and an enabling source of black juvenile and communal solidarity.

2

Rap Music and Black Culture: An Interview

QUESTION: In "Rap, Race, and Reality," you offered a brief summary of the history of rap music, from its initial stage of boastful partying, through a social critique phase (epitomized by Grandmaster Flash's "The Message"), to the "pluralization" phase of Run-D.M.C. and others. Since that essay appeared, rap has not only busted out commercially, but also has intensified a cultural debate via the religious- and education-oriented rap of such groups as Boogie Down Productions, Public Enemy, and more recent Islamic-centered groups (not to mention the controversies surrounding groups like N.W.A. and 2 Live Crew). I'm interested in your assessment of these developments. How might a theomusicological perspective inform the current state of rap?

ANSWER (Dyson): Well, I think the kind of recent explosion of what Boogie Down Productions' head rapper and guiding spirit KRS-One calls "edutainment" is a noteworthy and salutary development in the evolution of rap music. Rap music is a profoundly oral culture that exhibits the quest for literacy that has impelled the African-American community forward since its inception, certainly since its pilgrimage here on American soil. And I think what BDP and Public Enemy and other progressive, education-oriented, message-centered rap groups do is consistent with and consonant with that historic legacy. I think that these groups show us the best of what the rap culture has to offer—they combine the powerful rhetorical traditions that have been honed in African-American oral practices, the most noteworthy of which is black preaching (the black homiletical tradition), with the powerful musical culture that is a vibrant subculture of African-Americans (including the improvisational movement of jazz, so that sampling represents in one sense a kind of rap improvisation).

So I think the expansion of rap's territory into serious educational forums (Chuck D. calls rap music a kind of CNN of black culture) is salutary to the degree that it represents a powerful identification with historic forms of oral practices that have been honed in black culture: long narrative poems called "toasts," the raps of earlier generations (Bessie Smith, the Last Poets, Gil Scott-Heron), and so forth. I think rap music in that sense combines the *drum* and the *word* in a powerful fusion. And to that degree, then, these education-oriented rappers represent both a powerful past and a powerful future. What I mean by "a powerful future" is the possibility for expanding the didactic functions, the teaching functions of rap music—people are now talking about adopting rap music in the classroom, and it's primarily because of the powerful positive messages that these groups convey.

QUESTION: You've written that the "dis" or "dissing" rap, in which a rapper verbally attacks and belittles an opponent, is "a musical expression of the Afro-American cultural phenomenon [of] 'capping' or 'topping.' " It seems that this cultural context of rap was ignored and/or missed by the district attorneys and others who tried to censor 2 Live Crew last summer. Do you agree with literary theorist Henry Louis Gates's testimony that 2 Live Crew, while their misogyny should be condemned, must be understood in the context of the signifying practices of African-American oral tradition?

ANSWER: Yes, I think it is very important to understand that, as Henry Louis Gates pointed out, they're engaging in rhythmic teasing, appealing to oral practices that use lewd or bawdy humor to make their point. So the signifying, or parody, is very crucial, and one must not miss that.

On the other hand, we must place those oral practices into a larger African-American cultural perspective that allows *other* features of that culture to be juxtaposed to signification: moral criticism, sage advice, commonsense admonitions against out-of-bounds behavior—all of these are crucial elements of African-American culture that, when juxtaposed to this parody, inform the construction of these verbal practices and allow us to make some sense out of them. Because first we've got to understand them, but, second, we've got to be allowed to criticize them, but on their own terms, so that there's a kind of internal criticism going on. I mean, we understand and allow for the fact that these may be certain oral practices, but that doesn't absolve us from the responsibility to say that the use of parody, when expressing misogynistic, woman-bashing sentiments, needs to be criticized.

QUESTION: Do you see a similar need to critique and evaluate the black nationalism of some rap groups?

ANSWER: Sure, I think that's true with the nationalism also. It's interesting and intriguing to understand the perspective of young people who have a sense of revived cultural appreciation. They are resuscitating, if you will, former forms of black consciousness. They are engaging in a kind of minirenaissance that extends beyond rap culture, of course, with the valorization of Malcolm X as a central icon of the revived black neonationalist consciousness, with the preoccupation with Minister Louis Farrakhan (and earlier with George Stallings), with the movies of Spike Lee. I mean, there's a wide variety of cultural phenomena that express the revival of neonationalism. Black nationalism has informed, at every crucial juncture of American culture, the political ideology and cultural reflections of black culture.

On the other hand, nationalism needs to be placed into a larger context and dialogue within African-American culture itself *and* with the wider American culture so that it will not be insular and so that it has serious dialogue with other features of the wider culture that transcend *mere*, or exclusive, racial consciousness. Not that it must repudiate racial consciousness, because one does not want to repudiate, but instead acknowledge, the specificity of racial consciousness. But one wants to make contacts with and connections with wider cultural phenomena that then inform, criticize, and expand the possibility of expression for those varied practices and inflections.

QUESTION: Earlier you mentioned the influence of the black homiletic, or preaching, tradition on rap. I'm curious to hear your thoughts about M. C. Hammer's combination of rap and the church in "Pray."

ANSWER: Well, that's a very powerful fusion. M. C. Hammer

has come under serious scrutiny and criticism because of his popularization of rap—you know, the compromise of the Afrocentric perspective, the refusal to engage in more political raps—but I think that his "Pray" is an interesting fusion of the sacred and the secular, if you will. "Pray" is an admonition and an exhortation at once, that without prayer we won't make it, and if we do pray is the only way we *can* make it. So I think that is a very fascinating kind of fusion. It's reaching a wide range of people, and the message of the church, then, is being projected into the secular arena with the powerful motifs that are common to the church, and yet they transcend the narrow, sanctuary-bound messages that don't reach a wider populace who increasingly are not going *to* church. So I think that M. C. Hammer does a tremendous service in his own way in "Pray."

QUESTION: We see a similar phenomenon, I think, when Arsenio Hall, on national television, interviews the preteen vocal group "The Boys," and asks them if they pray. This kind of dialogue would be inconceivable on David Letterman or Johnny Carson.

ANSWER: That's exactly right. It's a powerful cultural moment because what you have with Arsenio Hall is a projection of a specific African-American male perspective filtered through the various strands of American popular culture. One of those strands is African-American popular culture, but he's reaching and appealing to a much wider audience, with the projection of that sensibility every night into millions of American homes. I mean, the way he comes on, the way he enacts from popular culture certain stances of the B-boy Weltanshauung, if you will, the way he engages in certain linguistic innovations, the way in which he stylizes his body in that space every night while millions of Americans are both able to consume those images and also react to them in a very limited way at their home—he permits a kind of voyeurism into and a vision of the B-boy and street culture in diluted but yet powerful ways.

QUESTION: In an essay on Michael Jackson [see chapter 4 in this volume], you contrast the commodification of the black body during slavery, in which the body "was articulated as the primal other, the form of difference *par excellence*," with redemptive uses of the body in both black religious practices and popular music. Can you extend that discussion to comment on recent expressions of the body, especially in the dance forms, for instance, of M. C. Hammer?

ANSWER: Well, the body for M. C. Hammer becomes a vehicle of praise and celebration. And it's an alluring admixture of sensuality/sexuality on the one hand and sacrality/spirituality on the other hand. Because even in the "Pray" video, for instance, we see the kinetic eroticism that animates his video and the smooth sensuality and the spiritualized celebrative moment, a kind of festive carnival spirit, that are all intermingled there. So you have the sacred moment and the secular moment mingled together, and the body for M. C. Hammer becomes the intersection of the sacred and the secular at the celebrative pole.

I think it's very intriguing. Some people see it as a mixed message in one sense, because here he is, he has these tight body suits for the females and the bare chests for the males, and they're doing ecclesiastical gyrations, one might say. But what they're really enacting, then, is a kind of festive religious moment that is filtered through the sexuality of Hammer's own dancing and the sensual moment of African-American culture. So I think it's an intriguing admixture, where the body becomes the site of the intersection of the sacred and the secular, the spiritual and the sensual.

QUESTION: Considering the struggles churches face in being relevant for, and in holding the interest and commitment of, youth, do you consider "secular spirituality" as exhibited in pop musicians like Michael Jackson and M. C. Hammer to be the predominant form of religious experience for today's young people? Is music, as the cliché goes, a new religion?

ANSWER: Well, it's a subgenre, I would say. It wouldn't be a religion of its own in one sense, but it's certainly a primary means by which these young people are experiencing religious reality and receiving a religious message. Traditional church attendance has diminished across the board in American culture, and the black church has not been exempt from this larger trend. So a majority or at least a significant segment of this culture of young people experiences religious reality in alternate forms.

So I think that when they hear M. C. Hammer's "Pray," or when other artists refer to God or invoke divine reality, whether it be a Muslim or a Christian one, it *is* a way that these young people *hear* a message. And rap musicians then fulfill the role of being cultural griots, urban griots dispensing a message of prophetic criticism, and also of being peripatetic preachers, in that sense. I mean, they're in one sense priests of a culture that has fixated itself on the oral dimension of popular culture, but who also then use that as a means of distributing powerful religious messages. And, yes, young people are flocking to them and viewing them and giving to them a sense of authority and authenticity that heretofore had been associated with the church. So there is a competitive dimension to this.

But also, I think, to see it in a wider sense, there is a more powerful appeal to the very means by which young people express themselves, which is this new orality, and it then is used to express *traditional* religious virtues. For example, "Pray": "We got to pray just to make it today." So it's a powerful traditional expression and practice—prayer—filtered through a nontraditional, postmodern, if you will, black cultural phenomenon of rap music. Rap music is a peculiar and specific phenomenon produced by conditions under late monopoly capital in postindustrial urban America, where the hemorrhaging of resources in the inner city, the evaporation of social services to address those specific conditions, has left a gaping void in both the culture of African-Americans and Americans in general. So the filling of that void and vacuum by rap music is a means by which people sustain themselves and maintain certain forms of sanity.

QUESTION: I think that would apply also to the technofunk dance forms of Janet Jackson, her *Rhythm Nation* videos.

ANSWER: *Rhythm Nation* is very crucial. Janet Jackson says it herself, you know, she's reaching out to people who ordinarily wouldn't get the message. I mean, she's not preaching to the choir—many people are already preaching to the choir. She wanted to get to the people who *weren't* socially conscious, who wanted to party and dance.

QUESTION: Essayist Michael Ventura sees the Africanization, or more accurately, the African-Americanization, of Euro-American culture, especially as revealed in music, as a healing process whereby the mind-body split inherited from Cartesianism and certain forms of Christian thought is transcended. I'm reminded of one of the connotations of "salvation" being wholeness, a making whole. Do you see a similar process at work?

ANSWER: That's fascinating. I think also we can add what the anthropologists call the "deification of accident." This is what happens in African culture, which is this constant living on what Cornel West calls "the slippery slope" or "the edge." The deification of accident, then, is the perennial process of being preoccupied by creative energies that are then enacted against perceived limits, whether we're talking about the various dunks of a Michael Jordan or the jazz riffs of a Wynton Marsalis. So that along with this kind of appropriation, this kind of Africanization of the European process, there's also a kind of hybridity that is going on, too. Because it does take certain moments of Eurocentric culture, which are inevitable and unavoidable given our hybrid existence in American culture, but also a kind of interjection or an *appeal* to an African moment yielding a unique and hybrid moment, the African-American moment.

So I think it's the fusion of the best of these traditions as it is enacted by a peculiarly African-American perspective and practice, which could be the dancing of M. C. Hammer or the dancing of Sammy Davis or the singing of Anita Baker or Regina Belle or Aretha Franklin. Or the powerful writings of Toni Morrison or Alice Walker or Charles Johnson.

3

Spike Lee's Neonationalist Vision

In 1986, a distinct phase in contemporary African-American cinema commenced. Spike Lee wrote, produced, directed, and acted in *She's Gotta Have It*, an independently made sex comedy that cost $175,000 but grossed over $6 million after distribution by Island Pictures. Since then Lee, and an expanding cadre of black filmmakers, including Robert Townsend, Keenen Ivory Wayans, and Euzhan Palcy, have written and directed a number of films that explore various themes in black life. Lee in particular creates films that are part of a revival of black nationalism (neonationalism), a movement that included provocative expressions in the cultural sphere (elements of rap music, the wearing of African medallions), interesting interventions in the intellectual sphere (articulation of Afrocentric perspectives in academic disciplines), and controversial developments in the social sphere (symbolized by Louis Farrakhan's Nation of Islam ideology, which enjoys narrow but significant popularity among blacks). Lee, foremost among his black director peers, is concerned with depicting the sociopolitical implications of his Afrocentric film aesthetic and neonationalist worldview.

But he is also determined to display the humanity of his characters, and he insists upon exploring the unacknowledged diversity and the jarring and underappreciated contradictions of black life. Lee, however, is confronted with a conflict: how to present the humanity of black folk without lapsing into an ontology of race that structures simplistic categories of being for black people and black culture that are the worst remnants of old-style black nationalism. Such constructions of black character and culture fail to express the complex diversity of black humanity.

On the one hand, because Lee is apparently committed to a static conception of racial identity, his characters appear as products of an archetypal mold that predetermines their responses to a range of sociohistorical situations. These characters are highly symbolic and widely representative, reflecting Lee's determination to repel the folkloric symbols of racism through racial countersymbol. On the other hand, Lee must revise his understanding of racial identity in order to present the humanity of black characters successfully. He must permit his characters to possess irony, self-reflection, and variability, qualities that, when absent—no matter the high aims that underlie archetypal representation—necessarily circumscribe agency and flatten humanity. It is in the electric intersection of these two competing and at times contradictory claims, of black cultural neonationalism and black humanism, that Lee's art takes place.

In *Do the Right Thing*, Lee's black neonationalism leaps off the screen through brilliant cinematography and riveting messages. As most Americans know, *Do the Right Thing* is about contemporary racism. The film's action is concentrated in a single block of Brooklyn's "Bed-Stuy" neighborhood on a scorching summer day. The heat, both natural and social, is a central metaphor for the film's theme of tense race relations. The pivotal place of social exchange in this compact, ethnically diverse, and highly self-contained community is Sal's Famous Pizzeria, the single vestige of white-owned business in Bed-Stuy. Sal (Danny Aiello) owns and operates the restaurant along with his two sons, Pino (John Turturro) and Vito (Richard Edwon), proud Italians who make the daily commute from the suburb of Bensonhurst. Lee plays Mookie, the hardworking but responsibility-shirking delivery man for Sal's and the primary link between the community and the pizzeria. Mookie seems able to maneuver easily between two worlds—until late in the film, when the community erupts in a riot at Sal's, prompted by an egregious instance of police brutality.

In choosing to explore the racial tension between Italian-Americans and African-Americans, Lee makes explicit reference to Howard Beach, employing it as an ideologically charged conceptual foil for his drama about American racism. Lee makes allusions to the Howard Beach incident throughout the movie: Sal brandishes a baseball bat in conflicts with various black patrons; the crowd chants "Coward Beach" at the riot. Lee wants his movie to provoke discussion about racism in the midst of a racially repressive era, when all such discourse is either banished to academia (although not much discussion goes on there, either) or considered completed in the distant past. Lee rejects the premises of this Reagan-era illogic and goes straight to the heart of the mechanism that disseminates and reinforces racial repression: the image, the symbol, the representation. *Do the Right Thing* contains symbols of racism and resistance to racism, representations of black life, and images of black nationalist sensibilities and thought.

Lee creates symbols that reveal the remorseless persistence of racism in quotidian quantity, exposing the psychopathology of everyday racism as it accumulates in small doses, over the course of days not unlike the one we witness in *Do the Right Thing*. Lee shows us the little bruises, the minor frustrations, and the minute but myriad racial fractures that mount without healing. There is the riff of the prickly relations between the black residents and the Koreans who own the neighborhood market. There is the challenge of Radio Raheem (Bill Nunn), a menacing bundle of brawn who wields his boom box as a weapon to usurp communal aural space as he practices his politics of cultural terrorism. But the central symbol of racial conflict is the ongoing tiff between Buggin' Out and Sal over the latter's refusal to place photos of black people on Sal's Wall of Fame, reserved for the likes of DiMaggio, Stallone, and Sinatra. Sal and Buggin' Out's battle over the photographs, over the issue of *representing* black people, makes explicit the terms of the film's representational warfare.

Lee's decision to provoke discussion about racism is heroic. He exposes a crucial American failure of nerve, a stunning loss of conscience about race. But beyond this accomplishment, how much light does he shed by raising the question of racism in the manner that he does? Lee's perspective portrays a view of race and racism that, while it manages to avoid a facile Manichaeanism, nevertheless slides dangerously close to a vision of "us" and "them," in which race is seen solely through the lens of biological determinism.

The problem with such biological determinism is that it construes racial identity as a unidimensional, monocausal reality that can be reduced to physically inheritable characteristics. Racial identity is an ever-evolving, continually transforming process that is never fully or finally exhausted by genetics and physiology. It is constantly structured and restructured, perennially created and recreated, in a web of social practices, economic conditions, gendered relations, material realities, and historical situations that are themselves shaped and reshaped. As the feminist critique of Freud asserts, anatomy is not destiny; likewise, biology is not identity.

Black cultural neonationalism obscures the role of elements such as gender, class, and geography in the construction of racial identity, and by so doing limits its resources for combating racial oppression. Consider the film's end, in which Lee juxtaposes quotes from Martin Luther King, Jr., and Malcolm X that posit the harm versus the help of violence in aid of black liberation. Lee has not stumbled serendipitously toward an interpretive framework that summarizes the two options open to black folk in fighting racism: Lee's neonationalist perspective has regulated his presentation of the problem of racism in the movie all along.

Furthermore, Lee's neonationalism determines which quotes he uses. As Lee knows, it can be argued that, before their deaths, King and X were converging in their understanding of race and racism. Both of them were developing understandings of racial identity and racism that were much more complex, open-ended, ecumenical, and international than the views they had previously held. King was changing because of his more radical comprehension of the relationship between race and class, and thus began to promote a more aggressive version of nonviolent resistance. X was changing, too, because of his visit to Mecca and his expanding conception of the possibilities of interracial solidarity. Each man also borrowed elements of analysis from the other, appropriating those lessons in ways that had the potential to chart a much different path for resistance to oppression in the seventies and on. By using these quotes from King and X, free of context, Lee gives an anachronistic and historical reading of the two figures. Presenting these quotes as a basis of present options may provide some conceptual and emotive resources for debate, but does little to enlighten. Lee freezes the meanings of these two men, instead of utilizing their mature thought as a basis for *reconceiving* the problem of racism to address *our* particular set of historical circumstances.

Lee's neonationalist leanings also affect his characters, who become mere archetypes. Buggin' Out (Giancarlo Esposito) is the local radical, a caricature of deep commitment, who is more rabble-rouser than thoughtful insurgent. Smiley (Roger Guenevcur Smith) is the stuttering conscience, first seen in front of the Yes Jesus Can Baptist Church. He hawks photographs of the famous meeting between King and X to reluctant passersby. Ossie Davis plays Da Mayor, the neighborhood drunk, who represents older black men who were scathed by economic desperation and personal failure, and whose modus vivendi is shaped by the bottle. Ruby Dee (Davis's real-life wife) is Mother Sister, a lonely black woman who represents the neighborhood's omniscient eye. She is a possible victim of desertion by a man like Da Mayor, or a woman who was determined and independent before her time (or perhaps both). Joie Lee, Spike's real-life sister, plays Mookie's sister Jade, and represents the responsible and stable black woman. She must support and suffer Mookie, her affectionately irascible brother, whom she chides for not taking care of his son. Mookie's son's mother, Tina (Rosie Perez), is the Latin firebrand who extemporizes in colorful neologism about Mookie's domestic shortcomings. And a trio of middle-aged black men, Sweet Dick Willie, ML, and Coconut Sud (Robin Harris, Paul Benjamin, and Frankie Faison), represent the often humorous folk philosophy of a generation of black males who have witnessed the opening of socioeconomic opportunity for others, but who must cope with a more limited horizon for themselves.

In one respect, Lee's use of archetypal black figures is salutary, as it expands the register of black characters in contemporary cinema. But the larger effect is harmful, and is a measure both of Hollywood's deeply entrenched racism and of the limitation of Lee's neonationalist worldview. Lee follows a tradition of sorts, as the attempt to decenter prevalent conceptions of racial behavior began in earnest in the twenties in Oscar Micheaux's films. A much later attempt to shift from stereotype to archetype in black film was crudely rendered in Melvin Van Peebles's *Sweet*

Sweetback's Baadasssss Song (1971). Although Lee is light-years ahead of Van Peebles in most respects, he still adopts a crucial element of Van Peebles's work: the representative archetype.

Lee is unable to meld his two ambitions—to present the breadth of black humanity while proclaiming a black neonationalist aesthetic. His attempt to present a black universe is admirable, but that universe must be one in which people genuinely act and do not simply respond as mere archetypal constructions. Because the characters carry such weighty symbolic significance (resonant though it might be), they must act like symbols, not like humans. As a result, their story seems predetermined, a byproduct of a complicated configuration of social, personal, and political situations.

The archetypal model accounts for the manner in which Lee portrays the white characters, particularly Sal and sons. Pino is the vicious ethnic chauvinist who clings tightly to his Italian identity and heritage for fear of finding himself awash in the tide of "nigger"-loving that seems to soak his other family members. Vito is the ethnic pluralist, an easygoing and impressionable young man whose main distinction is that he has no major beef with the blacks and Puerto Ricans. Only Sal, who splits the difference between his two sons, manages to rise in some complexity. He is a proud businessman whose long-standing relationship with the community has endeared him to most of the neighborhood's residents. But when provoked, he is not above hurling the incendiary racial epithet, which on one fateful occasion seals his destiny by beginning the riot that destroys his store.

This Saturday night Sal keeps the store open late to accommodate a group of neighborhood kids. That is when Radio Raheem (boom box in tow and pumping loud) and Buggin' Out shout a final request to place photos of blacks on the wall. After Radio Raheem refuses to lower the volume of his box, Sal, driven to an understandable frenzy, crushes the radio with his baseball bat. Radio Raheem also behaves understandably. He grabs Sal, pulls him over the counter, and the two men struggle from the store into the street. The police arrive and attempt to restrain Radio Raheem using the infamous New York Police "chokehold," a potentially lethal technique, especially when applied to black male necks. The police let Radic Raheem drop dead to the ground, kick him, and drag him into a police car. Meanwhile, they have handcuffed Buggin' Out and carted him away. The crowd is horror-stricken. Mookie, until now the mediator of disputes between Sal and the community, takes sides with his neighbors and throws a trash can through Sal's window, catalyzing the riot. The crowd destroys the pizzeria, overturning tables and equipment and taking money from the cash register. But it is stuttering Smiley who starts the fire. In African-American religious tradition, the Holy Spirit appears before believers in the form of fire. Smiley's torch is the articulation of his religious passion.

Lee's portrayal of police brutality, which has claimed the lives of too many black people, is disturbingly honest. The encounter between Radio Raheem and Sal is poignant and instructive. It shows that a black person's death may be provoked by incidents of racial antagonism gone amok, and that it is easy for precious young black life to be sacrificed in the gritty interstices between anger and abandonment. Thus, we can understand the neighborhood's consuming desire to destroy property—avenging the murder of a son whose punishment does not fit his crime.

It is also understandable that the crowd destroys Sal's place, the pizzeria being the nearest representative of destructive white presence, a white presence that has just denied Radio Raheem his future. But Sal certainly doesn't represent the "powers" that Public Enemy rapped about so fearlessly on Radio Raheem's box. As Lee knows, the character of racism has changed profoundly in the last few decades, and even though there are still too many ugly reassertions of overt racism, it is often the more subtle variety that needs to be identified and fought.

For instance, after viewing Lee's film many people may leave the theater smugly self-confident that they are not racists because they are not petit bourgeois Italian businessmen, because they don't call people "niggers," and because they are not policemen who chokehold black men to death. But contemporary racism is often the teacher who cannot take a black student seriously, who subtly dismisses her remarks in class because they are "not really central," or because he has presumed, often unconsciously, a limit to her abstract reasoning. (The double whammy of race and gender operates here.) Contemporary racism is often middle-class black managers hitting a career ceiling that is ostensibly due to their lack of high-level management skills, which, of course, are missing not because of lack of intelligence but because they have not acquired the right *kinds* of experience. Contemporary racism is not about being kept out of a clothes store, but rather about not being taken seriously because the store clerk presumes you won't spend your money or that you have none to spend.

To assert that racism is most virulent at Sal's level misses the complex ways in which everyday racism is structured, produced, and sustained in multifarious social practices, cultural traditions, and intellectual justifications. Sal is as much a victim of his racist worldview as he is its perpetrator. By refusing to probe the shift in the modus operandi of American racism, Lee misses the opportunity to expose what the British cultural critic Stuart Hall calls inferential racism, the "apparently naturalized representation of events and situations relating to race, whether factual or 'fictional,' which have racist premises and propositions inscribed in them as a set of unquestioned assumptions."

Those who strive to resist the new-style racism must dedicate themselves to pointing out slippery attitudes and ambiguous actions that signal the presence of racism without appearing to do so. This strategy must include drawing attention to unintended racist statements, actions, and thoughts, which nevertheless do harm. These strategies must be accompanied by sophisticated, high-powered intellectual dialogue about how the nature of particular forms of Western discourse provide the expression, reproduction, and maintenance of racist ideology and practices. People must form interracial, international lines of solidarity and develop analyses of racism in tandem with similar analyses of sexism, classism, anti-Semitism, anti-Arabism, homophobia, ecological terrorism, and a host of other progressive concerns.

Perhaps nothing does more to symbolize the shadowed brilliance of Lee's project, the troubled symbiosis of his black neonationalist vision and his desire to represent black humanity, than a scene in which Mookie is completing an argument with Jade. After they depart, the camera fixes on the graffiti on the wall: "Tawana told the truth!" It is understandable, given Lee's perspective, that he chooses to retrieve this fresh and tortured signifier from the iconographical reservoir of black neonationalists, some of whom believe Tawana transcends her infamous circumstances and embodies the reality of racial violence in our times. Racial violence on every level is vicious now, but Tawana is not its best or most powerful symbol. Lee's invocation of Tawana captures the way in which many positive aspects of neonationalist thought are damaged by close association with ideas and symbols that hurt more than help. Yes, it is important to urge racial self-esteem, a vision for racial progress, the honoring of historical figures, and the creation of powerful culture, but not if the result is a new kind of bigotry. For this reason we must criticize Lee's proximity to Louis Farrakhan's ideological stances. Real transformation of our condition will come only as we explore the resources of progressive thought, social action, and cultural expression that were provided by figures like King, X, Paul Robeson, W. E. B. Du Bois, Lorraine Hansberry, Pauli Murray, and Ida B. Wells. But we can't wallow in unimaginative mimesis. These people's crucial insights, cultural expressions, and transformative activities must inspire us to think critically and imaginatively about our condition and help us generate profound and sophisticated responses to our own crises. Only then will we be able to do the right thing.

Improvisation

On African-American Oral Culture

The desire for literacy has characterized the culture of African-Americans since their arrival here under the myriad brutalities of slavery. Although reading and writing were legally prohibited, black folk developed a resourceful oral tradition that had cultural precedence in African societies. From animal fables to slave reminiscences, from spirituals and blues to ghost tales, black folk generated an oral tradition that expressed and reinforced their cultural values, social norms, and religious beliefs.

Even with the subsequent development of literate intellectual traditions, a resonant orality continues to shape and influence black cultural expressions, including the novels of Toni Morrison, the sermons of Gardner Taylor, and the rap artistry of Kool Moe Dee. Beyond a general connection to black oral culture, however, what do such distinct art forms and intellectual traditions have in common? As *Talk That Talk: An Anthology of African-American Storytelling*, edited by Linda Goss and Marian E. Barnes (Simon and Schuster, 1989), makes clear, it is the genius of story that is the unifying heart of those diverse expressions.

Talk That Talk is a collection of African-American animal tales, family reminiscences, poems, legends, raps, sermons, and biographies, all of which tell stories—of joy and suffering, hope and heartbreak, violence and love. Accompanying each of the book's seven sections are short essays by scholars and professional storytellers, which provide often insightful commentary on various aspects of the black oral tradition.

Animal tales and fables are among the best-known elements of the black storytelling tradition, in which figures like Brer Rabbit represent specific personality and cultural traits. For instance, Brer Rabbit is a small animal who employs cunning to outmaneuver his larger opponents. The tortoise, although burdened by chronic inertia, exhibits plodding persistence. The spider's fragility conceals an iron determination to employ trickery as a survival strategy.

Animal fables also communicate moral lessons about acceptable community behavior. In "Brer Tiger and the Big Wind," the rabbit teaches the other animals the importance of unity in defeating their enemy. The Ghanaian tale "Why Anansi Hides in Corners," in which the spider selfishly refuses to help the rabbit make a drum, admonishes against improper treatment of friends. As Ivan Van Sertima's provocative essay on the trickster figure reveals, the animal fable also expressed the slave's longing for freedom. Thus, the fables were cathartic, didactic, and subversive.

The historical accounts included here present often poignant personal vignettes of difficult times. Jack and Rosa Maddox capture the traumatic transition from slavery to freedom, as Jack speaks of his wife: "She says all we was freed for is to starve to death." Martin Luther King's account of his struggle for clarity and courage in the early stages of the civil rights movement gathers added luminosity when viewed in the context of these stories of personal valor amid suffering and pain.

Although it is short, the selection of sermons provides a refreshing plunge into the richly textured and rhetorically complex world of African-American preaching. Its most able contemporary practitioners, from Frederick Sampson to Carolyn Knight, continue to draw wide portions of the black community to churches throughout America. James Weldon Johnson's "The Creation" remains a classic poetic expression of the black preaching idiom, and C. L. Franklin's "The Prodigal Son" is a real gem.

Franklin, father of soul-music great Aretha Franklin, recorded over sixty sermons for Chess Records. But even in print "The Prodigal Son" displays his deft use of metaphor to expound sophisticated theological truth, his skillful use of repetition to clarify his point, and his brilliant use of "whooping" (chanted speech) to seal his message's emotional authenticity.

The stories of family and home are amusing and revealing. In "The Case of the Missing Strawberry Pie," renowned storyteller Jackie Torrence recounts how her mother and uncle, as little children, robbed the pie safe of a strawberry pie intended for the minister on Sunday. In order to punish the mystery thief, her grandmother had all fourteen children line up and blow their breath into a shotgun, which she said would, when it detected the strawberries on their breath, "go off, and blow your head off."

The ghost and witch tales and the humorous tales and anecdotes brim with portents. Constance Garcia-Barrio's "The Monkey Woman" tells of a monkey who adorned himself in female human flesh in order to marry a man. Her plan ended in misery when their child, who had seen his mother change from monkey to woman, warned the father. At an auspicious moment, the father coolly played music that appealed to monkeys, and as his wife transformed before his very eyes, he cut her head off.

The section devoted to raps, rhythms, and rhymes includes jump-rope rhymes, lyrics from legendary blues performer Leadbelly, and a version of "Signifyin' Monkey" by performer Oscar Brown, Jr. The original "Signifyin' Monkey" is much more raucous and is an outstanding exemplar of the genre of long narrative oral poems called "toasts." This section is especially useful in showing how rap music has both cultural and linguistic antecedents in surviving black oral practices. Two raps are included, but surprisingly no lyrics from prominent, practicing rappers appear. Instead, we have a rap about African-American history and another about the storytelling tradition, both by professional storytellers. This unfortunate and undoubtedly unintended oversight may be an ironic reflection on the already weakened relations between black bourgeois literate culture and the literate subculture of hip-hop.

All in all, though, *Talk That Talk* is an invaluable contribution to those whose vocation it is to examine black cultural practices. Equally important, this anthology may whet the appetite for black storytelling among a new generation of African-Americans.

4

Michael Jackson's Postmodern Spirituality

> *[Michael Jackson] will not swiftly be forgiven for having turned so many tables, for he damn sure grabbed the brass ring, and the man who broke the bank at Monte Carlo has nothing on Michael.*
>
> *—James Baldwin*

> *Sometimes when you're treated unfairly it makes you stronger and more determined. Slavery was a terrible thing, but when black people in America finally got out from under that crushing system, they were* stronger. *They knew what it was to have your spirit crippled by people who are controlling your life. They were never going to let that happen again. I admire that kind of strength. People who have it take a stand and put their blood and soul into what they believe.*
>
> *—Michael Jackson,* Moonwalk

Michael Jackson is, arguably, the greatest *entertainer* of the twentieth century. As an international superstar, Jackson has captured the devotion of a large segment of the world's population in a manner reserved for a select few historic personages. Jackson strikes a deep, primal chord in the human psyche, fascinating us, perhaps, because he so easily and eerily represents us, even mirrors us (all of us) at the same time. Thus, if he is not a Nietzchean *Übermensch,* he is a Promethean allperson who traverses traditional boundaries that separate, categorize, and define differences: innocent/shrewd, young/old, black/white, male/female, and religious/secular.

Perhaps this is also why he frightens us. In his cosmos, Jackson is guided by a logic of experience that flees the comfortable core of life to its often untested periphery. In some senses, Jackson celebrates the dissolution of Yeats's center and exults in the scamper for the edge. If at times his pace to the uncharted is dizzying, his achievements in the wake of his pursuit are dazzling, and at times monumental. It is the nature of these achievements that I want to examine in this essay. I understand Michael Jackson to represent a postmodern form of African-American secular spirituality that is primarily televisual and performance oriented in its medium of expression, and that wrestles in a poignant fashion with moral themes that reflect black cultural and religious consciousness.

However, to suggest that Michael Jackson's art harbors religious significance and spiritual meaning is contentious for many observers of American culture. For some, Jackson is a self-styled Peter Pan figure who is securely nestled in a fantasy world of childlike make-believe, buffered by Disney characters and exotic animals.[1] To others, Jackson is a surpassingly shrewd businessman, capable of amassing a catalogue of publishing rights to songs by such artists as Sly Stone and the Beatles.[2] To others still, Jackson is a victim of the vicious processes of commerce that commodify his image and capitalize on his persona.[3] Certainly these and many other characterizations of Jackson may ring true, but they do not reflect the central truth of his cultural significance, nor do they capture the peculiar and unique genius of his art. Above all else that he may symbolize, central to Jackson's career is an abiding spiritual and religious consciousness that is expressed in his body of work as a performer.

Admittedly, part of the difficulty in discerning the presence of positive spiritual values and redemptive religious consciousness in Jackson's art may be its nontraditional expression. In both its style and substance, Jackson's spirituality exhibits elements that may be understood as postmodern.[4] Postmodernism's broad spectrum of expression—characterized by pastiche, quotation, fragmentation, stylistic merging, transgression, and eclecticism—suggests a dismantling of the hardened distinction between high artistic expression and lowbrow, popular cultural production. These and other postmodernist practices call into question settled beliefs and rigid formulations about art and culture in American life.

For some, postmodernist culture survives, in Roland Barthes's phrase, as the "civilization of the image."[5] Jackson's spirituality exhibits a keen awareness of the important function of imagery. His spirituality is filtered through the televisual apparatus, symbolizing (and symptomatic of) the Gutenberg shift in cultural consciousness marked by the move in our society from the literate to the cinemate, and the hegemony of the visual over the verbal. True to form, Jackson's spirituality is not primarily embodied in a series of written texts, nor is it exclusively articulated in song lyrics. Jackson's postmodern spirituality surfaces in the brilliant, haunting, and sometimes disturbing images and visions portrayed in his music videos and (films of his) live performances.

For Marxist critic Fredric Jameson, postmodernism is linked to and materially precipitated by the globalization of American capital in the late 1950s, expressing the "logic of late capitalism."[6] His early analysis accentuated the negative aspects of postmodernism, with its loss of the sense of history and its exemplification of commodification. Recently, however, Jameson has at least acknowledged some positive characteristics of postmodernism, such as its stress on the wide accessibility of culture and its recuperation of the art of storytelling in literary texts.[7] Other American theorists have uncritically adopted French poststructuralist readings of postmodernism that accentuated marginality, differance, and peripheralization as articulated by figures like Derrida and Lyotard, while ignoring the development of more indigenous expressions in the United States.

Ironically, as Cornel West has noted, these theorists have sought illumination of our American postmodern contexts by borrowing from such figures while neglecting exemplary postmodern African-American cultural producers, particularly artists and musicians.[8] These artists and musicians, from Charlie Parker to Wynton Marsalis, from Romare Bearden to Betye Saar, have wrestled existentially and artistically with disenabling forms of otherness and difference. Thus their artistic production heralds unexamined but crucial resources for contesting the disempowerment that can result from political, economic, social, and cultural marginality.

As a result, these African-American artists offer the possibility of accentuating elements of postmodern cultural experience and artistic expression that are, in Hal Foster's words, "resistant" and not "reactionary."[9] This suggests that these resistant forms of postmodernist production do not simply replicate older forms of artistic production in a nostalgic sense of mimetic play, but extend in their recuperative artistic process the boundaries of cultural expression. This may be viewed in Michael Jackson, who, while drawing upon the enormously skillful performance and dancing of James Brown and the electrifying showmanship of Jackie Wilson, yet manages to insert a unique brand of spiritual consciousness into his performances, yielding powerful forms of artistic, cultural, and religious expression.

Jackson's spiritual and religious awareness can be glimpsed in his persistent preoccupation with images, symbols, and themes that are informed by his own religious background. Jackson was reared as a Jehovah's Witness by his mother, whose faith he shared and, until recently, faithfully practiced. Although the particular character of Jackson's religious reflections and moral musings were shaped by his experience as a Jehovah's Witness, his art reflects perceptions and consciousness that are easily generalizable to the larger stream of African-American spirituality. Thus we may without extensive complication, for example, draw similarities between Jackson's work and the artistic achievements of his musical comrades Stevie Wonder and Marvin Gaye.

Suffice it to say that Jackson's religious sensibilities are expressed in his wrestling with religiously informed, morally shaped, and culturally conditioned themes that include an examining of the nature of good and evil; an exploring of the potentialities for transformation of the self, human nature, and society; a probing of the true nature of manhood in American culture, as opposed to disenabling versions of machismo; a confronting of the material lures and sexual seductions of everyday life in postmodern American culture; a proclaiming of the place of peace and love in transforming the world; and a surveying of the politics of American racial identity and awareness.

These themes recur in Jackson's song lyrics and music videos, and form the basis for the articulation of his own vision of African-American secular spirituality. Jackson is acutely aware of the importance of a morally informed and spiritually grounded perspective on such themes. For instance, in speaking of his role in the

"We Are the World" song-video-event that helped raise money for starving Ethiopians, Jackson, in his autobiography *Moonwalk*,[10] illumines the spiritual theme in the song's message and explains the impetus for his participation:

> In early 1985 we cut "We Are the World" at an all-night all-star recording session that was held after the ceremony for the American Music Awards. I wrote the song with Lionel Richie after seeing the appalling news footage of starving people in Ethiopia and the Sudan. . . . I think that "We Are the World" is a very spiritual song, but spiritual in a special sense. I was proud to be a part of that song and to be one of the musicians there that night. We were united by our desire to make a difference. It made the world a better place for us and it made a difference to the starving people we wanted to help. (pp. 261–62)

While Jackson does not specify the "special" nature of the song's spirituality, it is sufficiently clear that this spirituality bears social ramifications and is at minimum linked to expressing authentic and concrete concern for other human beings. In short, Jackson emphasizes the material consequences of his spiritual Weltanschauung, redeeming it from the possible infamy of an abstract mysticism that uncritically valorizes sentimental and emotive modes of expression. Furthermore, it is apparent elsewhere in Jackson's text that this spirituality is a gift from God and must be expressed in the particular vocational calling for which God has chosen him, namely his music and performance:

> I've always joked that I didn't ask to sing and dance, but it's true. When I open my mouth, music comes out. I'm honored that I have this ability. I thank God for it every day. I try to cultivate what He gave me. I feel I'm compelled to do what I do. (p. 272)

In discussing the spiritual character of his gift, Jackson speaks about his mother's faith:

> She instilled in me a love of Him that I will always have. She taught me that my talent for singing and dancing was as much God's work as a beautiful sunset or a storm that left snow for children to play in. Despite all the time we spent rehearsing and traveling, Mom would find time to take me to Kingdom Hall of the Jehovah's Witnesses, usually with Rebbie and LaToya. (pp. 12–13)

Moreover, Jackson is driven by a desire to enflesh this spirituality, to enable others to perceive the vision that energizes and empowers him, and in the process to transform people's lives with his art, with the stories that he sings and "tells":

> I've always wanted to be able to tell stories, you know, stories that came from the soul. I'd like to sit by a fire and tell people stories—make them see pictures, make them cry and laugh, take them anywhere emotionally with something as deceptively simple as words. I'd like to tell tales to move their souls and transform them. . . . In a way, songwriting uses the same skills, creates the emotional highs and lows. . . . There are very few books written on the art of storytelling, how to grip listeners. . . . No costumes, no makeup, no nothing, just you and your voice, and your powerful ability to take them anywhere, to transform their lives, if only for minutes. (pp. 5–6)

Jackson's art, then, is intentional and goal oriented, and self-consciously related to the spiritual roots that have nourished its beginning and that continue to sustain its expanding identity.

Jackson's spirituality, though, is a secular spirituality, which may at first appear to be an oxymoronic formulation. Jackson's spirituality is secular precisely because its primary site of execution and expression is not the church sanctuary but the concert stage, and because it is not embedded in conventional ecclesiastical structures or transmitted in traditional religious linguistic or liturgical practices. Furthermore, his secular spirituality does not assume that a prior grounding in the shared language of a religious community is needed in order to grasp its basic premises.

Neither does it make identity formed in intellectual exchange or conceptual dialogue needed for comprehension or participation. Jackson articulates powerful forms of human identity in images, symbols, and language that are shaped by, but not limited to, his own religious experience. Thus, the many traditions of moral reflection and ethical analysis that derive from a common Judeo-Christian heritage in American society are consonant in many crucial respects with Jackson's own vision of peace, love, and justice. Similar to the way that devotees of African-American religion participating in the civil rights movement appealed to a language of rights, thus allowing them to express their conceptions of peace, justice, and liberation in secular terms, so does

Jackson's spirituality find a "language" that is understood by members of an American culture not sharing his own religious experience.[11]

Furthermore, Jackson's spirituality is secular because it is created for, and best thrives in, the cultural, psychic, and social spaces of the concert world, and not the *ekklesia*. It is not situated in, or sustained by, conventional procedures of church participation, service, or worship. This does not mean, however, that Jackson's spirituality is devoid of religious drama involving rituals, pageantry, and spectacles.[12] On the contrary, Jackson's secular spirituality, particularly as performed on the concert stage, is replete with references to certain African-American religiocultural practices that signify in the musical arena.

For instance, Jackson's concerts thrive on call and response. Jackson's live performances mediate ritual structures of antiphonal oral and verbal exchange between artist and audience. Such antiphonal exchange permits the artist to articulate his or her vision and authorizes the audience to acknowledge its reception and even shape its meaning by responding to the emotion being expressed, refracting the message being sent, or reaffirming the idea being communicated. In this context, meaning is an open-ended process that resists premature or permanent closure. This secular koinonia of communicants (artist and audience) constitutes a text whose understanding necessitates mutual participation in order to explore and unpack its multiple meanings. In the best of the African-American religious tradition, meaning is produced by an ever-evolving, perennially transforming, historically conditioned set of cultural practices, rhetorical strategies, and religious signifiers. Jackson's phenomenal and protean energies in live performance exemplify this point.

Furthermore Jackson's performances richly fuse Bakhtinian conceptions of carnival with African-American forms of spiritual ecstasy, producing a highly animated hybrid that creates space for cultural resistance and religious agency.[13] Both carnival and African-American religious ecstatic experience have been devalued as cathartic, excessive, and celebrative of the "low" in human nature. But it is just this emphasis on the "low" religious expression of ecstasy, empathy, and subjective experientialism—versus the "high" religious expression of control, stolidity, and objective experientialism—that marks, in part, the subversive potentialities and powers of African-American religion.

Also, it is the "low" cultural expression of laughter, bodily pleasure, and vernacular language—versus the "high" cultural expression of solemnity, repression, and classical language—that expresses the powers of culturally degraded masses to revolt and survive. Carnival prevents rank and social hierarchy from tyrannizing social expression, much as progressive Christian conceptions of democracy allow the free social expression of equal beings.[14] Bakhtin says, "Carnival celebrated temporary liberation from the prevailing truth and from the established order: it marked the suspension of all hierarchical rank, privileges, norms and prohibitions."[15] Jackson taps into and ties these traditions together in a highly skillful and empowering fashion.

The primary form of Jackson's secular spirituality is televisual. In fact, the major moments in Jackson's vocation have been catalyzed by the visual medium, either on television or in music video. For instance, Jackson's passage from music superstar to a world historical and cultural figure was ritually enacted on May 16, 1983, with his mythic dance performance of the "moonwalk" on the "Motown 25" television special, which was beamed to almost 50 million viewers around the globe. Jackson's uncanny dexterity, disciplined grace, and explosive imagination coalesced in a series of immortal movements, which, in their turn, freeze-framed the recrudescent genius of street dance, summarized the important history of Fred Astaire–like purposeful grace in executing dance steps, and extended the brilliant tradition of African-American performers like Bojangles, Sammy Davis, and Katherine Dunham surging against the odds to create vital art.

Jackson's epochal routine skyrocketed his record sales and catapulted him into the stellar reaches of fame, landing him on the cover of the *Guiness Book of World Records* for selling over 40 million copies of his album *Thriller*, the most in music history. His autobiography *Moonwalk*, edited by Jackie Onassis, was aptly named, for it captures the watershed moment in Jackson's career and symbolizes his transformation into a personality of almost universal appeal.

The televisual medium, then, is central to Jackson's expression of his musical vision of life. When he was making the album *Thriller*, Jackson writes,

> I was determined to present this music as visually as possible. At the time I would look at what people were doing with video, and I couldn't understand why so much of it seemed so primitive and weak. I saw kids watching and accepting boring videos because they had no alternatives. My goal is to do the best I can in every area, so why work hard on an album and then produce a terrible video? I wanted something that would *glue* you to the set, something you'd want to watch over and over. . . . So I wanted to be a pioneer in this relatively new medium and make the best short music movies we could make. I don't even like to call them videos. On the set I explained that we were doing a *film*, and that was how I approached it. (pp. 201–2)

Since the televisual medium is so crucial to Jackson's vision of life, it is here that I want to concentrate my analysis in examining the confluence of music, medium, and message in Jackson's art. In the remaining part of the essay, then, I will trace some of the themes that constitute Jackson's African-American secular spirituality as they are presented in a major (but not exclusive) mode of expression for him—the music video. These themes include, as stated above, the nature of good and evil; the potentialities for transformation of the self, human nature, and society; the nature of real manhood in American culture; the politics of racial identity in America; and the place of love in changing the world. In exploring these themes in Jackson's art, I will examine two representative Jackson videos, "Thriller,"[16] and "Bad,"[17] and a live performance of "Man in the Mirror"[18] at the 1988 Grammy Awards.

Jackson's "Thriller" marked a revolutionary use of the music video. As Jackson indicated in the quote cited above, he intended to make a singular contribution to the field. In fact all of his videos are distinct and defy easy categorization.[19] "Thriller" (which capped Jackson's first period of music video creation) presents a fantastical, wild, even scary vision of human transformation that rests upon conventions developed in the horror-film genre and utilizes the werewolf figure as a metaphor of the potential for personal transmogrification. "Thriller" employs a variety of horror film staples, such as sophisticated makeup, special effects, eerie music, and even the chillingly familiar voice of thrill-master Vincent Price. It is a mark of Jackson's unique imaginative powers that he is able to explore questions of human nature and identity in this film genre.

The video begins with a written disclaimer: "Due to my strong personal convictions, I wish to stress that this film in no way endorses a belief in the occult." Jackson was then still connected to the Jehovah's Witness, and this statement was a concession to their concern about the possible misinterpretation of the video's content. The opening scene of "Thriller" depicts Jackson and his girlfriend, portrayed by Ola Ray, driving in a white 1950s Buick. Suddenly they are out of gas, and Jackson faces the embarrassing task of reporting this to Ray, knowing his companion will suspect a typical male ruse to initiate romantic tomfoolery. Jackson says that they are honestly out of gas, to Ray's incredulous ears. They get out of the car and begin to walk. Finally, however, Ray apologizes for her initial disbelief.

Jackson's character then begins to talk with Ray, expressing his affection for her and hoping that she will return a similar affection to him. As they embrace, Jackson asks her to be his "girl." To make it official, Jackson gives her a ring. He then tells her that he must vouchsafe a piece of important information to her, namely that he is "not like other guys." This, of course, is a statement with which Jackson observers, fans and detractors alike, would heartily agree. After Ray says she understands this, Jackson insists that she is missing his point, that he is different in a way much different than she appreciates.

Until now, the sterile placidity of the couple's nocturnal surroundings remain undisturbed, and only reinforce the engaging and affectionate emotions being mutually expressed between Jackson and Ray. But Jackson's announcement of Derridean differance shatters the unity of natural and personal calm. The pain of his self-awareness is the occasion for subsequent turmoil in Jackson and his companion. It is at the very point of Jackson's announcement that he begins to exhibit the specific and exaggerated character of his difference. The physiological structure of Jackson's countenance becomes radically altered, as he commences an ontological descent into animalistic debasement: he becomes a werewolf.

The transformation is now complete, and Jackson is the Freak, the one whose being and appearance cause utter horror and total repulsion (much like London's famed "Elephant Man," with whose remains Jackson is fascinated). He begins to chase his companion, who runs shrieking from the immense vulgarity of his transformed visage. Just as the werewolf corners her, we see a movie audience and understand that what we have just seen is a film being watched by an audience on film.

In the audience are Jackson and Ray, she horrified by what she has seen, Jackson relishing the gore of every cut, slice, and painful grimace. Ray removes herself from the audience, and Jackson, after savoring a final glimpse, follows her. After assuring Ray that "it was just a movie," the music to "Thriller" begins, with its menacing bass line foreshadowing the ominous events about to occur. Jackson sings the words to "Thriller," speaking about the evil lurking in the dark, the terror-filled night visions, and the paralysis that results from such visions. As he continues to sing, graves begin to open up, and unseemly creatures begin to emerge from long sleep, recalling some night of the living dead.

Just as the words indicate that "no mere mortal can resist the evil of thriller," Jackson is transformed into one of the creatures, growing fangs and developing dark circled eyes. In the next scene, Jackson's face is returned to normal, as he continues to warn of the consequences of the "Thriller night." Once again, Jackson is transformed, even transmogrified, into a horrible creature, and along with other ghoulish "demons" he begins to pursue Ray. They chase her into a house, where her crying screams are met with more creatures coming out of the floorboards and through the windows. As they crowd in for the final assault, Ray offers her ultimate terror-struck shriek, and Jackson, once again changed to his normal face, greets her and asks her what is wrong. As he helps her to her feet and they leave, he turns to the camera, with fangish mouth and devilish yellow eyes.

It would be obviously stretching the truth to suggest that "Thriller" offers Jackson's self-conscious attempt to theologically thematize his conception of human nature and human identity. Also, there are troubling aspects to Jackson's adoption of the horror film genre, which has notoriously sexualized victimization by constituting women as objects of male monster violent desire. However, I believe that "Thriller" does provide a lens on aspects of Jackson's views about human nature and on problems of evil that reflect his religious and moral views.

The lyrics to "Thriller" were not written by Jackson, but by Rod Temperton, a former member of the group Heatwave, itself a product of diverse American and British cultural and musical elements in the mid-1970s. In his lyrics, Temperton represents the threat of horror approaching from the outside. The human beings (Jackson and Ray) are victimized by events external to their nature or control, and evil intent is expressed through creatures radically unlike themselves:

> It's close to midnight and something evil's lurking in the dark / Under the moonlight you see a sight that almost stops your heart / . . . You hear the door slam and realize there's nowhere left to run / You feel the cold hand and wonder if you'll ever see the sun / You close your eyes and hope that this is just imagination / But all the while you hear the creature creepin' up behind / You're out of time / . . . There ain't no second chance against this thing with forty eyes

Jackson provides Ray protection, however, from the marauding monsters:

> Now is the time for you and I to cuddle close together / All through the night I'll save you from the terrors on the screen, I'll make you see

The further innuendo points to Jackson's ability to romantically thrill Ray:

> . . . It's a thriller, thriller night / 'Cause I can thrill you more than any ghost would dare to try / Girl, this is thriller, thriller night / So let me hold you tight and share a killer, diller, chiller, / Thriller here tonight

In his minimovie version of "Thriller" (which was nominated for an Oscar in the short film category), Jackson extends its range of meaning and expands its spectrum of signifiers, with the result that he expresses some of his views about human nature. First, Jackson represents the horror of evil as both an external event embodied in transhuman creatures and as an internal experience embodied in human creatures. Even more pointedly, the terrain of evil embodiment is the self, which has grave consequences for the human being, especially in altered behavior, attitudes, and physiological appearance. It is a totalizing process that affects, even infects, the whole human organism. In the movie, Jackson's turn from magnanimous protector to malicious pursuer indicates the dialectical tension of good and evil that defines the human predicament and illumines the difficult context of choice between moral opposites, particularly when they are embedded in the same human being.

For Jackson's "Thriller," human identity is an imperfect, messy amalgam of good and evil, of *humanitas* and *animalis*, of oppositional tendencies that inhabit the same psychic, spiritual, and biological space. A full comprehension of the social practices, personal habits, and cultural behavior manifested in acts of goodness must be chastened by an awareness of the potential for wrong and harm. Likewise, the judgment of the expression of evil social practices, personal habits, and cultural behavior must be tempered by the recognition of the human possibilities to do good acts and to generate productive lifestyles. In short, there are discernible traces of religious conceptions of human nature and identity in Jackson's video version of "Thriller" that acknowledge the limits of human capacities for good and also acknowledge an awareness of the human capability to do harm. It is not altogether unlike the view of human nature that informed Reinhold Niebuhr's political realism and influenced Martin Luther King, Jr.'s, thought.[20]

Furthermore, in "Thriller" Jackson has, at least inadvertently, raised the issue of marginality, difference, and otherness in much the same way that he indirectly precipitates conversations about such topics in real life (especially because of his alleged multiple cosmetic surgeries). The werewolf signifies the Embodied Other, the spectacle of a difference so gross that it evokes responses of fear, terror, or horror in gasping onlookers. Some may view this as a proleptic revelation of Jackson's own existential grappling with his Otherness, to be subsequently revealed in the "horrifying" spectacle of Jackson's transformation of his own face.

On the matter of his plastic surgery, Jackson complains that as he went from a "cute," chubby-faced kid to a lean young man, "the press started accusing me of surgically altering my appearance, beyond the nose job I freely admitted I had" (p. 229). Jackson denies having his cheeks altered, his lips thinned, or his skin peeled. In exasperation, he asks rhetorically, "What does my face have to do with my music or my dancing?" (p. 230). Apparently Jackson fails to understand that, as a cultural icon, the seeming de-Africanization of his face and the Europeanization of his image reflect a wrestling with profound questions of identity and self-image that influence the way his artistic achievements are perceived. In any regard, the werewolf character, although a highly stylized signifier rooted in Jackson's fantasy life, communicates the aesthetic dissonance, social terror, and personal repulsion that may result from (racial, sexual) forms of otherness and difference.

That the site of otherness would be the body (versus the mind, for example, in forms of madness) speaks volumes of the African-American confrontation with debilitating forms and uses of embodiment. The socially, morally, and economically repugnant uses of African-American embodiment, rooted in the commodification of the black body, began under slavocracy in American culture. The black body was articulated as the primal other, the form of difference par excellence. Such uses of the black body were repudiated in African-American religious practices, which redeemed the use of the body by employing it in rites of sanctification, rituals of purification, and acts of celebration. Jackson's expression of religious joy through his celebrative dance routines captures at least one pole of the redemptive use of the black body articulated in black religious practices.

In "Thriller" Jackson has managed, in his own peculiar and idiosyncratic manner, to encapsulate and represent certain of his views about evil and about human nature and human identity. Jackson as werewolf indicates the possibility of the radical instability of human nature and reflects the underlining of absolute distinctions between good and evil. The werewolf indicates the possibility of human beings embodying radical forms of evil and inflicting evil on other human beings, whether psychologically or in empirical events of social malevolence. The werewolf also indicates the Other, whose very embodiment occasions fear in those he or she encounters.

In his song and video "Bad," Jackson turns to more familiar cultural and social territory, as he examines the terms of existence for those who must straddle barriers between two worlds divided by race and class. Jackson searingly probes the complexities of making judgments about moral issues generated in the urban inner city. "Bad" is a takeoff on the Edmund Perry story.[21] Edmund Perry was a brilliant Harlem youth who graduated with honors from Phillips Exeter Academy, a prestigious prep school in New Hampshire, and was awarded a full scholarship to Stanford University. Ten days after his graduation, while back home in Harlem, he was killed on New York City's Upper West Side by a white policeman, Lee Van Houten, who claimed that Perry and his brother Jonah had viciously beaten him during a robbery attempt. Perry's story is told in a controversial book, *Best Intentions*, by Robert Sam Anson.[22]

"Bad" opens with a full camera view of Duxston prep school, couched in winter snow and obvious opulence, supported by ominous strains of music. As with "Thriller," the serenity and wholesome environment masks the potential for evil that lurks within, as Hitchcock's proverbial clean suburban landscape conceals the absurdity underneath. We then see the empty hallways and neat stairways of Duxston, followed by a full-face shot of Jackson slowly raising his head from a bowed position, indicating that the story and world we will see are his. The camera breaks to students running down the stairs and halls of Duxston, exulting in glee over the apparent winter break. Jackson is seen running down the hall and being stopped by a white male student who says that he wants to tell Darryl (Jackson's character) that he has done a good job this term, that he has worked hard, and that he is proud of Darryl. Darryl thanks him, after which the white student says, "High five, man. Take care." Darryl exchanges the high five gesture with the white student, and other students are shown running out of school.

The next scene switches to Jackson riding on the train, viewing the world outside his window. The camera pans back to a full view of the aisle and seats, showing Darryl talking to a white schoolmate while other white schoolmates make a mess of the train. To the left corner of the camera, and the train, sits a student of Latino descent with an open book, unsmilingly surveying the scene of recreative havoc created by the white students and glancing toward Darryl as he continues his conversation with the white student.

The scene dissolves, and Darryl and the Latino student are now the focus of the camera, with a mostly deserted background, indicating the passage of time. The Latino student begins to look at Darryl, peering at him as Darryl now sits alone. Over the loudspeaker, the announcer declares that the next station is Grand Central Terminal, the final stop of the train. The camera then pans in to a full-faced shot of the Latino student directing a piercing smirk and cutting glance at Darryl, who is foregrounded in a visually blurred manner while strains of troubling music insinuate themselves in the background. Darryl looks at the Latino student and gives a tentative smile that tests the tension of their nonverbal exchange, then looks away. The two of them, along with the few other passengers, get off the train.

The next scene shows a crowded subway, as the camera pans down a row of riding passengers: first a middle-aged black woman with her eyes closed after an apparently hard day of work; a pensive white woman; an elderly couple who look to be slightly worried; a young black woman looking down; a stern white woman blankly staring forward, the perfect exemplar of a person dulled by mind-numbing, alienated work in a Marxist vision; and finally the Latino student with Darryl next to him, both of their heads involuntarily shaking to the rhythm of the subway's movement.

The Latino student turns to Darryl, and as the camera focuses on Darryl's face, the Latino student asks him, "How many guys proud of you?" Darryl quietly counts with his lips and, without looking at the Latino student, says, "Three." With an ironic smile, the Latino student holds up four fingers and says, "Shoot, four guys proud of me!" Darryl looks at him and they smile, both recognizing that it is a source of perennial surprise to their fellow white students that they are able to excel at school. This is a subtle but powerful critique by Jackson of white liberalism, which has the power to stigmatize and punish with its often unconscious condescension even as it intends to single out and celebrate. This form of critique, of course, is linked to potent traditions of African-American religious and cultural criticism developed over centuries of protest against injustice and struggle for freedom.

As the Latino student prepares to leave his stop on the subway, he gives Darryl a soul brother handshake and says, "Be the man." Darryl responds to him, "Be the man." The significance here is that the high five of the white student earlier is juxtaposed against the soul handclasp of the Latino student. The high five, in this case, is a stylized, fashionable handshake that signifies an ephemeral, external code of relationship between Darryl and the white student. Alhough the white student is expressing attempted camaraderie and friendship, the high five is more a testament of the cultural distance between them than an acknowledgment of their bonds of social intimacy.

The Latino student's soul handclasp, however, is a meaningful, internal code of unspoken solidarity generated out of common circumstances of victimization and objectification. Furthermore, the Latino student's parting exhortation to Darryl to "be the man" is a culturally encoded signifier that subverts the usual semantic meaning of the terms and counsels a steadfast resolve to remain strong and rooted in one's own cultural identity while achieving success at "the man's" (white man's) institution.

The next scene shows a row of dilapidated, boarded-up brownstones in Harlem and a row of men standing around twenty-gallon oil drums, warming themselves over the fires they have started within, not an inappropriate metaphor for the condition of black men in contemporary American culture. As Darryl walks down the street a black man hollers at him, "Yo. Yo, blood. Yo." When Darryl does not answer him (perhaps because he knows that what the man wants he cannot give, or that what he wants he should not have), the man shrugs him off with hand gestures that say, "Forget it."

As Darryl continues to amble down the street, three other "brothers" catch sight of him, and one of them declares, as he hugs Darryl, "The Black is back. Yo. Black is back, my man," and the other two fellows joyfully greet him. After this, Darryl goes up into his apartment telling the "fellas" that he'll be down later. After Darryl goes into his apartment and reads a note of welcome from his mother who has to work late, until seven, he finds a window and looks out over the material morass and spiritual squalor that litter his neighborhood, a Harlem gutted by social misery and urban stench. The next scene shows Darryl and his three friends in the hallways of a building engaging in harmless chitchat and ribbing, as one of his friends inquires about Darryl's major. When Darryl responds that he is in high school, which requires no major, the friend asks, "Then what's your minor?" All of them, including Darryl, have a good laugh. Not so funny later on, and indicative of the trouble to come, is when Darryl is asked if the "white boys" at his school wear "turtle shells." "That's tortoise shells," Darryl replies. There is icy silence in the room, thick with resentment over Darryl's benignly intentioned correction.

After the leader of the group indicates that it is time to "go" (i.e., engage in petty criminal behavior), the scene changes to a street corner, where a man with a cane is transacting a drug sale with another man. After the man with the cane completes the sale, Darryl and his friends are seen leaning against a car, regarding him with a cautious silence. The man pulls back his jacket to reveal a revolver and asks if they are looking for somebody. The fellas, getting the message, depart.

Later, back in a building, the leader declares to Darryl, "Hunts up. Hunts up, homeboy. There are victims out there waitin' for us." Darryl utters a defiant question—"What?"—that rebuts the leader's criminal intentions. The leader declares, " 'What?' Shit! Homeboy ain't home. Naw, see he up at Dunesbury playin' tennis with his turtle shells." Thus, the struggle to maintain one's integrity and to construct a stable identity as a member of the underclass in the inner-city community surfaces. Jackson's video focuses sharply on the central problems of defining identity and examining the moral character of decisions that take account of the social and economic forces that form the background against which these choices must be made. Darryl responds to the leader, "Back off." After a rough verbal encounter, the leader grabs Darryl and says, "Yo man, what's wrong? Are you bad? Or is that what they teach you up at that sissy school of yours: how to forget who your friends are? Well let me tell you somethin', I don't care what they teach you up there. You either down or you ain't down. So the question is, are you bad or what?" The basis of their past relationship is shattered, and Darryl must renegotiate the terms of his relationship to his "in-group" if any form of that relationship is to survive.

Darryl tells the leader to leave him alone, that he's tired of him "messin' " with him. Finally he takes off his gloves and jacket and says that if the leader really wants to see what is bad, then he will show him. At this point we (and Darryl) are still in a morally ambiguous position, because we cannot ascertain the particular nature of Darryl's challenge, whether it will be a show of neighborhood machismo that revels in theft and crime, or whether it will be to subvert neighborhood conceptions of what is "bad," similar to what happened between Darryl and the Latino student's subversion of the code of success in the white world. This is an implicit appeal to the culturally encoded practice that uses words like "tough" and "bad" to mean something different, often their opposite. Jackson skillfully displays the dual tensions that define Darryl's world and that, in much more detail and depth, defined Edmund Perry's world. Moral choice is seen against a background of several factors that must be considered when one judges the actions of inner-city youth who resort to a life of crime to "make it." Jackson's moral vision, unquestionably formed by his own religious views, is able to appreciate these subtleties and promotes a vision that combines compassion and criticism.

The next scene shows Darryl and the fellas at a deserted section of the subway, awaiting a lone man walking down the corridor. Darryl, under the pressure to prove his "badness," is poised to pounce and prey upon the man, but at the last moment decides to tell him to flee. The man speaks no English, reinforcing the fact that victims of ghetto machismo or criminal activity are often other underclass and struggling people. The fellas become angry with Darryl, and declare, "You aren't down with us no more," and Darryl responds, "You ain't bad, you ain't nothin.' " Here again, Jackson's own moral perspective is informed by an understanding of human nature that acknowledges that all human beings embody the potential for wrongdoing. But as is clear in his reading of the story, all human beings have the ability to contribute to their own future by the choices they make and the options they exercise. This is no static conception of human nature and identity, no social determinism that locks human beings into predestined choice. It is rather a Christian understanding of human nature that appreciates the complexity and ambiguity that surrounds our moral choices, that posits an ambivalent disposition toward the desires that occupy our social landscape, and that accentuates the historical formation of the virtues we attempt to nourish.

At this juncture, the scene, until now black and white, blooms in full color, as dancers emerge from either side of the columns in the subway, rupturing the realism that has informed the video to this point. From then on, Darryl's message is communicated in Jackson's powerful singing voice, accompanied by extraordinarily skillful dancing that choreographs his message to the fellas. Jackson reverses the power arrangement between Darryl and the fellas that has defined their relationship as he sings:

> Your butt is mine / Gonna tell you right / Just show your face / In broad daylight / I'm telling you / On how I feel / Gonna hurt your mind / Don't shoot to kill / . . . I'm giving you / On count of three / To show your stuff / Or let it be . . . / I'm telling you / Just watch your mouth / I know your game / What you're about / Well they say the sky's the limit / And to me that's really true / But my friend you have seen nothin' / Just wait 'til I get through . . . / Because I'm bad, I'm bad —come on

At the climax of his melodied oration, Darryl comes face to face with the leader of the fellas in a dramatic encounter reminiscent of the machismo-laden staredowns between prize fighters. Darryl scorns their wrongdoing in a fusion of speech and song that is the strongest evocation of the African-American religious rhetorical practice of "whooping," "chanting," or "tuning" since the advent of rap music. Darryl's lyrical preachment is accented by the antiphonal response of his amen chorus of backup dancer-singers, who meet his every word and gesture with a rising spiral of vocal support that crescendos with a hissing noise meant to seal their message and admonish their hearers.

At the end, Darryl and the leader lock arms and finally engage in a soul handshake, sealing the leader's respect for Darryl, as he intones, "That's the way it goes down, huh?" The soul handshake reinstitutes the possibility for personal and social solidarity between Darryl and the leader, functioning, as it did with the Latino student, to strengthen the ties of mutuality and community. As the fellas depart, one of the brothers removes his hat, acknowledging the power of Darryl's perspective, even as the scene returns to black and white and Darryl's garb returns to his jacket and street clothes.

Jackson's "Bad" video premiered on a CBS television special that aired August 31, 1987, before a national viewing audience. It conveyed a moving message about struggling with racial identity, forms of machismo, and the problems of underclass black men in a potent mix of song and dance. It also testified to the national, even worldwide, influence of Jackson's African-American secular spirituality.

Perhaps the most poignant and powerfully explicit display of Jackson's brand of secular spirituality was reserved for the 1988 Grammy Awards Show, beamed to millions of people around the world. As the auditorium faded to dark, a white screen was shown, silhouetting Jackson's lithe image, his head topped by a dark brown fedora, his palm facing outward to the right on the end of his stiffened right arm, and his left leg extended, capped off by his trademark high-water pants, with a blue shirt circled at the waist by a white sash, and white socks and black shoes. As the audience screamed, strains of harmonies filled the air, and Jackson enacted ten seconds of solo dance movements, pantomiming some of his most agile poses. As the screen rose, Jackson began to sing, in an impassioned voice, a slow gospel-cadenced version of his song, "The Way You Make Me Feel." As Jackson gyrated on stage, the female dancer-actress Tatiana, famous from the video version of the song, emerged from the side of the stage. Jackson was also joined by four dancers who, with him, recreated the moves performed in the video.

Jackson then did a phenomenal foursquare version of the moonwalk, the dance that he made famous. The auditorium again faded to dark, with the spotlight on Jackson. He bowed, took the microphone handed to him, and began singing stanzas to "Man in The Mirror:"

> I'm gonna make a change, for once in my life / It's gonna feel real good, gonna make a difference / Gonna make it right . . . / As I turn up the collar on my favorite winter coat / This wind is blowin' my mind / I see the kids in the street, with not enough to eat / Who am I, to be blind? / Pretending not to see their needs / A summer's disregard, a broken bottle top / And a one man's soul / They follow each other on the wind, ya' know /

> 'Cause they got nowhere to go / That's why I want you to know / I'm starting with the man in the mirror / I'm asking him to change his ways / And no message could have been any clearer / If you wanna make the world a better place / Take a look at yourself, and then make a change

As he sang, the camera panned into his face as people from either side of the stage emerged from the wings. To his left were two singers, including Siedah Garrett, coauthor of "Man in The Mirror." To his right were three singers, including contemporary gospel great Andrae Crouch.

Jackson was singing, with their support, about the necessity for beginning the change in the world with one's self. As he stated in "Moonwalk:"

> "Man in the Mirror" is a great message. I love that song. If John Lennon was alive, he could really relate to that song because it says that if you want to make the world a better place, you have to work on yourself and change first. It's the same thing Kennedy was talking about when he said, "Ask not what your country can do for you; ask what you can do for your country." If you want to make the world a better place, take a look at yourself and make a change. Start with the man in the mirror. Start with yourself. Don't be looking at all the other things. Start with you. That's the truth. That's what Martin Luther King meant and Gandhi too. That's what I believe. (pp. 267–68)

As Jackson, Crouch, Garrett, and the others continued to sing, the choir from New York's New Hope Baptist Church emerged from the back of the stage, augmenting the vocal power of Jackson's message. The religious nature of Jackson's interpretation became visually apparent, and the implicitly religious sensibilities of his performance became explicitly captured in the religious symbols surrounding Jackson. Jackson spun and fell on his knees, dramatizing his message of the dialectical relationship between personal change and social transformation. Back on his feet, Jackson pleaded once more for the world to change. Again he fell to his knees, but this time he succumbed to the spirit and passion of the moment and remained there. Jackson was spontaneously touched by what was occurring, as if he were a spectator to the event, as if he were only a vehicle, an agent of a transcendent power. Jackson was as shaken by the power of the message as if he were hearing and delivering it for the first time, a lesson that great gospel singers and preachers have mastered. Andrae Crouch then moved over from the side of the stage, as if he were in a church service where someone was "slain in the spirit," and after wiping Jackson's brow, he helped him to his feet. Jackson, with new vitality breathed into him, "got happy" again, turning several times, spinning joyously, and spontaneously jumping up and down, shaking his hands, and doing a complex walk-skip-jump movement.

Jackson's choreography of his religious joy, as he transformed the Grammy stage into a sanctuary, was infectious, and his audience, his faithful congregation, responded in the ecstatic glee of emotional abandon to his every move, groan, and gesture. Jackson exhorted them by telling them that everyone has to make a change, that the black man has to make a change, and that the white man has to make a change. As he dropped to his knees yet another time, the twenty-person choir moved ever closer to him, cutting off the stage and reducing it to a diamond, both in its shape and substance. It was priceless and invaluable because Jackson was projecting the power of African-American spirituality forward and having it rearticulated back to him in the reverberating emotion of the audience and the escalating ecstasy of his singers. Jackson went down, like a martyr figure delivering a messianic message, sinking to his knees that his audience might, as he repeatedly implored them, "stand up, stand up, stand up." Jackson then resorted to his best exhortative deep-throated vocal to release a volcanic melisma and syllabic repetition of the word you, in "you-you-you-ou-ow-ow got to make a change," catalyzing a tumultuous response in the Grammy audience.

At the consummation of his homily in song, Jackson whispered, "Make that change," and his congregation came to their feet, thundering their applauded amen at Jackson, yielding their total love and trust to his expressed desire to change the world by their changing themselves. The camera displayed a felicitous complicity in the spirit of the moment and scouted the audience for the converted and the committed, finding them scattered throughout the auditorium's scene of pandemonium.

Quincy Jones was clapping in recognition of his young charge's genius and in graceful acknowledgment of their amazingly productive and satisfying partnership over the last decade. Prince, typically unsmiling, was nonetheless on his feet, giving Jackson his due. Jody Watley was smiling broadly and clapping with joy. Behind her was Anita Baker, raising her hand in testimony to the spirit's presence and ejaculating an incendiary "yeah" in verbal testimony to her spiritual enthusiasm. There, too, was Little Richard, a cultural icon himself, whose face was brushed with a deep and clear joy, perhaps vicariously exulting in Jackson's glorious fulfillment, a fulfillment denied Little Richard, a real pillar of rock 'n' roll. (Jackson would return the joy later, as he was the first to his feet when Little Richard playfully chided the recording academy for not recognizing his original genius by awarding him a Grammy.) Finally there were the Houstons, Whitney and Cissy, exhibiting in their individual persons what Jackson combined: powerful forms of traditional, black, gospel-inflected music wed to crossover, rich, hook-laden music supported by diluted but still driving African-American beats.

Jackson's performance revealed a crucial aspect of his vocation: a theatricalization of spirituality, a festive choreography of religious reality that is often present in his live performances. The manner in which Jackson is able to evoke a virtually religious response from even secular concert attenders, a response that transcends mere emotional expression or simple cathartic release, is astonishing. He articulates a vision of the world that, although it includes idiosyncratic and fantastical elements, nonetheless communicates powerful religious truths and moral themes that are expressed in his riveting music and videos.

Michael Jackson seizes the parameters of the artistically possible and expands them to dimensions beyond most of our imaginations. He increases the influence of black religious experience and practices by articulating through televisual media his brand of African-American secular spirituality and institution-transcending piety, rife with appropriate religious and cultural imagery. He also transforms the stage into a world-extending sanctuary on which he enacts rituals of religious ecstasy, moral courage, and spiritual passion that mediate substantive concerns about love, peace, and justice, simultaneously subverting cultural consensus about what constitutes the really "bad" and the "good." He embodies a postmodern version of African-American secular spirituality that has the opportunity to spread its influence into the next century and to ensure the presence in the larger American and world culture of some of the most poignant and creative art developed from an enormously rich and resourceful tradition.

Notes

1. See Larry Black, "The Man in the Mirror," *Maclean's*, May 2, 1988, p. 67; Michael Goldberg and David Handelman, "Is Michael Jackson for Real?" *Rolling Stone*, September 24, 1987, p. 55; Jay Cooks and Denise Worrell, "Bringing Back the Magic," *Time*, July 16, 1984, p. 63; and Jim Miller and Janet Huck, "The Peter Pan of Pop," *Newsweek*, January 10, 1983, pp. 52–54.

2. See Peter Petre, "The Traumas of Molding Crazes into Cash," *Fortune*, July 23, 1984, p. 48; Alex Ben Block, "Just One More Thriller," *Forbes 400*, October 1, 1984, pp. 232–34; "Michael Jackson Says 'Beat It' to Bootleggers," *Businessweek*, June 4, 1984, p. 36; and Goldberg and Handelman, "Is Michael Jackson for Real?" p. 140.

3. See, for example, "The Prisoner of Commerce," *New Republic*, April 16, 1984, p. 4.

4. For an explication of the European (especially French) contexts of postmodernism, see Jean-François Lyotard, *The Postmodern Condition: A Report on Knowledge*, trans. Geoff Bennington and Brian Massumi (Minneapolis: University of Minnesota Press, 1984); for an exploration of contemporary American postmodernism, see Hal Foster, ed., *The Anti-Aesthetic: Essays in Postmodern Culture* (Port Townsend, Wash.: Bay Press, 1983); see also Andreas Huyssen, *After the Great Divide: Modernism, Mass Culture, Postmodernism* (Bloomington: Indiana University Press, 1986); see also his essay, "Mapping the Postmodern," in *New German Critique* 33 (Fall 1984), for a historical situating of German, French, and American arguments on postmodernism. Also see the excellent collection of essays edited by Andrew Ross, *Universal Abandon? The Politics of Postmodernism* (Minneapolis: University of Minnesota Press, 1988).

5. Quoted in Richard Kearney, *The Wake of Imagination: Toward a Postmodern Culture* (Minneapolis: University of Minnesota Press, 1988).

6. Fredric Jameson, "Postmodernism or the Cultural Logic of Late Capitalism," in *New Left Review*, no. 145 (1984): 53–91.

7. Anders Stephanson, "Regarding Postmodernism: A Conversation with Fredric Jameson," in *Universal Abandon? The Politics of Postmodernism*, ed. Andrew Ross (Minneapolis: University of Minnesota Press, 1988), pp. 11–12.

8. Cornel West, *Prophetic Fragments* (Trenton, N.J.: Africa World Press, 1988), pp. 168–70.

9. Hal Foster, *Postmodern Culture* (Concord, Mass.: Pluto Press, 1985), pp. xii–xiii.

10. Michael Jackson, *Moonwalk* (New York: Doubleday, 1988), p. 13. All future references will be cited in the text.

11. Cornel West makes this salient point about the use of a language of rights by African-American religionists involved in the civil rights movement, in West, *Prophetic Fragments,* pp. 22–24.

12. For a useful summary of the meaning of ritual in religious experience, see Leszek Kolakowski, *Religion* (New York: Oxford, 1982), pp. 165–70.

13. For Bakhtin on carnival, see Mikhail Bakhtin, *Rabelais and His World* (Cambridge: Massachusetts Institute of Technology Press, 1968).

14. See Cornel West's insightful discussion of a Christian understanding of democracy in his *Prophesy Deliverance! An Afro-American Revolutionary Christianity* (Philadelphia: Westminster Press, 1982), especially the introduction and chapter 4.

15. Bakhtin, *Rabelais,* p. 10.

16. Michael Jackson, "Thriller," *Thriller*, Epic/CBS Records, 1983.

17. Michael Jackson, "Bad," *Bad*, Epic/CBS Records, 1987.

18. Michael Jackson, performer, "Man in the Mirror," (co-written by Siedah Garrett and George Ballard), *Bad*, Epic/CBS Records, 1987.

19. For a penetrating examination of rock music videos and a plausible way of categorizing MTV videos, see E. Ann Kaplan's *Rocking around the Clock: Music Television, Postmodernism, and Consumer Culture* (New York: Methuen, 1987), especially chapter 4. Many of Jackson's videos are more closely akin to short films, and thus demand a reading that regards them as such. Also, the religious, cultural, and racial contexts of Jackson's video-films must be examined, as I attempt in my analysis of two of Jackson's video-films and of a live performance on the 1988 Grammy's telecast.

20. For the effect of Niebuhr on King's thought, see his essay, "Pilgrimage to Nonviolence," in *A Testament of Hope: The Essential Writings of Martin Luther King, Jr.*, ed. James M. Washington (San Francisco: Harper & Row, 1986), pp. 35–36.

21. Goldberg and Handelman, "Is Michael Jackson for Real?" p. 138.

22. Robert Sam Anson, *Best Intentions: The Education and Killing of Edmund Perry* (New York: Random House, 1987). For a hard-hitting and highly critical review essay of Anson's book, see my "Edmund Perry: The Help That Hurts," *Christianity and Crisis* 48 (February 1, 1988) 17–21, expanded as "The Liberal Theory of Race," chap. 9, this volume.

Improvisation

Luther Vandross, Anita Baker, and the State of Soul

In the most perfect world, the outstanding balladeer of his generation would perform live with one of the most sumptuous female voices in pop music, wreaking havoc among the heartstrings of millions of music lovers across America. In Hartford's Civic Arena on a Friday night in 1989, for two and one-half hours, the world was perfect. Luther Vandross and Anita Baker brought "The Heat," their aptly titled concert tour, to town, and seared every soul under the sound of their extraordinary voices. True to the black religious roots that nurtured their enormous talents, Baker and Vandross understand that church is a verb, not a noun. That being so, they transformed the Civic Arena into a sanctuary, and ministers Baker and Vandross spiced the service with heavy doses of call and response and sizable portions of articulate passion.

Baker appeared first, after a brilliant comedy routine by young comic Tommy Davidson. Detroit's diminutive dynamo proceeded to ply her trade of lush, fiery, and imaginative love songs, mostly from her quadruple-platinum breakthrough album, *Rapture.* Baker worked her congregation thoroughly, exhorting them with "Sweet Love," rebuking them with "Watch Your Step," and healing them with "You Bring Me Joy." She also applied a steamy blue rendition of Billie Holiday's classic, "God Bless the Child," and displayed her funky chops with a rousing cover of Michael Jackson's "Another Part of Me." Her job well done, Baker pronounced her benediction with "Giving You the Best That I Got." She certainly had.

Then Senior Minister of Soul Vandross appeared, accompanied by a portable amen corner of backup singers. Vandross's art is subtle, his craft delicate and well wrought. If Baker electrified, Vandross mesmerized. Vandross supplied a rich and luscious array of intricately constructed, flawlessly executed love ballads whose force was peaked by stunning melisma and impeccable control. He spread his good news about love's ability to evoke pathos and longing on "Any Love" and chanted a plea of deep desire on his brilliant remake of Major Harris's "Love Won't Let Me Wait." Vandross displayed a mastery of the echo effect as he used it to tasteful advantage on Burt Bacharach's standard "A House Is Not a Home." Vandross lifted the audience to spiritual ecstasy, however, on his compelling rendition of the now classic "Superstar/Until You Come Back to Me." From the song's symphonic opening chords to its hauntingly otherworldly crescendo, Vandross stripped layer upon layer of inhibition away, until all that was left was pure feeling breathing ecstatic freedom. A chorus of amens thundered forth.

Baker's and Vandross's stellar performances make one wonder if they are alone in producing state-of-the-art music, or are there other artists in soul/R & B/black music who are plumbing its depths as well as expanding its scope? Fortunately, the answer is yes. Especially noteworthy is the development of the "new jack swing" sound, inspired and engineered by the work of one Teddy Riley, a member of the new group "Guy." The new jack swing sound marries the street smarts and hard edge of rappers (ebony prophets engaging in social and cultural criticism) with the sweet seduction of the crooners (amorous savants lamenting love's loss or celebrating its gain). The new jack swing sound places staccato beats and riveting drum programming over often entrancing, hypnotic rhythms. Other participants in the new jack sound include Bobby Brown, Keith Sweat, Aleese Simmons, Al B. Sure!, the group New Edition, and now, of course, Michael Jackson.

Then there is the phenomenally prolific output of the songwriting, production, and singing team of L.A. and Babyface, formerly of the group "The Deele." L.A. and Babyface are past masters of techno-soul, a deft merging of the best of the R & B/soul tradition with the most advanced sounds that can be managed from humanized technology. They are mining the harmonic riches of the Motown sixties, tapping the rhythmic subtleties and lyrical inventiveness of the seventies Philly Sound, and even buffing the outer perimeters of new jack grooves into a refined sheen of danceable technofunk. Their magic has touched Karyn White, the Mac Band, Sheena Easton, Bobby Brown, and Whitney Houston.

Like Baker and Vandross in the early stages of their careers, there are extremely talented artists deserving wider exposure and acclaim. An outstanding example is Vaneese Thomas, a highly intelligent singer-songwriter-producer who creates tasteful and well-crafted music, her forte the ballad. The Swarthmore-educated songstress is the daughter of R & B pioneer Rufus Thomas and the sister of the talented Carla Thomas, who produced many sixties hits. Her first album, the self-titled *Vaneese Thomas,* displayed enormous vocal dexterity and plenty of what may be termed "intelligent feeling." Her lyrics wed passion and thought in powerful abundance. She (and her very talented partners

Wayne Warnecke and Ernie Poccia) have written for Melba Moore, Sarah Dash, Freddie Jackson, and Regina Belle. Thomas is a talent to look out for. With Baker and Vandross at the vanguard, and Riley, L.A. and Babyface, and Vanesse Thomas marching right along, the soul of black music is doing well.

5

Be Like Mike? Michael Jordan and the Pedagogy of Desire

Michael Jordan is perhaps the best, and best-known, athlete in the world today. He has attained unparalleled cultural status because of his extraordinary physical gifts, his marketing as an icon of race-transcending American athletic and moral excellence, and his mastery of a sport that has become the metaphoric center of black cultural imagination. But the Olympian sum of Jordan's cultural meaning is greater than the fluent parts of his persona as athlete, family man, and marketing creation. There is hardly cultural precedence for the character of his unique fame, which has blurred the line between private and public, between personality and celebrity, and between substance and symbol. Michael Jordan stands at the breach between perception and intuition, his cultural meaning perennially deferred from closure because his career symbolizes possibility itself, gathering into its unfolding narrative the shattered remnants of previous incarnations of fame and yet transcending their reach.

Jordan has been called "the new DiMaggio" (Boers 1990, 30) and "Elvis in high-tops," indications of the herculean cultural heroism he has come to embody. There is even a religious element to the near worship of Jordan as a cultural icon of invincibility, as he has been called a "savior of sorts," "basketball's high priest" (Bradley 1991–92, 60), and "more popular than Jesus," except with "better endorsement deals" (Vancil 1992, 51). But the quickly developing cultural canonization of Michael Jordan provokes reflection about the contradictory uses to which Jordan's body is put as a seminal cultural text and ambiguous symbol of fantasy, and the avenues of agency and resistance available especially to black youth who make symbolic investment in Jordan's body as a means of cultural and personal possibility, creativity, and desire.

I understand Jordan in the broadest sense of the term to be a public pedagogue, a figure of estimable public moral authority whose career educates us about productive and disenabling forms of knowledge, desire, interest, consumption, and culture in three spheres: the culture of athletics that thrives on skill and performance, the specific expression of elements of African-American culture, and the market forces and processes of commodification expressed by, and produced in, advanced capitalism. By probing these dimensions of Jordan's cultural importance, we may gain a clearer understanding of his function in American society.

Athletic activity has shaped and reflected important sectors of American society. First, it produced communities of common athletic interest organized around the development of highly skilled performance. The development of norms of athletic excellence evidenced in sports activities cemented communities of participants who valorized rigorous sorts of physical discipline in preparation for athletic competition and in expressing the highest degree of athletic skill. Second, it produced potent subcultures that inculcated in their participants norms of individual and team accomplishment. Such norms tapped into the bipolar structures of competition and cooperation that pervade American culture. Third, it provided a means of reinscribing Western frontier myths of exploration and discovery-as-conquest onto a vital sphere of American culture. Sports activities can be viewed in part as the attempt to symbolically ritualize and metaphorically extend the ongoing quest for mastery of environment and vanquishing of opponents within the limits of physical contest.

Fourth, athletic activity has served to reinforce habits and virtues centered in collective pursuit of communal goals that are intimately connected to the common good, usually characterized within athletic circles as "team spirit." The culture of sport has physically captured and athletically articulated the mores, folkways, and dominant visions of American society, and at its best it has been conceived as a means of symbolically embracing and equitably pursuing the just, the good, the true, and the beautiful.

And finally, the culture of athletics has provided an acceptable and widely accessible means of white male bonding. For much of its history, American sports activity has reflected white patriarchal privilege, and it has been rigidly defined and socially shaped by rules that restricted the equitable participation of women and people of color.

Black participation in sports in mainstream society, therefore, is a relatively recent phenomenon. Of course, there have existed venerable traditions of black sports, such as the Negro (baseball) Leagues, which countered the exclusion of black bodies from white sports. The prohibition of athletic activity by black men in mainstream society severely limited publicly acceptable forms of displaying black physical prowess, an issue that had been politicized during slavery and whose legacy extended into the middle of the twentieth century. Hence, the potentially superior physical prowess of black men, validated for many by the long tradition of slave labor that built American society, helped reinforce racist arguments about the racial regimentation of social space and the denigration of the black body as an inappropriate presence in traditions of American sport.

Coupled with this fear of superior black physical prowess was the notion that inferior black intelligence limited the ability of blacks to perform excellently in those sports activities that required mental concentration and agility. These two forces—the presumed lack of sophisticated black cognitive skills and the fear of superior black physical prowess—restricted black sports participation to thriving but financially handicapped subcultures of black athletic activity. Later, of course, the physical prowess of the black body would be acknowledged and exploited as a supremely fertile zone of profit as mainstream athletic society literally cashed in on the symbolic danger of black sports excellence.

Because of its marginalized status within the regime of American sports, black athletic activity often acquired a social significance that transcended the internal dimensions of game, sport, and skill. Black sport became an arena not only for testing the limits of physical endurance and forms of athletic excellence—while reproducing or repudiating ideals of American justice, goodness, truth, and beauty—but it also became a way of ritualizing racial achievement against socially imposed barriers to cultural performance.

In short, black sport activity often acquired a heroic dimension, as viewed in the careers of figures such as Joe Louis, Jackie Robinson, Althea Gibson, Wilma Rudolph, Muhammad Ali, and Arthur Ashe. Black sports heroes transcended the narrow boundaries of specific sports activities and garnered importance as icons of cultural excellence, symbolic figures who embodied social possibilities of success denied to other people of color. But they also captured and catalyzed the black cultural fetishization of sport as a means of expressing black cultural style, as a means of valorizing craft as a marker of racial and self-expression, and as a means of pursuing social and economic mobility.

It is this culture of black athletics, created against the background of social and historical forces that shaped American athletic activity, that helped produce Jordan and help explain the craft that he practices. Craft is the honing of skill by the application of discipline, time, talent, and energy toward the realization of a particular cultural or personal goal. American folk cultures are pervaded by craft, from the production of cultural artifacts that express particular ethnic histories and traditions to the development of styles of life and work that reflect and symbolize a community's values, virtues, and goals. Michael Jordan's skills within basketball are clearly phenomenal, but his game can only be sufficiently explained by understanding its link to the fusion of African-American cultural norms and practices, and the idealization of skill and performance that characterize important aspects of American sport. I will identify three defining characteristics of Jordan's game that reflect the influence of African-American culture on his style of play.

First, Jordan's style of basketball reflects the *will to spontaneity*. I mean here the way in which historical accidence is transformed into cultural advantage, and the way acts of apparently random occurrence are spontaneously and imaginatively employed by Africans and African-Americans in a variety of forms of cultural expression. When examining Jordan's game, this feature of African-American culture clearly functions in his unpredictable eruptions of basketball creativity. It was apparent, for instance, during game two of the National Basketball Association

1991 championship series between Jordan's Chicago Bulls and the Los Angeles Lakers, in a shot that even Jordan ranked in his all-time top ten (McCallum 1991, 32). Jordan made a drive toward the lane, gesturing with his hands and body that he was about to complete a patent Jordan dunk shot with his right hand. But when he spied defender Sam Perkins slipping over to oppose his shot, he switched the ball in midair to his left hand to make an underhanded scoop shot instead, which immediately became known as the "levitation" shot. Such improvisation, a staple of the will to spontaneity, allows Jordan to expand his vocabulary of athletic spectacle, which is the stimulation of a desire to bear witness to the revelation of truth and beauty compressed into acts of athletic creativity.

Second, Jordan's game reflects the *stylization of the performed self*. This is the creation and projection of a sport persona that is an identifying mark of diverse African-American creative enterprises, from the complexly layered jazz experimentation of John Coltrane, the trickstering and signifying comedic routines of Richard Pryor, and the rhetorical ripostes and oral significations of rapper Kool Moe Dee. Jordan's whole game persona is a graphic depiction of the performed self as flying acrobat, resulting in his famous moniker "Air Jordan." Jordan's performed self is rife with the language of physical expressiveness: head moving, arms extending, hands waving, tongue wagging, and legs spreading.

He has also developed a resourceful repertoire of dazzling dunk shots that further express his performed self and that have garnered him a special niche within the folklore of the game: the cradle jam, rock-a-baby, kiss the rim, lean in, and the tomahawk. In Jordan's game, the stylization of a performed self has allowed him to create a distinct sports persona that has athletic as well as economic consequences, while mastering sophisticated levels of physical expression and redefining the possibilities of athletic achievement within basketball.

Finally, there is the subversion of perceived limits through the use of *edifying deception*, which in Jordan's case centers around the space/time continuum. This moment in African-American cultural practice is the ability to flout widely understood boundaries through mesmerization and alchemy, a subversion of common perceptions of the culturally or physically possible through the creative and deceptive manipulation of appearance. Jordan is perhaps most famous for his alleged "hang time," the uncanny ability to remain suspended in midair longer than other basketball players while executing his stunning array of improvised moves. But Jordan's "hang time" is technically a misnomer and can be more accurately attributed to Jordan's skillful athletic deception, his acrobatic leaping ability, and his intellectual toughness in projecting an aura of uniqueness around his craft than to his defiance of gravity and the laws of physics.

No human being, including Michael Jordan, can successfully defy the law of gravity and achieve relatively sustained altitude without the benefit of machines. As Douglas Kirkpatrick points out, the equation for altitude is $1/2g \times t2 = VO \times t$ ("How Does Michael Fly?"). However, Jordan appears to hang by *stylistically* relativizing the fixed coordinates of space and time through the skillful management and manipulation of his body in midair. For basketball players, hang time is the velocity and speed with which a player takes off combined with the path the player's center of gravity follows on the way up. At the peak of a player's vertical jump, the velocity and speed is close to, or at, zero; hanging motionless in the air is the work of masterful skill and illusion ("How Does Michael Fly?"). Michael Jordan, through the consummate skill and style of his game, only appears to be hanging in space for more than the one second that human beings are capable of remaining airborne.

But the African-American aspects of Jordan's game are indissolubly linked to the culture of consumption and the commodification of black culture.[1] Because of Jordan's supreme mastery of basketball, his squeaky-clean image, and his youthful vigor in pursuit of the American Dream, he has become, along with Bill Cosby, the quintessential pitchman in American society. Even his highly publicized troubles with gambling, his refusal to visit the White House after the Bulls' championship season, and a book that purports to expose the underside of his heroic myth have barely tarnished his All-American image.[2] Jordan eats Wheaties, drives Chevrolets, wears Hanes, drinks Coca-Cola, consumes McDonald's, guzzles Gatorade, and, of course, wears Nikes. He and his shrewd handlers have successfully produced, packaged, marketed, and distributed his image and commodified his symbolic worth, transforming cultural capital into cash, influence, prestige, status, and wealth. To that degree, at least, Jordan repudiates the sorry tradition of the black athlete as the naif who loses his money to piranha-like financial wizards, investors, and hangers-on. He represents the new-age athletic entrepreneur who understands that American sport is ensconced in the cultural practices associated with business, and that it demands particular forms of intelligence, perception, and representation to prevent abuse and maximize profit.

From the very beginning of his professional career, Jordan was consciously marketed by his agency Pro-Serv as a peripatetic vehicle of American fantasies of capital accumulation and material consumption tied to Jordan's personal modesty and moral probity. In so doing, they skillfully avoided attaching to Jordan the image of questionable ethics and lethal excess that plagued inside traders and corporate raiders on Wall Street during the mid-eighties, as Jordan began to emerge as a cultural icon. But Jordan is also the symbol of the spectacle-laden black athletic body as the site of commodified black cultural imagination. Ironically, the black male body, which has been historically viewed as threatening and inappropriate in American society (and remains so outside of sports and entertainment), is made an object of white desires to domesticate and dilute its more ominous and subversive uses, even symbolically reducing Jordan's body to dead meat (McDonald's McJordan hamburger), which can be consumed and expelled as waste.

Jordan's body is also the screen upon which is projected black desires to emulate his athletic excellence and replicate his entry into reaches of unimaginable wealth and fame. But there is more than vicarious substitution and the projection of fantasy onto Jordan's body that is occurring in the circulation and reproduction of black cultural desire. There is also the creative use of desire and fantasy by young blacks to counter, and capitulate to, the forces of cultural dominance that attempt to reduce the black body to a commodity and text that is employed for entertainment, titillation, or financial gain. Simply said, there is no easy correlation between the commodification of black youth culture and the evidences of a completely dominated consciousness.

Even within the dominant cultural practices that seek to turn the black body into pure profit, disruptions of capital are embodied, for instance, in messages circulated in black communities by public moralists who criticize the exploitation of black cultural creativity by casual footwear companies. In short, there are instances of both black complicity and resistance in the commodification of black cultural imagination, and the ideological criticism of exploitative cultural practices must always be linked to the language of possibility and agency in rendering a complex picture of the black cultural situation. As Henry Giroux observes:

> The power of complicity and the complicity of power are not exhausted simply by registering how people are positioned and located through the production of particular ideologies structured through particular discourses. . . . It is important to see that an overreliance on ideology critique has limited our ability to understand how people actively participate in the dominant culture through processes of accommodation, negotiation, and even resistance. (Giroux 1992, 194–95)

In making judgments about the various uses of the black body, especially Jordan's symbolic corporeality, we must specify how both consent and opposition to exploitation are often signaled in expressions of cultural creativity.

In examining his reactions to the racial ordering of athletic and cultural life, the ominous specificity of the black body creates anxieties for Jordan. His encounters with the limits of culturally mediated symbols of race and racial identity have occasionally mocked his desire to live beyond race, to be "neither black nor white" (Patton 1986, 52), to be "viewed as a person" (Vancil 1992, 57). While Jordan chafes under indictment by black critics who claim that he is not "black enough," he has perhaps not clearly understood the differences between enabling versions of human experience that transcend the exclusive gaze of race and disenabling visions of human community that seek race neutrality.

The former is the attempt to expand the perimeters of human experience beyond racial determinism, to nuance and deepen our understanding of the constituent elements of racial identity, and to understand how race, along with class, gender, geography, and sexual preference, shape and constrain human experience. The latter is the belief in an intangible, amorphous, nonhistorical, and raceless category of "person," existing in a zone beyond not simply the negative consequences of race, but beyond the specific patterns of cultural and racial identity that constitute and help shape human experience. Jordan's unclarity is consequential, weighing heavily on his apolitical bearing and his refusal to acknowledge the public character of his private beliefs about American society and the responsibility of his role as a public pedagogue.

Indeed it is the potency of black cultural expressions that not only have helped influence his style of play, but have also made the sneaker industry he lucratively participates in a multi-billion-dollar business. Michael Jordan has helped seize upon the commercial consequences of black cultural preoccupation with style and the commodification of the black juvenile imagination at the site of the sneaker. At the juncture of the sneaker, a host of cultural, political, and economic forces and meanings meet, collide, shatter, and are reassembled to symbolize the situation of contemporary black culture.

The sneaker reflects at once the projection and stylization of black urban realities linked in our contemporary historical moment to rap culture and the underground political economy of crack, and reigns as the universal icon for the culture of consumption. The sneaker symbolizes the ingenious manner in which black cultural nuances of cool, hip, and chic have influenced the broader American cultural landscape. It was black street culture that influenced sneaker companies' aggressive invasion of the black juvenile market in taking advantage of the increasing amounts of disposable income of young black men as a result of legitimate and illegitimate forms of work.

Problematically, though, the sneaker also epitomizes the worst features of the social production of desire and represents the ways in which moral energies of social conscience about material values are drained by the messages of undisciplined acquisitiveness promoted by corporate dimensions of the culture of consumption. These messages, of rapacious consumerism supported by cultural and personal narcissism, are articulated on Wall Street and are related to the expanding inner-city juvenocracy, where young black men rule over black urban space in the culture of crack and illicit criminal activity, fed by desires to "live large" and to reproduce capitalism's excesses on their own terrain. Also, sneaker companies make significant sums of money from the illicit gains of drug dealers.

Moreover, while sneaker companies have exploited black cultural expressions of cool, hip, chic, and style, they rarely benefit the people who both consume the largest quantity of products and whose culture redefined the sneaker companies' raison d'être. This situation is more severely compounded by the presence of spokespeople like Jordan, Spike Lee, and Bo Jackson, who are either ineffectual or defensive about or indifferent to the lethal consequences (especially in urban black-on-black violence over sneaker company products) of black juvenile acquisition of products that these figures have helped make culturally desirable and economically marketable.

Basketball is the metaphoric center of black juvenile culture, a major means by which even temporary forms of cultural and personal transcendence of personal limits are experienced. Michael Jordan is at the center of this black athletic culture, the supreme symbol of black cultural creativity in a society of diminishing tolerance for the black youth whose fascination with Jordan has helped sustain him. But Jordan is also the iconic fixture of broader segments of American society, who see in him the ideal figure: a black man of extraordinary genius on the court and before the cameras, who by virtue of his magical skills and godlike talents symbolizes the meaning of human possibility, while refusing to root it in the specific forms of culture and race in which it must inevitably make sense or fade to ultimate irrelevance.

Jordan also represents the contradictory impulses of the contemporary culture of consumption, where the black athletic body is deified, reified, and rearticulated within the narrow meanings of capital and commodity. But there is both resistance and consent to the exploitation of black bodies in Jordan's explicit cultural symbolism, as he provides brilliant glimpses of black culture's ingenuity of improvisation as a means of cultural expression and survival. It is also partially this element of black culture that has created in American society a desire to dream Jordan, to "be like Mike."

This pedagogy of desire that Jordan embodies, although at points immobilized by its depoliticized cultural contexts, is nevertheless a remarkable achievement in contemporary American culture: a six-foot-six American man of obvious African descent is the dominant presence and central cause of athletic fantasy in a sport that twenty years ago was denigrated as a black man's game and hence deemed unworthy of wide attention or support. Jordan is therefore the bearer of meanings about black culture larger than his individual life, the symbol of a pedagogy of style, presence, and desire that is immediately communicated by the sight of his black body before it can be contravened by reflection.

In the final analysis, his big black body—graceful and powerful, elegant and dark—symbolizes the possibilities of other black bodies to remain safe long enough to survive within the limited but significant sphere of sport, since Jordan's achievements have furthered the cultural acceptance of at least the athletic black body. In that sense, Jordan's powerful cultural capital has not been exhausted by narrow understandings of his symbolic absorption by the demands of capital and consumption. His body is still the symbolic carrier of racial and cultural desires to fly beyond limits and obstacles, a fluid metaphor of mobility and ascent to heights of excellence secured by genius and industry. It is this power to embody the often conflicting desires of so many that makes Michael Jordan a supremely instructive figure for our times.

Notes

1. I do not mean here a theory of commodification that does not accentuate the forms of agency that can function even within restrictive and hegemonic cultural practices. Rather, I think that, contrary to elitist and overly pessimistic Frankfurt School readings of the spectacle of commodity within mass cultures, common people can exercise "everyday forms of resistance" to hegemonic forms of cultural knowledge and practice. For an explication of the function of everyday forms of resistance, see Scott, *Domination and the Arts of Resistance*.

2. For a critical look at Jordan behind the myth, see Sam Smith, *The Jordan Rules* (New York: Simon and Schuster, 1992).

Works Cited

Boers, Terry. "Getting Better All the Time." *Inside Sports*, May 1990, pp. 30–33.

Bradley, Michael. "Air Everything." *Basketball Forecast*, 1991–92, pp. 60–67.

Giroux, Henry. *Border Crossings: Cultural Workers and the Politics of Education*. New York: Routledge, 1992.

"How Does Michael Fly?" *Chicago Tribune*, February 27, 1990, p. 28.

McCallum, Jack. "His Highness." *Sports Illustrated*, June 17, 1991, pp. 28–33.

Patton, Paul. "The Selling of Michael Jordan." *New York Times Magazine*, November 9, 1986, pp. 48–58.

Scott, James. *Domination and the Arts of Resistance*. New Haven, Conn.: Yale University Press, 1990.

Vancil, Mark. "Playboy Interview: Michael Jordan." *Playboy*, May 1992, pp. 51–164.

Improvisation

The Media and American Culture

Most people agree that the media influences American culture and the complex bulwark of beliefs, ideals, opinions, and ideologies that make up its values. But disagreement ranges wide and deep over the *degree* of influence the media exerts and whether this is a generally positive development or the manifestation of unhealthy tendencies in American society. To appreciate the role of media in shaping cultural values, determining social relations, and constructing visions of the politically plausible, it is necessary to understand how institutional power, social hegemony, and corporate interests combine to determine what is seen, heard, thought, and even felt in American society. Four recent books help us achieve these goals.

Elayne Rapping's insightful *The Looking Glass World of Nonfiction TV* (South End Press, 1987) probes local news formats, documentaries, magazine and talk shows, commercials, and the rise of cable television in explaining how they help socialize Americans to the underlying ideals, values, and visions of our society. Rapping artfully synthesizes and thoughtfully wields an impressive body of theoretical discussions of television as a cultural form and mode of technological expression, while contributing a powerful analysis of the aesthetic dimensions of the televisual experience. Although she concludes that television can provoke reflections on important social issues, Rapping shows how television most often expresses the political and economic interests of its owners.

The themes of political and economic interests, particularly in regard to the corporate domination of the cultural sphere, are given a provocative reading in Herbert Schiller's *Culture Inc.: The Corporate Takeover of Public Expression* (Oxford, 1989). Schiller skillfully explores the consolidation of corporate power and its largely negative effects on creative work through sponsorship of cultural expression in museums, theaters, performing-arts centers, street fairs, and even parades. Schiller details the expansion of American capitalism in the post–World War II period, showing how it aided in the establishment of corporate values in politics, law, education, and culture. He also discusses the repression and censorship of artists whose work challenges big business in museums and galleries that receive corporate sponsorship, while deftly tracing the social, economic, and political developments that have reinforced corporate power in centers of social interaction such as shopping malls. Despite its sometimes vulgar Marxist economic determinism, Schiller's important book is a must-read for those who would grasp the complicated corporate conditions under which cultural expression takes place in American society.

Another book that attempts to track the influence of media on the construction of American identity and values is *Cultural Politics in Contemporary America*, edited by Ian Angus and Sut Jhally (Routledge, 1989). The book brings together a broad array of writers who probe the often intricate, mostly masked relationships among American culture, political power, and the media in shaping social values and determining cultural practice. The book's singular contribution is the insistence that American society is constructed through the production, dissemination, and consumption of images of truth, beauty, and goodness. Over twenty cultural critics elaborate the racial, sexual, economic, social, and political dimensions of analysis and bases of struggle that define present cultural activity.

Finally, Richard Lentz's *Symbols, the News Magazines, and Martin Luther King* (Louisiana State University Press, 1990) is an important study of how *Newsweek*, *Time*, and *U.S. News and*

World Report responded to the shifting features of King's platform of social protest. While he accentuated reform, each magazine staked out distinct responses to King in relation to their middle-class readers—if *Time* was the center, *Newsweek* was left of that center and *U.S. Report* was to the right. Each magazine's reporting reflected how the media shape interpretive frameworks for understanding important symbols of American values such as King. As he shifted to radical territory, and especially after his death, the magazines scrambled to recreate versions of King that fit their ideological purposes, devaluing or dismissing his more militant stances and reasserting the symbolic importance of his conciliatory and reformist social strategies. Lentz's absorbing narrative is a skillful examination of the media's direct role in creating and reproducing images of acceptable social change and cultural values.

6

Bill Cosby and the Politics of Race

Bill Cosby is a formidable national icon. He is a powerful symbol of the graceful confluence of talent, wealth, and industry that are the American Dream. His television series, "The Cosby Show," has singlehandedly revived the situation comedy, spawning numerous imitations within the genre, surely the sincerest form of media flattery. His show has even spun off the highly successful "A Different World," a sitcom about contemporary black college life, second only to "The Cosby Show" in ratings and popularity. As if that weren't enough, "The Cosby Show" is now in syndication, with the prospect of generating almost a billion dollars in revenue.

Cosby's philanthropic gestures, too, have matched his larger-than-life television persona. He and his wife Camille's recent gifts to black colleges and universities, totaling almost 25 million dollars, have both aided the beleaguered black academy and generated renewed interest in black charitable activity. At Harlem's famed Apollo Theatre, Cosby raised more than one hundred thousand dollars for Jesse Jackson's 1988 presidential campaign. And at the beginning of the Tawana Brawley case, Cosby and Essence Communications' chief executive Ed Lewis offered a twenty-five-thousand-dollar reward, in part to signal their disdain for all forms of violence.

It is somewhat ironic, then, that until almost the last season of "The Cosby Show," there was continuing controversy about its treatment of the issue of race. From the very beginning, the Cosby series has been shadowed by persistent questions growing out of the politics of racial definition: Is "The Cosby Show" really black enough? Does "The Cosby Show" accurately reflect most African-American families, or should it attempt to do so? Shouldn't "The Cosby Show" confront the menacing specter of the black underclass and address a few of its attendant problems, such as poverty and unemployment? And so on.

The answers to these questions are not so simple, because they involve larger issues of how one defines racial identity and the role of television in catalyzing or anesthetizing social conscience. Needless to say, however, "The Cosby Show" does not exist in a sociohistorical vacuum, either in film and television history or in the larger history of American culture.

Part of the pressure on Cosby (fair or not) results from the paucity of mass media images that positively portray African-Americans. Most black American characters in early film were celluloid enfleshments of stereotypes existing in the minds of white directors, reinforcing notions of black character and culture that prevailed in society at large. Whole categories of black personality were socially constructed and then visually depicted, including the coon, the buck, the clown, the mammy, the darky, the spook, the shiftless shine, and the shuffling Negro.

The history of television has not improved much on this sad state of affairs. In most cases, TV has merely updated conventional film practices with newfangled glosses on old character types, such as with Amos 'n Andy and Rochester (Jack Benny's valet, played by Eddie Anderson). Even when there has been growth in representing black characters, television has often presented problematic versions of racial progress. With the likes of George Jefferson, J.J. "Kid Dyn-o-mite," and Arnold or Webster, blacks were either high-class variations on the theme of clown, or filling another social slot as a stereotypical slum dweller, or beneficiaries of white patrons-cum-adoptive parents, whose largesse brought domestic stability and upward mobility to chosen black children. Each of these options simply served to reinforce the narrow range of options open to black actors, to reinscribe the stereotype-creating practices of white directors and writers in the construction of black characters on television, and to downplay the increasing diversity and robust complexity of African-American culture.

Cosby's series is a marked departure from racial stereotyping, a leap made possible in large part by the social transformation of race relations under the aegis of the civil rights movement. The role of innovator not alien to him, Cosby was the first black to appear in a regular role in a television series, starring opposite Robert Culp for three years in "I Spy." "The Cosby Show" has shattered narrow conceptions of African-American identity and culture, presenting an intact, two-parent, upper-middle-class black family. Indeed, "The Cosby Show" has assumed authoritative status in popular culture, establishing the Cosby viewpoint on many matters as an authentic lens on the American Weltanschauung. Cosby's television brood, the Huxtables, now occupy privileged territory within the folklore of American family relations. The show, in many respects, is a televisual compendium of received wisdom about adults and adolescents where Spock and McLuhan easily embrace. Cliff, an obstetrician, and Clair, a lawyer, are an exemplary dual-career couple. They smoothly meld tradition and change into a formula of tender devotion and tough love, blending parental authority and adolescent autonomy in perfect measure.

Despite all of this, or perhaps because of it, the question persists: Is the Huxtable family "authentically black"? Such a question raises the ire of Cosby and his show's consultant, well-known Harvard psychiatrist Alvin Poussaint. First of all, such a question presumes a monolithic conception of racial identity and a narrow view of the diversity of black culture. Poussaint, in an October 1988 issue of *Ebony,* comments:

> As opportunities for Blacks expand, it is reasonable to expect that certain styles and actions, which might have typified past Black behavior, will change and vary widely in the future. . . . The Huxtable family is helping to dispel old stereotypes and to move its audience toward more realistic perceptions. Like Whites, Blacks on television should be portrayed in a full spectrum of roles and cultural styles, and no one should challenge the existence of such an array of styles within a pluralistic society.

Both Cosby and Poussaint have argued that no other sitcom is expected to address the issue of racism, and that it is unfair to hold

"The Cosby Show" responsible for such racial and cultural didacticism. "No one asks whether 'Three's Company' is going to deal with racism," Cosby has remarked. Furthermore, they argue that the sitcom, designed to entertain, is not well suited to handle such weighty matters as racism, and an attempt to do so would only compromise the possible impact of addressing such an important social issue in a more responsible fashion. Poussaint writes, "The sitcom formula also limits the range of what are considered appropriate story lines; audiences tune in to be entertained, not to be confronted with social problems. Critical social disorders, like racism, violence and drug abuse, rarely lend themselves to comic treatment; trying to deal with them on a sitcom could trivialize issues that deserve serious, thoughtful treatment."

Cosby's and Poussaint's arguments are certainly on target when they suggest the difficulty of addressing (especially with integrity) social problems such as racism. But it is certainly not impossible. In fact, one encouraging sign derives from the very success of "The Cosby Show" in addressing other tough social issues. For instance, "The Cosby Show" has consistently addressed the issue of sexism, creatively and comically showing how it should be debunked and resisted. There have been many humorously insightful encounters between Clair and her Princeton-educated son-in-law Elvin, a bona fide chauvinist. Cliff and Clair have continually attempted to counsel Elvin away from his anachronistic patriarchal proclivities, cajoling him, for example, about the folly of gender-conscious division of domestic labor.

Also, Cliff has occasionally confronted the issue of misdirected machismo, promoting a fuller meaning of manhood and a richer understanding of fatherhood. He has influenced the husbands of clients who thought the responsibility of child rearing was "woman's work." Cosby has said that in deciding to make his character an obstetrician, besides wanting to make women feel comfortable about giving birth, he wanted

> to talk to their husbands and put a few messages out every now and then. . . . That fathering a child isn't about being a macho man, and if you think it is, you're making a terrible mistake. It's about becoming a parent. . . . In one episode last season, a new husband comes into Cliff's office and says, "I'm the man, the head of the household. Women should be kept barefoot and

> pregnant." Cliff tells the guy that being a parent has nothing to do with that kind of concept of manhood. And he really straightens him out by telling him that neither he nor his wife will be in charge of the house—their children will.

And Cliff is often seen in the kitchen preparing meals for the family.

Such positive images of responsible male participation in all aspects of life on Cosby's show reflect a real-life concern and no mean influence on such matters, as attested to by his best-selling book *Fatherhood,* and his new book on marriage. Thus, "The Cosby Show" has shown how a complex social issue such as sexism can be addressed in humorous ways, producing socially responsible entertainment. The juxtaposition of comedy and conscience is not impossible, nor does it necessarily cost ratings.

Of course, as Cosby and Poussaint maintain, other sitcoms are not pressed about addressing issues of race. One implication of their point suggests that other shows should shoulder responsibility for addressing crucial social concerns. And that is right. Similar to what occurs in American culture, real progress in race relations is not made until white persons introduce norms of social equality within their own communities, workplaces, and homes, not simply waiting for a black spokesperson to deliver that message. Other sitcoms and dramatic series, therefore, must reflect a heightened degree of social awareness in regard to many issues, including race, sex, and class.

But that doesn't mean that "The Cosby Show" shouldn't touch such issues, even within the context of a half-hour sitcom. One of the most useful aspects of Cosby's dismantling of racial mythology and stereotyping is that it has permitted America to view black folk as *human beings*. The Cosby show has shown that much of what concerns human beings transcends race, such as issues of parenting, family relations, work, play, and love. This fact does not, however, negate the reality that some issues and concerns affect particular groups in more harmful ways than other groups. The fact that black people continue to be burdened with racial stereotyping in the workplace, for example, cannot be avoided, even as Cosby clarifies the ways in which black folk are just human beings. The two insights must not be considered mutually exclusive.

Cosby has amassed a good deal of moral authority and cultural capital and has captured the attention of millions of Americans who may have otherwise not tuned in or who would have categorized "The Cosby Show" as "just another black sitcom." Thus, he is in a unique position to show that concern for issues of race need not be merely the concerns of black folk, but can, and should, be the concern of human beings. To the degree, then, that his show is about an upper-middle-class family that "happens to be black," his show, like others, bears part of the responsibility of dealing with social issues, which he has proven can be effectively done without sacrificing his large viewing audience or humorous effect.

"The Cosby Show" can also indicate that being concerned about issues of race as black American human beings is legitimate and healthy and should not be avoided. It must communicate the reality that despite the upward social mobility experienced by an increasing number of black people, racism continues to plague African-Americans, although in new and different ways. For instance, while the architecture of legal segregation has been largely dismantled, the undeniable persistence of inequitable socioeconomic conditions for many limits the range of opportunities to the educated upper and middle classes. And even among those blacks who make substantial economic and social progress, the subtlety of racist ideologies, social practices, and cultural expressions means that racism's hibernation in slippery presuppositions, ambiguous attitudes, and equivocal behavior (which have the benefit of appearing neutral, but which actually endorse racist thought or deed) must be exposed and repudiated. To a captive white audience, Cosby's message could create useful awareness about the subversive shift in the ways racism persists and continues to manifest itself.

It is certainly healthy for Cosby not to be obsessed with race consciousness, which would indicate that black life is lived only in response to white racism, that black culture is merely reactive and is incapable of forming visions of life beyond the reach of race. That is not the same, however, as acknowledging that race continues to determine social relations and influence employment opportunities. Even obstetricians, lawyers, and upper-middle-class black children are not exempt from the prospect of racial tensions of some sort.

More pointedly, issues of race, sex, and class could be handled in a way that avoids the banal stereotyping that prevails elsewhere on television. Cosby's show has a responsibility to address these issues precisely because he has created cultural space for the legitimate existence of upper-middle-class blacks on television. The progressive vision of his show as exhibited in its insightful handling of the issue of sexism, then, creates the reasonable expectation of addressing such matters. Thus, the very skillful debunking of racial stereotypes that is generated by his show, and not the insistence that "black shows should do black stuff," is the reason Cosby's show must at least in some form address the problems of race and class.

"The Cosby Show" reflects the increasing diversity of African-American life, including the continuous upward social mobility by blacks, which provides access to new employment opportunities heretofore closed and expands the black middle class. Such mobility and expansion insures the development of new styles of existence for blacks that radically alter and impact African-American culture. Cosby's show is a legitimate expression of one aspect of that diversity. Another aspect is the intraracial class division and differentiation introduced as a result of this diversification of African-American life.

"The Cosby Show" is, therefore, also emblematic of the developing gulfs between black Americans who occupy varying social and class slots in American life, and is a symbol of the gap between the upper and under classes. As I have argued before, black track from the ghetto, which mimicked earlier patterns of white flight from the inner city, has resulted in severe class changes in many black communities. A sense of social isolation has also resulted as upper-middle-class blacks leave and those left behind experience loss of economic support, role models, and social continuity and cultural contact with more well-to-do blacks.

Cosby is certainly not expected to answer the enormously complex problem of the underclass and its relationship to the black middle and upper middle classes, a problem that social scientists continue to heatedly debate. But what is certain is that the silence and invisibility of the underclass in American life, and in television, except in threatening, stereotypical, or negative ways, continues to reinforce the belief that *all* occupants of the underclass are black and are active participants in illegal criminal behavior. Cosby's silence on the underclass and their complete invisibility on his show are therefore troubling. Cosby could go a long way toward helping America to see that many occupants of the underclass are conscientious people who are victimized, often by socioeconomic forces beyond their immediate control. "The Cosby Show" could certainly brush the fringes of the problem and at least give passing acknowledgment to the crisis that so many Americans who are black live with. Some indication of the existence of less fortunate blacks—some visiting relative whose situation is desperate, some deserving youth whose intellectual brilliance is not matched by material resources—could *both* alert America to the vicious effects of poverty on well-meaning people and send the message that the other side of the American Dream for many is the American Nightmare.

It is perhaps this lack of acknowledgment of the underside of the American Dream, the avoidance of its division of blacks by class, that is the most unfortunate feature of the Huxtable opulence. Cosby defends against linking the authenticity of the Huxtable representation of black life to the apparently contradictory luxury and comfort the family lives in when he says, "To say that they are not black enough is a denial of the American dream and the American way of life. My point is that this is an American family—an *American* family—and if you want to live like they do, and you're willing to work, the opportunity is there." But surely Cosby knows better than this. Such a statement leads us to believe that Cosby is unaware that there are millions of people, the so-called working poor, who travail in exemplary assiduity daily, but who nonetheless fall beneath the poverty level. Surely Cosby understands that Martin Luther King indicated in 1967, less than a year before his death, that he had lived long enough to see his American Dream turn into an American Nightmare on the streets of too many northern cities, and that King died in the midst of a campaign that accentuated the structurally denied opportunities for the poor across racial and ethnic lines.

Such a statement about opportunity provokes even closer scrutiny of the trajectory of Cosby's career, which has made him a cultural icon. He has risen to such phenomenal stature precisely because he embodies so much of the power of the ideology of Americanism: an individual who, despite a poor beginning, overcame problems of race and class in order to become a great stand-up comedian, actor, and spokesperson for several companies, including Jell-O, E. F. Hutton, Ford, and Coke. Cosby's career, too, is a lesson about how the management and commodification of staggering talent leads to even more staggering success, which is then recycled in the production of American fantasies about duplicating or somehow participating in that success.

Cosby's career also reveals the consolidation of the hegemonic relationship among television, the generating and shaping of consumptive desires and appetites for material goods, and the dissemination and perpetuation of the myths of universal access to the American dream. Inevitably, too, his career entails some contradictions that attest to the powerful ability of that success to transform, for good and ill, one's perspective. For instance, in his dissertation, cited by Daniel Okrent in the February 1987 *New England Monthly,* Cosby stated: "Each day advertisers bombard millions of viewers with their products to satisfy all the sensory needs, both internal and external. This mesmerized audience chases one fad after . . . another in the effort to 'build a . . . healthier, happier, [more] beautiful you.' " Cosby's subsequent endorsements as the most highly esteemed pitchman in American culture speak volumes about the price of progress.

We must certainly celebrate material progress, social advancement, educational attainment, and professional development, but not at the expense of remembering that for too long access to the higher reaches of the American Dream has been based on structural factors like race, class, and gender. This awareness, then, must inform the African-American construction of television images, characters, and families. Black folk, like Cosby, who are influential in television must, like the rest of us, engage in a self-criticism that perennially scrutinizes the values and visions that contribute to the development of lifestyles, the adoption of beliefs, or the formation of social conscience, especially as they are represented on TV.

Perhaps the greatest lesson from "The Cosby Show" is that being concerned about issues that transcend race and therefore display our humanity is fine, but that does not mean we should buy into a vacuous, bland universality that stigmatizes diversity, punishes difference, and destroys dissimilarities. As we painfully learned in the past, we cannot be thrown into the pot and melted down into one phenomenon called The American Experience. Although Cosby unquestionably runs up against the limits of the televisual medium, which seeks the lowest common denominator in human experience as a basis of blurring the differences between peoples and cultures and which seeks to maintain present power relations, systems of distributing wealth, and ways of assigning cultural authority, his show should teach us how to display the diversity of African-American life without compromising conscience, or consciousness, about those closed out of the American dream.

Similar to Spike Lee, but with a much different aesthetic feel, Cosby presents a black universe as the norm, feeling no need to announce the imposition of African-American perspectives, since they are assumed. But it is probably the case that many upper-middle-class black folk continue to talk about the racism of American culture, whether discussing its diminishing impact, its paralyzing persistence, or its prayed-for demise. Cosby has certainly shown us that we need not construct the whole house of our life experience from the raw material of our racial identity and that black folk are interested in issues that transcend race. However, such coming-of-age progress should not lead to zero-sum social concern, so that to be cognizant of race-transcending issues *replaces* or cancels out concern, for example, about the black poor or issues that generate intraracial conflict. "The Cosby Show" is an important advance in the fight to portray the profound complexity and rich diversity of black life on the small screen, because it shows a side of African-American life that is rarely seen on television. But "The Cosby Show" (and other TV sitcoms and drama series) must be pushed to encompass and attend to parts of that diversity that, although badly misrepresented under the plague of past stereotyping, must be addressed within the worldview that Cosby has the power and talent to present.

Improvisation

Gordon Parks: Prometheus in Motion

Near the middle of Gordon Parks's latest and most poignant self-portrait, *Voices in the Mirror* (Doubleday, 1990), he speaks of Paris as "a feast, a grand carnival of imagery." The same may be said of Parks's fourth autobiographical book, an eloquent missive from the front line of poetry and pain. His life lends a unifying logic to the telling shards and splintered narratives of twentieth-century black life—shards and narratives whose survival alone has proved their invincible dignity. In *Voices in the Mirror,* the narrative threads of the individual and the racial are so tightly woven together that they are virtually one.

Gordon Parks was reared by protective parents on the stubborn soil of the Kansas prairie. The youngest of fifteen siblings, Parks felt secure in the quiet strength of his father, Jackson, and the love of his mother, Sarah. That security was shattered when his mother died during Gordon's fifteenth year, and he spent the night next to her lonely coffin, an experience he remembers as both "terror-filled and strangely reassuring." Sent to live with a sister and her husband in Minnesota after his mother's death, Parks was violently thrown out of his new home by his Scrooge-like brother-in-law near Christmas. Parks was thrust into an unsolicited confrontation with racism and poverty in which adulthood beckoned immediately.

Parks records with unsparing candor the material deprivations, psychic thrashings, and moral agonies wrought by his initiation into maturity. It is amazing that he never allowed the ubiquity of racial animosities to obstruct his exploration of the mystery of life or wither his reverence for imagination and experience. Such reverence only fed his appetite for intellectual and artistic pursuits, executed without the benefit of a high-school education. Parks became a world-renowned photographer, painter, writer, musical composer, and filmmaker because, he says, he had a "fear of failure," a fear that compelled him to "fight off anything that might abet it—bigotry, hatred, discrimination, poverty or hunger" (p. 21).

As a photographer and writer, he has recorded the rich and the famous, the poor and the obscure, the black and the white. The first black photojournalist to work for *Life Magazine,* he has captured the plight of young Harlem gang warriors, portrayed the circumstances of a Brazilian family plunged into suffering by poverty, and tracked the profound ideological transformations wrought within a mellowing Malcolm X, including his departure from the Nation of Islam and his subsequent assassination at the hands of Nation loyalists. Parks also covered the latest European fashions and chronicled the life of deposed monarchs and dictators from around the globe.

Parks later transformed into a film his autobiographical novel, *The Learning Tree,* becoming the first black person to write and direct a Hollywood movie. Almost as varied in his personal relations as he is in his multiple careers, Parks has been thrice married and is now willing to absorb his share of the blame for each marital failure. "No doubt my inability to reach the summit of their expectations had a lot to do with the storms and disasters" (p. 339). He had four children from his three marriages, and endured the ultimate pain of parenthood—the loss of his son, Gordon Parks, Jr. The younger Parks, who died in a plane crash while filming a movie in Africa, had directed three other films, including the black cult classic, *Superfly.* Parks himself eventually made five Hollywood movies, including the important *Shaft,* which provided black youth "their first cinematic hero comparable to James Cagney or Humphrey Bogart" (p. 305).

As Parks sifts through the cache of memories his Promethean talents have created, he refuses to be bitter about the denials, limits, and indignities that have been, at one time or another, imposed upon his world. His trials have made him widely empathetic toward victims of *any* prejudice and skeptical about the privileges of race, class, or nation to establish the proper basis for human interaction. Through the power of his words, this intelligent and sensitive interpreter of human experience has now turned the mirror toward us, as well as himself; we, like Parks, must be judged by the integrity of our response to what we hear and see. Let us hope that we are half as successful as he has been.

7

Between Apocalypse and Redemption: John Singleton's *Boyz N the Hood*

By now the dramatic decline in black male life has become an unmistakable feature of our cultural landscape—although of course the causes behind the desperate condition of black men date much further back than its recent popular discovery. Every few months, new reports and conferences attempt to explain the poverty, disease, despair, and death that shove black men toward social apocalypse.

If these words appear too severe or hyperbolic, the statistics testify to the trauma. For black men between the ages of 18 and 29, suicide is the leading cause of death. Between 1980 and 1985, the life expectancy for white males increased from 63 to 74.6 years, but only from 59 to 65 years for black males. Between 1973 and 1986, the real earnings of black males between the ages of 18 and 29 fell 31 percent, as the percentage of young black males in the work force plummeted 20 percent. The number of black men who dropped out of the work force altogether doubled from 13 to 25 percent.

By 1989, almost 32 percent of black men between 16 and 19 were unemployed, compared with 16 percent of white men. And while blacks constitute only 12 percent of the nation's population, they make up 48 percent of the prison population, with men accounting for 89 percent of the black prison population. Only 14 percent of the white males who live in large metropolitan areas have been arrested, but the percentage for black males is 51 percent. And while 3 percent of white men have served time in prison, 18 percent of black men have been behind bars.[1]

Most chilling, black-on-black homicide is the leading cause of death for black males between the ages of 15 and 34. Or, to put it another way, "One out of every 21 black American males will be murdered in their lifetime. Most will die at the hands of another black male." These words appear in stark white print on the dark screen that opens John Singleton's masterful new film, *Boyz N the Hood*. These words are both summary and opening salvo in Singleton's battle to reinterpret and redeem the black male experience. With *Boyz N the Hood* we have the most brilliantly executed and fully realized portrait of the coming of age odyssey that black boys must undertake in the suffocating conditions of urban decay and civic chaos.

Singleton adds color and depth to Michael Schultz's groundbreaking *Cooley High*, extends the narrative scope of the Hudlin Brothers' important and humorous *House Party*, and creates a stunning complement to Gordon Parks's pioneering *Learning Tree*, which traced the painful pilgrimage to maturity of a rural black male. Singleton's treatment of the various elements of contemporary black urban experience—gang violence, drug addiction, black male-female relationships, domestic joys and pains, friendships—is subtle and complex. He layers narrative textures over gritty and compelling visual slices of black culture that show us what it means to come to maturity, or die trying, as a black male.

We have just begun to understand the pitfalls that attend the path of the black male. Social theory has only recently fixed its gaze on the specific predicament of black men in relation to the crisis of American capital, positing how their lives are shaped by structural changes in the political economy, for instance, rather than viewing them as the latest examples of black cultural pathology.[2] And social psychology has barely explored the deeply ingrained and culturally reinforced self-loathing and chronic lack of self-esteem that characterizes black males across age groups, income brackets, and social locations.

Even less have we understood the crisis of black males as rooted in childhood and adolescent obstacles to socioeconomic stability and moral, psychological, and emotional development. We have just begun to pay attention to specific rites of passage, stages of personality growth, and milestones of psychoemotional evolution that measure personal response to racial injustice, social disintegration, and class oppression.

James P. Comer and Alvin F. Poussaint's *Black Child Care*, Marian Wright Edelman's *Families in Peril*, and Darlene and Derek Hopson's foundational *Different and Wonderful* are among the exceptions that address the specific needs of black childhood and adolescence. Jewell Taylor-Gibbs's edited work, *Young, Black and Male in America: An Endangered Species*, has recently begun to fill a gaping void in social-scientific research on the crisis of the black male.

In the last decade alternative presses have vigorously probed the crisis of the black male. Like their black independent filmmaker peers, authors of volumes published by black independent presses often rely on lower budgets for advertising, marketing, and distribution. Nevertheless, word-of-mouth discussion of several books has sparked intense debate. Nathan and Julia Hare's *Bringing the Black Boy to Manhood: The Passage*, Jawanza Kunjufu's trilogy, *The Conspiracy to Destroy Black Boys*, Amos N. Wilson's *The Developmental Psychology of the Black Child*, Baba Zak A. Kondo's *For Homeboys Only: Arming and Strengthening Young Brothers for Black Manhood*, and Haki Madhubuti's *Black Men: Obsolete, Single, Dangerous?* have had an important impact on significant subsections of literate black culture, most of whom share an Afrocentric perspective.

Such works remind us that we have too infrequently understood the black male crisis through coming-of-age narratives and a set of shared social values that ritualize the process of the black adolescent's passage into adulthood. Such narratives and rites serve a dual function: they lend meaning to childhood experience, and they preserve and transmit black cultural values across the generations. Yet such narratives evoke a state of maturity—rooted in a vital community—that young black men are finding elusive or, all too often, impossible to reach. The conditions of extreme social neglect that besiege urban black communities—in every realm from health care to education to poverty and joblessness—make the black male's passage into adulthood treacherous at best.

One of the most tragic symptoms of the young black man's troubled path to maturity is the skewed and strained state of gender relations within the black community. With alarming frequency, black men turn to black women as scapegoats for their oppression, lashing out, often with physical violence, at those closest to them. It is the singular achievement of Singleton's film to redeem the power of the coming-of-age narrative while also adapting it to probe many of the very tensions that evade the foundations of the coming-of-age experience in the black community.

While mainstream American culture has only barely begun to register awareness of the true proportions of the crisis, young black males have responded in the last decade primarily in a rapidly flourishing independent popular culture, dominated by two genres: rap music and black film. The rap music of Run-D.M.C., Public Enemy, Boogie Down Productions, Kool Moe Dee, N.W.A., Ice Cube, and Ice-T and the films of Spike Lee, Robert Townsend, and now Matty Rich and Mario Van Peebles have afforded young black males a medium in which to visualize and verbalize their perspectives on a range of social, personal, and cultural issues, to tell their stories about themselves and each other while the rest of America consumes and eavesdrops.

John Singleton's new film makes a powerful contribution to this enterprise. Singleton filters his brilliant insights, critical comments, and compelling portraits of young black male culture through a film that reflects the sensibilities, styles, and attitudes of rap culture.[3] Singleton's shrewd casting of rapper Ice Cube as a central character allows him to seize symbolic capital from a real-life rap icon, while tailoring the violent excesses of Ice Cube's rap persona into a jarring visual reminder of the cost paid by black males for survival in American society. Singleton skillfully integrates the suggestive fragments of critical reflections on the black male predicament in several media and presents a stunning vision of black male pain and possibility in a catastrophic environment: South Central Los Angeles.

Of course, South Central Los Angeles is an already storied geography in the American social imagination. It has been given cursory—though melodramatic—treatment by news anchor Tom Brokaw's glimpse of gangs in a highly publicized 1988 TV special, and has been mythologized in Dennis Hopper's film about gang warfare, *Colors*. Hopper, who perceptively and provocatively helped probe the rough edges of anomie and rebellion for a whole generation of outsiders in 1969's *Easy Rider*, less successfully traces the genealogy of social despair, postmodern urban absurdity, and yearning for belonging that provides the context for understanding gang violence. Singleton's task in part, therefore, is a filmic demythologization of the reigning tropes, images, and metaphors that have expressed the experience of life in South Central Los Angeles. While gangs are a central part of the urban landscape, they are not its exclusive reality. And although gang warfare occupies a looming periphery in Singleton's film, it is not the defining center.

Boyz N the Hood is a painful and powerful look at the lives of black people, mostly male, who live in a lower-middle-class neighborhood in South Central Los Angeles. It is a story of relationships—of kin, friendship, community, love, rejection, contempt, and fear. At the story's heart are three important relationships: a triangular relationship between three boys, whose lives we track to mature adolescence; the relationship between one of the boys and his father; and the relationship between the other two boys and their mother.

Tre (Cuba Gooding, Jr.) is a young boy whose mother Reva Devereaux (Angela Bassett), in an effort to impose discipline upon him, sends him to live with his father across town. Tre has run afoul of his elementary school teacher for challenging both her authority and her Eurocentric curriculum. And Tre's life in his mother's neighborhood makes it clear why he is not accommodating well to school discipline. By the age of ten, he has already witnessed the yellow police tags that mark the scenes of crimes and has viewed the blood of a murder victim. Fortunately for Tre, his mother and father love him more than they couldn't love each other.

Doughboy (former N.W.A. rapper Ice Cube, in a brilliant cinematic debut) and Ricky (Morris Chestnut) are half brothers who live with their mother Brenda (Tyra Ferell) across the street from Tre and his father. Brenda, as a single black mother, belongs to a much-maligned group, whose members, depending on the amateurish social theory that wins the day, are vilified with charges of promiscuity, judged to be the source of all that is evil in the lives of black children, or at best stereotyped as helpless beneficiaries of the state. Singleton artfully avoids these caricatures by giving a complex portrait of Brenda, a woman who is plagued by her own set of demons, but who tries to provide the best living she can for her sons.

Even so, Brenda clearly favors Ricky over Doughboy—and this favoritism will bear fatal consequences for both boys. Indeed in Singleton's cinematic worldview both Ricky and Doughboy seem doomed to violent deaths because—unlike Tre—they have no male role models to guide them. This premise embodies one of the film's central tensions—and one of its central limitations. For even as he assigns black men a pivotal role of responsibility for the fate of black boys, Singleton also gives rather uncritical "precedence" to the impact of black men, even in their absence, over the efforts of present and loyal black women who more often prove to be at the head of strong black families.

While this foreshortened view of gender relations within the black community arguably distorts Singleton's cinematic vision, he is nonetheless remarkably perceptive in examining the subtle dynamics of the black family and neighborhood, tracking the differing effects that the boys' siblings, friends, and environment have on them. There is no bland nature-versus-nurture dichotomy here: Singleton is too smart to render life in terms of a Kierkegaardian either/or. His is an Afrocentric world of both/and.

This complex set of interactions—between mother and sons, between father and son, between boys who benefit from paternal wisdom or maternal ambitions, between brothers whose relationship is riven by primordial passions of envy and contempt, between environment and autonomy, between the larger social structure and the smaller but more immediate tensions of domestic life—define the central shape of *Hood*. We see a vision of black life that transcends insular preoccupations with "positive" or "negative" images and instead presents at once the limitations and virtues of black culture.

As a result, Singleton's film offers a plausible perspective on how people make the choices they do—and on how choice itself is not a property of autonomous moral agents acting in an existential vacuum, but rather something that is created and exercised within the interaction of social, psychic, political, and economic forces of everyday experience. Personal temperament, domestic discipline, parental guidance (or its absence) all help shape our understanding of our past and future, help define how we respond to challenge and crisis, and help mold how we embrace success or seem destined for failure.

Tre's developing relationship with his father, Furious Styles (Larry Fishburne), is by turns troubled and disciplined, sympathetic and compassionate—finely displaying Singleton's open-ended evocation of the meaning of social choice as well as his strong sensitivity to cultural detail. Furious Styles's moniker vibrates with double meaning, a semiotic pairing that allows Singleton to signify in speech what Furious accomplishes in action: a wonderful amalgam of old-school black consciousness, elegance, style, and wit linked to the hip-hop fetish of "dropping science" (spreading knowledge) and staying well informed about social issues.

Only seventeen years Tre's senior, Furious understands Tre's painful boyhood growth and identifies with his teen aspirations. But more than that, he possesses a sincere desire to shape Tre's life according to his own best lights. Furious is the strong presence and wise counselor who will guide Tre through the pitfalls of reaching personal maturity in the chaos of urban childhood—the very sort of presence denied to so many in *Hood*, and in countless black communities throughout the country.

Furious, in other words, embodies the promise of a different conception of black manhood. As a father he is disciplining but loving, firm but humorous, demanding but sympathetic. In him, the black male voice speaks with an authority so confidently possessed and equitably wielded that one might think it is strongly supported and valued in American culture, but of course that is not so. The black male voice is rarely heard without the inflections of race and class domination that distort its power in the home and community, mute its call for basic respect and common dignity, or amplify its ironic denial of the very principles of democracy and equality that it has publicly championed in pulpits and political organizations.

Among the most impressive achievements of Singleton's film is its portrayal of the neighborhood as a "community." In this vein Singleton implicitly sides with the communitarian critique of liberal moral autonomy and atomistic individualism.[4] In *Hood* people love and worry over one another, even if they express such sentiments roughly. For instance, when the older Tre crosses the street and sees a baby in the path of an oncoming car, he swoops her up and takes her to her crack-addicted mother. Tre gruffly reproves her for neglecting her child and insists that she change the baby's diapers before the baby smells as bad as her mother. And when Tre goes to a barbecue for Doughboy, who is fresh from a jail sentence, Brenda beseeches him to talk to Doughboy, hoping that Tre's intangible magic will "rub off on him."

But Singleton understands that communities, besides embodying resistance to the anonymity of liberal society as conceived in Aristotle accordig to MacIntyre, also reflect the despotic will of their fringe citizens who threaten the civic pieties by which communities are sustained. *Hood*'s community is fraught with mortal danger, its cords of love and friendship under the siege of gang violence and of what sociologist Mike Davis calls the political economy of crack.[5] Many inner-city communities live under what may be called a "juvenocracy": the economic rule and illegal tyranny exercised by young black men over significant territory in the black urban center. In the social geography of South Central L.A., neighborhoods are reconceived as spheres of expansion where urban space is carved up according to implicit agreements, explicit arrangements, or lethal conflicts between warring factions.

Thus, in addition to being isolated from the recognition and rewards of the dominant culture, inner-city communities are cut off from sources of moral authority and legitimate work, as underground political economies reward consenting children and teens with quick cash, faster cars, and sometimes, still more rapid death.[6] Along with the reterritorialization of black communal space through gentrification, the hegemony of the suburban mall over the inner-city and downtown shopping complex, and white flight and black track to the suburbs and exurbs, the inner city is continually devastated.

Such conditions rob the neighborhood of one of its basic social functions and defining characteristics: the cultivation of a self-determined privacy in which residents can establish and preserve their identities. Police helicopters constantly zoom overhead in *Hood*'s community, a mobile metaphor of the ominous surveillance and scrutiny to which so much of poor black life is increasingly subjected. The helicopter also signals another tragedy, which *Hood* alludes to throughout its narrative: ghetto residents must often flip a coin to distinguish Los Angeles' police from its criminals. After all, this is Darryl Gates's L.A.P.D., and the recent Rodney King incident only underscores a long tradition of extreme measures that police have used to control crime and patrol neighborhoods.[7]

This insight is poignantly featured in a scene just after Tre comes to live with his father. One night, Furious hears a strange noise. As an unsuspecting young Tre rises to use the toilet, Furious eases his gun from the side of his bed, spies an intruder in the living room and blasts away, leaving two holes in the front door. After they investigate the holes and call the police, Furious and Tre sit on the front porch, waiting an hour for the police to arrive. Furious remarks that "somebody musta been prayin' for that fool 'cause I swear I aimed right for his head." When Tre says that Furious "shoulda blew it off," Furious censors his sentiment, saying that it would have simply been the senseless death of another black man.

After the interracial police team arrive, the black policeman expresses Tre's censored sentiment with considerably more venom. "Be one less nigger out here in the streets we'd have to worry about." As they part, the policeman views Furious's scornful facial expression and asks if something is wrong. "Yeah," Furious disdainfully responds, "but it's just too bad you don't know what it is—brother." The black policeman has internalized the myth of the black male animal and has indiscriminately demonized young black males as thugs and dirt.

As fate would have it, this same police team accosts seventeen-year-old Tre and Ricky after they have departed from a local hangout that was sprayed by bullets. The policeman puts a gun to Tre's neck, uttering vicious epithets and spewing words that mark his hatred of black males and, by reflection, a piteous self-hatred. It recalls the lyrics from an Ice Cube rap, "F— tha Police": "And don't let it be a black and a white one / Cause they'll slam ya down to the street top / Black police showin' out for the white cop."

Furious's efforts to raise his son in these conditions of closely surveilled social anarchy reveal the galaxy of ambivalence that surrounds a conscientious, community-minded brother who wants the best for his family, but who also understands the social realities that shape the lives of black men. Furious's urban cosmology is three-tiered: at the immediate level, the brute problems of survival are refracted through the lens of black manhood; at the abstract level, large social forces such as gentrification and the military's recruitment of black male talent undermine the black man's role in the community; at the intermediate level, police brutality contends with the ongoing terror of gang violence.

Amid these hostile conditions, Furious is still able to instruct Tre in the rules of personal conduct and to teach him respect for his community, even as he schools him in how to survive. Furious says to Tre, "I know you think I'm hard on you. I'm trying to teach you how to be responsible. Your friends across the street don't have anybody to show them how to do that. You gon' see how they end up, too." His comment, despite its implicit self-satisfaction and sexism (Ricky and Doughboy, after all, do have their mother, Brenda), is meant to reveal the privilege of a young boy learning to face life under the shadow of fatherly love and discipline.

While Tre is being instructed by Furious, Ricky and Doughboy receive varying degrees of support and affirmation from Brenda. Ricky and Doughboy have different fathers, both of whom are conspicuously absent. In Doughboy's case, however, his father is symbolically present in that peculiar way that damns the offspring for their resemblance in spirit or body to the despised, departed father. The child becomes the vicarious sacrifice for the absent father, although he can never atone for the father's sins. Doughboy learns to see himself through his mother's eyes, her words ironically recreating Doughboy in the image of his invisible father. "You ain't shit," she says. "You just like yo' Daddy. You don't do shit, and you never gonna amount to shit."

Brenda is caught in a paradox of parenthood, made dizzy and stunned by a vicious circle of parental love reinforcing attractive qualities in the "good" and obedient child, while the frustration with the "bad" child reinforces his behavior. Brenda chooses to save one child by sacrificing the other—lending her action a Styronian tenor, Sophie's choice in the ghetto. She fusses *over*

Ricky; she fusses *at* Doughboy. When a scout for USC's football team visits Ricky, Brenda can barely conceal her pride. When the scout leaves, she tells Ricky, "I always knew you would amount to something."

In light of Doughboy's later disposition toward women, we see the developing deformations of misogyny. Here Singleton is on tough and touchy ground, linking the origins of Doughboy's misogyny to maternal mistreatment and neglect. Doughboy's misogyny is clearly the elaboration of a brooding and extended ressentiment, a deeply festering wound to his pride that infects his relationships with every woman he encounters.

For instance, at the party to celebrate his homecoming from his recent incarceration, Brenda announces that the food is ready. All of the males rush to the table, but immediately before they begin to eat, Tre, sensing that it will be to his advantage, reproves the guys for not acting gentlemanly and allowing the women first place in line. Doughboy chimes in, saying, "Let the ladies eat; ho's gotta eat, too," which draws laughter, both from the audience with which I viewed the film and from the backyard male crowd. The last line is a sly sample of Robert Townsend's classic comedic sendup of fast-food establishments in *Hollywood Shuffle*. When his girlfriend (Meta King) protests, saying she isn't a "ho," Doughboy responds, "Oops, I'm sorry, bitch," which draws even more laughter.

In another revealing exchange with his girlfriend, Doughboy is challenged to explain why he refers to women exclusively as "bitch, or ho, or hootchie." In trying to reply, Doughboy is reduced to the inarticulate hostility (feebly masquerading as humor) that characterizes misogyny in general: " 'Cause that's what you are."

"Bitch" and "ho," along with "skeezer" and "slut," have by now become the standard linguistic currency that young black males often use to demonstrate their authentic machismo. "Bitch" and equally offensive epithets compress womanhood into one indistinguishable whole, so that all women are the negative female, the seductress, temptress, and femme fatale all rolled into one. Hawthorne's scarlet A is demoted one letter and darkened; now an imaginary black B is emblazoned on the forehead of every female.

Although Singleton's female characters do not have center stage, by no means do they suffer male effrontery in silent complicity. When Furious and Reva meet at a trendy restaurant to discuss the possibility of Tre returning to live with his mother, Furious says, "I know you wanna play the mommy and all that, but it's time to let go." He reminds her that Tre is old enough to make his own decisions, that he is no longer a little boy because "that time has passed, sweetheart, you missed it." Furious then gets up to fetch a pack of cigarettes as if to punctuate his self-satisfied and triumphant speech, but Tre's mother demands that he sit down. As the camera draws close to her face, she subtly choreographs a black woman's grab-you-by-the-collar-and-set-you-straight demeanor with just the right facial gestures, and completes one of the most honest, mature, and poignant exchanges between a black man and a black woman in film history.

> It's my turn to talk. Of course you took in your son, my son, our son and you taught him what he needed to be a man, I'll give you that, because most men ain't man enough to do what you did. But that gives you no reason, do you hear me, no reason to tell me that I can't be a mother to my son. What you did is no different from what mothers have been doing from the beginning of time. It's just too bad more brothers won't do the same. But don't think you're special. Maybe cute, but not special. Drink your café au lait. It's on me.

Singleton says that his next film will be about black women coming of age, a subject left virtually unexplored in film. In the meantime, within its self-limited scope, *Hood* displays a diverse array of black women, taking care not to render them as either mawkish or cartoonish: a crack addict who sacrifices home, dignity, and children for her habit; a single mother struggling to raise her sons; black girlfriends hanging with the homeboys but demanding as much respect as they can get; Brandi (Nia Long), Tre's girlfriend, a Catholic who wants to hang on to her virginity until she's sure it's the right time; Tre's mother, who strikes a Solomonic compromise and gives her son up rather than see him sacrificed to the brutal conditions of his surroundings.

But while Singleton ably avoids flat stereotypical portraits of his female characters, he is less successful in challenging the logic that at least implicitly blames single black women for the plight of black children.[8] In Singleton's film vision, it is not institutions like the church that save Tre, but a heroic individual—his father Furious. But this leaves out far too much of the picture.

What about the high rates of black female joblessness, the sexist job market that continues to pay women at a rate that is 70 percent of the male wage for comparable work, the further devaluation of the "pink collar" by lower rates of medical insurance and other work-related benefits, all of which severely compromise the ability of single black mothers to effectively rear their children?[9] It is the absence of much more than a male role model and the strength he symbolizes that makes the life of a growing boy difficult and treacherous in communities such as South Central L.A.

The film's focus on Furious's heroic individualism fails, moreover, to fully account for the social and cultural forces that prevent more black men from being present in the home in the first place. Singleton's powerful message, that more black men must be responsible and present in the home to teach their sons how to become men, must not be reduced to the notion that those families devoid of black men are necessarily deficient and ineffective. Neither should Singleton's critical insights into the way that many black men are denied the privilege to rear their sons be collapsed to the idea that all black men who are present in their families will necessarily produce healthy, well-adjusted black males. So many clarifications and conditions must be added to the premise that *only* black men can rear healthy black males that it dies the death of a thousand qualifications.

In reality, Singleton's film works off the propulsive energies that fuel deep and often insufficiently understood tensions between black men and black women. A good deal of pain infuses relations between black men and women, recently dramatized with the publication of Shahrazad Ali's infamous and controversial underground bestseller, *The Blackman's Guide to Understanding the Blackwoman*. The book, which counseled black women to be submissive to black men and which endorsed black male violence toward women under specific circumstances, touched off a furious debate that drew forth the many unresolved personal, social, and domestic tensions between black men and women.[10]

This pain follows a weary pattern of gender relations that has privileged concerns defined by black men over feminist or womanist issues. Thus, during the civil rights movement, feminist and womanist questions were perennially deferred, so that precious attention would not be diverted from racial oppression and the achievement of liberation.[11] But this deference to issues of racial freedom is a permanent pattern in black male-female relations, womanist and feminist movements continue to exist on the fringe of black communities.[12] And even in the Afrocentric worldview that Singleton advocates, the role of black women is often subordinate to the black patriarch.

Equally as unfortunate, many contemporary approaches to the black male crisis have established a rank hierarchy that suggests that the plight of black men is infinitely more lethal, and hence more important, than the condition of black women. The necessary and urgent focus on the plight of black men, however, must not come at the expense of understanding its relationship to the circumstances of black women.

At places, Singleton is able to subtly embody a healthy and redemptive vision of black male-female relations. For instance, after Tre has been verbally abused and physically threatened by police brutality, he seeks sanctuary at Brandi's house, choreographing his rage at life in South Central by angrily swinging at empty space. As Tre breaks down in tears, he and Brandi finally achieve an authentic moment of spiritual and physical consummation previously denied them by the complications of peer pressure and religious restraint. After Tre is assured that Brandi is really ready, they make love, achieving a fugitive moment of true erotic and spiritual union.

Brandi is able to express an unfettered and spontaneous affection that is not a simplistic "sex-as-proof-of-love" that reigns in the thinking of many teen worldviews. Brandi's mature intimacy is both the expression of her evolving womanhood and a vindication of the wisdom of her previous restraint. Tre is able at once to act out his male rage and demonstrate his vulnerability to Brandi, thereby arguably achieving a synthesis of male and female responses and humanizing the crisis of the black male in a way that none of his other relationships—even his relationship with his father—are able to do. It is a pivotal moment in the development of a politics of alternative black masculinity that prizes the strength of surrender and cherishes the embrace of a healing tenderness.

As the boys mature into young men, their respective strengths are enhanced and their weaknesses exposed. The deepening tensions between Ricky and Doughboy break out into violence when a petty argument over who will run an errand for Ricky's girlfriend provokes a fistfight. After Tre tries unsuccessfully to stop the fight, Brenda runs out of the house, divides the two boys, slaps Doughboy in the face, and checks Ricky's condition. "What you slap me for?" Doughboy repeatedly asks her after Ricky and Tre go off to the store. She doesn't answer, but her choice, again, is clear. Its effect on Doughboy is clearer still.

Such everyday variations on the question of choice are, again, central to the world Singleton depicts in *Hood*. Singleton obviously understands that people are lodged between social structure and personal fortune, between luck and ambition. He brings a nuanced understanding of choice to each character's large and small acts of valor, courage, and integrity that reveal what contemporary moral philosophers call virtue.[13] But they often miss what Singleton understands: character is not only structured by the choices we make, but by the range of choices we have to choose from—choices for which individuals alone are not responsible.

Singleton focuses his lens on the devastating results of the choices made by *Hood*'s characters, for themselves and for others. *Hood* presents a chain of choices, a community defined in part by the labyrinthine array of choices made and the consequences borne, to which others must then choose to respond. But Singleton does not portray a blind fatalism or a mechanistic determinism; instead he displays a sturdy realism that shows how communities affect their own lives and how their lives are shaped by personal and impersonal forces.

Brenda's choice to favor Ricky may not have been completely her own—all the messages of society say that the good, obedient child, especially in the ghetto, is the one to nurture and help—but it resulted in Doughboy's envy of Ricky and contributed to

Doughboy's anger, alienation, and gradual drift into gang violence. Ironically and tragically, this constellation of choices may have contributed to Ricky's violent death when he is shot by members of a rival gang as he and Tre return from the neighborhood store.

Ricky's death, in turn, sets in motion a chain of choices and consequences. Doughboy feels he has no choice but to pursue his brother's killers, becoming a more vigilant keeper to his brother in Ricky's death than he could be while Ricky lived. Tre, too, chooses to join Doughboy, thereby repudiating everything his father taught and forswearing every virtue he has been trained to observe. When he grabs his father's gun and is met at the door by Furious, the collision between training and instinct is dramatized on Tre's face, wrenched in anguish and tears.

Although Furious convinces him to relinquish the gun, Furious's victory is only temporary. The meaning of Tre's manhood is at stake; it is the most severe test he has faced, and he chooses to sneak out of the house to join Doughboy. All Furious can do is tensely exercise his hands with two silver balls, which in this context are an unavoidable metaphor for how black men view their fate through their testicles, which are constantly up for grabs, attack, or destruction. Then sometime during the night, Tre's impassioned choice finally rings false, a product of the logic of vengeance he has desperately avoided all these years; he insists that he be let out of Doughboy's car before they find Ricky's killers.

Following the code of male honor, Doughboy kills his brother's killers. But the next morning, in a conversation with Tre, he is not so sure of violence's mastering logic anymore, and says that he understands Tre's choice to forsake Doughboy's vigilante mission, even as he silently understands that he is in too deep to be able to learn any other language of survival.

Across this chasm of violence and anguish, the two surviving friends are able to extend a final gesture of understanding. As Doughboy laments the loss of his brother, Tre offers him the bittersweet consolation that "you got one more brother left." Their final embrace in the film's closing moment is a sign of a deep love that binds brothers, a love, however, that too often will not save brothers.

The film's epilogue tells us that Doughboy is murdered two weeks later, presumably to avenge the deaths of Ricky's killers. The epilogue also tells us that Tre and Brandi manage to escape South Central as Tre pursues an education at Morehouse College, with Brandi at neighboring Spelman College. It is testimony to the power of Singleton's vision that Tre's escape is no callow Hollywood paean to the triumph of the human spirit (nor is it, as some reviewers have somewhat perversely described the film, "life-affirming"). The viewer is not permitted to forget for a moment the absurd and vicious predictability of the loss of life in South Central Los Angeles, a hurt so colossal that even Doughboy must ask, "If there was a God, why he let mothefuckers get smoked every night?" Theodicy in gangface.

Singleton is not about to provide a slick or easy answer. But he does powerfully juxtapose such questions alongside the sources of hope, sustained in the heroic sacrifice of everyday people who want their children's lives to be better. The work of John Singleton embodies such hope by reminding us that South Central Los Angeles, by the sheer power of discipline and love, sends children to college, even as its self-destructive rage sends them to the grave.

Notes

1. These statistics, as well as an examination of the social, economic, political, medical, and educational conditions of young black men and public policy recommendations for the social amelioration of their desperate circumstances, are found in a collection of essays edited by Jewelle Taylor Gibbs, *Young, Black, and Male in America: An Endangered Species*.

2. William Julius Wilson has detailed the shift in the American political economy from manufacturing to service employment and its impact upon the inner city and the ghetto poor, particularly upon black males who suffer high rates of joblessness (which he sees as the source of many problems in the black family) in *The Truly Disadvantaged*. For an analysis of the specific problems of black males in relation to labor force participation, see Gerald David Jaynes and Robin M. Williams, Jr., eds., *A Common Destiny*, pp. 301, 308–12.

3. I have explored the cultural expressions, material conditions, creative limits, and social problems associated with rap, in "Rap, Race and Reality," "The Culture of Hip-Hop," "2 Live Crew's Rap: Sex, Race and Class," "As Complex As They Wanna Be: 2 Live Crew," "Tapping into Rap," "Performance, Protest and Prophecy in the Culture of Hip-Hop," and in Jim Gardner, "Taking Rap Seriously:

Thcomusicologist Michael Eric Dyson on the New Urban Griots and Peripatetic Preachers (An Interview)'' (see chap. 3, this volume).

4. I have in mind here the criticism of liberal society, and the forms of moral agency it both affords and prevents, that has been gathered under the rubric of communitarianism, ranging from MacIntyre's *After Virtue* to Bellah et al.'s *Habits of the Heart*.

5. See Mike Davis's and Sue Riddick's brilliant analysis of the drug culture in "Los Angeles: Civil Liberties between the Hammer and the Rock."

6. For an insightful discussion of the relationship between the underground or illegitimate economy, and people exercising agency in resisting the worse injustices and effects of the legitimate economy, see Don Nonini, "Everyday Forms of Popular Resistance."

7. For a recent exploration of the dynamics of social interaction between police as agents and symbols of mainstream communal efforts to regulate the behavior and social place of black men, and black men in a local community, see Elijah Anderson, *Streetwise*, pp. 163–206.

8. According to this logic, as expressed in a familiar saying in many black communities, black women "love their sons and raise their daughters." For a valiant, although flawed, attempt to get beyond a theoretical framework that implicitly blames black women for the condition of black men, see Clement Cottingham, "Gender Shift in Black Communities." Cottingham attempts to distance himself from arguments about a black matriarchy that stifles black male social initiative and moral responsibility. Instead he examines the gender shifts in black communities fueled by black female educational mobility and the marginalization of lower-class black males. But his attempt is weakened, ironically, by a prominently placed quotation by James Baldwin, which serves as a backdrop to his subsequent discussions of mother-son relationships, black male-female relationships, and black female assertiveness. Cottingham writes: "Drawing on Southern black folk culture, James Baldwin, in his last published work, alluded to black lower-class social patterns which, when set against the urban upheaval among the black poor from the 1960s onward, seem to encourage this gender shift. He characterizes these lower-class social patterns as 'a disease peculiar to the Black community called 'sorriness.' 'It is,' Baldwin observes, 'a disease that attacks black males. It is transmitted by Mama, whose instinct is to protect the Black male from the devastation that threatens him from the moment he declares himself a man.' "

"Apart from its protectiveness toward male children, Baldwin notes another dimension of 'sorriness.' 'Mama,' he writes, 'lays this burden on Sister from whom she expects (or indicates she expects) far more than she expects from Brother; but one of the results of this all too comprehensible dynamic is that Brother may never grow up—in which case the community has become an accomplice to the Republic.' Perceptively, Baldwin concludes that the differences in the socialization of boys and girls eventually erode the father's commitment to family life."

When such allusive but isolated ethnographic comments are not placed in an analytical framework that tracks the social, political, economic, religious, and historical forces that shape black (female) rearing practices and circumscribe black male-female relations, they are more often than not employed to blame black women for the social failure of black children, especially boys. The point here is not to suggest that black women have no responsibility for the plight of black families. But most social theory has failed to grapple with the complex set of forces that define and delimit black female existence, too easily relying upon anecdotal tales of black female behavior preventing black males from flourishing, and not examining the shifts in the political economy, the demise of low-skilled, high-waged work, the deterioration of the general moral infrastructure of many poor black communities, the ravaging of black communities by legal forces of gentrification and illegal forces associated with crime and drugs, etc. These forces, and not black women, are the real villains.

9. For a perceptive analysis of the economic conditions that shape the lives of black women, see Julianne Malveaux, "The Political Economy of Black Women."

10. The peculiar pain that plagues the relationships between black men and black women across age, income, and communal strata was on bold and menacing display in the confrontation between Clarence Thomas and Anita Hill during Senate hearings to explore claims by Hill that Thomas sexually harassed her while she worked for him at two governmental agencies. Their confrontation was facilitated and constructed by the televisual medium, a ready metaphor for the technological intervention into contemporary relations between significant segments of the citizenry. Television also serves as the major mediator between various bodies of public officials and the increasingly narrow publics at whose behest they perform, thus blurring the distinctions between public good and private interest. The Hill-Thomas hearings also helped expose the wide degree to which the relations between black men and black women are shaped by a powerful white male gaze. In this case, the relevant criteria for assessing the truth of claims about sexual harassment and gender oppression were determined by white senatorial surveillance.

11. Thus, it was unexceptional during the civil rights movement for strong, articulate black women to be marginalized, or excluded altogether, from the intellectual work of the struggle. Furthermore, concerns about feminist liberation were generally overlooked, and many talented, courageous women were often denied a strong or distinct institutional voice about women's liberation in the racial liberation movement. For a typical instance of such sexism within civil rights organizations, see Carson's discussion of black female dissent within SNCC, in Clayborne Carson, *In Struggle*, pp. 147–48.

12. For insightful claims and descriptions of the marginal status of black feminist and womanist concerns in black communities and for helpful explorations of the complex problems faced by black feminists and womanists, see bell hooks's *Ain't I a Woman*, Michele Wallace's *Invisibility Blues*, Audre Lorde's *Sister/Outsider*, and Alice Walker's *In Search of Our Mother's Garden*.

13. Of course, many traditional conceptions of virtue display a theoretical blindness to structural factors that circumscribe and influence the acquisition of traditional moral skills, habits, and dispositions and the development of alternative and nonmainstream moral skills. What I mean here is that the development of virtues, and the attendant skills that must be deployed in order to practice them effectively, is contingent upon several factors: where and when one is born, the conditions under which one must live, the social and communal forces that limit and define one's life, etc. These factors color the character of moral skills that will be acquired, shape the way in which these skills will be appropriated, and even determine the list of skills required to live the good life in different communities. Furthermore, these virtues reflect the radically different norms, obligations, commit-

ments, and socioethical visions of particular communities. For a compelling critique of MacIntyre's contextualist universalist claim for the prevalence of the virtues of justice, truthfulness, and courage in all cultures and the implications of such a critique for moral theory, see Alessandro Ferrara's essay, "Universalisms: Procedural, Contextual, and Prudential." For an eloquent argument that calls for the authors of the communitarian social vision articulated in *Habits of the Heart* to pay attention to the life, thought, and contributions of people of color, see Vincent Harding, "Toward a Darkly Radiant Vision of America's Truth: A Letter of Concern, An Invitation to Re-Creation."

Works Cited

Anderson, Elijah. *Streetwise*. Chicago: University of Chicago Press, 1991.

Bellah, Robert N., Richard Madsen, William N. Sullivan, Ann Swidler, and Steven M. Tipton. *Habits of the Heart: Individualism and Commitment in American Life*. Berkeley: University of California Press, 1985.

Carson, Clayborne. *In Struggle: SNCC and the Black Awakening of the 1960s*. Cambridge: Harvard University Press, 1981.

Cottingham, Clement. "Gender Shift in Black Communities." *Dissent*, Fall 1989, pp. 521–25.

Davis, Mike, and Sue Riddick. "Los Angeles: Civil Liberties between the Hammer and the Rock." *New Left Review*, July/August 1988, pp. 37–60.

Dyson, Michael Eric. "As Complex As They Wanna Be: 2 Live Crew." *Z Magazine*, January 1991, pp. 76–78.

——. "The Culture of Hip-Hop." *Zeta Magazine*, June 1989, pp. 44–50.

——. "Performance, Protest and Prophecy in the Culture of Hip-Hop." In *The Emergency of Black and the Emergence of Rap*, ed. Jon Michael Spencer, pp. 12–24. Durham, N.C.: Duke University Press, 1991.

——. "Rap, Race and Reality." *Christianity and Crisis*, March 16, 1987, pp. 98–100.

——. "Tapping into Rap." *New World Outlook*, May/June 1991, pp. 32–35.

——. "2 Live Crew's Rap: Sex, Race and Class." *Christian Century*, January 2–9, 1991, pp. 7–8.

Ferrara, Alessandro. "Universalisms: Procedural, Contextual and Prudential." In *Universalism vs. Communitarianism: Contemporary Debates in Ethics*, ed. David Rasmussen, pp. 11–38, Cambridge: MIT Press, 1990.

Gardner, Jim. "Taking Rap Seriously: Theomusicologist Michael Eric Dyson on the New Urban Griots and Peripatetic Preachers (An Interview)." *Artvu*, Spring 1991, pp. 20–23.

Gibbs, Jewelle Taylor, ed. *Young, Black, Male in America: An Endangered Species*. Dover, Mass.: Auburn House, 1988.

Harding, Vincent. "Toward a Darkly Radiant Vision of America's Truth: A Letter of Concern, an Invitation to Re-Creation." In *Community in America: The Challenge of "Habits of the Heart,"* ed. Charles H. Reynolds and Ralph V. Norman, Berkeley: University of California Press, 1988, pp. 67–83.

hooks, bell. *Ain't I a Woman: Black Women and Feminism*. Boston: South End Press, 1981.

Jaynes, Gerald David, and Robin Williams, Jr., eds. *A Common Destiny: Blacks and American Society*. Washington, D.C.: National Academy Press, 1989.

Lorde, Audre. *Sister/Outsider*. Freedom, Calif.: Crossing Press, 1984.

MacIntyre, Alisdair. *After Virtue*. Notre Dame, Ind.: University of Notre Dame Press, 1981.

Malveaux, Julianne. "The Political Economy of Black Women." In *The Year Left 2—Toward a Rainbow Socialism: Essays on Race, Ethnicity, Class and Gender*, ed. Mike Davis, Manning Marable, Fred Pfeil, and Michael Sprinker, pp. 52–72. London: Verso, 1987.

Nonini, Don. "Everyday Forms of Popular Resistance." *Monthly Review: An Independent Socialist Magazine*, November 1988, pp. 25–36.

Walker, Alice. *In Search of Our Mother's Garden*. New York: Harcourt Brace Jovanovich, 1983.

Wallace, Michele. *Invisibility Blues: From Pop to Theory*. London: Verso, 1990.

Wilson, William Julius. *The Truly Disadvantaged: The Inner City, the Underclass, and Public Policy*. Chicago: University of Chicago Press, 1987.

Improvisation

On the *Mo' Money* Soundtrack

In the most recent spate of black films, music has played a crucial part in accenting plot and enlarging themes. The sound track that songwriter-producers Jimmy "Jam" Harris and Terry Lewis have assembled for Damon Wayans's *Mo' Money* is an invigorating companion to the film, a freestanding cache of black musical styles—from rap to ballads, gospel to funk—whose common theme is the virtues and vicissitudes of love.

Mo' Money's first single, "The Best Things in Life Are Free," deftly melds Janet Jackson's airy delivery with Luther Vandross's yearning, softly insistent vocals. The duo effortlessly floats a sparkling melody and lyrics about love's inestimable value over a slinking Jam and Lewis rhythm track that showcases the rapping of New Edition mates Michael Bivens, Ronnie DeVoe, and Ralph Tresvant. Tresvant expands the track's sentiments on "Money Can't Buy You Love," rescuing the title's potential for cliché through sheer emotional intimacy and directness of expression. Put across by a rubbery bass line and a jaunty, irresistible mid-tempo groove, the tune renews Tresvant's standing debt to Marvin Gaye.

The raps on *Mo' Money* work so well because they confirm that genre's preeminence as the poetry of everyday life. MC Lyte, for instance, seductively embellishes a conceit drawn from quotidian experience on "Ice Cream Dream," a delicious ode to erotic desire. "Get Off My Back," by Public Enemy's Flavor Flav, juxtaposes P-Funk grooves and a subtle James Brown synthesized shuffle against Flav's classic off-kilter commentary. The monkey he implores to quit his back is not only a potent symbol of cocaine addiction, but an image as well of his pedigree as a musical trickster, a legacy he shares with George Clinton.

Gospel's glorious power unfurls in Ann Nesby's roof-shattering wails, plaintive shouts, and rollicking melisma, which crease the Sounds of Blackness's "Joy"; built on a swaggering house rhythm, "Joy" shows once more that gospel's genius is its spiraling, hypnotic repetition. Nesby, meanwhile, also takes a turn on Big Daddy Kane's humorous rap "A Job Ain't Nuthin' but Work," on which Kane insists, "I'm so against work I wouldn't even take a blow job." And Krush's "Let's Get Together (So Groovy Now)"—with its blistering pastiche of sixties girl-group grooves, seventies organ funk, eighties rap chants, and nineties swinging R & B—exhorts universal community in the lines "I think it would be just nifty / We could learn so much from the sixties."

Some of Jam and Lewis's most noteworthy recent work has emerged in collaboration with Johnny Gill, one of his generation's most gifted vocalists. Gill delights again on "Let's Just Run Away," a searing, moody love ballad backed by minimal, edgy sequencing. In the same sonic vein, the enchanting Caron Wheeler, formerly of Soul II Soul, delivers an eerily affecting performance on "I Adore You," earthily scatting over the song's sputtering beats.

There are some misses on *Mo' Money*—a couple of throw-away instrumental tracks—and a screeching heavy metal rocker (the Harlem Yacht Club's "Brother Will") doesn't quite measure up to the album's other efforts. But harmony-dense ballads by Color Me Badd and Mint Condition partially redeem these excesses. Overall, Jam and Lewis have produced an incandescent collage of musical genres that reveals the imagination and creativity of the best contemporary black music.

Part II

Beyond the Mantra: Reflections on Race, Gender, and Class

8

Probing a Divided Metaphor: Malcolm X and His Readers

In *The Autobiography of Malcolm X* the charismatic black religious nationalist recalls his momentous 1964 pilgrimage to Mecca, a visit that would alter the course of his life and career. After twelve years in which this minister of the Nation of Islam trumpeted a doctrine of the intrinsic evil of whites, likened the dream of American equality to a "nightmare" for American blacks, and championed a plan to redeem black Americans by saving them from the tide of brainwashing that had drowned awareness of the black race's true superiority, X writes of an incident in Jedda, in which he is treated with great hospitality by a man who, in America, would be considered white:

> That white man . . . related to Arabia's ruler, truly an international man, . . . had given up his suite to me, for my transient comfort . . . . He had followed the American press about me. If he did that, he knew there was only stigma attached to me. I was supposed to have horns. I was a "racist." I was "anti-white." . . . Everyone was even accusing me of using his religion of Islam as a cloak for . . . criminal practices and philosophy. . . . That morning was when I first began to reappraise the "white man." It was when I first began to perceive that "white man," as commonly used, means complexion only secondarily; primarily it described attitudes and actions. In America, "white man" meant specific attitudes and actions toward the black man, and toward all other non-white men. But in the Muslim world, I had seen that men with white complexions were more genuinely brotherly than anyone else had ever been.

> That morning was the start of a radical alteration in my whole outlook about "white" men.

His life-changing encounters were recorded in letters from Africa to family members and other followers in the United States. The revealing missives detailed X's view of the color blindness of Muslim society and religion. This series of experiences forced X to "rearrange much of my thought-patterns previously held, and to toss aside some of my previous conclusions."

Less than a year later, Malcolm X was gunned down by assassins in New York's Audubon Ballroom. By the time of his apocalyptic martyrdom, X had seceded from the Nation (after bitter disappointment in the moral failures of its leader Elijah Muhammad and the tensions within the Nation concerning his own increased public presence) and had begun two organizations, one religious, the other political. Each group reflected X's transformed perspective about racial and religious matters, especially his belief that broad social engagement permitted blacks their best chance to oppose the lethal legacy of American racism.

It is around Malcolm's increasingly independent political activity during the final fifty weeks of his life, combined with his startling reversal of feeling about the possibility of redemption for white America, that so much controversy and confusion have gathered. Although X made many overtures to a broader philosophy of human community, he simply didn't live long enough to fulfill the promise of his significant but tentative first steps. While we may conclude with certainty that X had rejected the whites-are-devils pronouncements that helped to focus his earlier life and brought him the attention and vilification of a nation, we are brought up short in trying to definitively detail the universal humanitarianism of his later days.

Although his entire legacy until recently has been demonized and dismissed by the traditional academy, Malcolm's popularity never flagged among a cadre of black nationalist activists, journalists, and independent intellectuals who for a quarter century have debated intensely his significance to black politics, black culture, and American society. These debates have had a trickle-up effect; they created the ground swell for the fierce war of interpretation being waged over Malcolm's meaning in our times.

In the face of the grim recurrence of a racism many believed had been greatly diminished, the renewed popularity of Malcolm X—both his image and his ideology—have taken on new importance. The signs of his ascent—from posters, ubiquitous X baseball hats, and sampling of his voice on rap records to the recording of the opera *X* created by Anthony and Thulani Davis; this month's release of the epic film biography directed by Spike Lee; and the forthcoming release of his speeches edited to reveal his ideological evolution—all are a function of both need and mythology: the current and deeply felt need for a confrontational stance toward America's continuing racism and the seductive mythology of the perfect black man.

Thus it is that Malcolm X's name no longer belongs to him, no longer refers simply to his tall body or to his short life. Like Martin Luther King, Jr., X has come to mean more than himself. For some, X is an unreconstructed nationalist, while for others he wed his nationalist beliefs to socialist philosophy. Still others subject X to Marxist and Freudian analysis, while others emphasize his vocation as a public moralist. His stature derives as much from his detractors' exaggerated fears as from his admirers' exalted hopes. He has become a divided metaphor: for those who love him, he is a powerful lens of self-perception, a means of sharply focusing political and racial priorities; for those who loathe him, he is a distorted mirror that reflects violence and hatred.

Malcolm himself anticipated the confusion his views would cause (he confessed, "Even I was myself astounded"). At the time, he had not fully gauged the disquiet his new beliefs would cause among supporters already thrown by his earlier break with the Nation of Islam. Among the black religious sect's powerful dramatis personae—its leader the Honorable Elijah Muhammad; the world champion boxer Muhammad Ali; and Louis X, now Minister Louis Farrakhan, Malcolm's associate turned enemy—it was Malcolm who emerged as the major player in the Nation of Islam's dramatic attempts to rescue black Americans from what they viewed as the bankrupt religious and social values of white society.

Yet Malcolm X has received nothing like the intellectual attention devoted to King. As the central figure of the civil rights movement, King justifiably has been the subject of extensive scholarship, but his cultural visibility has also to do with the style, content, and aims of his leadership, which for most of his life were easily translatable and largely attractive to white America. On the other hand, X's complex leadership, which visited rhetorical scorn on white supremacy and which appealed especially to working and poor blacks, has invited derision, caricature, and dismissal, forces that undermine extensive and balanced scholarly investigation.

To be sure, numerous writings about X's legacy have been published in alternative and black newspapers, journals, pamphlets, and books; they have been vigorously discussed in conferences, rap sessions, and panel discussions throughout the black communities of America. Yet with notable exceptions, the literature on Malcolm X has often missed the mark, offering praise where critical judgment is called for, trapping itself in intellectual frameworks that neither illumine nor surprise.

Of course, *The Autobiography of Malcolm X*, as told to Alex Haley (New York: Grove Press, 1964), is the Ur-text of contemporary black nationalism. Activists and intellectuals tote it in their back pockets and briefcases in ready reference in debates about black America, while rappers imitate its radical tones and students often quote it as sacred verse. As X's faithful and creative scribe—he had written two articles about X and interviewed him for *Playboy* magazine when a publisher tapped him to write X's autobiography in 1963—Haley placed his considerable narrative skills at Malcolm's disposal. It was Haley who brought X's life to full color, crafting a classic of African-American letters. But as Malcolm opened his life to Haley, he was also reinventing it on the spot. X was improvising a personal narrative that drew from both the virtues and failures of memory. But the lapses in accuracy that he exhibited were often rooted less in mendacity than in the human need to tell stories in ways that make our lives make sense.

Despite the crucial role of his autobiography in expanding black cultural consciousness, the full meaning of Malcolm X's life inevitably must be judged using more than a story that draws from a single source. Thus it is especially important now to explore a select group of books published over the past two decades that offer widely divergent views of Malcolm X's complex political journey.

In the early anthology *Malcolm X: The Man and His Times* (New York: Collier Books, 1969; Trenton, N.J.: Africa World Press, 1990), the first anthology dedicated to exploring Malcolm's life and thought, the black historian and Hunter College professor emeritus John Henrik Clarke has edited a collection of voices that undermine a single understanding of Malcolm's place in history. What many of the essays share is a reverential regard for his black nationalist legacy.

In his contribution to this collection of thirty-four essays, interviews, and organizational statements, the black theologian Albert Cleage (who knew and worked with X) boldly defends Malcolm's black nationalist reputation by concluding that "if in Mecca he had decided that blacks and whites can unite, then his life at that moment would have become meaningless in terms of the world struggle of black people." Cleage seeks to rebut the beliefs that Malcolm at the end of his life was becoming either an integrationist, an advocate of the internationalization of black struggle, or a socialist.

The activist and political theorist James Boggs criticizes both Malcolm's black nationalist heirs, whom he views as preoccupied with Black Power sloganeering and as bereft of sufficient analytic depth, and "white radicals who lend a grudging support to Black Power," patronizing black revolutionaries as " 'unfinished products' who will one day see the light and recognize the superiority of Marxist theory and the necessity of an alliance with the white working class." The writer Charles Wilson insightfully discusses Malcolm's "failure of leadership style and a failure to evolve a sound organizational base for his activities," concluding that Malcolm was a "victim of his own charisma."

Clarke's anthology mattered: in the days following Malcolm X's death, its contributors addressed urban blacks and nationalist intellectuals confronting their deepening social crisis. It argued that black nationalism was an important and thriving alternative to black bourgeois protest, which held out as its goal black integration into white society. Clarke's book also countered the demonization of a man believed by most whites (and many blacks) to be the embodiment of evil. But its goal of redeeming Malcolm X's legacy rather than evaluating it lessens its value; the collection's tone suggests an exercise in beatification, with cultural interpreters working to preserve fragments of Malcolm's memory against abuse or amnesia.

Fortunately, the books that primarily understand Malcolm in relation to the moral abomination of racism to which his views forcefully responded supply the needed critical attention to his career. Black theologian James Cone's *Martin & Malcolm & America: A Dream or a Nightmare* (Maryknoll, N.Y.: Orbis Books, 1991) treats the religious roots of Malcolm's moral vision; journalist Louis Lomax's *To Kill a Black Man* (Los Angeles: Holloway House, 1968) addresses the social and political dimensions of Malcolm's moral perspective. But it is in their roles as comparative studies of King and X that the Cone and Lomax books seize our interest, as they critically pair the defining figures of contemporary black culture. Cone, the widely regarded founder of black theology and a professor at New York's Union Theological Seminary, has been profoundly influenced by both King and X, and his book is a public acknowledgment of intellectual debt and inspiration.

Most Americans believe that X and King occupied violently opposed ethical universes, that their positions on the best solution to America's racial crisis led them to a permanent parting of paths. More likely, though, they were the yin and yang of black moral responses to white racism, complementing more than contradicting each other in their last years. Cone even suggests that King and X were in important ways *converging*, saying that "Malcolm and Martin moved away from the extremes of their original positions and began to embrace aspects of each other's viewpoints." Thus, King began in 1966 to emphasize black pride and to explore the virtues of "temporary segregation" to foster the economic health of black communities, and he became more radical about the limits of social protest. And X for his part became publicly political, acknowledged the militancy of integrationists, and even encouraged voter registration.

Although King and X met only once for a brief moment—resulting in the famed photo of both figures smiling broadly at the U.S. Capitol in 1964—X did, in 1965, journey to Selma, Alabama, where King was in jail, to speak to civil-rights workers before leaving for a speaking engagement in London. His remarks on that occasion to Coretta King—less than a month before his death—

reveal X's poignant awareness and acceptance of the distinct roles he and King played in the black freedom movement. "I want Dr. King to know that I didn't come to Selma to make his job difficult. I really did come thinking I could make it easier. If the white people realize what the alternative is, perhaps they will be more willing to hear Dr. King."

In the Lomax book, the author, a friend to both leaders, characterizes each figure more rigidly; the book outlines vividly how distinct X's openness to violent self-defense was from King's advocacy of nonviolence as a strategy of social change. Written in the torturous aftermath of King's assassination in 1968, Lomax's volume has all the virtues of historical immediacy—impassioned narration, proximity to the moment's true feeling, unvarnished insight. What it lacks is the greater virtue of historical perspective, which comes from long and mature reflection upon events. This is the virtue that Cone's book possesses, along with an analytical acumen that explores the development of King's and X's lives and thought in larger scope and richer detail than many of his nationalist predecessors.

But like them, Cone is plagued by an overreliance on the theme of racial unity as an intellectual principle to explain his twin subjects' failures and achievements, limiting his understanding of King and X and skewing his view of their complex uses (especially King's) of history and culture. Nevertheless, Cone's book is an invaluable aid in comprehending the similarities and differences between the two towering influences on contemporary black culture.

Malcolm X lived for most of his life in opposition to the fundamental assumptions of American moral judgment that innocence and corruption are on a continuum, that justice and injustice are on a scale, and that proper moral behavior depends on making the right choices between existing options of good and evil. Such a vision of X is presented in Peter Goldman's *The Death and Life of Malcolm X* (Urbana: University of Illinois Press, 1979). Goldman, a senior editor at *Newsweek*, met X in 1962 and spent hundreds of hours interviewing him. Goldman's book captures with eloquence and imagination the forces of white racial oppression that made life hell for northern poor blacks and the minimal resources apparently at their disposal before Malcolm's defiant rhetoric rallied black rage and anger to their defense.

Goldman's Malcolm is one whose "life was itself an accusation," a "witness for the prosecution" of white injustice, a "public moralist." With each aspect of X's life that Goldman treats—whether it is Malcolm's foreshadowing of the forthcoming Black Power Movement or his withering assaults on white society—Goldman's narrative subtly and skillfully illumines Malcolm's career.

What Goldman fails to do is properly convey the mammoth scope of competing economic, cultural, and historical forces that erupted during the 1940s, 1950s, and 1960s and that reflected not only racial antagonism, but class conflict and gender oppression as well. Nor does he present a sufficient analysis of the extreme political limitations placed on black militant men of either religious or secular sensibility. Still, Goldman's book, the first full-scale life of X, remains an indispensable biography of the enigmatic leader.

If the task of biography is to cast as bright a light as possible over the shadowed areas of human behavior, then psychobiography doubles the effort, using the insights gleaned through psychological theory to illumine the full range of human experience. Over the last decade, several journal articles and two books have notably applied the psychobiographical approach, with varying results. UCLA social theorist and Marxist psychoanalyst Eugene Victor Wolfenstein's *The Victims of Democracy: Malcolm X and the Black Revolution* (London: Free Association Books, 1989) is a work of considerable intellectual imagination and rigor that represents the best of this trend.

Wolfenstein takes ample measure of the energies that created X and the demons that drove him. Recalling X's "earliest vivid memory"—being traumatically awakened in the middle of the night in 1929 because the family house in Lansing, Michigan, was burning to the ground—Wolfenstein contends that Malcolm's "consciousness began in a moment of racist violence." Starting from that point, he brilliantly maps Malcolm's developing awareness both as a black man in a racist culture and as a member of a violent family. Wolfenstein says that Malcolm's father "made himself, by his own hand, both the defender and destroyer of his family."

In Wolfenstein's scheme, because Freudian theory "provides no foundation for the analysis of interests, be they individual or collective," and Marxism "provides no foundation for the analysis of desires," he uses both to explain Malcolm's life. But his book has deficits; besides his lack of clarity about the importance of religion in providing social cohesion among northern urban black communities, he focuses exclusively on biological definitions of race. More recent race theorists have maintained that race is not only a biological reality, but carries socially created meanings as well. Such an approach to race might help Wolfenstein explain how Malcolm and other blacks understood and employed race in their defense against white racism and how rigid views of race held by black nationalists like X limited their range of social response. Wolfenstein's major limitation lies in his overuse of X's autobiography for information about Malcolm. Nonetheless, Wolfenstein's book is the most astute treatment to date of Malcolm's intellectual and psychological roots.

If Wolfenstein, despite his flaws, represents the best of the psychobiographical impulse, Bruce Perry's *Malcolm: The Life of a Man Who Changed Black America* (Barrytown, N.Y.: Station Hill Press, 1991) may represent the worst. In Perry's eyes, Malcolm's troubled childhood holds the key to his subsequent career as a black leader. According to Perry, the physical abuse of his mother by Malcolm's father, his parents' extramarital affairs, the breakup of the family after the father's death and the mother's mental collapse, Malcolm's inheritance of his mother's obsession with color, and his hatred of women learned during childhood are all factors that contributed to the mature Malcolm's contorted leadership style.

Perry says Malcolm's "war against the white power structure evolved from the same inner needs that had spawned earlier rebellions against his teachers, the law, established religion, and other symbols of authority." Perry portrays Malcolm's family as besieged by unremitting violence, criminality, and pathology. The mature Malcolm is equally tragic, a man of looming greatness whose self-destructing personality "contributed to his premature death." It is here that Perry's project folds in on itself, its rough edges puncturing the center of its explanatory purpose.

True enough, he does unearth new information about Malcolm. For instance, he reveals that in 1961 X held a secret meeting with the Klan on Elijah Muhammad's behalf, seeking the Klan's aid (since both groups opposed racial mixing) in obtaining land for the Nation of Islam to employ in implementing its separatist philosophy. Perry also discusses Malcolm's alleged homosexual activity, both as an experimenting adolescent and as a hustling young adult "who sold himself, as if the best he had to offer was his body." Perry's discussion of X's alleged homosexuality taps into an interpretive powder keg, especially since so many among the constituency that supports Malcolm's renewed importance are young, black, and male and are avid participants in a male-driven revival of black nationalism that thrives on the machismo of rap culture. But Perry's revelations are less striking for their threat to Malcolm's image as the quintessential black man than for the pedestrian interpretation he offers of Malcolm's homosexual motivations: absent male role models and a history of tyrannical females.

Since Perry makes a plausible case for their occurrence, a discussion of X's homosexual alliances might have served Perry as a powerful interpretive wedge beneath the cultural weight of oppressive black machismo, and as a way of exploring and explaining the cruel varieties of homophobia that afflict black communities. Instead Perry's treatment of Malcolm's sexuality is manifestly impotent; his analysis fails to make a substantive contribution to our understanding of black sexual politics or its relationship to social liberation. Perry fills in details about Malcolm's last year, but again his tendentious reading of Malcolm's career mars his perspective. For instance, he concludes that Malcolm's forays onto foreign soil were an attempt to secure funding for his fledgling organization. But this is only partially true; by his trips abroad, X was seeking to expand the scope of his views about the black struggle as his philosophy took on international dimensions.

And while Perry convincingly argues that X had forsaken his views about "devil" whites as early as 1959, during his first trip to the Middle East and long before his trip to Mecca in 1964, he cynically concludes that X's press conference held at New York's

Kennedy Airport after his return from Africa in May 1964 was a "fitting culmination to the public-relations campaign that had begun with his letter-writing campaign." Although X's last year was undoubtedly a year of sometimes frantic searching for the right road to take, Perry portrays Malcolm's final year as a series of opportunistic ploys to expand his support among nonblack audiences. Further, although Perry concedes X's "extraordinary capacity for political ambiguity," he more often characterizes X as a "political chameleon." Perry's book finally impresses as little more than a sniping account that makes a complex figure smaller than life.

To fully grasp X's complexity, it is necessary to probe his radical shift to a broader base of racial protest during his last year. Perhaps the most prominent and controversial interpreters of Malcolm's last year have been a group of intellectuals associated with the Socialist Workers party, a Trotskyite group that took keen interest in Malcolm's views after his return from Mecca and sponsored some of his last speeches. For the most part, their views have been articulated by the social critic George Breitman, author of *The Last Year of Malcolm X: The Evolution of a Revolutionary* (New York: Pathfinder, 1967) and editor of two volumes of Malcolm's speeches, organizational statements, and interviews he gave during his last years, *Malcolm X Speaks* (New York: Grove Weidenfeld, 1965) and *By Any Means Necessary* (New York: Pathfinder, 1970).

Breitman passionately argues that Malcolm's split with Elijah Muhammad was a major shock, however inevitable. Thus X needed time to rethink his beliefs and determine his organizational direction. Breitman divides Malcolm's independent phase into two parts: a transition period, lasting the few months between his split in March 1964 until his return from Africa at the end of May 1964, and the final period, lasting from June 1964 until his death in February 1965.

Breitman maintains that this final period marked Malcolm's maturation as "a revolutionary—increasingly anti-capitalist and pro-socialist as well as anti-imperialist," although these are labels that Breitman acknowledges Malcolm himself never adopted. But the truth is we have only the bare-bones outlines of Malcolm's emerging worldview, including his views on socialism. Malcolm's speeches throughout these collected volumes showcase a common feature: X displays sympathy for socialist philosophy without committing himself to its practice as a means of achieving liberation for African-Americans. X confessed in the "Young Socialist" interview near the end of his life that "I still would be hard pressed to give a specific definition of the overall philosophy which I think is necessary for the liberation of the black people in this country."

As a speculative study, Breitman's book is fascinating and provocative; as a definitive study of Malcolm's evolving intellectual positions, it is much less convincing. X left behind fragments of political speech more than systematic social thought, suggestive ideological gestures more than substantive political activity. Breitman is attempting to saddle X with a set of views he didn't live long enough to clarify or adopt.

The rebirth of black nationalism has sparked renewed interest in Malcolm X's life and thought. With its emphasis on racial pride and self-esteem; its support of black religious, business, and educational institutions; and the importance it gives to cultural and racial unity, black nationalism is prominently displayed throughout contemporary black America—witness the popularity of Nation of Islam leader Minister Louis Farrakhan; the broad appeal and controversy of rap music; the adoption of African hairstyles, pendants, and clothing; the expression of Afrocentric ideas by scholars such as Temple University Afro-American Studies chair Molefi Asante and Rutgers University professor Ivan van Sertima; and of course, the cultural deluge that is Malcomania.

But black nationalism has in the past, as well as in its most recent revival, suffocated the achievements of black women. The same may be said for the civil rights movement, where talented black and white women were often reduced to hewers of pencils and carriers of coffee. That most public interpreters of black nationalism and the civil rights movement are men reflects not only the sexism of these organizations, but the ongoing sexism of our society, which continues to discourage and prevent women from gaining intellectual authority in the debates that shape national perceptions about crucial social movements and public figures. As these facts are more broadly acknowledged and confronted, the number of women who have a voice in these debates should increase. Black feminist perspectives on Malcolm X will deepen our understanding of a figure who has only recently begun to receive wide reconsideration.

Malcolm X is now a part of the American imagination that once relegated him to its margins; he has become, in death, the source of our constant reinventions of his life. This transcendent status, however, does not free us from the obligation to demand more from our examination of the life that really was his. More than ever, we must forsake uncritical celebrations—not by denying his myth, but by taking it into account, by probing for the continuing wellsprings of his appeal and in so doing understanding our need to romanticize or revile him. Battered by unprincipled opponents, smothered by well-meaning loyalists, Malcolm's past is not yet settled; it never will be. Nonetheless, he must in the end receive what every important historical figure deserves: a comprehensive examination of both word and deed. To do less would be to fail ourselves and the history Malcolm X so boldly helped to create.

A Select Bibliography

Breitman, George; Porter, Herman; and Smith, Baxter. *The Assassination of Malcolm X*. New York: Pathfinder, 1976; 2nd ed., 1988; 3rd ed., 1991. A collection of essays and book reviews, mostly by Breitman, that purport to prove a government conspiracy to kill X.

Carson, Clayborne. *Malcolm X: The FBI File*. Introduction by Spike Lee, edited by David Gallen. New York: Carroll & Graf, 1991. Extensive excerpts from X's FBI files, arranged in nineteen sections; provides invaluable information about X's activities and progress as activist and thinker. Carson argues that the files place X in the context of American racial politics of the fifties and sixties.

Davis, Lenwood G., comp., with Marsha L. Moore. *Malcolm X: A Selected Bibliography*. Westport, Conn.: Greenwood Press, 1984. Indicates the wide debate about Malcolm carried on in the popular press, especially alternative newspapers, and in journals, magazines, and books.

Epps, Archie, ed. *Malcolm X: Speeches at Harvard*. New York: Paragon House, 1991. Previously published as *The Speeches of Malcolm X at Harvard*. New York: Morrow, 1968. Three speeches of X at Harvard during the sixties, edited and introduced by Epps, who knew X. An imaginative introduction compares X's views to Shakespeare's plays, but almost swallows the speeches themselves.

Essien-Udom, E. U. *Black Nationalism. The Search for an Identity in America*. Chicago: University of Chicago Press, 1962. An excellent standard treatment of black nationalist belief and practice during the fifties that includes analysis of Black Muslims.

Johnson, Timothy V. *Malcolm: A Comprehensive Annotated Bibliography*. New York: Garland, 1986. See comment following Davis.

Karim, Iman Benjamin, ed. *The End of White World Supremacy: Four Speeches by Malcolm X*. New York: Arcade, 1971. As a historical document that records X's thinking during the crucial year before he departed from the Nation of Islam, these speeches are valuable. But it is marred by the attempt by the editor (who knew and served under X and introduced him on the day of his assassination) to validate through X's own words views he lived to reject, making the book an act of ironic ventriloquism achieved by editorial manipulation.

Lee, Spike, with Ralph Wiley. *By Any Means Necessary: The Trials and Tribulations of the Making of* Malcolm X. New York: Hyperion, 1992. Vintage Lee chronicling of the economic, racial, and political obstacles he faced in completing his magnum opus. Also contains insightful comments from the film's principals—from producers, cinematographer, and actors—and the film's script, penned by James Baldwin, Arnold Perl, and Lee.

Lincoln, C. Eric. *The Black Muslims in America*. Boston: Beacon Press, 1961; rev. ed., 1973. The classic treatment of the Black Muslims during the leadership of Elijah Muhammad and Malcolm X. Unsurpassed as a sociological study of the sources of Black Muslim belief and practice.

Lomax, Louis. *When the Word Is Given: A Report on Elijah Muhummad, Malcolm X, and the Black Muslim Movement*. Cleveland: World, 1963. An informal and perceptive attempt by a journalist to unveil the movement's mysterious shroud of religious rituals, puritanical behavior, and unorthodox beliefs, which have to this day intimidated and intrigued outsiders. Lomax is a literate reporter whose lucid prose and imaginative reporting evoke the electricity and immediacy of the events he describes.

Perry, Bruce, ed. *Malcolm X: The Last Speeches*. New York: Pathfinder, 1989. A valuable collection of six X speeches and interviews, including two speeches X delivered during the last week of his life. The collection is especially helpful in documenting X's mature metamorphosis as a social activist and intellectual who began to conceive of the problems of blacks within an international framework.

T'Shaka, Oba. *The Political Legacy of Malcolm X*. Richmond, Calif.: Pan Afrikan, 1983. A clear exposition of Malcolm's political ideas as a revolutionary black nationalist. T'Shaka's critical examination, however, doesn't vigorously probe the contradictions of X's black nationalist thought.

Wood, Joe, ed. *Malcolm X: In Our Own Image*. New York: St. Martin's Press, 1992. An excellently conceived and wide ranging collection of essays by fourteen black intellectuals expands the critical dialogue about X's legacy. A useful anthology to read in tandem with Clarke's more celebratory collection.

Improvisation

On Contemporary Black Nationalism: A Response to Gary Peller

Gary Peller, in "Race against Integration" (*Tikkun,* Jan./Feb. 1991), presents a thoughtful and provocative critique of the ideologies that have shaped modern racial debate. Slashing away at liberal myths of integrationism's rational necessity and historical inevitability, Peller skillfully historicizes contemporary racial relations in order to show their roots in particular social and cultural traditions.

But Peller's arguments for adopting a black nationalist approach to racial politics are less persuasive. Indeed the terms of debate within the black community should prompt us to reconsider whether modern nationalism can easily be juxtaposed with integrationism as its ideological antithesis. Black nationalism and integrationism are complex, heterogeneous, and varied traditions. Although Peller concedes that black nationalism is not a monolithic tradition, he more often than not portrays *both* integrationism and nationalism in monolithic terms. This leads him to overlook conflicting and contradictory elements within each tradition, as well as important points of contact that they share. For instance, even an avowed integrationist like Martin Luther King, Jr., showed considerable flexibility in the course of his own ideological evolution. Although King eschewed the tactics of violent confrontation that many nationalists advocated, he readily embraced their wider goals of political empowerment, racial pride, and community solidarity.

King's initial strategy was to bring blacks within the larger compass of the American social, political, and cultural mainstream. But he later reconsidered this position. He began to believe that simple and uncritical integration tacitly endorsed the inequitable distribution of wealth, health care, employment, and other social goods that shaped the course of American capitalism both at home and abroad. This emergent radicalism informed, for example, King's early opposition to the war in Vietnam, as well as his growing solidarity with urban working-class blacks—and whites as well. One need only remember that King was organizing garbagemen on strike in Memphis at the time of his death to see how the integrationist position could converge with important points of the nationalist program.

And Malcolm X, beginning from a position of narrow nationalism, moved toward a parallel point of affinity with a politics of transracial coalition. Social contact—the cultural value, as Peller observes, that was the centerpiece of integrationist reform—with traditional Muslims and black Africans provided him with empirical validation of transracial life as a social fact and political possibility. He was thereby compelled to rethink the racial exclusionism of Elijah Muhammad's Nation of Islam and to begin promoting a more tolerant race-specific consciousness that could build alliances between races and nations. The radicalization of Martin and the race-specific tolerance of Malcolm thus exhibited the complex interaction of the diverse traditions of integrationism and nationalism.

The sharp distinctions Peller draws between integrationists and nationalists do help us understand how these traditions have diverged, but his analysis sheds less light on important points of convergence these disparate traditions have reached on issues of racial pride and varieties of black economic development. And this is why he falters as well in adapting his psychocultural critique of white liberal integrationism to explain the motivations of black integrationists. Blacks within the integrationist camp—with some notable exceptions—were far less disposed than their white counterparts to view black nationalists as reverse racists. Black nationalism has a long tradition of influencing black social thought and has been prominent at every crucial juncture of black American political history. Various strands of nationalist ideology have informed the thought of many black integrationists and progressives, in much the same way as they informed important elements of King's political development.

Black nationalism boasts a rich theoretical and cultural history that includes what some intellectuals have called its "golden age," from 1850 to 1925. Far from being founded on a narrow platform of mere secessionism, this phase of nationalism commanded the allegiance of a wide range of black intellectuals, from Alexander Crummel to W. E. B. Du Bois, and achieved its widest popularity in the black community under the imaginative and controversial leadership of Marcus Garvey. It is thus puzzling that Peller finds nationalism's most compelling moment to be the 1960s—particularly the Black Power movement and the Nation-of-Islam-era pronouncements of Malcolm X. We have good reason to question whether that brand of nationalism can serve as a basis of a viable contemporary racial and cultural politics. Some form of black nationalism will always be present in racial debate, by virtue of its dialectical relationship to integrationism and its parasitic relationship to liberal society at large. But the rampant sexism of 1960s-era (and for that matter, contemporary) nationalism, its ethnic exclusivism, and its racial separatism prevent its adherents from forging necessary and healthy coalitions with other progressive groups. And this in turn has meant that it has been severely handicapped in its efforts to win material and political gains. A nationalism symbolically tied to the 1960s-era legacy is thus an unlikely candidate to achieve the goals that Peller has thoughtfully envisioned for it.

Contemporary black nationalism, or neonationalism, is primarily a cultural affair: witness rap music, Spike Lee's films, and the symbolic adoption of Egypt as a trope of racial origins. Although these cultural achievements are often significant and provocative, they do not by themselves promise a racial or cultural politics that can deliver the political vision, economic rehabilitation, moral renewal, and social reconstruction that the black community so desperately needs. Nor does it effectively address those who are the most desperate: the black poor, mostly women and children, who suffer silent death by suffocation in the decay of our inner cities. The kind of black nationalism that Peller defends cannot claim even the limited successes that integrationism can in addressing the demoralizing and destructive social forces that blight America's racial landscape. Only forms of racial consciousness such as the race-specific universalism of the mature Malcolm X can begin to supply the materials for the urgent task at hand. They can analyze the specific conditions of black oppression, while linking this analysis to other important categories of social identity and solidarity such as gender and class. Only with such linkages can we hope to immediately ameliorate and ultimately eradicate the structural impediments to real black liberation.

9

The Liberal Theory of Race

The abysmal state of race relations in American culture is a continuing source of bewilderment and frustration. The reappearance of overt racist activity, especially on college and secondary school campuses, forces us to reevaluate our understanding of race as we approach the last decade of the twentieth century. In particular, the liberal theory of race, which has dominated the American understanding of race relations, has exhibited a crisis of explanation, manifested in its exponents' inability to elucidate persistent forms of Afro-American oppression.

Robert Anson's book *Best Intentions: The Education and Killing of Edmund Perry* (New York: Random House, 1988), which recently appeared in paperback, reflects the crisis in liberal race theory. Anson's perspective is rooted in a theory of race that prevents him from understanding the complex ways in which racism continues to exert profound influence over the lives of millions of black people. In particular, his explanation of the social and personal forces that besieged Edmund Perry's life, and caused his death, is severely limited by Anson's approach. By examining issues raised in Anson's treatment of Perry's life and death, I want to comment upon the limits of the liberal theory of race and show how Anson's use of it distorts crucial issues that need to be addressed.

In 1981, Edmund Perry, a black teenager "of exceptional promise," left Harlem for Exeter, New Hampshire, in order to attend one of the nation's most prestigious prep schools. On June 2, 1985, he graduated from Phillips Exeter Academy with honors, having been awarded a full scholarship to Stanford University. Ten days later, a short distance from Harlem on New York City's Upper West Side, Perry was killed by Lee Van Houten, a young white plain-clothes police officer. Van Houten reported that Perry and an accomplice had beaten him viciously during a robbery attempt on the night of June 12.

Van Houten stated that after yelling that he was a police officer, he managed, with blurred vision and failing consciousness, to pull his gun from its ankle holster and fire three shots. One attacker, who held him from behind, fled; Perry, who assaulted him frontally, lay on his back on the sidewalk, stilled by a wound to his stomach. At 12:55 A.M., after being taken to nearby St. Luke's Hospital, Edmund Perry was pronounced dead. (Perry's brother Jonah, then a nineteen-year-old engineering student at Cornell University, was said to have been the accomplice that night. Jonah Perry was later formally charged and cleared by a grand jury.)

Robert Anson is a freelance magazine writer and author. At the time of Perry's killing his son was also a student at Exeter and, in fact, had sat behind Perry every day during school assembly. This connection accounts, in part, for Anson's interest in the Perry story, even after widespread public shock over the shooting subsided. An even more powerful motivation, however, was the apparent contradiction Edmund Perry represented. On the one hand, Perry had "all the things anyone was supposed to need to climb out of poverty and make it in America." On the other hand, if Perry had actually died trying to mug Van Houten, then something had gone "dreadfully haywire," despite the "best intentions" of Harlem and Exeter. Anson's book is his search for an understanding of Perry's life, education, and killing, and thereby of racism in U.S. society.

Anson begins by looking for a conclusive account of what happened on the night of June 12. His investigation is fatally compromised by the fact that Lee Van Houten was the only eyewitness to the event. What Anson does is piece together circumstantial evidence that he believes supports Van Houten's story. (The official police inquiry ruled the killing of Edmund Perry "justifiable homicide" and within departmental guidelines.)

Several factors—Perry's personal reputation, the number of

shootings of black men by New York City police, and especially the lack of concrete proof against Edmund and Jonah Perry and Van Houten's inability to identify Jonah as one of the two assailants—lead me to conclude we will never be certain about the events of June 12. We should, however, still look seriously at other issues Anson raises (and doesn't raise) in his search for an explanation of Perry's life: the position of racial minorities in predominantly white institutions, the consequences of juggling two cultures, the ongoing racism of United States culture, and the inability of most existing race theory to illuminate racism's malignant persistence.

Since Anson's investigation leads him to rule out foul play or police attempts at cover-up, he follows the lead of one of the principal police investigators—a garrulous detective who tells him the streets had eaten Perry alive. Thus, Anson goes to Harlem.

Through a set of interviews that are the greatest strength of the book, Anson tries to piece together a picture of Edmund Perry's life and the environment that produced and shaped him. We hear the proud voices of women who had driven dope dealers from the streets by their sheer physical presence; the admiring voices of friends who were inspired by Perry's discipline and dedication to his ambitious goals; the knowing voices of former cosurvivors of the vicious circle of drugs, poverty, and violence, one of whom contended that "Edmund died a natural death up here"; the perceptive voice of a pastor who appreciated Perry's religious values and his ability to maneuver between two cultures; the empathetic voices of other blacks who had struggled with the difficulty and guilt of their departure from desolate and beleaguered circumstances; the pained voices of former teachers and mentors who identified and nurtured Perry's powerful intelligence and talent.

Above all, we hear the strikingly ambitious and sacrificial voice of Perry's mother. Veronica Perry emerges as a powerful woman who fought tooth and nail the despair and cynicism that too often conform Harlem life to its ugly mold—a woman who sent both her sons to prestigious prep schools, successfully ran for the school board, and worked ceaselessly to raise the quality of life in her neighborhood.

The picture of Edmund Perry that formed was one of an extremely bright, hard worker who possessed a mature vision of life's purpose and an infectious compassion for his people—a vision nurtured by strong religious beliefs. But Anson, sensing a canonizing impulse at work in the stories of friends, teachers, and mentors, searches for a fuller picture. He wants Edmund Perry, warts and all, and so he begins interviewing classmates, teachers, and administrators at Exeter.

Many at Exeter spoke of Perry's intelligence, his eagerness to perform well, his quick wit, his enormous love for his mother, his pride in (and rivalry with) his brother, Jonah. Exeter's chaplain said Perry was guarded, rarely revealing much about himself. Some black classmates, especially women, thought that initially Perry could be "pushy" or "cocky"—something they attributed to his neighborhood roots. Some white classmates were disturbed by what they perceived to be an extraordinary "racial sensitivity." David Daniels, then one of only three blacks on the faculty and the adult closest to Perry at Exeter, conceded that point: Perry "was sensitive about race, probably more so than the other black students. I never saw any racial hostility though. Instead, there was frustration, exasperation."

Anson also reports on the year Perry spent in Barcelona, as well as his troubled final year at Exeter. Perry told many people he experienced no racism in Spain, but Anson contends this was deliberate misrepresentation of the facts. He observes that in this case, as in others, "it was becoming apparent that Eddie had a propensity for telling different stories to different people."

During his final year at Exeter, Perry's work fell off, and he became increasingly hostile. Anson details Perry's participation in a club that demanded a sexual initiation, and discusses his (and others') low-level drug dealing. Perry also delivered a "tough and angry" speech to a schoolwide assembly on Martin Luther King's birthday. The speech, written immediately after King's assassination by a former black Exeter student, used Black Power rhetoric to make a bristling declaration of black independence.

Overall, the picture of Perry that emerged from Exeter was one of a deeply troubled young man whose racial identity caused him and, by extension, those around him a great deal of pain. Now Anson is sure: "Edmund Perry had indeed been killed while trying to assault an officer of the law. Why he had done so was less apparent to me."

Unfortunately, the assumptions that Anson brings to his search for an adequate explanation of Perry's death guarantee that he will not find one. The backdrop for most of his reflections on Perry is a scissors-and-paste version of the liberal theory of race—a theory that even in its more sophisticated manifestations has never come to terms with the reality of structural racism.

The liberal understanding of race in the United States is modeled on the white European immigrant experience.[1] In making this experience paradigmatic, liberal theorists have lumped race together with other variables—religion, language, and nationality, for example—and taken them all to constitute a larger ethnic identity that is more crucial than race in explaining the condition of black people. The focus on ethnicity means that liberal theories of race are primarily concerned either with ethnic assimilation or with the maintenance of ethnic identity through cultural pluralism.

Thus lawyer Madison Grant advanced his angloconformity theory of ethnicity in the 1920s, contending that there must be total assimilation and conformity to Anglo-American life in order for white Americans to retain their racial purity. Historian Frederick J. Turner and Jewish immigrant Israel Zangwill composed the melting-pot theory, which asserted that America is best seen as a pot in which all ethnic groups are melting and merging together. Horace Kallen proposed the notion of cultural pluralism, saying that each culture maintains its own character while coexisting with other groups. And Moynihan and Glazer promoted the emerging culture theory, maintaining that cultures interact and the resultant combination produces a political and cultural tertium quid, the phenomenon of the hyphenated American (e.g., African-American).

The liberal theory of race has informed the party practices, jurisprudential reasoning, and legislative agendas of its most ardent and aggressive political proponents, the liberal Democrats. Liberal race theory experienced a fragile inception in FDR's New Deal, a tentative strengthening under Truman's Fair Deal, and a substantial solidification in Kennedy's and Johnson's Great Society due to the civil rights movement. In sociopolitical dress, liberal race theory has argued for a greater black share in jobs, for integration of housing and education, and for desegregation of interstate transportation as strategies to assure black inclusion and assimilation in the larger circle of American privilege.

The problem with the theory is that it encounters an insurmountable obstacle: the irreducible reality of race. Because it conceives of race as merely a part of one's broader ethnic identity, liberal race theory is unable to make sense of the particular forms of oppression generated primarily by racial identity. Much of the time, it cannot explain why blacks have failed to "assimilate" because it has not acknowledged the unique structural character of racism or historical content of racial oppression slavery, Jim Crow laws, structural unemployment, gentrification of black living space, deeply ingrained institutional racism. At this point, however, instead of revising their fundamental assumptions, liberal race theorists tend to explain blacks' failure to "assimilate" successfully by looking almost exclusively at problems *within* black culture and by treating these problems as givens.

More specifically, liberal theory opts for an explanation of the debilitating effects of racism that reduces them to their psychological effects on the black personality. It does not weave its psychological analysis into a dynamic understanding of the persistent social, historical, and political aspects of racism. While it is undeniable that racism's effect on the black psyche is deleterious, to perceive that as racism's *primary* damage obscures the persistent structural factors that enforce and *reinforce* perceptions of personal inferiority, rage, and hostility. That kind of reductionism hinders our understanding of personal identity as a construct of several different elements—social, psychological, political, and historical—and makes it likely that we will mislocate the causes of black failure to "assimilate."

This psychological reductionism is nowhere more apparent than in the second half of *Best Intentions*. As Anson interviews Perry's classmates, teachers, and administrators, he draws a psychological portrait of Perry as an angry, hostile, and belligerent person. True, but Anson never really tells us why. He does not connect his psychological portrait to any social structural analysis—either of Exeter or of Harlem as Perry experienced them. When we do get hints of an explanation of Perry's actions—from either his white classmates or Anson—they are usually by way of further appeals to psychological factors. His classmates say Ed had a chip on his shoulder because of race, indeed that he was a racist himself. Anson wonders whether the stories of white racism that Veronica Perry told Ed "shaped" him, because he was "impressionable," possibly causing him to attempt to mug a New York police officer.

To his credit, Anson considers the possibility that Ed's psychic turmoil was occasioned by the clash of cultures between Harlem and Exeter. But aside from a brief review of common understandings of race relations, liberal social policy, and Harlem history of the last few decades, he doesn't even begin to cover the moral, political, socioeconomic, and historical ground that psychology shares in a plausible explanation of Perry's life and behavior. The condition of the black underclass, the way in which gentrification of black living space continues to shrink black life options, an understanding of the psychic, spiritual, and physical attack on black men—all these factors would help chart a comprehensive approach to Perry's life and death.

Such an approach would avoid merely personalistic explanations that totally blame Perry. It would also avoid merely structural explanations that totally absolve Perry of any responsibility for the choices he made. In short, it would provide the richest detail possible about the circumstances of Perry's life so that he is rendered as a human being faced with difficult choices, choices that must be made within a complicated configuration of personal and structural constraints. Anson simply has not done this.

Instead, he gets mired in a great myth of liberal theory—the myth of meritocracy—and fails to comprehend how a person of Perry's talent could have failed. The dominant belief that legitimates the central place of achievement in U.S. culture and explains the distribution of goods and privileges is that all things being relatively equal, one gets what one merits, based upon intelligence, industry, and a host of other American character traits. The single most important social issue that has focused the problems and contradictions of the meritocratic approach is affirmative action.

Throughout *Best Intentions* Anson employs Perry as an example of the "legitimate" complaints white Exeter students had against blacks for receiving "preferential treatment." He says that Perry's race helped him gain admission to Stanford and Yale. Furthermore, Anson reports, several Exeter faculty members admitted this point, referring to the experience of the white valedictorian in Perry's senior year "who possessed an academic and extracurricular record far more distinguished than Eddie's," and who applied to Stanford, "but was not admitted." This example is intriguing because throughout the book Anson reports that Perry was, by most accounts, an extremely intelligent, articulate youngster "sought after by name" by places like Princeton and Yale. But its importance lies elsewhere. It reflects the confusion of effect with cause that underlies Anson's view of Perry. Anson seems to forget that affirmative action was instituted to redress inequality of opportunity; whites who inherit the privileges of economic resources, old boy networks, and the like are not making it on "merit" alone.

The kind of assumptions that inform Anson's thinking are precisely what exacerbated Perry's situation as a black student at a predominantly white institution. On the one hand, many "liberals" want to address past wrongs by admitting qualified minority students to elite educational institutions. On the other hand, these same students are then blamed for extending and perpetuating inequality by being the recipients of "preferential treatment." Unfortunately the terrain on which this battle is fought is the lives of minority students. How can Anson grasp Perry when he, too, is a victim of the same limited understanding?

Anson might have overcome the limits of his approach if he had made a more sustained attempt to acquaint himself with Afro-American culture. But as is clear in several places in *Best Intentions,* he just doesn't understand the general concerns or basic themes of Afro-American life.

Anson asks whether the stories Veronica Perry told her son, stories about the evils of white racism and the need not to "judge all whites harshly," had made Perry "racially proud" or "angry enough, possibly, to have vented that rage on a seemingly innocuous white boy on a darkened city street." What Anson apparently doesn't understand is that in telling her son these stories Veronica Perry was performing the tragically necessary task most black parents face: telling her child about the viciousness of racism while ratifying her Christian belief that hate is not the proper response for victimized blacks. Thus, she was preparing Edmund Perry to negotiate the difficult process of identifying and acknowledging racism while channeling the resulting, and justifiable, anger into creative and redemptive strategies for coping.

Anson remarks that Perry told different stories to different people, pointing to the obvious fact that he was "pretending" in order to augment his image as a ghetto street tough. But there is more. As is obvious throughout the book, Perry more easily (although sometimes only after extensive scrutiny) formed close associations with other blacks and especially sympathetic whites, able to tell and share one story with them and another with the rest of Exeter. Perry most likely learned, as do most black people, that he could not afford to bare his soul often—either because truth telling could not be borne by particular moods of the white conscience or because it could not be tolerated by many aspects of the white worldview. For example, when told by a teacher that he needed counseling, Perry said there wasn't anyone on campus he could talk to, that the only people he could talk to were black, and that "anytime he tried to open up to whites and be honest, he always wound up hurting someone's feelings." Or again: a white student who shared many classes with Perry told him that "people are just people," and that "some people are white and some people are black, and if you are going to get bummed out about it, it's pretty dumb."

Thus, in order to avoid a discourse of perpetual blame (whose payoff is usually only increased frustration) and the pain of having to explain oneself, to argue for the logic or legitimacy of one's being, Perry adopted a familiar coping strategy: he knew when, and when not, to open and reveal himself. While, as a maturing youth, Perry undoubtedly "pretended" and lied, it is important not to confuse this with strategies adopted to deal with an environment that is hostile and insensitive to one's identity. Ironically, Anson's psychological perspective does not comprehend this crucial point.

More poignantly, throughout the book Anson quotes and refers to Veronica Perry's strong religious beliefs, which Anson thinks are "extremely intense." He sees Veronica Perry's swing from profound belief in the wisdom of God in taking her son to a bitter denouncement of the police system that killed him as a possible indication of her emotional instability. (She had had a nervous breakdown.) In fact, her "mood swing" may be understood as ad hoc theodicy, an attempt to come to grips theologically as best she could with the evil that killed her child. It is an attempt to vindicate—through faith—belief in a good and loving God who may appear absent or silent in the face of human suffering, without at the same time excusing the human beings who inflict that suffering. It is a theme that runs through the Afro-American Christian engagement with the world, and it is a central problem in Christian theology.

Finally, a most telling moment comes when, in speaking of what led to Perry's death, Anson concludes, "The only villain I found was something amorphous, not a person or thing, just a difference called race." He then checks his conclusion with "the only black friend I really had." It happens that Anson's phantom friend also knew Edmund Perry. The disturbing aspect of this is that Anson checks the viability of his interpretive vision against the understanding, insight, and knowledge of *one* black man, who, Anson says, offered to "guide me as my reporting went along, not by providing specific leads, but by confirming whether or not what I came up with was correct." We are thus left with the definite impression that Anson does not know very much about the *diversity* of Afro-American thought and culture. In what constitutes an irony of liberalism, he depends upon his only black friend, thereby tokenizing that thought and culture and segregating himself from a powerful tradition that might have deepened his reflections on Perry's life and death.

The upshot of Anson's approach is that even though he unearths the conflicts and consequences of being socially and culturally amphibious, of negotiating the psychological demands of two different worlds, his findings just pass him by. He cannot fashion an understanding of Edmund Perry's life and death. All we hear is the restatement of a "difference called race" without any attempt to explain what difference that difference makes.

Two other approaches to race might have helped Anson understand what made Edmund Perry's life hell. The first is the racial formation theory advanced by Michael Omi and Howard Winant in their book *Racial Formation in the United States*. In going beyond liberal race theory, Omi and Winant want to avoid the economic determinist and class reductionist elements in most progressive and leftist race theory, and conceive race as an irreducible category, like gender and class, for social theorizing about oppression. Racial formation theory, then, seeks to capture the process by which racial categories are formed, transformed, destroyed, and reformed. Furthermore, it treats race as a central axis of social relations that resists being subsumed under a larger category like ethnicity. It takes seriously the psychological, social, political, cultural, and historical as crucial explanatory strands in a full-blown theory of race.

The second theory is Cornel West's analysis of race, first articulated in *Prophesy Deliverance!* and now developed in an essay in his new book, *Prophetic Fragments.*[2] West, like Winant and Omi, seeks to avoid reductionist accounts of racism. West's theory permits him to trace the emergence and development (or genealogy) of the idea of white racism and supremacy in modern Western discourse. Such an approach promotes the unearthing of the material, economic, political, cultural, psychological, sexual, and spiritual forces that express and respond to the social practices of racism within the cultural traditions of Western civilization. West's theory has three stages: (1) a radical historical investigation of the emergence, development, and persistence of white supremacy; (2) an analysis of the mechanisms that develop and maintain the logic of white supremacy in the everyday lives of people of color; and (3) an examination of how class exploitation, state repression, and bureaucratic domination operate in the lives of people of color. Both theories, then, offer an analysis of racism that takes seriously the psychological, social, political, cultural, and historical as crucial explanatory strands. They therefore offer a much more comprehensive picture, in alliance with the broader and deeper perspective of Afro-American culture, of the complex, stubborn reality Edmund Perry faced.

In a revealing passage early in the book, Anson tells of the time Martin Luther King came to Chicago to march for open housing. It was the summer of 1966, and Anson, fresh out of Notre Dame, was a correspondent for *Time.* He marched with King and was present when King was hit on the head with a rock. He was one of the people who "pulled him up and shielded him." The supreme irony may be that twenty years later, while intending to shield King's legacy, Anson has left it more vulnerable and exposed.

Notes

1. My argument here is based on the important work of Michael Omi and Howard Winant in *Racial Formation in the United States* (New York: Routledge and Kegan Paul, 1986).

2. Cornel West, "A Genealogy of Modern Racism," in *Prophesy Deliverance! An Afro-American Revolutionary Christianity* (Philadelphia: Westminster Press, 1982), pp. 47–68, and *Prophetic Fragments* (Grand Rapids, Mich,: Eerdmans, 1988).

Improvisation

The Two Racisms

The racially motivated murder of Yusef Hawkins, a sixteen-year-old New Yorker, symbolizes the continuing and bitter crisis in American race relations. More poignant, his death is a dangerous point along the tortuous trajectory of New York's racial problem.

Young Hawkins was murdered on August 23, 1989, in Bensonhurst, Brooklyn, a predominantly Italian blue-collar neighborhood. He and three friends went there to meet the owner of an automobile that one of them hoped to purchase. En route they walked past the apartment of eighteen-year-old Gina Feliciano, who shortly before had severed a relationship with eighteen-year-old Keith Mondello and was now reputedly dating blacks and Latinos. Mondello was allegedly seeking revenge on Feliciano's date for her birthday party.

At least ten and perhaps as many as thirty youths, including Mondello, gathered in front of Feliciano's apartment, apparently unaware that she had canceled her party because of threats of trouble. As Hawkins and his friends approached, four shots were fired; Hawkins, hit twice in the chest, died shortly afterward. To lend absurdity to the tragedy, Hawkins was not Feliciano's new suitor.

In a year already marked by new rioting in Miami over a black man murdered by police and by steadily increasing racial violence on college campuses, Hawkins's senseless death is a forceful reminder of America's unresolved racist history, and the circumstances of the murder are rife with the iconography of New York's racial antipathy: baseball bats wielded by several of the white youths, the mostly black marches of protest in the aftermath, and the controversial police tactics in one of them. Those who deemed Spike Lee's portrayal of the deep divide between Italians and African-Americans in his film *Do the Right Thing* to be overdrawn, art intimidating life as it were, have now been tragically rebutted.

The ready temptation is to view the troubling escalation of racial violence in tightly turfed, blue-collar communities like Bensonhurst as isolated from other varieties of racism. Admittedly several factors intensify racism's violent expression in white working-class communities. For one, there is the machismo-laden bonding process fostered through loosely associated groups of young men. These gangs commit random acts of racial violence in retaliation against a perceived invasion of their turf by blacks or other minorities. Also, a generation removed from the immediate social, historical, and political background of the civil rights movement, these white youths find white supremacist groups like the Klan, the boot boys, and the skinheads appealing. Their racist message, coupled with the older generation's resentment of the limited racial progress that *has* been made, renders the white youths devoid of a sense of why strategies like affirmative action were developed. Furthermore, the dislocation of many blue-collar whites within the economy, with its shift from manufacturing to service employment, means that there is intense intraclass as well as racial conflict, especially in competition for low-skilled, high-wage jobs.

However, while racism is perhaps most violently expressed in blue-collar communities, both its logic and life are sustained across class lines. Racism is embedded and expressed in the classroom by racist teachers and professors, in the white-collar workplace by career ceilings on black managers, in the judicial system in recent Supreme Court attacks on the spirit of affirmative action, in housing by the ongoing real estate practice of "steering," in local government (New York City mayor Edward Koch's racial insensitivity stands out), and for most of this decade by national policies under Reaganism. What occurred in Bensonhurst, and in Howard Beach before it, is the conspicuous harvest of the seeds of bigotry sown in a thousand insidiously subtle gestures of racial antagonism, insensitivity, and resentment. Our task, in formulating strategies of resistance, is to understand the relationship between the two racisms. In so doing, we help reveal how racism's violent, working-class expression is linked to, and nourished by, its less visible but just as vicious middle- and upper-class counterparts. Otherwise, Yusuf Hawkins's tragic death will have been in vain.

10

Racism and Race Theory in the Nineties

Contemporary African-Americans are confronting the myriad and conflicted meanings of race, as well as a spiral of new cultural possibilities only partially revealed in the tortuous trajectory of American race relations since the civil rights revolution. Although Americans often give rhetorical assent to that era's lessons of justice, freedom, and equality that derived their force from the renegotiation of race relations, we are barely able to generate the vision or national will to institutionalize our ideals in transformed social structures, redistributed economic resources, and broad political struggle. Even a cursory survey of the state of soul of blacks on several fronts reveals the ominous amalgam of failure and gain that measure our progress from the reign of racial anarchy barely thirty years ago.

For most ebony citizens of our racially fractured polis, the national democratic experiment has produced decidedly mixed results. Although the number of black elected officials has climbed dramatically during the last twenty years, and although Jesse Jackson's two historic presidential quests have greatly expanded the horizon of possibility for black electoral politics, the real political payoffs of democracy have yet to be realized by a significant segment of black Americans. The irony of democracy denied is not lost, especially as students in China's Tiananmen Square, Germans dancing atop the Berlin Wall, and others in Budapest, Warsaw, and Prague have shaken off their nightmarish apprenticeship to tyranny and oppression in the name of American democracy.

Although the black middle class has boomed, representing a more sophisticated and complex population than the portrait of paranoia and insecurity penned by social scientist E. Franklin Frazier, its fragile ligaments are hardly able to pull the vast majority of blacks into its precincts of privilege. One-third of black Americans continue to live in poverty, and the ghetto poor continue to be victims of modern "progress," faring only slightly better with the ostensibly objective categories of social science and cultural criticism than with the vicious economic conditions that make their lives hell.

Strangely, the sphere of consumption unites a broad spectrum of our society in an ironic politics of diversity. The intersection of broad segments of American culture is at the point of consumption of goods, whose distribution is regulated by both legitimate and illegitimate markets and political economies. The relentless individualism and consumerism of the eighties played to the unlimited greed of a generation inebriated on material excess and pleasure. This ethic of consumption was reflected in the movement of the yuppies into the inner city and in the ecobabble that spewed from the frothing mouths of business elites in the clutches of a ruthless narcissism that drove them to pursue ever more wealth. It was also reflected in the expansion of the underground political economy of crack, deriving its force from the concomitant rising of an urban juvenocracy, which endangered not only whites, but inner-city blacks as well.

And the ugly renaissance of racism has only complicated the search for enabling responses to the political, social, and economic crises that plague Afro-America. How can we best understand racism in the nineties, in the midst of the complex entanglements of racism with classism and sexism? In order to grasp hold of the slippery challenge that contemporary racism presents, we must account for the differences between racism in the nineties and racism in the sixties, and then present a progressive race theory that addresses racism's cruel persistence.

Racism, it seems, refuses to die. The last few years have presented a growing list of racial debacles—from Howard Beach to the murder of Yusef Hawkins—that frame the reassertion of race as a subject of acrimonious debate and the source of painful feelings. The problem, of course, is that effectively confronting racism no longer consists of identifying racism's presence and then developing strategies for its elimination, as happened in the fifties and sixties. Present talk about race is dominated by debates about the very nature of racism's existence and about what evidence sufficiently proves its persistence in our day.

It will be easily conceded that before and during the sixties racism was much different from today's curious varieties. Racism before and during the sixties was marked by a nexus of socio-economic relations, ideological infrastructures, and political practices that created and reinforced clear lines of demarcation between whites and blacks. The long legacy of slavery was not yet resolved into even the patina of fluid social relations that resulted under the aegis of the civil rights movement. Instead the hegemony of race created a social, political, economic, and cultural atmosphere where the static division of every aspect of life was predicated upon color. Before the late sixties and early seventies, therefore, racism was distinguished by at least three characteristics: ideology, social practices, and clear evidences of racism.

The ideological infrastructure that accommodated the social toleration and political expression of racism derived from strong, long-standing beliefs about the inherent inferiority of black human beings. A complex network of beliefs about black character and personality were expressed under the disciplining eye of white racism. Whole categories of black personality were socially constructed and then depicted in novels, tracts, theological literature, and scientific writings that encapsulated prevailing notions of black being. Black folk were depicted as subhuman animals bereft of the mental skills associated with abstract reasoning. This led to images of the black as buck, mammy, coon, shuffling Negro, shiftless shine, darky, and spook. These images would survive for centuries, and even after legal emancipation they would insinuate themselves into the art, literature, cinema, and television of the modern era. Although there were variations on the theme, this basic ideological infrastructure remained in place at least until the early part of the twentieth century.

Even after the substantial intellectual accomplishments of figures like Frederick Douglass, W. E. B. Du Bois, Ida Wells Barnett, Phillis Wheatley, primal beliefs about inherent black inferiority persisted. Also, ancient black psychological and social hurts generated by racial violence continued to manifest themselves with calamitous consistency. The chronic lack of black self-regard had its ugly genesis in the unruly expression of racial debasement, and there is a virtually direct line that extends from racist beliefs about blacks to various social and psychological manifestations of black self-hate, especially black-on-black homicide.

By the early fifties and sixties, despite various movements for liberation originating in the African-American community, such as the Garvey UNIA, the educational achievements inspired by the talented tenth theory of Du Bois, the practical agrarianism of Booker T. Washington, and labor participation advocacy under A. Philip Randolph, this ideological infrastructure remained firm. Even though Du Bois, Garvey, Washington, Randolph, and others had been chipping away at the massive structure of racism, promoting black self-determination, black intellectual progress, industrial prowess, and labor unification, it was not until the civil rights movement that the powerful confluence of these various elements erupted in protest, resistance, and struggle to challenge the assumptions embedded in the ideological framework that had superintended American race relations. This ideological framework was apparent in significant ways to both blacks and whites—both understood what was at stake, the lines of racial division, and the terms of the debate—even as each responded in wildly different ways to its existence and expression.

Part of the reason blacks were able to successfully confront American racism is because it was characterized by a Cartesian clarity, a clear and distinct set of social, political, and economic ideas and practices that explicitly expressed and reinforced the prevailing ideological framework. Racial violence of every imaginable description was visited upon black Americans, particularly in the South, where 70 percent of black folk lived prior to the mass migration that began in the early years of this century. There was a distinct ordering and colonization of black social space and mobility in black water fountains, black sections of town, and black spheres of social and institutional organization, such as stores and churches. The legitimation of violence toward blacks, a common feature of black life linking past and present, found strong historical precedence in slavery's black codes. During the first half of this century, blacks were mercilessly hung, brutally beaten, and viciously murdered. With virtually no legal redress, blacks were continually subject to the unabated tyranny of white violence, which usually found protection by the law.

The political order was dominated by white elected officials whose interest in the extension of white rule allowed an infinite variety of practices that further insured the prevalence of injustice. With the complete disenfranchisement of most black people, the ability to effect their own destinies was further compromised. Economically, of course, black participation in the labor force had been severely limited to low-skilled, low-wage jobs that reinforced the economic inferiority of African-Americans. Sharecropping arrangements subverted economic independence and reinforced black dependence on white farm owners who duplicated as closely as possible the conditions of southern plantation slavery.

The whole regimen of racist social, political, and economic practices reflected the ideological base of its expression. More pointedly, these practices provided concrete evidence of the existence of the ideologies of racism. The evidence consisted of burned crosses, lynched bodies, buried corpses, and bullet-riddled men and women. There was overwhelming physical, psychic, and social testimony to the existence of racism that proved its reality. In the sixties, the civil rights movement understood what it was up against precisely because its enemy was visible and its goals well defined.

After the civil rights movement, and the legal establishment of equal opportunity for blacks, especially through affirmative action in education and employment, America endured a backlash against former racial goodwill and the evaporation of wide racial tolerance. The seventies and eighties witnessed the expression of racial hostility in subtle ways, indicating that racial transformation was not as substantial as many had formerly believed. In short, the character of American race relations permits the appearance of a level of success that can be easily exaggerated and exploited.

Contemporary race relations are mired in the bog of a torturous irony: the passion and vision of liberals—whose intent it was to vanquish the obvious and vile manifestations of racial animosity—have now been co-opted by conservative intellectuals who conceal the abated but still malicious expressions of racism. The constellation of metaphors once marshaled by liberals to resist racism's varied assault—from racism as disease, racism as loss of vision, racism as conscience spoiled and turned against its best and highest ends—has suffered a blasphemous reversal of fortune. Indeed, these metaphors symbolize a larger complex of forsaken ideas whose rejection points to the changed nature of American race relations: the front line of progressive resistance to racism has temporarily lost the battle of language, conceding the prerogative to narrate the most crucial features of American race relations to the political and cultural right.

American society has endured the unnatural disaster of a continental shift along the fault lines of the definition, description, and explanation of the state of race in our culture. And the belief that a collective American conscience would be the seconding vote to poignant (if sometimes sloppy) justifications of resistive action has been relieved of its moral innocence, while the fate of racial progress is thrust into the lion's den of so-called "rational" and "racially neutral" arguments.

More glumly, our era of racial desperation is marked by the varied evidences of race hatred's predictable revival. A decade ago, Eric Foner warned that in our day, as in the nineteenth century, a period of radical change followed by a desire for stability would give way to an explicit attack on the very achievements believed to be irreversibly established by federal law and the Constitution. More subtly, on elite college campuses the implications of difference, diversity, and pluralism are heatedly debated, but their hard lessons are mostly avoided or dissolved in the discourse of merit, objectivity, or standards.

In the face of such attacks, all usual roads of response falter in resolving the conundrum of persistent racism. Classic liberalism and neoliberalism continue to publish a laundry list of ancient racial indignities made fresh by today's news. But these liberalisms are burdened by a loyalty to a form of social analysis that obscures recognition of structural impediments to racial progress, a failure that only promises certain defeat of its goal of full integration of blacks into American society. Neonationalism continues to spin a contradictory ideological web, whose sometimes abrasive threads of racial pride, economic enhancement, and cultural achievement produce, at best, brilliant but diminished cultural expression and, at worst, self-defeating catharsis and impotent political windbagging.

And contemporary neoconservativism is drawn like a vulture to the linguistic carcasses of the liberal race rhetoric it helped defeat, infusing them with a foul new life, made all the more confusing because, while their present exterior resembles their former incarnation, the spirit is all wrong. Hence we have the spectacle of phrases like "racial fairness" and "equal playing ground," lifted straight from the transcript of liberal resistance to racism, newly and perversely employed to buttress ideals like justice and equality, which are forced to take a shortcut to their worst possible meaning.

The lesson that progressives should learn from all this is that racial meanings must be perennially contested, constantly redefined in an interpretive warfare that has its roots in a liberating vision of society, politics, economics, and culture. Progressive race theory must historicize the story of American racial history, emphasizing both its progresses and failures. We have witnessed the marginalization of an understanding of racial history that provides a sense of the heights scaled, of obstacles overcome, and of remaining roadblocks to the achievement of real racial liberation. The prevailing myth of racial history absorbs all racial complexities and contradictions into a narrative of uncomplicated linear progress, smoothing all racial mountains into a vast hinterland of unexplored possibility. This yarn of racial history, most often spun under the auspices of contemporary neoconservativism, deviously obscures the complicity of neoconservatives in opposing the racial progress that was achieved under the extraordinarily difficult circumstances that their social and political opposition helped create. In such a truncated narrative, racial meanings are often severed from their historical context, alienated from the nexus of social relations and catastrophes that called them into existence.

A progressive race theory must relentlessly historicize the development and genealogy of American race relations, meeting the prevailing conservative racial ideology blow for blow in contesting its whitewashed history of race. For instance, affirmative action, a shibboleth of conservative disdain and a key word in liberal race theory, is often said to begin with the Johnson administration in the 1960s, to devolve into inequitable preferential treatment for minorities, and to become ideologically debased as a thin veil for quotas, particularly in education and employment. A progressive race theory must admit that affirmative action has catalyzed the important but narrow amelioration of middle-class, professional, and well-educated blacks and women. But it must also insist that affirmative action was instituted to eradicate actual past harm and did not begin with Lyndon Johnson, but with Franklin Roosevelt in 1941. It took the construction of presidential executive orders from Roosevelt, Eisenhower, Truman, and Kennedy to pave the way for Johnson's Executive Order Number 11246, which realized in greater scope the ideals of fairness and equality only tentatively prefigured in previous executive actions.

Progressive racial theory must also highlight the strengths of liberalism, neonationalism, and conservativism, even as it avoids their weaknesses in reconceiving race relations. It agrees with liberals that the goal of full and meaningful participation in America has been frustrated, but it must move beyond immigrant analogies, cultural pathology, and psychological reductionism in seeking helpful explanations of black failure to integrate. Progressive race theory must highlight the specific conditions under which minorities have been oppressed, and then link an analysis of those conditions to enabling forms of social theory that attend to structural, root causes that reproduce oppression over space and time.

Progressive race theory squares with the insights of neoconservatives who claim that moral responsibility is a crucial ingredient to self-respect and an indispensable motivation for rising from the pits of poverty. But it must understand moral responsibility against the background of social options, cultural resources, and economic conditions that form the immediate environment within which people must live and make choices. In short, a theory of responsible moral agency must account for the conditions of possibility for such agency to be meaningfully exercised. Progressive race theory must also draw attention to the wide prevalence of destructive and narrow cultural messages about black identity and to the social forces that mystify the persistent obstacles to black racial mobility even when high degrees of individual motivation, talent, and skill are in place.

Progressive race theory must understand that neonationalism's appeal is that its exponents exploit the genius of racial particularity, grounding their vision of the world in a racial worldview that stresses pride in culture. But progressive race theory must point to the ideological insularity of neonationalists that obscures the role of factors such as gender and class in determining black people's life situation. Such a progressive understanding of race can provide powerful and liberating insights that yield greater understanding about neonationalism's most desperate constituency, the postindustrial urban black poor.

In its finest theoretical moments, progressive race theory explores the specific social, political, economic, ideological, and cultural factors that create and extend oppression in our contemporary historical moment. Progressive race theory also emphasizes transracial coalitions that pay attention to how race, class, gender, age, sex, and geography all play a crucial role in shaping the lives of people in our society. Only with such a progressive understanding of race can we hope to advance beyond the interminable ideological impasse that defines the state of contemporary race relations.

Improvisation

Affirmative Action and the Courts

On June 12, 1989, a five-four majority of the Supreme Court ruled that court-approved affirmative action plans, known as consent decrees, from now on may be challenged by white workers. A week earlier, the Court had overturned by the same margin a long-standing Burger Court interpretation of the law that had placed the burden on justifying discriminatory business practices on employers. And last January a six-three majority established debilitating restrictive criteria for minority set-aside programs. All three rulings directly threaten the foundation of equal employment opportunities for women and racial minorities. When it comes to civil rights, it is now clear that Reagan's Court has arrived.

The most recent case, *Martin v. Wilks*, involved white firefighters from Birmingham, Alabama, who claimed they were victims of reverse discrimination because of a 1981 court-approved plan to hire and promote blacks in equal numbers to whites until the number of black firefighters approached the proportion of blacks in the labor force. The ruling will inevitably cause future consent decrees to be constructed and implemented in a more cautious and tentative way. Because more than three hundred new consent decrees are adopted each year by government and private employers, the ruling may precipitate a flurry of aggressive litigation across the country aimed at dismantling the legal employment arrangements that address past discriminatory hiring and promotion practices.

In the wake of this decision, employers (especially in the private sector) may now decide to abandon affirmative action altogether. Chief Justice William Rehnquist's opinion for the majority clearly grants room for employers to maneuver away from implementing all but the most token of affirmative action policies, putatively for fear of violating the rights of those not covered by such plans. Moreover, even though the decision does not directly affect voluntarily adopted affirmative action plans, many such plans are now subject to litigation, and the attack on voluntary programs cannot be far behind.

By allowing white employers to challenge consent decrees years after they have been accepted in court, the decision threatens not only future affirmative action employment policies but past ones as well. Ironically, on the same day, the Court declared in a separate but related ruling that three women who worked for AT&T had waited too long to file suit challenging seniority rules that they claimed discriminated against them.

In one of the cruelest twists suffered by the civil rights movement, white men have successfully appropriate the language of victimization and articulated their own suffering compellingly enough to cancel out the claims of those whose suffering they in large part helped create. What is really on trial in these most recent Supreme Court decisions on employment discrimination, as perhaps it has been all along, is the very idea of affirmative action. The struggle over how best to resolve historic injury inflicted upon racial minorities as a group and on women as a group is forbiddingly complex and perennially frustrating. For the notion and, more acutely, the act of addressing past discrimination through affirmative action entails the denial of certain privileges to others, usually white men, who, although not always individually, at least as a group have benefited from past socioeconomic, educational, and employment arrangements that directly and unrelentingly discriminated against women and minorities. Although affirmative action, with its numerical timetables, quotas, and goals, is an imperfect means of achieving justice for the wronged, it is the best means currently available, and certainly no more unjust than the racism and sexism that precipitated its development and necessitates its continued existence.

Congress must now move to reassert its original intent in calling on employers to develop equal employment opportunities and affirmative action plans. But in light of the high court's demonstrated insensitivity to the concerns of minorities and women, we are forced to reassess a strategy that has proved vulnerable to legal rebuff. In particular, those minorities and women who have benefited from past affirmative action policies must take it upon themselves to reignite the fight against racism and sexism at a time when social lethargy threatens from within almost as ominously as Supreme Court decisions challenge from without.

11

Leonard Jeffries and the Struggle for the Black Mind

The whirlwind of controversy that surrounds the figure of Dr. Leonard Jeffries obscures the complex problems that must figure in an understanding of the nerve he has struck deep in the decadent cavity of race in America. The outspoken chairman of the black studies department of the City College of New York is the lightning rod for a gaggle of issues that embody a contemporary cultural crisis: theories of biological or environmental determinism, the rise of Afrocentric education, and claims about the African origin of civilization.

A speech Jeffries made in July 1991, in which he said Jews and Italians had collaborated in Hollywood to denigrate blacks and that Jews had financed the slave trade, drew outrage from many whites who felt that such alleged bigotry and anti-Semitism warranted disciplinary action from the college. On October 28, 1991, the trustees effectively put Jeffries on probation as department head, although his employment was protected by his tenured status. However, further allegations that Jeffries had also threatened the life of a Harvard student journalist during an interview put Jeffries in danger of being dismissed for "conduct unbecoming a member of the staff." City College had announced that it would investigate the allegations, which Jeffries called "scurrilous" and part of "a media lynching."

Jeffries continues to be a popular figure among black students on campus and certain activists in the community. What seems to draw their interest are his alleged statements about the role of the skin pigment melanin in shaping culture and behavior and his provocative use of the metaphor of sun people (who are warm, cooperative, and community-minded) versus ice people (who are cold, territorial, and aggressive). Few realize that the popular contemporary source of the sun people/ice people typology is a 1978 book, *The Iceman Inheritance: Prehistoric Sources of Western Man's Racism, Sexism and Aggression*, by white Canadian author Michael Bradley.[1]

The melanin theory, however, has its genesis in a broad body of literature published mostly by independent or black presses and in highly technical studies in scientific and medical journals. Black authors like psychiatrist Richard King, in his book titled *African Origin of Biological Psychiatry*,[2] Carol Barnes in his privately published monograph *Melanin,* and lecturers such as Baltimore psychiatrist Patricia Newton have stimulated interest in the role of melanin in biological, mental, and racial development. Newton and King have also been a motivating behind-the-scenes force in organizing a series of "Melanin Conferences," held annually since 1987 in San Francisco, New York, Washington, D.C., Dallas, and Los Angeles. Each conference has drawn more than five hundred participants—lay people and community activists joining with scholars.

But the most prominent figure to introduced a consideration of the possible behavioral and cultural consequences of melanin to broad public discussion has been black psychiatrist Frances Cress-Welsing. Cress-Welsing first articulated in 1970 the Cress Theory of color-confrontation and racism (white racism), which links the development of white supremacist ideology to white fear of genetic annihilation.[3] Her theory maintains that "whiteness is indeed a genetic inadequacy or a relative genetic deficiency state, based upon the genetic inability to produce the skin pigments of melanin (which is responsible for all skin color). The vast majority of the world's people are not so afflicted, which suggests that color is normal for human beings and color absence is abnormal. . . . Color always 'annihilates' (phenotypically and genetically speaking) the non-color, white."[4] Cress-Welsing further states that because of their "color inferiority," whites respond with a psychological vengeance toward people of color, developing "an uncontrollable sense of hostility and aggression," an attitude that has "continued to manifest itself throughout the history of mass confrontations between whites and people of color."[5]

Ironically, Cress-Welsing now says she believes that the recent preoccupation with her melanin theory is a diversion from the more immediate problem facing people of color: white supremacy. "I put the discussion of melanin on the board in order to [describe how pigmentation] was a factor in what white supremacy behavior was all about," she says. "If I had my way, there wouldn't be all the discussion about melanin. I would say discuss white supremacy. White supremacy has guided the discussion to multiculturalism, diversity, to anything [but white supremacy]."

Indeed, white supremacy is a theme that Cress-Welsing single-mindedly pursues in her book *The Isis Papers: The Keys to the Colors,* a text that has sold nearly forty thousand copies, principally through black-owned retail outlets. But despite her currently stated interest in refocusing her message on white supremacy, she continues to develop her melanin theory, for example, by expounding on the neurochemical basis of soul and evil. Moreover, since her theory links white injustice with the inability of whites to produce melanin, her focus on white racism leads ineluctably to a concern with melanin.

Jeffries, too, has been attempting to distance himself from possible racist implications of the melanin theory. When he appeared on "Donahue" last fall, his first time on a national TV show, he said, "We do not have a theory of melanin that says black people are superior. It's a joke. But it's been run and run and run into the ground." Jeffries contends that melanin is subsidiary to "the larger awakening of African peoples in terms of their real history," because there is "an African primacy to human experience."

But he just as often stressed the need for comprehending the crucial function of melanin in cultural and biological evolution. Jeffries noted that *Civilization or Barbarism: An Authentic Anthropology*, the landmark book by the late Senegalese scholar Cheikh Anta Diop, characterizes melanin as "the phenomenon which helps us establish that there's only one human race, and that human race is African. Melanin is that phenomenon that comes about as a result of the sun factor."

Jeffries says Diop links the development of melanin to a more involved theory about the origins of human civilization in Africa's

Nile River valley, where important distinctions in the qualities of persons and cultures would have been developed— hence his use of the reductionist sun people/ice people dichotomy to explain perceived differences in persons from the northern and southern cradles. "The value system of the northern cradle [ice people] . . . that rough survival value system, produces a premium on male physical strength and has produced this warrior value system," Jeffries opined, "whereas [in] the value system of the south [sun people] where you can look at the spiritual relationship within the human and the cosmic family . . . you see the male and female principle in harmony and balance, you see nature in harmony and balance, you see the relationship of the sky and the moon and the sun to human development." This amounts to biological, ecological, and racial determinism, and can hardly be substantiated.

Although Jeffries views himself as an Afrocentrist, Molefi Kete Asante, chairman of Temple University's Department of African American Studies and often described as the "father of the theoretical and philosophical movement of Afrocentricity" (he is the author of *Afrocentricity*, published by Africa World Press), contends that Afrocentricity itself "is not a theory of biological determinism [but] essentially the idea that African people must be seen as subjects of history and of human experience, rather than objects." Asante finds the melanin theory "intriguing" but disavows it as an Afrocentric theory.

Rigid categories based on essential, unvarying characteristics melt in the face of actual experience and human history. "Blacks are just as intellectual [as whites], and whites in some situations are just as feeling [as blacks]," says Cornell University professor Martin Bernal, author of *Black Athena: The Afroasiatic Roots of Classical Civilization.*[6] "My study of human societies and the way in which whites and blacks behave in their societies makes me believe that you can explain these things more satisfactorily in terms of society and social relations than you can in terms of physiology."

Bernal, a white Briton whose recent scholarship explores the Egyptian roots of Greek civilization, admits a personal affinity for Egypt in part because "here is an African culture [that is] analytical and intellectual. You can have African societies of both types, just as you can have European societies of both types." Bernal says his study of Egypt and Greece has taught him that both were such a "mixed culture."

Egypt was one of the great civilizations of the ancient world, but so were China, Mesopotamia in the Middle East, and other cultures in Central America. So in attempting to overcome the bruising absence of constructive discourse about Africa, Jeffries and his cohorts have distorted the variety and legitimacy of other ancient civilizations through the lens of a compensatory racial and cultural hierarchy that assigns African artificial and romantic superiority.

Indeed, it was Jeffries' courageous attempt to reverse the harmful effects of Eurocentrism through educational reform in the New York State school system that first brought him to national attention. Jeffries served as a consultant to the first of two task forces charged by the New York State Commission on Education with correcting deficiencies in the curriculum in regard to people of color. Not surprisingly, Jeffries and many of the task force members concluded that the experiences, histories, and contributions of nonwhite people were gravely underrepresented in New York's educational curriculum. Brutal internecine battles developed, especially between Jeffries and his ideological opponents, historian Arthur Schlesinger, Jr., and educator Diane Ravitch, but many of Jeffries' ideas were adopted in the committee's final report, "A Curriculum of Inclusion."

Schlesinger issued his dissenting opinions in *The Disuniting of America: Reflections on a Multicultural Society.*[7] In it he invoked the timeworn metaphor of national unity forged as ethnic groups melted into the American character, in contrast to what he saw as the vicious ethnic tribalism evinced by people of Jeffries' ilk. Apparently for Schlesinger, anyone who appeals to racial or ethnic identity as the basis of making radical social, political, or moral claims is what may be termed an ethnosaur, a recalcitrant ethnic loyalist who has not acknowledged the legitimacy of a superior and more sweeping national identity. Schlesinger contends that many Afrocentrists "not only divert attention from the real needs but exacerbate the problems."

The call by Schlesinger and others for more "objective" historical scholarship fails to address the persistent historical patterns of racist exclusion of minority perspectives that are manifest in varying degrees from the elementary school to university education. "[Schlesinger] probably really believes that he and his contemporaries have been writing objective history," says Bernal. "He seems to me remarkably lacking in self-consciousness and awareness and still sees white middle-aged men as the only people capable of rendering acceptable historical judgments."

In this context, Afrocentric attempts to articulate credible intellectual conceptions of the nature and shape of black racial experiences and to express profound disenchantment with the silence of majoritarian histories on the suffering and achievements of minority peoples are praiseworthy indeed. But while Jeffries' diatribes against Eurocentrism are sometimes accurate, his embrace of various ideas in support of his version of Afrocentrism seems plain wrongheaded. Jeffries is promoting a rigid and romantic notion of racial identity.

Ironically, Jeffries is arguing for the same sort of unanimity of vision and experience that racism has artificially imposed upon African-American life. Perhaps he would do well to heed the words of fellow Afrocentrist Asante that "the virtue of Afrocentrism is pluralism without hierarchy." Asante emphasizes that "Afrocentricity is not about valorizing your position and degrading other people. Whites must not be seen as above anyone; but by the same token they've got to be seen alongside everyone."

Moreover, Jeffries' romanticization of Egyptian culture as the seat of human civilization incorrectly views history through the idyllic lens of uncritical racial pride and narrow nationalist goals. Such simplistic distortions overlook the conflicts and corruption spawned by Egyptian civilization and repeat the fantastic egocentrism and therapeutic fables of Eurocentric history at its worst. "Eurocentric history as taught in schools and universities has had a very large ego-boosting, if not therapeutic, purpose for whites," acknowledges Bernal. "It's in a way normal for the idea that blacks should have some confidence building in their pedagogy." But he cautions against an uncritical celebration of racial and cultural roots. "I think there should be research history as well, and that will sometimes reveal facts that you don't like."

As mature African-American scholars, teachers, students, and citizens, we must embrace the rich and varied racial past that has contributed to our making. We must also acknowledge the profound degree to which we have alternately enjoyed and endured a terrible but sometimes fruitful symbiosis with European-American culture, how we have helped shape many of its cultural gifts to the world, even against its will, and how those expressions emerged in the crucible and turmoil of our uniquely African-American experience.

Notes

1. Michael Bradley, *The Iceman Inheritance: Prehistoric Sources of Western Man's Racism, Sexism, and Aggression* (New York: Kayode, 1978).

2. Richard King, *African Origin of Biological Psychiatry* (Germantown, Tenn.: Seymour-Smith, 1990).

3. See Frances Cress Welsing, "The Cress Theory of Color-Confrontation and Racism (White Supremacy)," in Welsing, *The Isis Papers: The Keys to the Colors* (Chicago: Third World Press, 1991), pp. 1–16.

4. Ibid., p. 4.

5. Ibid., p. 5.

6. Martin Bernal, *Black Athena: The Afroasiatic Roots of Classical Civilization* (New Brunswick, N.J.: Rutgers University Press, 1987).

7. Arthur Schlesinger, *The Disuniting of America: Reflections on a Multicultural Society* (Knoxville, Tenn.: Whittle Communications, 1991).

Improvisation

Columbus Redux: An African-American Perspective

The European Age of Discovery, which stretched from the fifteenth to the eighteenth century, is said to have begun when the Portuguese captured Ceuta on the North African coast opposite Gibraltar in 1415. For the rest of the fifteenth century Portuguese explorers, supported at first by Prince Henry the Navigator and subsequently by King John II, eventually moved to the western African coast in search of a path to the Indies. In 1488 Bartolomeu Dias doubled the Cape of Good Hope, while a mere decade later, Vasco da Gama made his way to Calicut in India. In 1513, the first Portuguese ship had landed at Canton. Under the leadership of Alfonso d'Alboquerque, the Portuguese had established strongholds in Goa in India in 1510, Malacca on the west coast of the Malay Peninsula in 1511, and Ormuz in the Persian Gulf in 1515.

In the meantime, a navigator serving Spain was busy helping establish a different sort of empire. In 1492 Christopher Columbus charted his way across the Atlantic to the Caribbean, "discovering" most of the major islands in that area and part of the eastern coast of Central America in three voyages from 1493 to 1504. The Portuguese were embittered over Spain's participation in a process of "discovery" they felt to be uniquely their own. But they compromised with the Treaty of Tordesillas in 1494.[1]

Spain and Portugal carved up the world by tracing an imaginary line north and south 370 leagues west of the Cape Verde Islands on the west coast of Africa. Everything west of their meridian line went to Spain, while everything to the east belonged to Portugal. But every part of the Americas and Africa that the Europeans "discovered" contained people with cultures and traditions of their own, which, in the embrace of European civilization, underwent radical transformation and, in some cases, outright destruction.

What, then, does the quincentennial celebration of Columbus's "discovery" of the New World mean to those of us who claim solidarity as and with the victims of European discovery? The ideal of European discovery has been indissolubly wedded to tropes, metaphors, and practices of conquest, pillage, and plunder. The process of European "discovery" was linked to the actual conquest of indigenous peoples in the Americas and Africa. Thus, we must question whether European practices of usurping the rights of indigenous and aboriginal peoples to self-determination and government is a theme to be celebrated.

It is a tough time to be raising such a question. The cultural fallout from so-called political correctness has created a hostile social climate. "Political correctness," or PC, is a concept first developed by the left in defense against the fabled pieties and cultural excesses of minority perspectives on race, class, and gender. But the concerted response to PC by neoconservatives have proved it to be a thinly veiled ideology. Critics of political correctness claim that people of color, feminists, and other radicals have scandalously victimized the academy and workplace by imposing virtually fascist notions of acceptable speech and behavior with regard to minorities. However, social realities tell a different tale. In spite of presumed PC pressure, there has been no real decline in Eurocentric dominance. While it is true that, in response to such hegemony, and in light of their attempts to redraw the maps of cultural, academic, and social dominance, proponents of "minority" perspectives have certainly erred (one thinks of monolithic conceptions of racial or gender identity advanced by some blacks and women), the lion's share of power to determine social, cultural, or academic practice still rests beyond the control of blacks and women. That Columbus's conquest and its lethal effect on entire groups of people is still viewed as worthy of celebration, with little consciousness of irony, is a case in point.

Columbus's discovery of the New World also displays the power of the European to define the aboriginal or native as "Other." This peculiar aberration from the normal process of acknowledging a coerced host and an invading discoverer marks the power of the European to absorb, disperse, and commodify the talents, gifts, bodies, and imaginations of the native peoples of America and Africa for the gain of the European Empire. In the process, indigenous ways of life are lost, native processes of cultural imagination are stymied, and self-determined privacy of community and nationhood are irrevocably undermined and destroyed.

Moreover, the enslavement of people from the Americas and Africa was aided by the European "discovery" of the aboriginal or native as "heathen." The establishment of a European Christian civilization in the newly "discovered" parts of the Americas, the Caribbean islands, and Africa helped foster the barbarous subversion of entire cultural traditions, and also helped consolidate the unity of European cultural and religious dominance of these parts of the world.

As a result, the shaping of the narratives of history that recount "discovery" have all but whitewashed the abominable strategies of conquest and domination employed by Europeans in the Americas and Africa, insisting that they were unavoidable costs of expansion and development. When the Columbus conquest is not placed in a critical social, cultural, and historical context, celebration is dishonest. Native American, African, and African-American intellectuals right now are yet in the midst of a compelling project to recover their histories. They are having to compel

American and European historians to revise and reexamine the magical idealism that has held Clio hostage over the last five hundred years.

When an honest historical reckoning is dutifuly avoided, the genocidal effects of European conquest and mastery of indigenous American and African lives is lost from common view. The real cost of such historical evasion is the severing of indigenous peoples from crucial elements of their history and their religious, cultural, and intellectual traditions. Thus the *initial* process of genocide is *continued* when the historical acknowledgment of its implementation is concealed beneath myths of European progress, expansion, and civilization.

In the five hundredth year of Columbus's "discovery" of America, Americans must *rediscover Columbus.* We must tell the whole story, and thus help redeem the real losses of indigenous and native peoples' stories—a loss that has made our country less than it could have become. In owning up to the European link between "discovery" and European armed conquest, with all of its genocidal effects, we are also able to accentuate the boldness, imagination, and vigor with which native and minority peoples and traditions have flourished under such inhuman circumstances. Such people have not simply been the *victims* of history but also *subjects* of their own making in the midst of cruel denials of culture, tradition, and sometimes even life.

The point is not that we must trash everything European. Nothing exists in cultural, racial, or even national purity. Neither is the point to indiscriminately valorize everything non-European. The point is to *tell the truth,* as clearly and intelligently as we are able. Only then will we be able to counter the forces of genocide, racism, and historical amnesia, the effects of which still linger in our contemporary cultural, religious, and national practices.

Note

1. For this section I am indebted to *The Columbia History of the World,* ed. John A. Garraty and Peter Gay (New York: Harper & Row, 1972), pp. 622–23.

12

Sex, Race, and Class: Two Cases

Sex, race, and class have played a critical role in numerous American cultural revolutions during this century. The civil rights, feminist, and labor movements reflect the power of this provocative trio to spark social transformation, help define personal identity, draw attention to salient categories for social theory, and create coalitions between groups targeted by racial, sexual, and class oppression. But sex, race, and class have also caused considerable conflicts and tensions between groups who compete for limited forms of cultural legitimacy, visibility, and support. Two recent incidents in the public racial memory, the obscenity trial of the rap group 2 Live Crew and the Central Park jogging case, show how sex, race, and class are intricately intertwined and the source of significant anxieties between various feminists, civil libertarians, and black youth culture advocates.

On the surface, the jury trial of 2 Live Crew was straightforward. The rap group, led by rapper Luther Campbell, was charged with violating obscenity laws in an adults-only concert in Hollywood, Florida, on June 10, four days after a federal judge had ruled that the group's album, "As Nasty as They Wanna Be," was similarly obscene. After two weeks of testimony by both sides, 2 Live Crew was found innocent of the charges. In the process of the trial, however, a flurry of commentary and criticism was evoked. The 2 Live Crew controversy is at the center of a vortex of powerful social and cultural issues such as First Amendment rights to free expression, the force and extent of misogynist cultural impulses, and the function of race in judging controversial artistic expressions. How should we think about the issues raised by 2 Live Crew's trial?

There is little doubt that 2 Live Crew's rap artistry hinges on pornographic desires, misogynist impulses, and raucous sexual experimentation:

> To have her walkin' funny we try to abuse it / A big stinking pussy can't do it all / So we try real hard just to bust the walls / . . . Suck my dick, bitch / And make it puke . . . / Lick my ass up and down / Lick it till your tongue turn doo-doo brown / I'll break you down / And dick you long / I'll bust your pussy / Then break your backbone / Cause me so horny

Although most rap lyrics do not explicitly endorse such graphic sexual sentiments, much of rap is rooted in assumptions about women as exclusive objects of male sexual satisfaction that underwrite 2 Live Crew's artistic vision.

More pointedly, 2 Live Crew's sexism expresses cultural sentiments that, although outwardly prohibited, are frequently expressed in the subterranean, pornographic fantasies of men in a patriarchal culture that thrives on strategies of domination in infinitely adaptable guises, including racial, sexual, and class domination. Thus, a double standard of explicit denial and secret permission prevails in regard to sexism. Indeed, that double standard is depended upon to prevent the rupturing of a delicate balance between conscience and guilt where strident offenses are sometimes punished, while the behaviors and attitudes that underwrite sexism's logic, furnish its rationale, and consolidate its manifold practices often remain invisible and unchallenged.

This is not to suggest that one example of sexism is indistinguishable from the next. Some expressions of sexism, patriarchalism, and misogyny are so nefarious that they demand immediate, uncompromising response. My point is that a complex infrastructure of sexist attitudes, behaviors, actions, and ideology is constructed around the issue of gender in everyday American culture, and that infrastructure provides the background for sexism's coarser manifestations. Similar to racism, sexism's cruder expressions (as in 2 Live Crew lyrics) are supported and reinforced by a complex and subtle network of social relations, intellectual justifications, and cultural practices (e.g., glass ceilings placed on the careers of female managers in corporate America).

The 2 Live Crew controversy also surfaces repressed American cultural attitudes toward black male sexuality. Few images have caused more anxiety in the American sexual psyche than the black male embodiment of phallic prowess. A sordid range of stereotypes, jealousies, and fears have been developed around black men wielding their sexuality in ways that are perceived as untoward, unruly, or uncontrolled. Beyond stereotypes and jealousies, a range of sometimes lethal punishments have been practiced against black men, from lynching for "reckless eyeballing" of white women to outright genital castration. Indeed, black male sexual activity has often been historically viewed as inherently vulgar, and particularly dangerous when not directed toward its suitable sexual goal—black women. Thus, the fires of fear of black male sexuality were stoked by imagined black male transgression of proper sexual limits, particularly when the subject was social and sexual intercourse with white women. Fear of black male sexuality is often at root a fear of miscegenation.

The recordings and performances of 2 Live Crew symbolize the black phallus out of control, respecting no sexual territory as sacred, and penetrating the barriers that divide civilized sexual behavior from brutally objectifying and demeaning sex. For many white audiences, they are the frightening embodiment of *Soul on Ice*–era Eldridge Cleaver sexual excesses, with stock rape-as-revenge fantasies in tow. For many black audiences, they are sexual villains whose transgressive sexual behavior represents the weakening of communal bonds and the decline of moral imagination.

This latter fact makes it difficult to write off 2 Live Crew's lyrics as mere examples of black oral practices that employ bawdy humor to make their point. Duke literary critic Henry Louis Gates, who served as an expert defense witness, is right to point out 2 Live Crew's use of the established black oral practice of signifying, a rhythmic teasing and cajoling, often laced with lewd or off-color remarks that employ parody to either compliment or insult. But black oral practices must be placed in a wider cultural context that permits parallel features of that culture, like moral criticism, sage advice, or common-sense admonitions against out-of-bounds behavior, to enter the field of discussion. Failure to adopt such a viewpoint prevents critical distance on black oral practices. Such critical distance is necessary to assess their worth, judge their effectiveness in relation to comparable expressions within the genre, and describe their wider cultural value and social function. To show how 2 Live Crew employs parody does not suspend the necessity to subject their art to cultural and moral criticism. Their use of parody expresses a point of view about women that is disturbing, not least because they couch their misogyny in humorous terms that fail to envision its lethal consequences for women in fantasies of abusive sex that may lead to, or result from, practices of vicious sexual domination.

We must be reminded that criticism of 2 Live Crew is also a form of self-criticism for most black communities, which continue to reflect the sexism of the larger society. A glaring example is the black church, where a kind of ecclesiastical apartheid is in effect: although black women constitute 70 percent of the membership of the church, they rarely have access to the central symbol of power, the pulpit—a more civilized expression of sexism, but sexism reinforced, sustained, and nourished, nonetheless.

The critique of 2 Live Crew must not, however, feign sociopolitical innocence, cultural purity, or moral neutrality. Similar cases for censorship and obscenity could be made against comedian Andrew Dice Clay's white racist routines and misogynist monologues, or rock group Guns N' Roses homophobic harangues and racist lyrics. Such examples point to the difficulty of deciding upon and describing national standards of obscenity and supplying convincing public arguments about the reasons that govern such judgments. According to the Supreme Court, an artistic creation is obscene if, by community standards, it appeals primarily to prurient interest or if it lacks serious artistic, literary, political, or scientific merit. One need not be steeped in contemporary moral or philosophical theory to understand that community standards of *anything* vary according to what community is being referred to; that interest-laden reason adjudicates competing claims about the true, the good, and the beautiful; and that our historical, political, economic, and social backgrounds affect our understanding of standards of obscenity, how to best apply them, and how to know when they have been fractured or offended.

That 2 Live Crew, as a result of the legal action its raps have occasioned, becomes the classic example of art combating censorship and claims of obscenity, when so many other prior examples abound, is plainly motivated by racial considerations, driven in part by the black male phallic paranoia discussed above. Furthermore, we must be aware of the social, economic, political, and cultural conditions that help shape the lives of young black males, and understand how rap music functions as a form of youthful black cultural resistance, artistic expression, and personal accomplishment.

Rap culture has provided a healthy and flourishing alternative to a burgeoning juvenocracy in the urban inner city, where young black (mostly) men under the age of twenty-five reign over significant segments of black postindustrial urban space, sustained on goods and services produced by an underground political economy of criminal activity that is centered on drugs. The chronic and structural unemployment of black men, the evaporation of social services to address the gap in black male income, and the deterioration of stable structures of institutional support have all contributed to the plight of black men. Rap music provides young black men with economic incentives, social goals, and cultural prominence to escape the urban inner city and avoid the political economy of criminal activity. Luther Campbell, 2 Live Crew's leader, emerged out of Miami's riot-torn Liberty City, beating poverty and crime through his rap vocation. The obscene conditions under which he matured should be outlawed.

Rap music has also transformed linguistic innovation and verbal experimentation, a staple of diverse African-American rhetorical traditions, into a lucrative art. It has employed the rap concert as a public space of symbolic rejection of black bourgeois sensibilities, an arena for the linguistic refusal to accommodate conservative cultural and political forces, and a refuge from the tyrannizing surveillance of black speech practices exercised in mainstream cultural institutions.

The freedom of expression for rappers, even 2 Live Crew, must be protected. The 2 Live Crew controversy tests the limits of free expression in an increasingly complex cultural sphere where issues of racial, sexual, and class difference provoke thoughtful reexamination of cherished ideals like democracy, equality, and liberty. The First Amendment right to free expression may be conceived as a compromise between the authoritarian regulation of social expression and the potential anarchy of totally unlimited social expression. As with all rights-based defenses of fundamental freedoms, the right to free expression permits conflicting and contradictory expressions within its scope of protection.

Furthermore, the right to free expression often entails an alliance of conscience between ideological opponents who disagree about substantive moral, political, and social issues, but who defend the rights of others to express their views. For instance, some Christians have defended the right of non-Christians *not* to pray in public schools, and some civil rights activists have defended the right of the Ku Klux Klan to verbally express its vitriolic ideology of white racist supremacy. Thus, the speech of civil rights activists and Ku Klux Klan terrorists, as well as feminists and misogynists, should receive, *theoretically*, equal legal protection.

Only political naiveté or insularity would conclude that the right to free expression has been equitably applied throughout its tortuous tenure; as the old saw goes, the right to a free press belongs to those who own the press. So it is with the right to free expression: it belongs to those who control, manipulate, and shape expression, whether they be powerful presses, major corporate media conglomerates, or groups sufficiently aware that their right to free expression has been repressed. But as the civil rights movement proved, rights have sufficient interpretive flexibility to be employed on behalf of those who, despite their exclusion from the vision of the original intent of the law, are able to marshal ample resources of moral courage, social conscience, and intellectual acuity to resist the erosion, misapplication, or negligence of rights in defense of their perspectives, or even their lives.

In the 2 Live Crew case, the right to free expression has exhibited the possibility for interpretive resiliency and broad-based application to a range of provocative social issues. The recent controversy occasioned by the late Robert Mapplethorpe's homoerotic photography and the current crisis of confidence afflicting the National Endowment for the Arts, particularly over the work of nontraditional performance artists, for example, raise the specter of repressed cultural expression and limited artistic freedom. The 2 Live Crew jury clearly and explicitly ratified the principle of free artistic expression, even when it severely threatens mainstream modes of artistic creation. In their view, Luther Campbell and Thomas Jefferson deserve equal protection.

My appeal to maintain the right to free expression, however, does not absolve progressive peoples of responsibility to act to oppose the substance of an offensive viewpoint or set of cultural practices. Indeed, civic responsibility, manifest in civil disobedience, social activism, political resistance, and cultural engagement, is the necessary complement to civil rights. Civil responsibility must be exercised in vigorous and thoughtful measure to eradicate offensive social expressions that the right to free expression permits, and to place legal limits on harmful social practices.

While 2 Live Crew's *right* to express its artistic worldview should be protected, even by the most fervent feminist, that artistic worldview, which has profoundly disturbing social and cultural meanings, must be strongly and vociferously criticized. But 2 Live Crew's artistic worldview must be criticized on the basis of a civilly responsible resistance to their rap narratives, which glorify malicious sexual machismo, vilify female sexuality not exclusively linked to the desires of men, and eroticize violent and vengeful sexual behavior. But the implicit and racist swipe at young black male culture in the whole affair must not be overlooked when calls for legal response go forward. Informed criticism, yes; reactionary censorship, no.

The rape of a young white New York woman by as many as eight black and Hispanic teens in Central Park on April 19, 1989, provoked a deeply divided body of opinion about both the rape's elusive cause and its deleterious effects. In a way that couldn't be totally anticipated, commentary flowed forward from every quarter of New York and the nation, from the right, center, and left, whose only unity perhaps lies in the common sense of bewilderment, helplessness, and anger felt in the face of such seemingly inexplicable behavior. In the fray of attempted answers, no one is exactly sure why it happened, and why *this* particular incident catalyzed the attention and studied outrage of an entire city and country. What are we to make of the Central Park rape and the reaction it has occasioned?

The Central Park incident is so explosive because it captures the thorny knot of problems that have increasingly made New York City a microcosm of the racial, sexual, and class miseries afoot in American culture at large, a laboratory of societal ills that mount daily without cease or cure. How we understand their intricate interrelationship will ultimately determine how we view this event and perhaps set the agenda for how we should reshape sociopolitical practices structured around race, class, gender, and age.

The tendency of existing commentary is to privilege one aspect of the incident (e.g., race, gender) in relation to the other elements that make it a volatile issue. Such privileging activity may only create more confusion than it seeks to eliminate and may generate alienation among groups that have sound reasons for cooperative alliance. This does not negate the existence of tensions between and within, for example, African-American and feminist communities, but it means that the most helpful dialogue emerges when we understand how race, class, gender, and age all contributed to what occurred in Central Park on April 19. Otherwise, we are left with a sort of musical chairs scamper for ideological legitimacy that always leaves out a crucial component in accounting for what happened, while masking the real social, economic, and political roots of the various problems that converged that evening.

The severity of the sexual brutality exerted against a lone woman by several males rightfully occasioned the outrage of New York and the nation. Few rapes make the front page, and the sad fact is that we live in a culture that has not confronted the laxity of its attitudes, customs, and laws that grant varying degrees of permission to men to intrude upon and violate the sexual ownership by women of their own bodies. In New York City alone, over 3,500 women are the victims of reported rape, not counting the thousands of women who do not report being raped. A woman is raped in the United States every six minutes, and one out of every ten women will be victimized by rape. There has been an enormous increase in rape arrests of teens in New York (27 percent for boys under 18, 200 percent for boys under 13).

Also, the startling increase in date rapes, particularly on college campuses, and a prevalent attitude that further victimizes women by making them feel responsible for their own rape (through alleged provocative dressing or sexual innuendo) make for a very sad and sick scene. Thus, these teens are not perverted monsters or animals who exhibited such totally asocial, deviant, or aberrant behavior. In a very tragic sense what these youth did was an extreme expression, and logical outcome, of the persistence of antiquated views about women as objects of male sexual satisfaction that remain deeply ingrained in the folkways and mores of American culture, despite two solid decades of resistance and protest by feminists. This does not exonerate these teens, but simply seeks to explain how their behavior is more connected to present social practices and cultural attitudes than we would like to admit.

Unfortunately, however, even when they are reported, all rapes do not receive equal media or legal attention for various reasons, the sheer number of such crimes being one, our jaded sensibilities in regard to even outrageous crime being another. However, a clear and consistent principle has asserted itself in regard to such attention that may be summarized in the following way: who you are makes a big difference as to what will be done and said when a crime happens to you. In general, race, class, and gender are primary factors in determining the level of media attention, legal scrutiny, state concern, and even public sympathy developed around a particular crime. That rape is rarely big news exemplifies this truth. But even in usually low-visibility crimes, hierarchy prevails.

For instance, the press coverage of the Central Park event has drawn such heavy criticism, particularly from black circles, because it makes one thing clear: crime that victimizes black folk is not as important as crime that victimizes white folk. How media coverage constitutes some events as "newsworthy" is practically indistinguishable from prevailing attitudes about race, class, and gender that render some events more important than others. In a culture that through institutional practices, personal attitudes, societal norms, and political behavior has reinforced the devaluation of black life, it is no surprise that the media, judicial system, and city government reflect apathy or cool interest about crimes against blacks, crimes often committed by other blacks.

Thus, when a black woman was gang raped on the roof of a New York building and then thrown three stories a few days after the Central Park rape, remaining in critical condition in a New York hospital, it received little attention in the papers, nor was it made a priority of police investigation. This and a thousand other crimes occur in black neighborhoods across America, and yet they are rarely given front-page exposure by the media or priority treatment by the police. The point here is merely to reiterate what passes for common knowledge in black communities: black life is at a low premium, and to hurt, maim, or murder a black person carries little punitive consequence or public concern. (Thus, the same group of teens terrorized black and Hispanic people in a couple of neighborhoods before the Central Park rape, to little police response or media fanfare.) This, too, rightfully occasions the anger of blacks who witness the callous disregard for crime that victimizes blacks and other poor people, who must then suffer the consequences of their victimization in the pain of anonymous silence.

Painful, too, is the way in which the Central Park incident exposed the sexism that continues to plague most black communities. The definition of sexism and patriarchy in black circles has always been a touchy and tricky affair, primarily because of the central preoccupation with racism. While it may be argued that, given the denial of broad access to institutional power, black men have not by and large been able to set the political, economic, and social terms that regulate women's lives, we have often victimized black women with a form of sexist, machismo-laden behavior that compensated for debilitating forms of social emasculation under the sting of racism. Black women, for the most part, were encouraged, and coerced, to subordinate and suppress concerns about feminist liberation in fierce loyalty to the assumed primacy of obtaining racial liberation, which often meant black male acquisition of white male privilege, power, and position.

This set of relations has formed the premise of black male-female relations: they are locked together in common struggle against racism, while sexism is deeply inscribed in the social practices of their limited, and limiting, world. Also, a high degree of violence often mediates black male-female relations. So while black folk have given a particular social twist and specific historical nuance to male/female relations, basic features of that relationship, including violence and repression, cut across lines of race, class, and regrettably, as Central Park shows, even age.

Simply put then, black communities must begin facing up to

the lethal consequences of our own sexism. The time is over for expecting black women to be silent about the sexual violence and personal suppression they experience in ostensible fidelity to our common cause. They must no longer be forced to choose between being women or being black—they are both. Rather, our moral purview must be expanded to include problems of sexism as central to the struggle of black communities across America. Subordinating the question of gender oppression to racism only means that we are complicit in encouraging sexist stereotypes, patriarchal posturing, and misogynistic behavior among a younger generation of black males, especially among our teens, adversely affecting the entire community.

What is also deeply disturbing about our youth in Central Park is that they exhibited a mobile nihilism, a denial of norms and sanctions in gratuitous violence that bespeaks an internalization of the terror that has besieged black urban communities, of both working-class and underclass varieties. There has been a definite shift in the balance of power in relations between young black teens and parental and other authority figures, largely because of the erosion of family life, the subversion of stable economic infrastructures in black communities, and the emergence of an underground political economy that thrives on illegal activity and dispenses an accompanying psychic and social capital of its own making. Thus, there is a burgeoning juvenocracy that is generating its own rules of behavior and establishing its own laws of survival. This explains in part the incident in Central Park, even among working-class youth, who fasten onto the folklore and culture of this juvenocracy, which is able to present strategies of survival in a tough, violent world by being (on the) offensive: set the terms of violence yourself, it seems to say, and you have a better chance of survival.

But in one sense, they are highly mimetic, and even parasitic. Central Park is not simply an exceptional event, outside the parameters of usual activity, and these youth are not animals deserving of "Trumped"-up xenophobia and class hatred. These youth are simply the newest twist on a classic American phenomenon: violence. Violence created America (the Revolution), was employed to secure free labor to build its economy and institutions (slavery), informed our national self-identity as the most potent purveyor of world destruction (Hiroshima, Nagasaki), and has been used in countless ways to maintain domestic civility, often stigmatizing specific groups in unconscionable strategies of containment (e.g., state repression aimed at blacks at the height of the civil rights movement).

Furthermore, violence is as fresh to America as the cowboy captivity of the presidency of Ronald Reagan, and is a pervasive part of the American social imagination as reflected in the cult of film stars and characters who reign as popular heroes. Indeed, these figures are a crucial part of the taxonomy of American violence, and each person or character has generated a justification of violence in various ways as they have become key words in our common cultural parlance. Witness our valorization of Rambo reflexes (passionate violence marshaled forward in face of personal injustice), Schwarzenegger sentiments (technically precise violence with merciless execution), the Eastwood ethic (Dirty Harry's cool, dispassionate violence wielded in the name of the state as antihero), Bronson brutality (vigilante violence directed against so-called social refuse, usually young black and Latino men), and Norris nuances (highly stylized violence tainted with strong traces of xenophobia).

In the final analysis, then, Central Park is not so distant from us as we would like to believe, not so far from our making as we would avow. Naive avoidance of hard realities will not do. Central Park is a relatively safe social space for many of New York's privileged, including upwardly mobile professionals. Part of the outrage, then, is occasioned by the perceived violation of the unwritten codes of protective distance that police that space. (Thus many responses were built upon the premise that "we" could take "our" park back.) It will not help to reinforce pernicious stereotypes about black men, increasing the already rampant sociosexual fear that continues to exist between black men and white women, and especially in the minds of many white men. Neither will it benefit us to deny the vicious violence toward women that these young teens expressed, violence that is nourished from sexist attitudes that prevail in most minority and mainstream communities. And finally, "wilding" is the social expression among particular groups of teens of the violence that is central to American culture and rooted in factors involving race, class, age, and gender. All of these factors are crucial in understanding what went wrong in Central Park. And all of these categories must be taken seriously in attempting to describe what it will take to make things go right, not only in New York, but in our nation at large.

The 2 Live Crew controversy, as well as the Central Park jogger case, have provoked animated discussions about First Amendment rights to free expression, feminist resistance to misogynist cultural expressions, the role of race in assessing and understanding controversial art, and the lethally sexist social and cultural environment that tolerate and promote violence toward women. To the degree that such discussion heightens not only our awareness of such vital issues, but also quickens our pulse for sustained cultural engagement around such crucial cultural themes, the discussions will prove fruitful. These two incidents also show how the postmodern politics of race, class, and gender gather and order complex and uncomfortable meanings, challenging any easy alliance among groups that have a desperate interest in coalitional survival. Only through careful thinking and conscientious action can we hope to benefit from our failed connections, our substantive disagreements, and our hard-won solidarity.

Improvisation

Toni Morrison's Vision

In her six published novels, Toni Morrison has evoked the byzantine complexities, contradictory desires, and tainted joys of African-American life with haunting eloquence and unsparing honesty. Morrison's eulogistic claim about James Baldwin—that he provided black people a language to live in—is true of her own work.

In *Playing in the Dark: Whiteness and the Literary Imagination* (Harvard University Press, 1992), she reflects upon the creative process and the route imagination takes when it is shaped by cultural and social forces, and proves herself to be an equally insightful and compelling guide. First delivered as the Tanner lectures at Harvard University, this is a book of multiple inversions:

a writer becomes critic, a woman reflects upon the work of mostly men, an African-American intellectual examines the literary construction by white intellectuals of an "American Africanism."

By that term, Morrison means "the ways in which a nonwhite, Africanlike (or Africanist) presence or persona was constructed in the United States, and the imaginative uses this fabricated presence served." In three compact and skillful essays, Morrison explores and illumines the gaggle of literary devices—conceits, tropes, metaphors—that have been mostly unconsciously deployed by white writers to refract the rays of blackness through the prism of literary silence, repression, or avoidance. Morrison ably applies her therapeutic textual intervention to make these rays visible and to imaginatively envision how an Africanist presence was crucial, indeed essential, in forming and extending an American national literature.

Morrison subtly exposes how racial realities affected the literary imagination, maintaining that "it may be possible to discover, through a close look at literary 'blackness,' the nature—even the cause—of literary 'whiteness.' " For the balance of her slim but big book, Morrison wrestles this symbiosis of coloration to consciousness, mapping its unwieldy influence on American literature by examining its representative symptoms in the work of Willa Cather, Edgar Allan Poe, Herman Melville, Mark Twain, Saul Bellow, and Ernest Hemingway. She avoids the intellectual seduction of narrow explanations of white literary uses of the Africanist presence by more subtly showing how black people were at the heart of strategies and processes of American self-definition and self-discovery in American literature. Moreover, Morrison exposes how asserting the meaninglessness of race to the American identity is, in literary discourse, "itself a racial act."

Morrison's book helps expose the fallacy of viewing race exclusively through the lens of biology by maintaining that race has become "metaphorical—a way of referring to and disguising forces, events, classes, and expressions of social decay and economic division far more threatening to the body politic than biological 'race' ever was." Such a redefinition challenges the notion that race is a natural and settled category of personal identity, instead showing how race is socially constructed and made concrete through an intermingling of literary images, religious beliefs, and cultural conventions that are mistakenly perceived as necessary and inevitable.

By going for the American literary jugular—the canon of books that have helped shape American perceptions of racial and national identities—Morrison places her arguments about the absent presence of the African-American at the very heart of contemporary public conversation about what is authentically and originally American. Boldly she reimagines and remaps the possibility of America through its forestalled but not defeated dark side, its shadow constituency nuancing at every crucial turn America's own truest and best identity.

In Morrison's readings and rereadings of classic American writers, the "parasitical nature of white freedom" becomes apparent, while the images of blackness as "evil *and* protective, rebellious *and* forgiving, fearful *and* desirable" and whiteness as "mute, meaningless, unfathomable, pointless, frozen, veiled, curtained, dreaded, senseless, implacable" are all expertly revealed and adroitly detailed.

If Morrison's book is about the white literary imagination—how it elides, silences, codifies, or distorts a dark agency without which the white literary imagination is unthinkable—*Playing in the Dark* is also about a black intellectual seizing interpretive space within a racially ordered hierarchy of cultural criticism. Blacks are usually represented through the lens of white perception rather than the other way around, in part because few black intellectuals have successfully warded off the domineering gaze of white intellectual surveillance. With Toni Morrison's impressive debut as a critical intellectual, a substantive change is portended.

13

The Plight of Black Men

On a recent trip to Knoxville, I visited Harold's barber shop, where I had gotten my hair cut during college, and after whenever I had the chance. I had developed a friendship with Ike, a local barber who took great pride in this work. I popped my head inside the front door, and after exchanging friendly greetings with Harold, the owner, and noticing Ike missing, I inquired about his return. It had been nearly two years since Ike had cut my hair, and I was hoping to receive the careful expertise that comes from familiarity and repetition.

"Man, I'm sorry to tell you, but Ike got killed almost two years ago," Harold informed me. "He and his brother, who was drunk, got into a fight, and he stabbed Ike to death."

I was shocked, depressed, and grieved, these emotions competing in rapid-fire fashion for the meager psychic resources I was able to muster. In a daze of retreat from the fierce onslaught of unavoidable absurdity, I half-consciously slumped into Harold's chair, seeking solace through his story of Ike's untimely and brutal leave-taking. Feeling my pain, Harold filled in the details of Ike's last hours, realizing that for me Ike's death had happened only yesterday. Harold proceeded to cut my hair with a methodical precision that was itself a temporary and all-too-thin refuge from the chaos of arbitrary death, a protest against the nonlinear progression of miseries that claim the lives of too many black men. After he finished, I thanked Harold, both of us recognizing that we would not soon forget Ike's life, or his terrible death.

This drama of tragic demise, compressed agony, nearly impotent commiseration, and social absurdity is repeated countless times, too many times, in American culture for black men. Ike's death forced to the surface a painful awareness that provides the chilling sound track to most black men's lives: it is still hazardous to be a human being of African descent in America.

Not surprisingly, much of the ideological legitimation for the contemporary misery of African-Americans in general, and black men in particular, derives from the historical legacy of slavery, which continues to assert its brutal presence in the untold suffering of millions of everyday black folk. For instance, the pernicious commodification of the black body during slavery was underwritten by the desire of white slave owners to completely master black life. The desire for mastery also fueled the severe regulation of black sexual activity, furthering the telos of southern agrarian capital by reducing black men to studs and black women to machines of production. Black men and women became sexual and economic property. Because of the arrangement of social relations, slavery was also the breeding ground for much of the mythos of black male sexuality that survives to this day: that black men are imagined as peripatetic phalluses with unrequited desire for their denied object—white women.

Also crucial during slavery was the legitimation of violence toward blacks, especially black men. Rebellion in any form was severely punished, and the social construction of black male image and identity took place under the disciplining eye of white male dominance. Thus healthy black self-regard and self-confidence were outlawed as punitive consequences were attached to their assertion in black life. Although alternate forms of resistance were generated, particularly those rooted in religious praxis, problems of self-hatred and self-abnegation persisted. The success of the American political, economic, and social infrastructure was predicated in large part upon a squelching of black life by white modes of cultural domination. The psychic, political, economic, and social costs of slavery, then, continue to be paid, but mostly by the descendants of the oppressed. The way in which young black men continue to pay is particularly unsettling.

Black men are presently caught in a web of social relations, economic conditions, and political predicaments that portray their future in rather bleak terms.[1] For instance, the structural unemployment of black men has reached virtually epidemic proportions, with black youth unemployment double that of white youth. Almost one-half of young black men have had no work experience at all. Given the permanent shift in the U.S. economy from manufacturing and industrial jobs to high-tech and service employment and the flight of these jobs from the cities to the suburbs, the prospects for eroding the stubborn unemployment of black men appear slim.[2]

The educational front is not much better. Young black males are dropping out of school at alarming rates, due to a combination of severe economic difficulties, disciplinary entanglements, and academic frustrations. Thus the low level of educational achievement by young black men exacerbates their already precarious employment situation. Needless to say, the pool of high-school graduates eligible for college has severely shrunk, and even those who go on to college have disproportionate rates of attrition.

Suicide, too, is on the rise, ranking as the third leading cause of death among young black men. Since 1960, the number of black men who have died from suicide has tripled. The homicide rate of black men is atrocious. For black male teenagers and young adults, homicide ranks as the leading cause of death. In 1987, more young black men were killed within the United States in a single year than had been killed abroad in the entire nine years of the Vietnam War. A young black man has a one-in-twenty-one lifetime chance of being killed, most likely at the hands of another black man, belying the self-destructive character of black homicide.

Even with all this, a contemporary focus on the predicament of black males is rendered problematical and ironic for two reasons. First, what may be termed the "Calvin Klein" character of debate about social problems—which amounts to a "designer" social consciousness—makes it very difficult for the concerns of black men to be taken seriously. Social concern, like other commodities, is subject to cycles of production, distribution, and consumption. With the dwindling of crucial governmental resources to address a range of social problems, social concern is increasingly relegated to the domain of private philanthropic and nonprofit organizations. Furthermore, the selection of which problems merit scarce resources is determined, in part, by such philanthropic organizations, which highlight special issues, secure the services of prominent spokespersons, procure capital for research, and distribute the benefits of their information.

Unfortunately, Americans have rarely been able to sustain debate about pressing social problems over long periods of time. Even less have we been able to conceive underlying structural features that bind complex social issues together. Such conceptualization of the intricate interrelationship of social problems would facilitate the development of broadly formed coalitions that address a range of social concern. As things stand, problems like poverty, racism, and sexism go in and out of style. Black men, with the exception of star athletes and famous entertainers, are out of style.

Second, the irony of the black male predicament is that it has reached its nadir precisely at the point when much deserved attention has been devoted to the achievements of black women like Alice Walker, Toni Morrison, and Terry McMillan.

The identification and development of the womanist tradition in African-American culture has permitted the articulation of powerful visions of black female identity and liberation. Michele Wallace, bell hooks, Alice Walker, Audre Lorde, and Toni Morrison have written in empowering ways about the disenabling forms of racism and patriarchy that persist in white and black communities. They have expressed the rich resources for identity that come from maintaining allegiances to multiple kinship groups defined by race, gender, and sexual orientation, while also addressing the challenges that arise in such membership.

Thus discussions about black men should not take place in an ahistorical vacuum, but should be informed by sensitivity to the plight of black women. To isolate and examine the pernicious problems of young black men does not privilege their perspectives or predicament. Rather, it is to acknowledge the decisively deleterious consequences of racism and classism that plague black folk, particularly young black males.

The aim of my analysis is to present enabling forms of consciousness that may contribute to the reconstitution of the social, economic, and political relations that continually consign the lives of black men to psychic malaise, social destruction, and physical death. It does not encourage or dismiss the sexism of black men, nor does it condone the patriarchal behavior that sometimes manifests itself in minority communities in the form of misdirected machismo. Above all, African-Americans must avoid a potentially hazardous situation that plays musical chairs with scarce resources allocated to black folk and threatens to inadvertently exacerbate already deteriorated relations between black men and women. The crisis of black inner-city communities is so intense that it demands our collective resources to stem the tide of violence and catastrophe that has besieged them.

I grew up as a young black male in Detroit in the 1960s and 1970s. I witnessed firsthand the social horror that is entrenched in inner-city communities, the social havoc wreaked from economic hardship. In my youth, Detroit had been tagged the "murder capital of the world," and many of those murders were of black men, many times by other black men. Night after night, the news media in Detroit painted the ugly picture of a homicide-ridden city caught in the desperate clutches of death, depression, and decay. I remember having recurring nightmares of naked violence, in which Hitchcockian vertigo emerged in Daliesque perspective to produce gun-wielding perpetrators of doom seeking to do me in.

And apart from those disturbing dreams, I was exercised by the small vignettes of abortive violence that shattered my circle of friends and acquaintances. My next-door neighbor, a young black man, was stabbed in the jugular vein by an acquaintance and bled to death in the midst of a card game. (Of course, one of the ugly statistics involving black-on-black crime is that many black men are killed by those whom they know.) Another acquaintance murdered a businessman in a robbery; another executed several people in a gangland-style murder.

At fourteen, I was at our corner store at the sales counter, when suddenly a jolt in the back revealed a young black man wielding a sawed-off, double-barreled shotgun, requesting, along with armed accomplices stationed throughout the store, that we hit the floor. We were being robbed. At the age of eighteen I was stopped one Saturday night at 10:30 by a young black man who ominously materialized out of nowhere, much like the .357 Magnum revolver that he revealed to me in an robbery attempt. Terror engulfed my entire being in the fear of imminent death. In desperation I hurled a protest against the asphyxiating economic hardships that had apparently reduced him to desperation, too, and appealed to the conscience I hoped was buried beneath the necessity that drove him to rob me. I proclaimed, "Man, you don't look like the type of brother that would be doin' something like this."

"I wouldn't be doin' this, man," he shot back, "but I got a wife and three kids, and we ain't got nothin' to eat. And besides, last week somebody did the same thing to me that I'm doin' to you." After convincing him that I really only had one dollar and thirty-five cents, the young man permitted me to leave with my life intact.

The terrain for these and so many other encounters that have shaped the lives of black males was the ghetto. Much social research and criticism has been generated in regard to the worse-off inhabitants of the inner city, the so-called underclass. From the progressive perspective of William Julius Wilson to the archconservative musings of Charles Murray, those who dwell in ghettos, or enclaves of civic, psychic, and social terror, have been the object of recrudescent interest within hallowed academic circles and governmental policy rooms.[3] In most cases they have not fared well and have borne the brunt of multifarious "blame the victim" social logics and policies.

One of the more devastating developments in inner-city communities is the presence of drugs and the criminal activity associated with their production, marketing, and consumption. Through the escalation of the use of the rocklike form of cocaine known as "crack" and intensified related gang activity, young black men are involved in a vicious subculture of crime. This subculture is sustained by two potent attractions: the personal acceptance and affirmation gangs offer and the possibility of enormous economic reward.

U.S. gang life had its genesis in the Northeast of the 1840s, particularly in the depressed neighborhoods of Boston and New York, where young Irishmen developed gangs to sustain social solidarity and to forge a collective identity based on common ethnic roots.[4] Since then, youth of every ethnic and racial origin have formed gangs for similar reasons, and at times have even functioned to protect their own ethnic or racial group from attack by harmful outsiders. Overall, a persistent reason for joining gangs is the sense of absolute belonging and unsurpassed social love that results from gang membership. Especially for young black men whose life is at a low premium in America, gangs have fulfilled a primal need to possess a sense of social cohesion through group identity. Particularly when traditional avenues for the realization of personal growth, esteem, and self-worth, usually gained through employment and career opportunities, have been closed, young black men find gangs a powerful alternative.

Gangs also offer immediate material gratification through a powerful and lucrative underground economy. This underground economy is supported by exchanging drugs and services for money, or by barter. The lifestyle developed and made possible by the sale of crack presents often irresistible economic alternatives to young black men frustrated by their own unemployment. The death that can result from involvement in such drug- and gang-related activity is ineffective in prohibiting young black men from participating.

To understand the attraction such activity holds for black men, one must remember the desperate economic conditions of urban black life. The problems of poverty and joblessness have loomed large for African-American men, particularly in the Rust Belt, including New York, Chicago, Philadelphia, Detroit, Cleveland, Indianapolis, and Baltimore. From the 1950s to the 1980s, there was severe decline in manufacturing and in retail and wholesale trade, attended by escalating unemployment and a decrease in labor-force participation by black males, particularly during the 1970s.

During this three-decade decline of employment, however, there was not an expansion of social services or significant increase in entry-level service jobs. As William Julius Wilson rightly argues, the urban ghettos then became more socially isolated than at any other time. Also, with the mass exodus of black working- and middle-class families from the ghetto, the inner city's severe unemployment and joblessness became even more magnified. With black track from the inner city mimicking earlier patterns of white flight, severe class changes have negatively affected black ghettos. Such class changes have depleted communities of service establishments, local businesses, and stores that could remain profitable enough to provide full-time employment so that persons could support families, or even to offer youths part-time employment in order to develop crucial habits of responsibility and work. Furthermore, ghetto residents are removed from job networks that operate in more affluent neighborhoods. Thus, they are deprived of the informal contact with employers that results in finding decent jobs. All of these factors create a medium for the development of criminal behavior by black men in order to survive, ranging from fencing stolen goods to petty thievery to drug dealing. For many black families, the illegal activity of young black men provides their only income.

Predictably, then, it is in these Rust Belt cities, and other large urban and metropolitan areas, where drug and gang activity has escalated in the past decade. Detroit, Philadelphia, and New York have had significant gang and drug activity, but Chicago and Los Angeles have dominated of late. Especially in regard to gang-related criminal activity such as homicides, Chicago and L.A. form a terrible one-two punch. Chicago had 47 gang-related deaths in 1987, 75 in 1986, and 60 in 1988. L.A.'s toll stands at 400 for 1988.

Of course, L.A.'s gang scene has generated mythic interpretation in the Dennis Hopper film *Colors.* In the past decade, gang membership in L.A. has risen from 15,000 to almost 60,000 (with some city officials claiming as much as 80,000), as gang warfare claims one life per day. The ethnic composition of the groups include Mexicans, Armenians, Samoans, and Fijians. But gang life is dominated by South Central L.A. black gangs, populated by young black men willing to give their lives in fearless fidelity to their group's survival. The two largest aggregates of gangs, composed of several hundred microgangs, are the Bloods and the Crips, distinguished by the colors of their shoelaces, T-shirts, and bandannas.

The black gangs have become particularly dangerous because of their association with crack. The gangs control more than 150 crack houses in L.A., each of which does over five thousand dollars of business per day, garnering over half a billion dollars per year. Crack houses, which transform powdered cocaine into crystalline rock form in order to be smoked, offer powerful material rewards to gang members. Even young teens can earn almost a thousand dollars a week, often outdistancing what their parents, if they work at all, can earn in two months.

So far, most analyses of drug gangs and the black youth who

comprise their membership have repeated old saws about the pathology of black culture and weak family structure, without accounting for the pressing economic realities and the need for acceptance that help explain such activity. As long as the poverty of young black men is ignored, the disproportionate number of black unemployed males is overlooked, and the structural features of racism and classism are avoided, there is room for the proliferation of social explanations that blame the victim. Such social explanations reinforce the misguided efforts of public officials to stem the tide of illegal behavior by state repression aimed at young blacks, such as the sweeps of L.A. neighborhoods resulting in mass arrests of more than four thousand black men, more than at any time since the Watts rebellion of 1965.

Helpful remedies must promote the restoration of job training (such as Neighborhood Youth Corps [NYC] and the Comprehensive Employment and Training Act [CETA]); the development of policies that support the family, such as child-care and education programs; a full employment policy; and dropout prevention in public schools. These are only the first steps toward the deeper structural transformation necessary to improve the plight of African-American men, but they would be vast improvements over present efforts.

Not to be forgotten, either, are forms of cultural resistance that are developed and sustained within black life and are alternatives to the crack gangs. An example that springs immediately to mind is rap music. Rap music provides space for cultural resistance to the criminal-ridden ethos that pervades segments of many underclass communities. Rap was initially a form of musical play that directed the creative urges of its producers into placing often humorous lyrics over the music of well-known black hits.

As it evolved, however, rap became a more critical and conscientious forum for visiting social criticism upon various forms of social injustice, especially racial and class oppression. For instance, Grandmaster Flash and the Furious Five pioneered the social awakening of rap with two rap records, "The Message" and "New York, New York." These rap records combined poignant descriptions of social misery and trenchant criticism of social problems as they remarked upon the condition of black urban America. They compared the postmodern city of crime, deception, political corruption, economic hardship, and cultural malaise to a "jungle." These young savants portrayed a chilling vision of life that placed them beyond the parameters of traditional African-American cultural resources of support: religious faith, communal strength, and familial roots. Thus, they were creating their own aesthetic of survival, generated from the raw material of their immediate reality, the black ghetto. This began the vocation of the rap artist, in part, as urban griot dispensing social and cultural critique.

Although rap music has been saddled with a reputation for creating violent outbursts by young blacks, especially at rap concerts, most of rap's participants have repeatedly spurned violence and all forms of criminal behavior as useless alternatives for black youth. Indeed rap has provided an alternative to patterns of identity formation provided by gang activity and has created musical vehicles for personal and cultural agency. A strong sense of self-confidence permeates the entire rap genre, providing healthy outlets for young blacks to assert, boast, and luxuriate in a rich self-conception based upon the achievement that their talents afford them. For those reasons alone, it deserves support. Even more, rap music, although its increasing expansion means being influenced by the music industry's corporate tastes and decisions, presents an economic alternative to the underground economy of crack gangs and the illegal activity associated with them.

However, part of the enormous difficulty in discouraging illegal activity among young black men has to do, ironically, with their often correct perception of the racism and classism still rampant in employment and educational opportunities open to upwardly mobile blacks. The subtle but lethal limits continually imposed upon young black professionals, for instance, as a result of the persistence of racist ideologies operating in multifarious institutional patterns and personal configurations, send powerful signals to young black occupants of the underclass that education and skill do not ward off racist, classist forms of oppression.

This point was reiterated to me upon my son's recent visit with me at Princeton near Christmas. Excited about the prospect of spending time together catching up on new movies, playing video games, reading, and the like, we dropped by my bank to get a cash advance on my MasterCard. I presented my card to the young service representative, expecting no trouble since I had just paid my bill a couple of weeks before. When he returned, he informed me that not only could I not get any money, but that he would have to keep my card. When I asked for an explanation, all he could say was that he was following the instructions of my card's bank, since my MasterCard was issued by a different bank.

After we went back and forth a few times about the matter, I asked to see the manager. "He'll just tell you the same thing that I've been telling you," he insisted. But my persistent demand prevailed, as he huffed away to the manager's office, resentfully carrying my request to his boss. My son, sitting next to me the whole time, asked what the problem was, and I told him that there must be a mistake, and that it would all be cleared up shortly. He gave me that confident look that says, "My dad can handle it." After waiting for about seven or eight minutes, I caught the manager's figure peripherally, and just as I turned, I saw him heading with the representative to an empty desk, opening the drawer and pulling out a pair of scissors. I could feel the blood begin to boil in my veins as I beseeched the manager, "Sir, if you're about to do what I fear you will, can we please talk first?" Of course, my request was to no avail, as he sliced my card in two before what had now become a considerable crowd. I immediately jumped up and followed him into his office, my son trailing close behind, crying now, tearfully pumping me with "Daddy, what's going on?"

I rushed into the manager's office and asked for the privacy of a closed door, to which he responded, "Don't let him close the door," as he beckoned three other employees into his office. I angrily grabbed the remnants of my card from his hands and proceeded to tell him that I was a reputable member of the community and a good customer of the bank and that if I had been wearing a three-piece suit (instead of the black running suit I was garbed in) and if I had been a white male (and not a black man) I would have been at least accorded the respect of a conversation, prior to a private negotiation of an embarrassing situation, which furthermore was the apparent result of a mistake on the bank's part.

His face flustered, the manager then prominently positioned his index finger beneath his desk drawer, and pushed a button, while declaring, "I'm calling the police on you." My anger now piqued, I was tempted to vent my rage on his defiant countenance, arrested only by the vision terrible that flashed before my eyes as a chilling premonition of destruction: I would assault the manager's neck; his co-workers would join the fracas, as my son stood by horrified by his helplessness to aid me; the police would come, and abuse me even further, possibly harming my son in the process. I retreated under the power of this proleptic vision, grabbing my son's hand as I marched out of the bank. Just as we walked through the doors, the policemen were pulling up.

Although after extensive protests, phone calls, and the like, I eventually received an apology from the bank's board and a MasterCard from their branch, this incident seared an indelible impression onto my mind, reminding me that regardless of how much education, moral authority, or personal integrity a black man possesses, he is still a "nigger," still powerless in many ways to affect his destiny.

The tragedy in all of this, of course, is that even when articulate, intelligent black men manage to rise above the temptations and traps of "the ghetto," they are often subject to continuing forms of social fear, sexual jealousy, and obnoxious racism. More pointedly, in the 1960s, during a crucial stage in the development of black pride and self-esteem, highly educated, deeply conscientious black men were gunned down in cold blood. This phenomenon finds paradigmatic expression in the deaths of Medgar Evers, Malcolm X, and Martin Luther King, Jr. These events of public death are structured deep in the psyches of surviving black men, and the ways in which these horrible spectacles of racial catastrophe represent and implicitly sanction lesser forms of social evil against black men remains hurtful to black America.

I will never forget the effect of King's death on me as a nine-year-old boy in Detroit. For weeks I could not be alone at night before an open door or window without fearing that someone would kill me, too. I thought that if they killed this man who taught justice, peace, forgiveness, and love, then they would kill all black men. For me, Martin's death meant that no black man in America was safe, that no black man could afford the gift of vision, that no black man could possess an intelligent fire that would sear the fierce edges of ignorance and wither to ashes the propositions of hate without being extinguished. Ultimately Martin's death meant that all black men, in some way, are perennially exposed to the threat of annihilation.

As we move toward the last decade of this century, the shadow of Du Bois's prophetic declaration that the twentieth century's problem would be the color line continues to extend itself in foreboding manner. The plight of black men, indeed, is a microcosmic reflection of the problems that are at the throat of all black people, an idiomatic expression of hurt drawn from the larger discourse of racial pain. Unless, however, there is vast reconstitution of our social, economic, and political policies and practices, most of which target black men with vicious specificity, Du Bois's words will serve as the frontispiece to the racial agony of the twenty-first century, as well.

Notes

1. For a look at the contemporary plight of black men, especially black juvenile males, see *Young, Black, and Male in America: An Endangered Species,* ed. Jewelle Taylor Gibbs (Dover, Mass.: Auburn House, 1988).

2. See William Julius Wilson, *The Truly Disadvantaged: The Inner City, the Underclass, and Public Policy* (Chicago: University of Chicago Press, 1987).

3. See Wilson, *The Truly Disadvantaged.* For Charles Murray's views on poverty, welfare, and the ghetto underclass, see his influential book, *Losing Ground: American Social Policy, 1950–1980* (New York: Basic Books, 1984).

4. This section on gangs is informed by the work of Mike Davis in his *City of Quartz* (New York: Verso Press, 1991).

Improvisation

Remembering Emmett Till

On Thursday, July 25, 1991, on what would have been Emmett Till's fiftieth birthday, the city of Chicago held an official ceremony to rename significant sections of Seventy-First Street "Emmett Till Road." Along with Emmett's mother, Mrs. Mamie Till Mobley, Mayor Richard Daley, and Mrs. Rosa Parks, I made comments at the ceremony. The substance of my remarks follows.

The meaning of Emmett Till's brief life and tragic death is so monumental we can scarcely grasp hold of it. Our attempts to honor his memory today—although necessary and appropriate—are poor recompense for his noble sacrifice of life under obscene and absurd conditions. And our efforts are pitifully inadequate to give gratitude to Mrs. Mamie Till Mobley, who without her knowledge or consent was called upon to sacrifice her only-begotten son. When Emmett lost his life in tender youth, the world shuddered in angry disbelief at the barbarous passions that could accomplish such a deed. But no American who had not spent energy to retard racism's unruly spread, who had not sought somehow to untangle the lethal knot of fear and ignorance that produce prejudice, could claim innocence. The blood of Emmett Till was on the hands of every person who watched in malignant silence as black men were lynched, black women were raped, and black children were intimidated and even murdered.

By choosing to honor the memory of Emmett Till, we make a covenant with our past to own its pain as our responsibility and to forgive its failures only if the wisdom we derive from their doing is made a conscious part of our present pacts of racial peace. After all, the repression of uncomfortable memories of racial calamity and the avoidance of past racial injustice have become all too common and convenient. But the only way old and deep wounds are healed is to confront their existence and to acknowledge their power to inflict even more suffering and harm if they go unchecked. By remembering Emmett Till's death, we confess that we are not yet done with the work of racial reconciliation, and that although important progress has been made, vast spaces of racial ignorance and animosity remain to be conquered before real justice is achieved.

We do no service to ourselves, and only great harm to Emmett's memory, if we overlook the specific events that caused his sainted sacrifice to acquire a luminous and universal symbolism. Emmett, who was nicknamed "Bo," enjoyed a normal childhood except for one distinguishing illness, which would later have an ominous effect on his short life: he contracted polio at the age of five, leaving him with a severe stutter. After visiting numerous physicians and trying several approaches to remedy his impediment of speech, Emmett's mother finally came upon a solution that worked. She instructed Emmett to whistle when he felt a stutter coming on, after which he was able to speak clearly.

On the surface, being a black teen with a stutter bore no power to shape one's destiny or to revolutionize the racial future of a nation. But with Emmett it was different. In the prime of his evolving adolescence Emmett faced the lethal limits imposed upon all black life, condensed to a single act of senseless murder. While completing a purchase in the grocery store in Money, Mississippi, where he had gone to visit his relatives, he made what appeared to be a whistling noise, which was interpreted as a "wolf whistle" to the white proprietor's wife.

If this indeed happened, what followed is still undeniably absurd. But in light of the fateful trajectory of Southern race relations, Emmett's stutter acquired a fatal meaning. His accidental biological trait, much like his race, collided with an ancient interracial sexual taboo that he barely understood and, in his northern freedom, had not learned to fear. Ironically, his very freedom from artificial racial distinctions was his doom.

For his unpardonable sin, Emmett was violently abducted from his uncle's house, brutally beaten, shot in the head, and tossed in the Tallahatchie River with a two-hundred-pound cotton gin motor tied around his neck. When his body was pulled from the water, his mother Mamie successfully prevented him from being buried in Mississippi, as the local sheriff had deviously planned. Instead, she brought Emmett's body back to Chicago, and for five days she held an open casket vigil that was eventually viewed by more than six hundred thousand people.

The unspeakable horror of Emmett's death caused shock to ripple through the entire nation. More importantly, his death galvanized a people perched on the fragile border between heroism and fear to courageously pursue meaningful and complete equality. In the curious mix of fortuity and destiny that infuse all events of epic meaning, Emmett's death gained a transcendent metaphoric value. Rosa Parks drew strength from his unintended martyrdom when she sat down with dignity so that all black people could stand up with pride. Medgar Evers cried bitter tears of frustration and pain, and he was charged to gird his loins and renew his commitment to shout justice in Mississippi's Dark Delta, leading to his own death and a rightful place at Emmett's side in the sacred pantheon of murdered martyrs. And Emmett's death gave Martin Luther King, Jr., the great social prophet and American visionary who himself answered the highest call to service and paid the greatest price of sacrifice, an irresistible symbol for the civil rights movement. And it continues to give contemporary fighters for freedom the inspiration and courage to love mercy and to help do justice.

And so what we do here today is in memory of all who have given their lives so that justice, freedom, and equality would not remain abstract principles on parchment, but become living ideas in action. For the purpose of monuments, whether statues of stone or street signs of steel, whether large or small, is to evoke the sacrament of remembrance. Monuments embody a communal choice to remember and to make intangible dreams permanent and concrete. But their real beauty consists in their power to complete the cycle of memory, and to transcend stone and steel and renew our hearts and illumine our minds with the passion and ideals for which they stand.

But above all, what we do here today is for all innocent children who, like Emmett Till, are the unwitting victims of sacrifice. It is for babies born to mothers addicted to crack; it is for children who are mentally and physically disabled; it is for children who endure emotional and bodily abuse in silent suffering; it is for orphaned and foster children who are robbed of the intimacies of family love and bereft of the benefit of parental wisdom; it is for homeless children who have no shelter from nature's changes or from the social environment's vengeful will; it is for poor children who are daily reminded by social theory and public policy that their lives are expendable and their basic needs unaffordable.

And in the harshest irony of all, it is for the young black Emmett Tills who are killed by other young black Emmett Tills in a culture of crime and violence that is the cruelest challenge to Emmett Till's great legacy. The disintegration of the moral fabric of urban communities, the thriving of the "political economy of crack," and the obscene incidence of black-on-black homicide threaten to make Emmett's untimely sacrificial death empty. Both black communities and American institutions must be held responsible. Black communities must develop cultural resources to restore ethical responsibility, place humane regard for life at their center once again, and generate transformative visions of black manhood that do not lead to self-destruction. American institutions, including government, school, and business, must restructure political economic practices that devalue black male labor, reshape academic settings that needlessly exacerbate and reinforce low self-esteem, and reconstruct practices such as police brutality that target black men with vicious particularity.

In reality, all black children who become men and women, who have benefited from the freedom to explore the entire range of their talents, owe a debt to Emmett Till, who was denied the opportunity to fully blossom. In the city of Emmett's birth, there would be no possibility for the nearly superhuman athletic feats of Michael Jordan or for the stunning two sports exploits of Bo Jackson without Emmett "Bo" Till's short life and tragic death. His sacrifice helped opened doors for them. And if we continue to recall his life and death, the memory of Emmett Till will continue to open doors of painful truth and tragic but redemptive history for us all.

14

Black Grass-Roots Leaders

Black leadership across America is entangled in the thickets of a punishing irony: it is riddled by uncertainty precisely when it should be enjoying its greatest impact in our nation's history. The problem derives from changing expectations generated by increased black participation in electoral politics since the civil rights movement and a consequent concern about a transition in leadership styles.

"Many black elected officials," observes University of Pennsylvania historian Mary Frances Berry, "are concerned about the same things that every other politician is concerned about—staying in office as long as they can, getting reelected, and moving up in politics—without having any commitment beyond the rhetorical to doing anything about issues and taking risks." The situation has resulted in heightened visibility, and even eagerness, in black America for so-called black grass-roots leaders.

But are grass-roots leaders actually more effective? Do such leaders have a superior vision of moral reconstruction and socioeconomic regeneration that can offset the chaos and civic decay ravaging most large cities? Or are they attempting to apply outmoded tactics to contemporary social and political problems because of a perilous naiveté about how political, economic, and social resources are distributed? And do the high degrees of hustling and opportunism resulting from loose organizational structures and virtually nonexistent accountability mechanisms undermine the good that grass-roots organizations and leaders accomplish?

Al Sharpton, thirty-seven, now a declared candidate for the U.S.

Senate seat held by Alfonse D'Amato, may be the most intriguing figure whose public career raises such issues. The president of the New York City–based National Action Network is best known for his flamboyant and often inflammatory presence at many of New York's most infamous racial catastrophes. "My mission," says Sharpton, "is to continue the social action that emanated from the movement started by Adam Clayton Powell and Martin Luther King, Jr., in this country—unpaid, uncompromising voices that will raise unashamedly the issues of black people and keep these issues at center stage until they are resolved."

Many observers have applauded Sharpton's appearances at public incidents of racial calamity, viewing his presence as a guarantee that precious media attention will be devoted to cases that might otherwise go unnoticed. Others feel that Sharpton, along with allied attorneys C. Vernon Mason and Alton Maddox, has exploited these tragedies and helped exacerbate New York's racial tensions. But University of Wisconsin law professor Patricia Williams contends that Sharpton's particular skill is to juxtapose events in a way that generates publicity. "It is a talent that black leadership needs, and few black leaders, even Jesse Jackson, seem to have the ability to create such attention." Williams is skeptical, however, of Sharpton's aims. He doesn't use his skills "to the best advantage of the black community," particularly because "his allegiances are quite confused," she says. Moreover, Williams maintains, "a roving spotlight is not the same as having a constituency." As Howard University political scientist Ronald Walters sees it, Sharpton symbolizes a style of leadership undercutting the belief that the needs of the black community are fundamentally addressed through legislative action.

"Sharpton is an anomaly," says Walters, "because he is one of the few people around to continue to lead mass mobilization and political strategies." Mass mobilization must not be discounted, Walters contends, because it has been the crucial basis for much of the most progressive legislation for blacks in the last two decades, including the Anti-Apartheid Act of 1986, the King holiday, and the Humphrey-Hawkins bill.

Although a figure like Sharpton provides symbolic leadership, the value of such leadership is severely limited when unable to deliver social services or political goods. While Sharpton, in the tradition of our best public moralists, often manipulates symbols of racial malaise in competing for the declining resources of public attention and communal shame, he lacks a commensurate ability to link racial pain to financial and social resources in a way that can relieve the material suffering of his followers.

Sharpton funds his organization from member donations at his weekly rallies in Harlem's P.S. 175, broadcast over New York's WWRL radio, and through donations from his radio audience. He claims that his organization refuses foundation grants and other corporate or governmental funding so that "we will not have to compromise." His annual budget, he says, is around one hundred fifty thousand dollars, which reflects what he adds to the till in fees received for speaking throughout the country. Looming over Sharpton, of course, is a cloud of suspicion created by well-known tax problems and allegations that he was once an informant for the FBI, charges he dismisses as attempts to undermine his leadership.

Nevertheless, Sharpton has undeniable appeal, even if it is largely symbolic—a leadership style that is important, according to Princeton philosopher Cornel West, because it is "directed toward frustrated and alienated people that don't seem to interest other politicians."

Dramatizing his community's condition has helped make Milwaukee alderman Michael McGee a hero to most of his constituency and a "clown" to Milwaukee mayor John O. Norquist. Despite McGee's status as an elected official since 1984, his long history of local activism has given him considerable cachet among various grass-roots communities in Milwaukee. His annual alderman's income is thirty-seven thousand dollars. He is up for reelection in 1992. And despite a loss of 60 percent of his base through redistricting, he is expected to retain his seat. Prior to taking public office, McGee was employed by a health organization while running a crime prevention program he founded in 1975 and headed for five years before it received funding from the federal government.

Because Milwaukee's black communities are besieged by despair and violence even as its white communities prosper, McGee urges urban guerrilla warfare by a black militia if Milwaukee's racist government has not responded to the black community's emergency conditions by 1995. "Urban guerrilla warfare, including sniping and sabotage, is necessary because of the lack of progress made," McGee contends. "Other tactics have failed. Urban guerrilla warfare is the escalation of tactics of sit-ins, marching, and direct action, which have been taken for granted. It is the continuation of the American Revolution." The results of that revolution more than two centuries ago, McGee maintains, have not yet reached most black Americans.

McGee's bleak assessment of Milwaukee's black community is borne out by troubling statistics. Unemployment for blacks is at 25 percent as against 5 percent overall. Of all public school dropouts, 62 percent are black, while the grade point average for blacks hovers at 1.3 (D+) and for whites at 1.9 (C). The average income for blacks is $10,000; for whites it is $21,600. Blacks are turned down for home loans at a rate of 24 percent, while only 6 percent of whites are rejected. And of the 333 children born to women under 16 years of age, 255 of the mothers were black women and 78 were white.

Fellow alderman Marvin Pratt agrees with McGee's analysis of Milwaukee's situation, as do many of the city's black leaders. He is uncomfortable, however, with McGee's advocacy of violence. But Walter Farrell, Jr., a professor of educational policy and community studies at the University of Wisconsin in Milwaukee, believes McGee is in the vanguard of local grass-roots leaders who embody the hopes of underclass citizens virtually unreached by traditional leadership.

Still, whether McGee's advocacy of urban guerrilla warfare is viewed as the outlandish antics of a media-savvy pol (he's been on both "Donahue" and "60 Minutes") or the bare-edged desperation of a man who has seen an apocalyptic vision (he claims divine inspiration), McGee has struck a deep nerve in Milwaukee and the nation. Sharpton and McGee arguably exhibit an approach to black leadership rooted in a charismatic, personality-centered model that has been highly visible in black culture from the black church to organizations such as Martin Luther King's Southern Christian Leadership Conference (SCLC) and Jesse Jackson's People United to Serve Humanity (PUSH) and Rainbow Coalition.

As University of Colorado historian and political scientist Manning Marable asserts, such leaders are the legatees of a tradition of "messianic figures who embody both spiritual aspirations and secular grievances." But, Marable contends, a number of charismatic leaders have been vulnerable to "co-optation and buy-out," and grass-roots leadership is often hampered by the "lack of a mechanism for accountability."

Accountability, however, is a crucial term in the leadership vocabulary of grass-roots figures like Mark Ridley-Thomas. Ridley-Thomas, a councilman elected last June from Los Angeles's eighth district, labored for ten years as the executive director of the L.A. branch of the SCLC. James Lawson, SCLC branch president, says that Ridley-Thomas has made crucial contributions to Los Angeles on a number of important issues, including "the environment, peace, justice, racism, sexism, and nonviolence." But, Lawson warns, "it's important for Mark, now that he's moved into the city council, to remember that the system will try to do everything it can to corrupt and knock leaders in the political arena. They need more than a voting base."

Ridley-Thomas, thirty-seven, says he is interested "not in building a cult of personality but progressive coalitions." As he sees it, the crisis in black leadership partially derives from a "shrinking from progressive politics," where leaders are "sidetracked or bought off because they are power hungry." The test of Ridley-Thomas's own political mettle has just begun, centering on whether he can successfully operate with his style of progressive politics in an atmosphere in which co-optation is the order of the day. Ridley-Thomas is paid a city council incumbent's annual salary of ninety thousand dollars. He raised close to four hundred thousand dollars during his campaign, mostly from individual contributions.

His duty, he says, is to take the "substantial resources that a councilman has in L.A. and bring them to bear in empowering a community that in many ways has been neglected." Ridley-Thomas argues that people should democratically participate in decisions that affect their lives. "Because of my commitment to empowerment of the neighborhoods," he says, "a developer can't come to me and get a sign-off on a project unless certain steps have been followed with respect to neighborhood participation."

Candor is rare among black leaders. Many have refrained from public criticism of each other, for example, because of the manipulative uses to which such criticism is often put by white media and political opponents. But unless honest and principled criticism of black leadership is encouraged within black communities, an unhealthy silence will be reinforced, tragically passing for communal loyalty and racial solidarity.

Such criticisms have broad application when examining the structures and practices of many lesser-known grass-roots organizations. Given Sharpton's perennial and nebulous organizational shifts, recyclings, and realignments, one questions whether his organization exists off paper, beyond the furious ad hoc gatherings that mark his episodic interventions in New York's public events of racial pain. And while McGee's promotion of urban guerrilla warfare is understandable, his romantic notions of organizing the ghetto poor, and even drug dealers, to commit civil rebellion has little chance to ameliorate the fundamental conditions of poverty, joblessness, and racism that make the lives of the ghetto poor hell. Grass-roots leaders face a stern challenge if they are to be more effective—the challenge of shaping black grass-roots followers into an effectively organized political constituency around nonelectoral political behavior, such as community organizing around employment, housing, and health issues, and the refusal to collapse all political activity into efforts aimed at placing people in office.

One of the most valuable functions of grass-roots leadership is a broad and bold social vision advocating strategic social and political action, whose aim is the increased viability of neighborhoods, a viability measured through the active participation of average persons in the process of making the claims and rewards, as well as the rights and responsibilities, of citizenship local and immediate. A further function of such leadership is to apply rigorous and constant pressure upon traditional political actors to deliver social goods and services to the people by whom politicians are elected. In this scenario of grass-roots leadership, critical thinking and social action reinforce one another.

The conditions that make black grass-roots leadership necessary are sadly perennial: the detrimental indifference to urban blight by politicians heady with power and privilege; the social marginalization and economic deterioration of the working class, the working poor, and the ghetto poor; the upsurge of racial antipathy in hundreds of white ethnic and mixed-race communities across America; the cultural and political fallout from claims about "political correctness" in universities and the workplace; and the vicious concentration of wealth in capital-crazy corporations and the hands of a few rich individuals while the middle and working classes and the poor grow more desperate by the hour. Black grass-roots leadership that is able to articulate the concerns of often voiceless persons is especially important during an era that has witnessed an exponential increase in black elected officials but a disappointing failure of black political nerve and attention to describing, understanding, and remedying our community's most crucial problems.

A black grass-roots leadership characterized by integrity, sharp intelligence, and political wisdom is of vital importance as politicians grow more concerned with political leadership. It is precisely this moral dimension, this unwillingness to be bought or bossed, that marks the contribution of black grass-roots leadership. Thus the needs of communities are placed before the personal priorities of political privilege, reward, and comfort, goods that, when indulged in to excess, cushion, absorb, or silence the prophetic criticism that grass-roots leadership often supplies.

Grass-roots leaders must also develop more persuasive and incisive analyses of social, economic, and political problems and must forge enabling links with other grass-roots organizations, including those focused on issues of gender, class, sexual orientation, age, and the environment. Coalitions can give leaders and organizations a richer set of social tools and relationships with which to address the problems black communities confront. Isolation affords little chance to affect American society. But in progressive solidarity, black grass-roots leaders and organizations have a real chance to help shape the future of black communities throughout the nation.

Improvisation

The Invisible Lives of Working-Class Black Men

Stereotypes about black men have been spread through much of American society not only by the wide-ranging organs of popular culture but also by the solemn utterances of scholarly research. And more than any group of scholars, it is the sociologists who have vigorously pursued the investigation of black men, producing several ethnographic classics in a genre of writing that has acquired its own special rules and peculiar prominence.

Among those classics are Elliot Liebow's *Talley's Corner*, Lee Rainwater's *Behind Ghetto Walls*, Ulf Hannerz's *Soulside*, and Elijah Anderson's *A Place on the Corner* and *Streetwise*—books that, for better and worse, have helped to shape cultural perceptions of black men and have influenced social policy that is aimed at the amelioration of their often difficult lives. Now we have Mitchell Duneier's *Slim's Table: Race, Respectability and Masculinity in America*, an imaginative and myth-shattering interpretation of the often neglected working-class and working-poor black man that is inspired by and dissents from its predecessors in the field.

For the most part, the lives of working black men have been shunted to the periphery of scholarly and cultural awareness, as a preponderance of attention has been devoted to ghetto poor and middle-class black men. Duneier rescues working black men from unjust sociological oblivion by narrating in stirring and fastidious detail the social rituals, cultural values, and personal virtues of the men who pass time at Valois, a Greek-owned South Side Chicago cafeteria that is the social hub of Hyde Park—the racially integrated, middle-class neighborhood that is home to the University of Chicago. Against received notions about such men—that they posture, brag about their sexual exploits, are fundamentally immoral—Duneier poses a resonant portrait of men who care deeply for one another, who display vulnerability in relationships with women, and who have a finely developed sense of personal dignity and respect.

There is Jackson, a semiretired crane operator who, despite his troubles with his ghetto apartment landlord, takes great pride in paying his bills. There is Billy Black, a repairman for the Chicago Transit Authority, and Harold, an exterminator, both of whom confessed that they were "victims rather than exploiters" in relationships with women. There is also Claude, a police officer who became a regular at Valois's after his divorce because he didn't "favor the solitude at home" and because he acknowledged that his fellow "men are like my family now. Because we eat together every day."

But neither does Duneier avoid talking of men like Willie, who "was one of a very few men at Valois whose outer-directed, attention-seeking, self-aggrandizing behavior actually did conform with sociology's typical portrait of the black male." Duneier also records how some of the men view with suspicion and disdain a younger generation of black males, thereby ironically internalizing the very stereotypes of black men rebutted by their own experience. And he captures the resentment some of the men feel for middle-class blacks and well-educated white students, resentment that leads occasionally to petty forms of harassment.

But most of the black men Duneier encountered in Valois were proud and moral figures whose personal behavior and work habits were exemplary. These perhaps unexpected virtues of character and community are most poignantly symbolized in the moral authority of Slim, for whom the book is titled and around whose serenely solid personality many of the lessons of Duneier's four years of field work are centered. It is at Slim's table in Valois that Duneier discerns that many of these men have the ability to make the features of their moral community work not only for themselves but for others as well. For instance, Slim, a sixty-five-year-old ghetto mechanic, showed compassion and care for Bart, a white retired file clerk ten years his senior who had grown to maturity in a racist South and who recalcitrantly retained many of his poisonous beliefs about blacks. But across this chasm of culture and color, Slim embraced Bart as his "father" and at least partially allowed the old man to relinquish his fear and prejudice.

Perhaps the most striking feature of Duneier's book is its portrayal of the quest for maintaining respectability, of "the black man's inner strength—his resolve, his pride, and his sincerity." The men of *Slim's Table* are embarrassed when they transgress "specific notions of moral worth" and are injured when "they are treated by others in a way that is inconsistent with their self-esteem.''

In the course of *Slim's Table*, Duneier takes on the icons of his field, including authors as various as Liebow, Charles Keil, Hannerz, Rainwater, St. Clair Drake and Horace Cayton (*Black Metropolis*), and Anderson. Duneier argues that although ''on some level'' their books have made

> some progress in liberating blacks from the images that are used to oppress them, when they confirm blacks in other stereotypes with insubstantial evidence they are even more insidious in their influence than an explicitly racist account, which would have no prospect of acceptance. This is evident in the wide respect the whole body of ethnography on black men has achieved, despite its tendency to make generalizations that would be intolerable if made about white ethnic groups without strong evidence.

Duneier also criticizes the influential thesis that William Julius Wilson propounded in *The Truly Disadvantaged* (and that Elijah Anderson's ethnographic studies have attempted to support). Duneier claims that Wilson argued that the departure of the black middle class to the suburbs has left the ghettos without role models, isolating ''poor blacks from mainstream values and behavioral patterns.'' But as Duneier notes, Wilson's and Anderson's explanations of ''what has been lost to the ghettos,'' with their use of phrases like ''hard work, perseverance, decency and propriety'' to describe middle-class blacks, imply ''that the majority of ghetto dwellers who work at low wage jobs do not have these characteristics.''[1]

However, Duneier responds, ''phrases like 'moral value' and 'decency' do not accurately distinguish the character of the blacks who have departed from the ones who are left behind.'' Further, it seems likely that men of Slim's moral authority have much to teach not only the ghetto but all segments of American society as well. Whatever one believes about the problems of black men and the books that have examined the sources of their sorrows and survival, *Slim's Table* is of immense value. Intellectually honest, self-critical, and willing to challenge old beliefs with his fresh investigations, Mitchell Duneier has given us an ethnography of black men that will provide debate and provide insight for years to come.

Note

1. In fairness to William Julius Wilson, he does not articulate the theory that Duneier ascribes to him. As Wilson responded in the *Chicago Tribune,* September 30, 1992: "My book points out that middle-class and working-class blacks—who have historically reinforced traditional patterns of work, family and education in the inner city—have departed many ghetto neighborhoods in significant numbers. I argue that there is a paucity of families with regularly employed individuals in these neighborhods not only because of the outmigration of higher income families, but also because of the declining employment opportunities associated with economic restructuring. In other words, the ranks of the employed, especially working males, in many inner-city neighborhoods have been severely reduced, not totally eliminated. . . . Just like the older men who eat regularly in this cafeteria in the affluent Hyde Park neighborhood and whom Duneier claims are representative of ghetto blacks, the people interviewed in their actual homes and neighborhoods by our research team spoke with dignity and reinforce values of work, family and education. But they also focused on issues that are not highlighted in the benign portraits in *Slim's Table*—the problems of racial segregation, class subordination and social isolation that not only make their efforts to survive very difficult but that have destroyed so many of their relatives, friends and neighbors."

15

Reflections on the 1988 Presidential Campaign

Any reflection on the 1988 presidential campaign's meaning for progressives must begin by acknowledging the general demoralization of the left, which is principally due to two factors. First, there is the continuing contraction of the boundaries of discourse in American political culture, resulting in the consolidation of the right and the ongoing marginalization of the left. In a presidential race that saw Bush forces employ a skillful treachery in undermining forms of political tolerance and notions of ideological inclusiveness, even the word "liberal" became the dirty "L" word, anathema to the progress of American civil and social life. In such a climate, then, it is small wonder that progressives of every ilk have been traumatized by the rhetorical terrorism of the right in its subversive rearticulation of political meanings, meanings that are now primarily understood from the narrow focuses of conservative ideology and "mainstream" politics.

A further source of demoralization is the desperate infighting now transpiring over the meaning of the watershed moment that gave greatest historical momentum and political point to the contemporary left: the sixties. Segments of the left are presently locked in interpretive warfare over the significance of the sixties, its place in defining and determining present courses of action and strategy, and are even involved in some brutal ideological skirmishes that sometimes amount to a lefter-than-thou context. The irony of this, of course, is that such interpretive combat is occurring precisely when the liberal logic that informed the Great Society agenda has been rebutted, when the measured progress that resulted from various sixties movements for liberation has been retarded, and when the sympathetic political sentiment and concern generated during that era has been rejected.

Given this background, then, the 1988 presidential election seems only to portend further demoralization and promise even greater polarization of the left. Upon further reflection, however, this view may be challenged by encouraging signs. First, the Bush victory does not represent an authoritative mandate "of the people." Indeed the degree to which the electoral process accurately reflects the political mood or positions of most Americans is highly questionable. Only 49 percent of the eligible electorate chose to vote, making it the lowest turnout in sixty-four years. Also, a disproportionate number of persons who voted for Bush were college-educated white males who earned more than fifty thousand dollars per year. Bush's mandate, then, is predicated on a narrow slice of the electorate, composed of wealthy, well-educated white men.

Furthermore there was manifested among those who chose to vote what may be termed a schizophrenic voting behavior. While the conservative agenda was ratified nationally, on the local, state, and federal levels the Democrats managed to hold on strong. For instance, the Democrats defied recent historical precedence and gained two seats in the Senate and five seats in the House of Representatives, making it the first time in twenty years that the winning party lost seats in the House.

This schizophrenic voting behavior suggests, on the one hand, that the Democrats project an inability to elect a national leader who is even able to develop consensus among, and bring relative unity to, the diverse and disparate groups that constitute the Democratic party. The most crucial priority of the Democratic party is to secure the commitment of a vast cross section of its historic constituency (blacks, labor, etc.) without sacrificing its most progressive elements under the banner of a bland (neo) liberal socioeconomic and political agenda. In sum, it must articulate a vision and develop programs that can catalyze the socioeconomic and political amelioration of the underclass, for example, and discover ways of registering its occupants to vote, while managing to capture the loyalty and imagination of broad sectors of its remaining constituency and the American public that chose not to vote in the 1988 election.

On the other hand, the bifurcated behavior of the voting populace also suggests the existence of significant segments of liberal sympathy, and possibly progressive sentiment, that can be built upon by the left. While it is true that the social visions of the left are far more expansive than most recent liberal versions of the Democratic party, we must be nondogmatic in seeking mass agency for sociopolitical change. In short, we must be willing to tap into existing structures of (quasi) progressive political organizations if they offer chances for authentic, even if limited, participation and transformation. This certainly chastens *chiliastic* conversation about, and *utopian* visions of, immediate radical sociopolitical amelioration through a third party (although this does not disqualify conversations or visions of third-party politics, just about what *kind* of conversation and visions we should have, and under what conditions they can be effective). It does not negate, however, the need for serious and sustained forms of progressive sociopolitical insurgency outside of the two major political parties (e.g., prophetic critique of political practices, economic policies, and social norms by blacks, feminists, community organizations, etc.). All of this counsels progressives not to capitulate to premature despair or fall prey to a final cynicism. These signs of hope may be small, but they are not insignificant.

The most promising sign of hope for progressives remains the Jackson campaign. Despite the Jackson campaign being beset by its own blindness and being laced with new challenges generated by its limited success, it still represents the best extant political option for the left. In his 1988 quest for the oval office, Jackson showed remarkable growth and maturity since his historic initial bid for the presidency in 1984. His adroit skills as an orator never in question, Jackson proved he possessed a commensurate political wisdom and savvy born of real experience in grappling with substantive social, political, and economic issues. As a result, Jackson's political base expanded beyond the black community, as he gained increasing support among many whites, particularly farm workers, labor, and feminists.

Jackson's campaign remained the sole voice for a progressive coalition made up of, among others, ecologists, feminists, blacks, gays, and so on. This kind of progressive coalition represents the most powerful challenge to the "business as usual" approach in American politics. Jackson consistently articulated a political stance and vision concerned with the politically, socially, and economically marginalized that captured the imaginations of millions of voters, and even more Americans alienated from the electoral process.

Jackson argued for the validity of "comparable worth" in an effort to destroy inequities in pay based on gender. He advocated a freeze in defense spending and the restoration of the maximum personal tax rate to 38.5 percent, which would affect the wealthiest six hundred thousand Americans and free up funds to finance a national health-care plan. He denounced the exploitative practices of U.S. and transnational corporations and urged the redirection of their profits from various foreign ventures to the development and sustenance of independent local economies. Jackson's campaign, too, was perennially preoccupied with helping factory laborers through federal activity to stop "factory flight" in the Sun Belt and with aiding farm workers through ceaseless efforts to retard the ruinous consequences of corporate agribusiness on family farms. In these and numerous other ways, Jackson advanced a progressive social vision for American society, often based on persuasive analyses of the multifarious forms of socioeconomic oppression and political marginalization that merit continued, serious consideration by the left.[1]

This is not to suggest, however, that Jackson's program was without blemish or shortcoming. A problematic aspect of Jackson's project remains the tension of definition: will he be a political insider or a prophetic outsider? In short, will he play within the parameters of traditional politics (i.e., remain within the folds of the Democratic party) and thus retain the option of staking out progressive territory within those boundaries? Or will he opt for the outside, and thus exercise the prerogative of uttering prophetic critique of the political order? In reality, this dilemma may already be resolved, as Jackson's two bids for the presidency have assured him of a certain (although still undefined) role within the established Democratic hierarchy. However, the unpredictability of Jackson's campaign movement, which is both its strength and its weakness, means that the exact configuration of his forthcoming political activity remains an open question.

The challenge to the left is to build upon and expand the parameters of Jackson's campaign and thus deepen engagement with the issues he has raised that have been abandoned by the right and even much of the neoliberal agenda. These issues include continued support for women's issues (reproductive rights, etc.); ongoing analysis and development of an agenda that confronts issues related to the underclass; grappling with the specificity of race as a determinant of oppression, in alliance with analyses that also take class seriously; commitment to the nuclear arms debate that stresses the need for the development of sane policy devoid of Red Scare Reaganism; ongoing support for the struggles of workers, especially farm and factory workers, in the Rust and Sun belts; the development of a foreign policy in the Middle East that respects the humanity and dignity of Israelis and Palestinians, moving beyond the uncritical, pro-Zionist posture that has dominated in recent years; and the development of plausible means of financing an effective national health-care plan.

This is indeed a daunting, although not unattainable, political order. Particularly on local, state, and federal levels, there is much space for the crafting of effective policies, the generation of concrete political support, and the development of creative programs that in various ways address these and other progressive concerns. Perhaps it would do the left well to remember the mayoralty of the late Harold Washington, to view the working of a flawed, although helpful, local government administration implementing progressive politics.

Washington took office as the result of a powerful urban grassroots political movement that supported him and continued to hold him accountable. In winning Chicago's highest office, Washington stepped into a treacherous political gap that placed urban reform politicians on one hand and Daley machine politicians on the other hand. Urban reform politics, which sought improved government efficiency, broadened political representation, and enhanced socioeconomic equality, had its political base depleted by radical demographic changes and was unable to get its representatives elected. Machine politics depended on a pernicious patronage arrangement whereby political favors were doled out in exchange for votes, and excluded women, blacks, Latinos, and other minorities.[2]

Into this political gap stepped Washington. His political ingenuity rested on the fact that he represented the transformation of the character of urban reform politics. This is the case largely because he unified the black poor, the working poor, and segments of the middle and upper classes, along with some traditional liberals, feminists, labor constitutents, and affluent "lakefront liberals." Washington was supported, in the main, by grass roots and community-based organizations that promoted constructive political activities, including voter education and registration, in getting him elected. Thus, a powerful black political movement, including groups like CBUC (Chicago Black United Communities, which sponsored conferences to raise voter awareness) and POWER (People Organized for Welfare Employment Rights, which registered public aid recipients), in alliance with other progressive people, was responsible for Washington's success.

Despite spending his first term dismantling the patronage system of the previous machine and being embroiled in brutal battles with Chicago's city council, Washington worked to make city government a more improved phenomenon than it had been under machine rule. Pregnant women and mothers of small children received coupons for baby foods, cereals, and dairy products. Washington generated mortgage money for eight thousand housing units, almost four times more than the previous administration. The Office of Professional Standards, which fields complaints against the police department, was removed from police headquarters to ensure fairness. Washington unsealed government files that had been kept from the public for decades. He recognized unions for forty thousand city workers, significantly diminishing the paternalism that had previously reigned. Washington also stressed extensive neighborhood economic development. For the most part, there was a downward redistribution of benefits to needful lower-income blacks and whites.[3]

As the left continues to wrestle with its role in organized political activity, examples such as Washington and even Jackson prevent wholesale cynicism about the uselessness of such ventures. Despite the shift to the right, there is much room to maneuver on the left, especially on local, state, and federal levels. Diligent work on these levels, in concert with continued sociopolitical agitation and resistance on a national basis, may yet result in the restructuring of political, economic, and social relations in a way that more clearly represents justice and equality.

Improvisation

Looking Back on the Eighties

As a decade, the eighties achieved an identity as much by erosion as through rupture. The psychic and social wounds left over from the sixties, coupled with the often narcissistic preoccupation with self of the seventies, wore heavily and strangely on the American conscience in the eighties. In turn, this provoked in many Americans alternating rhythms of denial of, and resentment of responsibility for, the worst excesses of the preceding two decades. The eighties, therefore, finessed the moral turbulence of the sixties by adopting a subtle spiritual coldness and resolved the banal selfishness of the seventies into an ironic but staunch refusal to accept any personal blame for society's ills.

Such personal and social transformations have been skillfully explored over the last twenty years by cultural critic and social historian Barbara Ehrenreich, who has served as a gadfly both to a socially anesthetized American right and to a demoralized and sometimes self-serving American Left, notably in her book *Fear of Falling: The Inner Life of the Middle Class* (1989).

Ehrenreich has also developed a reputation for the occasional essay, and *The Worst Years of Our Lives: Irreverent Notes from a Decade of Greed* (Pantheon, 1990) is a rich collection of her pungent social analysis and cultural criticism. Addressing a wide range of topics, including "classism," cultural consumerism, and Yuppiedom, her essays are informed by a resonant feminism and nondogmatic democratic socialism. And although Ehrenreich is dead serious about her commitments, she doesn't take herself too seriously.

In the first essay, "Spudding Out," she addresses the culture of television, which has produced that passive recipient of the beams emanating from the square tube, the so-called couch potato. There is, Ehrenreich says, an arresting contradiction at the heart of this phenomenon, for "when you watch television, you will see people doing many things . . . (but) you will never see people watching television." Thus "we love television, because television brings us a world in which television does not exist."

In "Premature Pragmatism" she addresses the surrender of idealism on the part of Ivy League college students in exchange for a realism about the world that translates into lucrative salaries in supposedly comfortable careers. But for these undergraduates, she wryly motes, "idealism" was "defined as an ordinary, respectable profession in the human services. 'Realism' meant plunging almost straight from prepubescence into the stone-hearted world of finance capitalism."

Addressing the fury and frustration that has attended our national drug crisis, Ehrenreich cuts right to the sources of our addictive behavior. "No street-corner crack dealer ever had a better line than the one Madison Avenue delivers at every commercial break: Buy now! Quick thrills! You deserve it! . . . Drug frenzy, we might as well acknowledge, is displaced rage at the consumer culture to which we are all so eagerly, morbidly addicted."

In "Liberals' Disappearing Act," written in 1986, two years before George Bush's presidential campaign made liberalism the "L" word, Ehrenreich displayed a prescient awareness of the right's agenda. "One of its most venerable themes," she explains, "is that real men don't get all hot and bothered by issues like poverty, inequality, or the nuclear threat; only women and wimps vote liberal."

"The Moral Bypass" is a sharp but sympathetic review of *Habits of the Heart,* in which Robert Bellah and others "attempt to assess the American character" and "find that we have, for the most part, lost the way but that the stuff of redemption lies around us, if we are only willing to give it a try." Wading through the book's rich description of the therapeutic mentality and depoliticized culture of the white middle class, Ehrenreich then lays her analytic hands on what for her is the troubling suggestion that religion will provide the glue of salvation, transcendent purpose and community for fragmented individuals.

The trouble with religion, Ehrenreich contends, besides its tendency toward bigotry and meanness, is that it reflects the very therapeutic mentality that the authors of *Habits of the Heart* lament. In religion's stead, she suggests, we should place an overlooked but resourceful alternative: socialism.

Ehrenreich's socialism is a viable alternative, she says, because it attempts to link private notions of decency and morality with the political economy. Moreover, socialism is desirable because it represents the only modern vision that reconciles individual desire with collective need.

The problem, though, is that the tension in the modern world between the ideals and practices of socialism is no less great than the tension that has prevailed between the ideals and practices of religion, particularly those of western Christianity. Perhaps it might be useful for Ehrenreich to explore the ground that democratic socialism shares with progressive religion. A variety of liberation theologies that attempt to link religious belief to democratic ideas and egalitarian practices, and more importantly, to the quest for meaning in life beyond sectarian and religious concerns, might add fruitfully to Ehrenreich's vision.

Although she casts herself an outsider in many senses—as woman, as democratic socialist, and as feminist—Ehrenreich's essays might have troubled themselves more about the ways in which she is also an insider, as a white woman and a relatively privileged intellectual. But in the main, her essays reflect the work of an engaged intellectual for whom mere description of the world, no matter how incisive, will not suffice. Her aim is to change the world, and her persuasive analyses of many of America's most difficult problems make a valuable contribution toward that end.

Notes

1. *Keep Hope Alive: Jesse Jackson's 1988 Presidential Campaign,* ed. Frank Clemente and Frank Watkins (Boston: South End Press, 1989).

2. William Grimshaw, *Bitter Fruit: Black Politics and the Chicago Machine 1931–1991* (Chicago: University of Chicago Press, 1992), pp. 167–96.

3. Ibid., pp. 197–224.

Part III

This Far by Faith: Black Religion

16

Mixed Blessings: Martin Luther King, Jr., and the Lessons of an Ambiguous Heroism

The establishment of a national holiday to honor the life and achievements of Martin Luther King, Jr., is a reason for critical celebration. Only the second American and the first African-American to be feted with this singular honor, the celebration of King's birthday is an occasion of national, religious, and racial significance. It acknowledges that King was the supreme embodiment of American citizenship and political engagement, the highest manifestation of the American religious genius, and the richest expression of the multifaceted character of the black experience in America.

On the other hand, the King birthday celebration also presents the danger of losing the challenging and uncomfortable dimensions of King's thought and life by romanticizing his career. The nature and scope of King's accomplishments, which center in nothing short of a specific revolution in how black people live and are perceived in American culture, inevitably invite historic embellishment and social myth. But neither a puerile romanticization of King as Safe Negro nor a caricatured mythologization of King as Great American Hero will do. King's life was too complex, his achievements too profound, and his thinking too provocative to warrant such naive responses. We must transcend such unrealistic assessments of King and concentrate on the substantive contributions of his life and thought.

An especially helpful and illuminating way to view King's life and justly assess his accomplishments is through a reflection upon the ethics and politics of hero celebration. This context permits us to examine the beneficial and harmful uses to which the King holiday may be put in creating or preserving images of King that avoid disturbing history or dodge painful truth. This context also provides a healthy framework in addressing recent revelations about King's character, including charges of plagiarism and womanizing. In this essay, I will examine some characteristics of heroism, exploring the ways it makes sense to call King a hero, treat two central tensions that arise in asserting that King's heroism is ambiguous, and briefly suggest that King's birthday is indeed worth celebrating.

In my brief examination of some characteristics of heroism, I do not intend to provide a theory of heroism or trace its varied genealogy. Rather, I will discuss heroism within the limits of existing understandings of the concept and then seek to apply them to King in analyzing the effects of hero worship on the ideals for which he gave his life.

In his work on George Washington, cultural critic and historian Gary Wills reminds us that hero worship "is a hard assignment for many people today—one they think they cannot fulfill, or should not. Hero worship is elitist. It reduces the science of history to mere biography, if not to anecdote. It suggests that individual talent is a more important force than large economic processes. . . . The attitude of many in our time is captured by Bertolt Brecht's Galileo, who says: 'Unhappy the land that needs a hero.' "[1] While Wills's larger point about the suspicion of many Americans toward hero worship may be valid, explaining the diminished field of activity over which heroism is spread, it is equally true that American hero worship is presently focused in two social spheres: competitive sports and the military.

Contemporary forms of American heroism are often displayed within the context of sports competition, where individual or team exploits are lauded for embodying particular virtues, skills, and mastery. For example, basketball heroes are often said to embody the virtues of rigorous habits of practice, expert skills of physical dexterity, and mastery of the overall complexity of their craft necessary to perform excellently and unselfishly in a team sport.

Military heroes, as well, figure prominently in the comparatively constricted sphere of heroism celebrated today. America's recent war in the Gulf shows how eager Americans are for clear embodiments of American values of national patriotism, personal valor, and sacrifice for the common good. That Generals Norman Schwarzkopf and Colin Powell are instant heroes testifies to the peculiar hunger of many Americans for reassurance about the integrity and rightness of this country's values and ways of life.

Perhaps this last point clearly demonstrates a telling feature of heroism: it is intimately related to ideals felt to be worthy of support because they say something important about national self-identity. Part of the difficulty in deciding upon a genuine and truly national hero is connected to the increasing diversity of American culture. Because of the bewildering pluralization of perspectives about what it means to be an American, growing dispute about what goods are worthy of pursuit, strong disagreement about how to measure various forms of moral and social excellence, and the unraveling of a unified concept of the public good, the virtuous as well as the heroic is subject to radical revision and heated debate. Occasionally, however, a person or movement so decisively captures the nation's imagination that a variety of Americans come to believe that their truest selves and deepest beliefs are embodied in the vision and life of that figure or movement. Such was the case for many Americans in relation to Martin Luther King, Jr., and the civil rights movement.

The civil rights movement provided a social context, cultural framework, and racial worldview for blacks and other similarly excluded Americans to argue for inclusion within the larger circle of privilege, rights, and status from which they had been socially and legally barred. Civil rights leaders and activists built upon the symbol systems of black religion, the resonant traditions of radical protest within black culture, and a progressive understanding of liberal democracy in articulating demands for equality, justice, and freedom. Because of this potent mix of elements, the civil rights movement had the advantage of appealing to specific values nourished within a black cultural cosmos, while linking them to the iconic structures, symbolic worldviews, and heroic values that undergirded much of American society. As symbolic representative of the civil rights movement, Martin Luther King, Jr., embodied the virtues of black religious culture and black traditions of protest, as well as the best impulses of Western liberal democracy.

On the other hand, King wove into his rhetorical and strategic tapestry threads of prophetic religious utterance and radical social criticism that sorely tested the limits of liberal tolerance of forces of fundamental social challenge and transformation. The fact that some state and national politicians who represent the forces of stasis and regression that King opposed are now in part responsible for presiding over the public rituals to commemorate his memory only attests to the ambiguous character of the heroism King embodies.

King figures prominently in a distinct line of social prophets whose ideals can sometimes only be truly honored by their remaining, in significant measure, outside of the totemic processes of official acceptance, which cloak their status as prophetic characters whose memory judges American moral practice. The ambiguity that surrounds King's memory is healthy because it creates suggestive tensions within the developing edifice of King worship and draws attention to those troubling aspects of King's thought that have the potential to shatter the rigid constructions of official truth.

In reflecting upon the ambiguity of King's heroism, it will be helpful to discuss some characteristics of heroism and explore how King can be usefully understood as an American hero. A heroic figure undeniably possesses the ability to substantially alter and influence the course of events because of her mix of personal traits, skills, talents, and visions. This definition, of course, rests on the distinction that Sidney Hook made between two types of persons who qualify as potential heroes. After defining the hero in history as "the individual to whom we can justifiably attribute preponderant influence in determining an issue or even whose consequences would have been profoundly different if he had not acted as he did," Hook describes the difference in "eventful" persons and "event-making" persons.[2]

> The *eventful* man in history is any man whose actions influenced subsequent developments along a quite different course than would have been followed if these actions had not been taken. The *event-making* man is an eventful man whose actions are the consequences of outstanding capacities of intelligence, will, and

> character rather than of accidents of position. This distinction tries to do justice to the general belief that a hero is great not merely in virtue of what he does but in virtue of what he is.[3]

By Hook's measure, King certainly qualifies as a genuine hero, as someone whose combination of talents, intelligence, and vision considerably altered the course of events. This does not mean that King was the only person in the civil rights movement who possessed high degrees of intelligence, discipline, and skill. Numerous participants in the civil rights movement exhibited extraordinary leadership ability and qualities, ranging from the ingenious strategic skills of Bayard Rustin, the penetrating philosophic skills of Bob Moses, the uncanny organizational skills and folk wisdom of Fannie Lou Hamer, and the creative nonviolent theory of James Lawson.[4] While others possessed sharper skills than King in particular areas, King possessed a unique ability to inspire masses and maintain the loyalty of an impressive host of talented men and women. Perhaps this was best expressed by Benjamin Mays when he wrote:

> It may be that only one man in ten million could have led the Montgomery boycott without that city exploding into one of the worst race riots in history. . . . If the Montgomery Improvement Association had chosen a person other than King to communicate the Negroes' grievances to the city fathers, Dr. King might have gone through life as a successful Baptist preacher and no more. His rare ability to lead and inspire the classes as well as the masses, in a crusade for social justice, might never have been called forth.[5]

Furthermore, it may be argued that the force of King's personality, intelligence, and gifts helped create the conditions for social change in regard to race relations. King thus exhibited what Hook meant in a further clarification of the eventful versus the event-making person.

> The event-making man, on the other hand, finds a fork in the historical road, but he also helps, so to speak, to create it. He increases the odds of success for the alternative he chooses by virtue of the extraordinary qualities he brings to bear to realize it. At the very least, he must . . . display exceptional qualities of leadership. It is the hero as event-making man who leaves the

positive imprint of his personality upon history—an imprint that is still observable after he has disappeared from the scene.[6]

As Lerone Bennett observed, King's ability to create the conditions that led to social transformation was clearly demonstrated in Birmingham, Alabama, where it is widely believed that the civil rights movement gained its greatest symbolic victory because of a highly publicized clash with Sheriff Bull Connors's violent tactics to repel the civil rights demonstrators.

> No leader, of course, can create an event the time is not prepared for. But the genius of the great leader lies precisely in his apprehension of what the times require and in carrying through in the teeth of great opposition an act that changes the times. In Birmingham, King approached that kind of greatness, creating the occasion of the "Negro Revolution" by an act almost everyone said was ill-timed and ill-chosen. Birmingham . . . was *chosen*, not stumbled upon. It was created by a man who knew exactly what he wanted and how much he would probably have to pay to get it.[7]

King was certainly a figure who often precipitated change through conscious, decisive action.

The hero, particularly the one who advances an agenda of trenchant social criticism and sweeping ethical reform, also possesses the ability to create a situation in which it is untenable to remain unchanged or unchallenged by the hero's vision of how things should be. The hero, in short compass, forces us to make moral choices. As James Hanigan says:

> One thing that makes the hero's course a precarious one is that the very nature of the hero's role in history requires the more ordinary among us to make choices. It is not simply a matter for us of liking or disliking, of admiring or ignoring the hero. Rather, we are forced to choose for or against the hero, for or against the vision, or dream, or message, or course of action the hero proposes to us. One hallmark of the hero's authenticity as a hero is precisely that he or she forces us to choose; we cannot remain indifferent to this presence among us, even if we would. For not to be with the hero is automatically to be against him or her.[8]

This aspect of heroism was quite evident in King's life. He constantly envisioned America as a work in progress, a nation constructed by the redemptive or destructive choices it would make about its moral and social future. In this regard, King was quintessentially American, placing the notion of experiment and pragmatic moral revisionism at the heart of his creed of American social life.

The primary impact of King's life and career may consist in the clarity he brought to the choices that Americans must make in "living out" the principal ideals of the American creed, particularly as embodied in the Constitution and the Declaration of Independence. King's genius and heroic stature derived from his adroit skill at pointing out the disintegration of the American Dream and dramatically portraying the distance between American ideals of justice and equality and its contradictory antidemocratic practices. But it was his willingness to die for American ideals that made King so dangerous, because he forced America to examine itself with the instruments of equality, justice, and social morality America claimed as its own. Because of this quality in King's leadership, we may concede that "the possibility for heroism in our time will be tempered by the ideals we propose to ourselves—a thing proved in the heroic age of civil rights, when Dr. King and many others suffered and died for the concept of equality we profess but have not lived up to."[9]

Moreover, King's martyrdom also linked him to other American heroic figures, like Abraham Lincoln and John and Robert Kennedy, whose deaths made them the subjects of national memory through eulogies and memorials, and gained them even greater status as the vehicles of American moral and social redemption. As Conrad Cherry perceptively notes in writing about Robert Kennedy's funeral, and by extension other funerals of national significance,

> In this funeral Americans joined in a sacred ceremony, the scope of which crossed denominational religious boundaries. Many citizens had participated in another such ceremony only a few weeks earlier at the funeral for Dr. Martin Luther King, Jr., and in still another only a few short years earlier at the funeral for President John F. Kennedy. American history is, in fact, replete with leaders who have been canonized in the national consciousness as exemplars of American ideals and as particular bearers of American's destiny under God. When those leaders have met

> their deaths they have become, in the national memory as well as in the ceremonies and speeches that surround their deaths, martyrs for the American cause, even in some cases redeemers.[10]

Equally important, heroism often enables ordinary people to make a critical difference in their social and personal existence by linking their lives to larger social goals and movements that embody the virtues to which they aspire. The ideals of equality, justice, and freedom had for so long been uttered in public discourse and written in the creeds of American society and had in varying degrees been realized for particular segments of American culture. But freedom, equality, and justice often remained unrealized for many others, and King both envisioned how these ideals could be enfleshed and boldly envisioned how enormous obstacles to their realization could be overcome. In this scenario, the individual hero functions as an enabler for a group of people to rise above their limiting circumstances and participate in a drama of redemption, reconstruction, or transformation in which their roles, however small, are perceived as necessary and vital. Thus I will speak of this further when I discuss King's means of nonviolent transformation.

But the hero also looks to the group for insight and inspiration. Indeed, the group often serves a heroic function itself, engaging in what Max Weber called social heroism:

> Max Weber claimed that the Reformation and the attendant rise of capitalism were the last examples of middle class heroism. He is not alluding by this to the highly individualized gallantry of a John Wayne. Heroism for Weber is a social act. It occurs when a group of people no longer simply stand up for the system, but stand out against it. They critique the present and act to reclaim control over the future. The bourgeoisie of the Reformation era changed the circumstances of their existence and freed themselves from the dominance of aristocratic, social, political, and economic structures.[11]

In this scenario, the hero often functions to recall great past deeds as the basis for present and future action by masses of people. King understood this, and acted on it.

But the prospect of King's heroism becomes more problematic as we reflect on why he is presently being officially canonized, while near the end of his life he was roundly dismissed as a hopeless romantic and an irrelevant idealist. What was the real nature of King's achievements? In this section, I want to explore the nature of King's genius, and then proceed to address two tensions that further reinforce the ambiguity of King's heroism. Although King possessed many gifts, I think his genius lay in his moral vision and the choice of nonviolent means in attempting to achieve equality and real democracy for black Americans.

The idea that Martin Luther King was a man of moral vision raises questions about the nature of moral arguments, the particular content of moral statements, and the proper adjudication of competing moral claims. In our day, simply put, morality has fallen on hard times. This difficulty, though, does not absolve us of the responsibility to engage our every energy and resource in clarifying what we mean by morality and advancing a moral vision. King was willing, and able, to perform such a task. In fact, the historical conditions under which he and his comrades labored elicited from King and the civil rights movement a moral vision to guide and regulate its tasks and purposes.

Although King's moral vision may be variously conceived, I think, for my present purposes, it may be helpfully viewed in the following two ways. First, King's moral vision was not the work of one man. It expressed the hopes and aspirations of a long tradition of confrontation with and critical reflection upon the existential and social circumstances of black people in America. King did not invent or discover, but rather inherited, the imperative to rectify the evils of racism and impoverishment embedded in the legal, social, political, economic, and religious structures of American society.

King was the son, grandson, and great-grandson of Baptist preachers, so the very texture of his life from birth was religious and spiritual. He was reared under the powerful preaching of his father, the Rev. Martin Luther King, Sr., pastor of the Ebeneezer Baptist Church of Atlanta, Georgia. Martin Luther King, Jr., attended Morehouse College and came under the influence of, among others, the late Dr. Benjamin Elijah Mays, president of Morehouse and Dr. George Kelsey, who is now professor emeritus at Drew University. These men, both scholar-preachers, provided for King the paradigm of ministry as an intellectually respectable, socially engaged, and emotionally satisfying vocation. At nineteen Martin was ordained to the ministry and became associate pastor of Ebeneezer, and later its copastor, after serving six years as the pastor of Dexter Avenue Baptist Church in Montgomery, Alabama.

Given this background, King was firmly rooted in the institution that lies at the heart of Afro-American life, the black church. Throughout their history religion has been and remains the central ordering influence upon the vast majority of Americans of African descent. Albert Raboteau, in his ground-breaking work on the religion of Afro-American slaves, titled *Slave Religion,* writes,

> "Black religious institutions have been the foundation of Afro-American culture. An agency of social control, a source of economic cooperation, an arena for political activity, a sponsor of education, and a refuge in a hostile white world, the black church has been historically the social center of Afro-American life."[12]

From its inception the black church identified racism (whether embedded in vicious slavery or embodied in white Christianity's segregationist ethos) as a heinous sin, and resolved to make its extirpation a primary goal of the black church's existence. The black church message that all people are children of God and that everyone deserves to be treated with decency and respect found ample application in King's moral vision. The notion in the black church that God sides with the oppressed, as God sided with Israel against Egyptian bondage, inspired King's actions and was a central part of his moral vision, as reflected in his belief that Afro-Americans had "cosmic companionship" in the struggle for liberation.

The Afro-American religious notion of loving and praying for one's enemies, despite their decadence, hate, or brutality, had a strong affinity with the Gandhian philosophy of nonviolence as a teaching, technique, and lifestyle that King ardently preached and assiduously practiced. The black church understanding that all people, regardless of social standing, educational attainment, political sophistication, or cultural refinement, are equal heirs to God's promises found expression in King's concept of the beloved community where black and white, rich and poor, and powerful and powerless would be united in peace and harmony.

In these and many more significant ways King was organically linked to the living tradition of Afro-American religion. One aspect of King's genius was his ability to project this profoundly Afro-American religious sensibility into the American sociopolitical ethos and employ it as a base from which to argue for and, to a degree, effect social, political, and economic transformation.

This ability reflects the second characteristic of King's moral vision: it countered the narrow exclusivism of a vulgar patriotism and put forward a creative reinterpretation of America's central political concepts and documents. King's moral hermeneutic understood these concepts generally in relation to American moral improvement and specifically in relation to Afro-American freedom and liberation. In short, King appealed to the very documents that are central to American civil life—the Constitution, the Declaration of Independence—and pointed out their basis for a moral understanding and interpretation of concepts like equality, justice, and freedom. Furthermore, he employed these documents as a yardstick to judge the actual attainment by American society of the goals, norms, and ideals they articulated.

Not only, then, does King's moral vision have a religious moment, but it extends itself into the national civic realm, constituting its political moment. King's moral vision was predicated upon, in part, what he understood to be the best in American religious, civil, legal, social, and political history. He deemed his moral vision to be commensurate with American historic and national goals set forth in the Constitution and the Declaration of Independence, which help regulate American ideas about issues like freedom, justice, and equality.

In fact, in his famous "I Have A Dream" speech, King clearly stated that his dream was "deeply rooted in the American dream."[13] When King confronted the massive and abusive legal, social, and political structures that thwarted the materialization of Afro-American freedom, justice, and equality in any concrete sense, he appealed to these documents in calling for the realization of the norms and ideals they espoused. King said in Washington, "I have a dream that one day this nation will rise up and live out the true meaning of its creed, 'We hold these truths to be self-evident that all men are created equal.' "[14]

King believed, despite the fact that black people were slaves when this creed was written, that any fair-minded interpreter would be bound to enlarge its vision of liberty and equality to include all people. The principles articulated in the Constitution and the Declaration of Independence struck an authentic chord of truth for King that could not be nullified even by the shortsightedness of their original authors in regard to people of color. These documents provided a substantial foundation for American society to accord all people the status of persons with rights. King stated: "When the architects of our Republic wrote the magnificent words of the Constitution and the Declaration of Independence, they were signing a promissory note to which every American was to fall heir. This note was the promise that all men, yes black men as well as white men, would be guaranteed the unalienable rights of life, liberty and the pursuit of happiness."[15]

King refused to permit the interpretation of democracy, liberty, justice, and freedom to be monopolized by those who would truncate and distort the understanding of American history and ideals. King refused to allow either the overt barbarity of bigoted segregationists like the Ku Klux Klan and the White Citizens Council or the covert but no less pernicious racism of prejudiced politicians to define democracy. On the rhetorical battleground of American public ideology, King wrested from them the prerogative of describing and defining what is authentically American, and in the process transformed the terms of American political and civil discourse. Martin Luther King's moral vision, then, which was rooted in Afro-American religion and which advanced a creative American moral hermeneutic, was a powerful and often persuasive means for structuring a protest movement to secure basic rights for black Americans.

Another way of accounting for King's heroic character and genius is his insistence on militant nonviolence as the means of obtaining freedom, justice, and equality for black people. King's advocacy of militant nonviolence was important for two interrelated reasons. First, it appealed to the African-American religious heritage of black culture, while linking that heritage to other powerful models of resistance and social transformation. Second, it presumed the heroic character of everyday black folk to resist evil and located transformative agency within their grasp.

King's advocacy of nonviolence was deeply anchored in an African-American religious ethic of love that promoted the fundamental dignity of all creatures because of their relationship to a loving, all-powerful God. As I have already indicated, norms and values developed in the black church influenced King's theological ideals, but they also shaped his strategies of social reform and his beliefs about human potential for progress and change. What is crucial for the African-American religious ethic of love in relation to nonviolent means to attain social, economic, and political freedom is that in King's worldview, nonviolence was a *way of life* and not simply a strategy of social transformation.

This distinction is key to understanding how King maintained a consistent moral stance toward various forms of violence, including war and domestic policies that reinforced poverty and classism. King saw nonviolent resistance to oppressive social structures, policies, and persons as a means of acquiring basic necessities such as food, clothing, and shelter, as well as being the only viable and ethically legitimate way to obtain freedom, justice, and equality. Although the destruction of racism was a major goal of African-American nonviolent resistance, it was only one goal of the nonviolent lifestyle. As King matured politically, he began to expand his field of moral vision to include classism, poverty, and militarism as legitimate objects of social protest. He believed that conceiving of nonviolence as both a lifestyle and a means of resisting a variety of social and moral problems was consonant with the affirmation of life, liberty, and equality in the black religious experience.

But King's advocacy of nonviolence was also the result of disciplined study of its applications in a variety of national, social, and moral contexts. He examined the principled resistance to taxpaying advocated by Henry David Thoreau, as well as his seminal essay on civil disobedience. It is widely known that King also diligently studied the principles, methods, and lifestyle of Mohandas Gandhi, whose "experiments with truth" had a powerful impact on King's thinking. Gandhi's leadership of millions of Indians to resist the systemic social oppression of British colonialism inspired King to adapt Gandhi's methods of nonviolent resistance to American society.

Second, King's advocacy of nonviolence presumed the heroic character of everyday black people. Although this presumption contained romantic notions of black self-identity, it also located forms of transformative agency within the grasp of often powerless ordinary black folk. It is important to remember that at the beginning of the civil rights movement the lot of everyday black people remained even more circumscribed by the forces of segregation, race hatred, and class inequality from which the black middle class had only occasionally, and precariously, escaped. The civil rights movement provided an enormous boost to the self-identity of black people who had long believed that they were relatively powerless to change their condition.

However, Cornel West points out that King's presumption that black people could wield nonviolence as a means to social liberation contained a romantic notion of superiority over other racial groups, particularly white Americans. West also contends that King's doctrine of nonviolence

> tends to assume tacitly that Afro-Americans have acquired, as a result of their historical experience, a peculiar capacity to love their enemies, to endure patiently suffering, pain, and hardship and thereby "teach the white man how to love" or "cure the white man of his sickness." King seemed to believe that Afro-Americans possess a unique proclivity for nonviolence, more so than do other racial groups, that they have a certain bent toward humility, meekness, and forbearance, hence are quite naturally disposed toward nonviolent action. In King's broad overview, God is utilizing Afro-Americans—this community of caritas (other-directed love)—to bring about "the blessed community." . . . The self-image fostered . . . is defensive in character and romantic in content.[16]

While I think West's assessment is just, there is another dimension to King's assumption that must not be overlooked: his belief in the moral heroism of black people also assumed that the power to affect their destiny and to exercise transformative moral agency was achievable by ordinary black folk. Like that of Marcus Garvey before him and Malcolm X during his own day, the genius of King resided in the ability to appeal to his followers' heroic potentials by placing strict demands on their shoulders, challenging them to live up to a standard of moral excellence that neither they nor their opponents realized they possessed. King believed that black people could muster the resources they already had at their disposal, such as moral authority and a limited but significant economic base, to foster legitimate claims to social goods like education, housing, and enfranchisement.

Moreover, the standards of moral excellence that King expected through disciplined participation in nonviolent demonstrations, which included rites of self-examination and purification, were of inestimable worth not only in fighting for denied social privileges and rights, but in the healthy enlargement of crucial narratives of racial self-esteem. King understood the virtues of "everyday forms of resistance," and appealed to the "weapons of the weak" in opposing unjust social forces.[23]

While the above discussion specifies how it makes sense to call King a hero, now I want to explore two tensions that flow from the assertion of King's ambiguous heroism, which may be summed up in the following way: while King's contributions were heroic and significant, many African-Americans, particularly the working poor and the underclass, still suffer in important ways; and while King deserves great honor and praise of a particular sort, he is indebted to traditions of African-American religious protest, social criticism, and progressive democracy.

It must be conceded that despite the significant basic changes that King helped bring about, the present status of poor black Americans in particular presents little cause for celebration. Their situation does not mean that King's achievements were not substantial. Rather it reflects the deep structures of persistent racism and classism that have not yet yielded to sustained levels of protest and resistance.

In order to judge King's career, we must imagine what American society would be for blacks without his historic achievements. Without basic rights to vote, desegregated public transportation and accommodations, equal housing legislation, and the like, American society would more radically reflect what Gunnar Myrdal termed the American Dilemma. King and other participants in the civil rights movement wrought heroic change, but that change was a partial movement toward real liberation.

If it was once believed that King's vision was only a beginning, a mere foot in the door of civil rights, political empowerment, and economic equality, the tragic reality now is that the door has been shut fast in the face of many Afro-Americans. This is displayed particularly in two areas: the persistence of racism and the disintegration of postindustrial urban life.

It is fair to say that a climate of hostility has been generated toward those who assert that this country has not achieved the ideals of freedom, justice, and equality in any significant structural manner, as envisioned by the mature Martin Luther King, Jr. The early Martin Luther King was preoccupied with securing inclusion in American society as it is, without questioning the means by which wealth is distributed; without probing the mechanisms that determine privilege, prestige, and status; and without challenging the growing classism that shattered the notion of a monolithic black community.

The mature Martin Luther King, Jr., however, understood that economic injustice was just as great an impediment to black liberation as racial injustice. As I will show later, King's mature career was spent in attempting to draw out the implications of a coalition politics that transcended race to speak of economic injustice and class oppression. His Poor People's March was the first real attempt to enact a coalition politics that bound together the interests of various marginalized groups, including Latinos, poor blacks and whites, and peace activists.

Part of King's great frustration resulted from the fact that racism was much more complex and multifaceted than he realized at the beginning of his career, and he sought to educate himself and his colleagues about the structural, socially embedded nature of institutional racism and the structural nature of class oppression. This accounts in part for how we can claim that King's contributions were heroic while acknowledging that they were neither perfect nor permanent. Some of the gains King helped secure were structurally permanent, such as legally desegregated public housing and transportation. Other gains must be continually ratified by law, such as the civil rights bill, which must be renegotiated through legislation. Moreover, the logic of racial progress is subject to perennial reexamination and justification.

The project to make King a particular sort of hero has often presented a picture of completion and satisfaction with regard to the structural obstacles to African-American racial progress. However, a suggestive and subversive side of King's heroism views him as an iconic figure who inspires continued battle to implement the goals and dreams for which he gave his life. It is consistent to suggest that although the general perception of blacks has changed, the actual legal barriers to social mobility have been removed, and particular categories of blacks have made substantial gains economically, King's life equally symbolizes the continued battle for the truly disadvantaged, the ghetto poor. It is heroic in a distinctly Kingian sense to resist official efforts at King canonization that both whitewash actual racial history and deny the work that remains, and to support the belief that much more progress must be made before real liberation can be achieved.

To suggest this, however, is to counter the self-image of the reigning political view of things that is the framework of contemporary conservative and liberal American sociopolitical ideology. Conservative political thought as construed here maintains that the struggle for black self-determination is largely over and that sufficient energy has been devoted to the eradication of racism in American life. Liberal political thought, even when it acknowledges the continuing expression of certain forms of racial and economic inequality, rarely effectively examines the reasons for their malignant persistence.

The predominant political ideology shrinks space for radical dissent and marginalizes, absorbs, or excludes voices asserting that the American condition is in terrible disarray. In short, the ideological horizon and sociopolitical landscape have been dominated by conservative and liberal visions that constitute political realism, effectively preventing radical alternatives to their often mundane and pedestrian achievements.

Conservative ideology and politics have the effect of both offering limited and narrowly conceived options to Afro-American suffering and ensuring the continued hegemony of white, upper-middle-class politics. Liberal alternatives, while certainly an improvement, are nevertheless plagued by an inability to move beyond a provincial vision of what economic and political measures are necessary to better Afro-American life. Liberalism attends to symptoms rather than to root causes.

The tragic reality of the Afro-American condition is that, while in many respects blacks are certainly better off, in other respects many blacks continue to suffer. For instance, the disintegration of the moral, economic, and civic fabric of poor black communities is stunning and entails lethal social consequences. The arising of a subculture of crime, which thrives on the political economy of crack, is threatening to destroy the inner city. Also the gentrification of black urban living space means that inner-city residents are being squeezed out of marginal neighborhoods by an escalating tax rate that forces the working poor into even poorer neighborhoods.

Poverty, for example, affects black people in an especially pernicious manner. Since the 1970s, there has been an enormous increase in poverty in America. In 1970, 14.9 percent of all children were poor. Today the figure is almost 21 percent. For minorities, it is even worse. Two out of every five Hispanic children are poor, and almost one out of every two black children is poor. For black children under six, the poverty rate is a record high 51.1 percent. There is a continually widening gap between the wealthy and the poor in America, and this year it is the highest ever since the Census Bureau began collecting statistics in 1947. Last year, two-fifths of the population received 67 percent of all national income, the highest ever recorded. The poorest two-fifths, on the other hand, received only 15.7 percent of all income, the lowest ever recorded. Even worse, one-third of all black America remains below the poverty line.[17]

Another factor that has contributed to the current condition of black America for the better part of the eighties is the legacy of the Reagan era. The Reagan administration symbolized, and ominously expressed, a new breed of racism, generating policies pervaded by subtle forms of discrimination and prejudice that have had a devastating impact on black America. The Reagan administration's laissez-faire attitude toward the enforcement of laws and governmental policies that protect minorities and its outright attack on the hard-won rights of America's poor and dispossessed helped set the tone for an almost unmitigated viciousness toward these groups.[18] The Reagan years have fueled a subversive shift in the modus operandi of American racism. Often no longer able to openly express racial hatred through barbaric deeds, racists have found subtle and insidious forms of expression.

This racism not only is evident in upper-middle-class America, with its staunchly conservative values and sensibilities that problematize Afro-American progress, and in the white working and underclass, with its tightly turfed communities that cling to racial and ethnic identification as a means of exclusion and survival (e.g., Howard Beach and Bensonhurst),[19] but it also has, in a cruelly ironic twist, engendered a new reactionary group of black neoconservative political and intellectual figures. This group rejects civil rights as a means to black progress and naively contends that such measures as affirmative action cripple rather than aid black freedom by creating negative stereotypes about inferior black performance in education and employment. All of this suggests the deep dimensions of our current crisis.

The second tension in regard to King's heroism rests on the fact that, although his achievements merit praise and honor, those accomplishments are related to a larger tradition of African-American protest, as well as traditions of liberal democracy. For instance, the King holiday reminds us that by celebrating King's life and career in particular, America celebrates the profound accomplishments of black America in general. This recognition offers to American intellectual life the vital resources of a living Afro-American intellectual tradition that can continue to inform, challenge, and even transform American discourse about race, class, justice, freedom, and equality. More specifically, since, as I have stated above, King's life was developed and shaped in the ethos of a black church worldview and since the locus classicus of his moral vision was the Afro-American religious experience, our attention is redirected back to that experience as a crucial resource for the maintenance and extension of King's moral vision, in alliance with other progressive sociopolitical, historical, and economic thought.

Indeed, the notion that King himself was the producer, not the product, and the cause, not the effect, of Afro American libera tion potentials that had been long latent, and at times vitally visible, in the fabric of our national experience is entirely alien to King's thought. Although he believed historical forces, under the direction of a demanding but loving providence, had arranged his ascension to a leadership position, he always believed that he articulated what many black people thought, knew, and held to be true. King obviously understood that he was the voice for a protest movement that had been growing for a long while and that had finally gathered the strength to resist the cumulative evils visited upon black people by the apartheid-like conditions in the American South. In fact, in speaking about the experience that initially catapulted him into international fame, King wrote:

> When I went to Montgomery, Alabama, as a pastor in 1954, I had not the slightest idea that I would later become involved in a crisis in which nonviolent resistance would be applicable. After I had lived in the community about a year, the bus boycott began. The Negro people of Montgomery, exhausted by the humiliating experiences that they had constantly faced on the buses, expressed in a massive act of noncooperation their determination to be free. They came to see that it was ultimately more honorable to walk the streets in dignity than ride the buses in humiliation. At the beginning of the protest the people called on me to serve as their spokesman.[20]

The recognition that King was part of a larger tradition disallows America to escape its obligation to those King represented by relegating his thought to the fixed and static past. Instead, it forces America to critically engage and constantly examine the dynamic contemporary expressions of the thought and practices emerging from the tradition that birthed and buttressed King.

Furthermore, the need for a reinvigorated moral vision can only be immediately strengthened by portraying the explicit relationship among King, the civil rights movement, and the most recent and powerful popular expression of the Afro-American intellectual and religious tradition: the Jackson campaigns for president. No honest and complete assessment of the movements and forces made possible by King's and his comrades' achievements can be performed without mention of the Jackson candidacy. The Jackson campaigns, which have already in a fundamental way transformed the shape and contours of modern American politics, were made possible by a host of historical ingredients, not the least of which was the tradition of sociopolitical insurgency stimulated by the Afro-American religious tradition and the civil rights movement.

The Jackson campaigns in part enact a profound transformation in the ideas we inherit from the mature Martin Luther King. They underscore the need for a transition from an initial emphasis on civil rights to an appreciation of issues of class and economic inequality.[21] Thus the relationship between King and Jackson, as participants in the same tradition and in active pursuit of the goals of economic empowerment, racial harmony, and universal justice, regulated by a vision developed in an Afro-American religious perspective, must not be lost as we celebrate King's birthday.

Indeed, as we celebrate his birthday we must exercise extreme caution in retrieving images of King, especially those that avoid the painful truth of recent revelations about King's character. The latter includes charges that King plagiarized portions of his dissertation, that he was a womanizer, and that he possibly physically abused a woman the night before his death. In the face of these revelations, how can we proceed celebrating King's life?

First, it is important to remember that the celebration of King's achievements is not predicated upon a notion of human perfection. Before these revelations, it was well known that King was a great but flawed human being. He admitted on several occasions his own guilt over sexual indiscretions and pledged to remedy his infidelity with all the strength to resist temptation that lay in him. King's obvious recognition of his finitude and limitation serve as a worthy model of emulation for us as we seek to celebrate his moral legacy of protest for civil and social rights. But his legacy of self-examination, admission of fault, and the attempt to concretely rectify the wrong, even if it is not always successfully done, is a model we can usefully incorporate as responsible and mature moral agents.

Second, the charges of King's alleged plagiarism are disturbing and inexcusable. To use someone else's written work without proper recitation is a form of verbal thievery. This painful truth, however, forces us to raise even more questions about why it occurred. Since we cannot question King, we can only surmise, infer, and speculate. King's dissertation was completed while he was pastoring his first church in Montgomery and during the beginning of the Montgomery bus boycott. Undoubtedly, the pressures of the burgeoning movement tempted King to plagiarize Jack Boozer's dissertation in order to complete his own doctoral studies.

Moreover, although many black scholars had passed through Boston University's doctoral program in religion, one peculiar and tragic legacy of racism involved the pernicious self-doubts that could have plagued any developing black scholar. Qualities of self-worth, competence, talent, and skill are not developed in a vacuum, but are in part socially constructed and reproduced. In the mid-fifties it is certainly conceivable that a young talented black doctoral student who was uncertain of his real worth, despite the encouragement of professors and colleagues, and who was faced with an unpredictable and unfolding social crisis, could be tempted to rely on work that had already been accepted and viewed as competent.

The best approach to these charges, as well as charges about King's possible physical abuse, can be made by developing a healthy and realistic framework of assessment of King's life and career that will remain consistent even in the event of other revelations about his person and character. The power of King's achievements, the real force of his genius, consisted in his passion for justice to be done for the most lowly and oppressed inhabitants of American society. His moral authority as a spokesperson for truth, equality, and the embodiment of a particular slant on the American Dream cannot be compromised by revelations about his personal and student life.

What these revelations do achieve, however, is a sad reminder of the forces of wrong and dishonor by which we are all subject to be tempted and corrupted. King serves as a reminder that no figure establishes an Archimedean point of moral perfection from which to argue for social change, that all argument for transformation is immanent criticism rooted in the faults and limitations of being human, but those limitations do not ultimately destroy the truth for which limited and faulty humans stand. Although the vehicle for that truth is tarnished, enough of the truth's power and persuasion can emerge to convince others of its necessity and worth. We must view King in such a realistic fashion. These revelations show that King was an enormously complex human being, confirming what we know of him as we study his ideological evolutions and his political maturation.

As has been much remarked on, toward the end of his life King began to discern inadequacies in his former analyses of racial antipathy, social injustice, and economic inequality. He discovered that these problems were much more deeply rooted and structurally expressed than he had initially surmised.

As a result he focused his considerable critical skills on the larger national and international economic, political, and social contexts of Afro-Americans', and other oppressed people's, plight. King began to speak about the redistribution of resources, guaranteed incomes for the poor, and forming a multiracial coalition of the unemployed and the poor. This signified his changing perspective. In an article written just before his assassination and published after it, King wrote:

> We call our demonstration a campaign for jobs and income because we feel that the economic question is the most crucial that black people, and poor people generally, are confronting. . . . We need an economic bill of rights. This would guarantee a job to all people who want to work and are able to work. It would also guarantee an income for all who are not able to work. . . . I hope that a specific number of jobs is set forth, that a program will emerge to abolish unemployment, and that there will be another program to supplement the income of those whose earnings are below the poverty level.[22]

King had already begun to speak out against the war in Vietnam, decrying the lamentable manner in which resources for the poor were being pilfered by an ever-increasing war chest. He was criticized within the civil rights movement for squandering its social influence and political capital with the Johnson administration. He was attacked outside the movement for delving, even "meddling," into larger domestic and foreign affairs that were not the legitimate concern of a civil rights leader.

King's moral vision, however, could not abide the spurious schizophrenia that compartmentalized moral concern into distinct and separable spheres. Morality was of a piece to King, and his moral vision was integrated and unified. The whole of life fell under its searching purview and rigorous scrutiny. King's later efforts to unite poor blacks, whites, and other minorities, as well as labor and other progressive concerns, marked him as a highly dangerous man who was greatly feared in many governmental, political, and social quarters.

These facts must be recalled as we engage in the rituals of remembrance and rites of recovery of the meaning of King's moral vision. We must refuse those who would commodify King's career into acceptable packages of comfortable, and not dangerous, memory, to be consumed by the American public in the name of a mythologization project intent on subverting King's radical and disturbing memory. In short, we must engage in hermeneutical combat and interpretive warfare over the future of King's memory, making certain that the custodians of the King canon include and remember his provocative words and oppositional ideas, as well as his comforting thoughts and hopeful beliefs. Martin Luther King, Jr., was a man who possessed a profound moral vision that was rooted in the Afro-American religious experience and that advanced a creative American moral hermeneutic. Remembering his life and thought challenges us to examine the present condition of American moral life and discover it wanting in regard to its treatment of those King represented: the black, the poor, and the oppressed.

Construed in the above manner, King's birthday serves as an outpost in progressive terrain, creating space in which to collect the energies of protest and struggle as they are related to the visionary revival and recovery of the moral tradition within which King lived and labored. King Day can facilitate a broadly conceived coalition of the oppressed and suffering who have a desperate interest in recovering the symbol and substance of King's moral vision.

Celebrating Martin Luther King's birthday as an official holiday promises a poignant and profound change in the rhythm of public rituals commemorating events of ultimate national and historical significance. King Day structures in the recurring cycle of American holidays a period of time that concentrates attention upon the meaning of King's life and thought. It also extends beyond King, transcending his personal and individual meaning, and celebrates the ingenuity of black survival in an American political, social, and cultural ethos often inimical to Afro-American existence.

King Day also points us back to that Afro-American religious tradition that produced King and that continues to thrive in the midst of American religious, social, and political life. It also provides a means of reconstituting King's moral vision by challenging us each year to more closely approximate in our national and individual life and thought the goals and purposes for which he gave his life. In this sense, the name Martin Luther King, Jr., no longer merely represents the time and place of his life and body on earth, but symbolizes the hope of oppressed people everywhere that the dignity and worth of human life will be universally respected and uplifted.

Notes

1. Gary Wills, *Cincinnatus: George Washington and the Enlightenment* (Garden City, N.Y.: Doubleday, 1984), p. 109.

2. Sidney Hook, *The Hero in History: A Study in Limitation and Possibility* (New York: John Day, 1943), p. 153.

3. Ibid., p. 154.

4. For a good social characterization of the figures who surrounded King in the civil rights movement, see Taylor Branch's commanding social history, *Parting the Waters: America in the King Years, 1955–1963* (New York: Simon & Schuster, 1989).

5. This quote is from Benjamin Mays's introduction to Lerone Bennett, *What Manner of Man: A Biography of Martin Luther King, Jr.* (Chicago: Johnson, 1976), p. ii.

6. Hook, *The Hero in History*, p. 157.

7. Bennett, *What Manner of Man*, p. 131.

8. James P. Hanigan, *Martin Luther King, Jr., and the Foundations of Nonviolence* (New York: University Press of America, 1984), pp. 31–32.

9. Wills, *Cincinnatus*, p. 132.

10. Conrad Cherry, *God's New Israel: Religious Interpretations of American Destiny* (Englewood Cliffs, N.J.: Prentice-Hall, 1971), p. 6.

11. Paul G. King, Kent Maynard, and David O. Woodyard, *Risking Liberation: Middle Class Powerlessness and Social Heroism* (Atlanta, Ga.: John Knox Press, 1988), p. 15.

12. Albert J. Raboteau, *Slave Religion* (New York: Oxford University Press, 1978), p. iv.

13. Martin Luther King, Jr., "I Have A Dream," in *A Testament of Hope: The Essential Writings of Martin Luther King, Jr.*, ed. James Melvin Washington (New York: Harper & Row, 1986), p. 219.

14. Ibid., p. 219.

15. Ibid., p. 217.

16. Cornel West, *Prophesy Deliverance! An Afro-American Revolutionary Christianity* (Philadelphia: Westminster, 1982), pp. 74–75.

17. These Census Bureau figures are usually reported on annually by Robert Greenstein in *Christianity and Crisis*. For a good example of such reporting, see John Bickerman and Robert Greenstein, "High and Dry on the Poverty Plateau," *Christianity and Crisis*, October 28, 1985, pp. 411–12.

18. For example, the Supreme Court is now, in effect, "Reagan's Court," due to Reagan's appointees, who legally enact his conservative political agenda. For commentary on how the Supreme Court has turned back the clock on affirmative action, see my "Deaffirmation," *Nation*, July 3, 1989, pp. 4–5.

19. For a brief exploration of racism in both segments of society, see my article "The Two Racisms," *Nation*, July 3, 1989, pp. 4–5.

20. Washington, ed., *Testament of Hope*, p. 38.

21. Roger Hatch describes the relation between the perspective of the mature Martin Luther King, Jr., and Jackson's vision for America, and addresses Jackson's evolution into the second phase of the civil rights movement, which concentrates on equity in every area of life (particularly economic justice), in *Beyond Opportunity: Jesse Jackson's Vision for America* (Philadelphia: Fortress Press, 1988), esp. pp. 11–23.

22. Washington, ed., *Testament of Hope*, pp. 67, 70.

23. These terms refer to the important works of James Scott. See especially *Domination and the Arts of Resistance* (New Haven: Yale University Press, 1990).

Improvisation

Martin's Death, and Ours?

The death of Martin Luther King, Jr., on April 4, 1968, when I was nine years old, was the death of my innocence. Of all the events that have shaken my world, few have conspired so radically to alter the shape and content of my awareness as this event. Writ large on my mind, it came as a verdict: "You are no longer innocent, you are condemned to awareness."

I was sitting on the living room floor watching television, when suddenly a news bulletin interrupted the regular program. The newsman's voice, usually a lesson in impeccable cadence and inflection, now dragged in somber monotone. "Martin Luther King, Jr., has just been shot in Memphis, Tennessee," he managed. Behind me, sitting in his favorite chair, my father offered a seemingly involuntary response. His hurting "humh" summed up the whole mater in one word. Ejaculated in the midst of strained disbelief and shock, that "humh" became an unknowing utterance of eventual grief. My father's reaction gathered into its dismal tone told the horror black America felt about the loss of this black prophet. King's mellifluous baritone voice was stilled by a piece of metal that traveled with ungodly speed and precision to explode its message of death inside his neck.

After a few words by the newsman suggesting that Martin was not dead, but seriously wounded, that he was shot on a hotel balcony (an unholy shrine to the senseless murder of our dreams and hopes), the television permitted us to hear what became Martin's last speech. "I just want to do God's will," King declared. "And He's allowed me to go up to the mountain. And I've looked over. And I've se-e-n the promised land." The audience, now sensing the imminent climax of Martin's powerful speech, swelled its chorus of vocal support, perforating his oration with shouts of "Yes, sir, oh yes! Go ahead, yes, doctor." "And I'm happy tonight," Martin continued, he and his audience now united in a spiritual, almost mystical bond. "I'm not worried about anything. I'm not fearing any man. 'Mine eyes have seen the glory of the coming of the Lord.' "

The audience on film, and in my heart, responded with thunderous applause to this powerfully persuasive ebony seer whose words were crammed with the pathos and poetry of the black American experience. After showing the film, the television resumed its regular program, but my attention had been completely diverted. I had been electrified. Even then, the hair on my limbs stood at attention when that voice like a trumpet blew a clarion call for freedom. His charisma was intoxicating, and I immediately felt fraternal sympathy and instant allegiance to the cause he so eloquently articulated. But, in a matter of moments, the newsman again broke faith with the printed program to announce the final tragedy: "Martin Luther King, Jr., has been assassinated at thirty-nine years old."

Martin's death was the traumatic climax to a period of harsh history for black Americans, especially in my birthplace, the alternately famed and infamous "Motor City," Detroit. The riot of the summer of '67 undermined the fragile peace that had marked the relationship between the black and white communities, a microcosmic reflection of the Kerner Commission's incisive report on America's divided society, one black, one white. Already sensitive to the tension and turmoil of the riot, Martin's death brought into sharp focus the repulsive reality whose bare outline had taken form for me in the anarchy of the riot: race is explosive, volatile in America. My cocoon was assaulted, and the butterfly of consciousness yanked from its sleepy rest in innocence. It was a painful awakening, but I was not alone in it. The same thing is suffered by all black people at one time or another.

Painful awakening is being forced upon us again, now in 1988, exactly twenty years since Martin's assassination. In the interval between King's death and the current conspicuous reappearance of racism of the last few years (Howard Beach, the Citadel, Forsyth County), a subversive shift in the modus operandi of American racism has taken place. Often, no longer able to express racial hatred openly through barbaric deeds, racists have found more subtle and insidious forms of expression. What's more, in a cruelly ironic twist, the success of the civil rights movement has been turned in on itself. An unfortunate consequence of the civil rights movement's commitment to vanquish every visible sign of racism is that racism has gone underground. A subterranean network of slippery attitudes, ambiguous actions, and unfixed, equivocal meanings, which can accommodate racist intent and concomitantly permit the semblance of racial fairness, operates in most segments of American society. Implicit in this is a colossal effort to deny racism's existence. Incidents like Howard Beach are explained away, on the basis of statistical infrequency, as aberrations from the norm of racial tranquility. Since little "concrete" evidence can be evinced to substantiate its existence, racism is supposed to be gone. Out of sight, out of mind. The whole matter is now ensconced in an obfuscating demand to provide sixties-style proof for eighties-style racism.

In times like these, what can Martin's death mean for us? The brilliant and beautiful dream he articulated with intelligent fire was almost dead before he was, maimed by the intransigent refusal of America to see his vision and heed his voice. And while the King holiday is extremely important, one can almost hear Martin warning us from his grave not to be seduced by the display of unity that his birthday celebration rallies, when for the rest of the year the acrimonious legacy of racial bigotry continues to pollute the air of common life in America. Martin understood that, often, the only reward for speaking the truth unadorned, for voicing the uncomfortable reality and painting the plain picture, is a bullet. But he also understood that his death could be redemptive only if it forced our nation to comprehend the idiocy of racial hatred, and only if it brought the liberation of Americans, black and white, one day nearer. Given our present circumstances, however, Martin's death is in danger of being banalized, flattened out by the forces of historical regression in regard to race.

The only way Martin's death can be rescued from the infamy of national neglect is for us to engage in the moral action of occupying our living, doing, and thinking with the goals and purposes for which he sacrificed his life. We must balance our quotidian quest for peace and sanity with the vibrant and persistent pursuit of cosmic love and justice. Otherwise, we subvert the redemptive meaning Martin believed could come with the loss of his life—and his death will become ours.

17

Martin and Malcolm

Martin Luther King, Jr., and Malcolm X are the towering icons of contemporary African-American culture. Of course, King has transcended the boundaries of race. His iridescent image has been seized upon to illumine an astonishing array of social projects—and commercial products—whose humanitarian pedigree is thought to be vouchsafed by symbolic solidarity with an American hero. But the international fame and nearly universal respect he now commands have not diminished his appeal among common black people who will never know either. Millions of black homes continue to display portraits of King, his graceful humility radiating a perennial blessing to their domestic space. For many blacks, King's progressive civil protest, in which American ideals of justice engendered civil disobedience and social compromise, has become the definitive model for social transformation.

But for a generation of black youth reared on sound bites of history that mimic the rap culture that has shaped them, the voice of Malcolm X supplies the authentic timbre of social rebellion. And his serene but ominous countenance peering from countless posters forms the perfect portrait of black anger at American pride and prejudice. Unlike King, however, the hues of Malcolm's charisma have for the most part remained dark and radical. His reputation is shaped by the specific appeal to racial identity and cultural pride, heroic gestures in an era of political surrender and resurgent racism.

Rap artists, black youth culture's self-styled postmodern urban griots, dispense social criticism and history lessons with Malcolm's hot breath sampled between their fiery lyrics. Radical and black nationalist intelligentsia employ Malcolm's words as the touchstone of an independent and critical black cultural consciousness. And even black people for whom King's example provides an ideological north star draw solace from Malcolm at moments of uncertainty about the sanity of American culture or the sincerity of American democracy.

That Martin and Malcolm, therefore, represent two distinct traditions of response to homegrown American racism is undeniable. Captured in the useful but imprecise shorthand developed to distinguish the ways black people have resisted racism for more than two centuries, King's position represented an integrationist approach to the American dilemma, advocating equal inclusion of blacks in the drama of national privilege. And for most of his life Malcolm X advocated a separatist and nationalist strategy for black survival, seeking a space free from white racial violence. But what is even more intriguing, although more subtle and complex, is the way in which King's and Malcolm X's strategies, ideologies, and principles of racial combat seemed at *crucial points* to be of a piece, the fragmented components of a narrative whole of racial redemption.

This is a complicated point to make without homogenizing King and Malcolm X into a mythic unity, without creating consonance where there is none, and without imposing a grid on racial experience. The challenge to anyone who would interpret King and Malcolm X is to appreciate both overlap and opposition, but only after tracing the contours of their ideologies, exploring the nuances of their respective visions of racial transformation, and investigating the varied intellectual and social resources they brought to bear to the traditions in which they took part.

To this task James Cone seems particularly well suited. Born and reared in the Deep South, Cone has spent most of his career as a teacher and scholar in northern institutions. Educated as an undergraduate at a historically black college, Cone gained his doctorate degree at a white university, where he was trained in the thought of neo-orthodox German theologian Karl Barth. Soon thereafter, Cone came to reject many of the premises of white Western theology. In its place, he articulated a theology that reflected black religious experience and reshaped theological language in light of the guiding principle of black liberation and resistance to oppression. Indeed, Cone is widely regarded as the father of black theology.

In his incipient expression of intellectual dissent from traditional theology, the ground-breaking *Black Theology and Black Power*,[1] Cone proved to be the angry young man of the religious academy. He took traditional theology to task for its vicious complicity in the oppression of blacks by supplying theological comfort and philosophical justification to white racism. Although he failed to take seriously the important exceptions to his theological diatribe (a failure duly noted by equally blind white theologians), Cone's often shrill tone struck a highly responsive chord in important sectors of the theological academy.

But more importantly, Cone made theology suddenly attractive, and in some cases irresistible, for a whole generation of black religious intellectuals and church persons who questioned the power of their discipline and faith to facilitate social transformation after King's death. Cone integrated elements of traditional black church life (discourse about justice, God, and judgment) with radical social ideas (black power, a black God, and trenchant criticism of white racism). Here was a black man trained like Martin who spoke like Malcolm, an X in King's clothing.

In more than twenty years and several books since then, Cone has refined his vision of the scope and tasks of the black theological enterprise. He has introduced a vibrant idiom in theological language from his academic base as Charles Briggs Distinguished Professor of Systematic Theology at New York's Union Theological Seminary. Cone has lectured across the hemisphere, his books have been translated into several languages, and his ideas have spawned dissertations, conferences, and books in many parts of the world.

Like King and Malcolm X, Cone is a revolutionary figure, and like them, he has endured the pain and risk of growth. He has integrated new strands into his arguments over the years to address his former weaknesses, particularly on issues of gender and social theory. Each new book has reflected his continuing dialogue with an expanded group of interlocutors. Cone's latest book, *Martin & Malcolm & America: A Dream or a Nightmare*, takes us forward by looking backward. He examines two figures who have influenced black Americans, and more specifically, the shape and character of his own thought. In a sense, his book is a public reckoning with his own intellectual and personal heritage. It is, in many ways, an impressive achievement and perhaps his best book.

Cone's book is organized in a methodical fashion, with his characteristic clarity of expression on generous display. While obfuscatory and insular jargon hold sway in so many academic disciplines, Cone never lets the language he is using get in the way of the story he is telling. Other fine studies have compared King and Malcolm X, along with other black religious and intellectual figures, such as Peter Paris's *Black Leaders in Conflict* and Robert Franklin's *Liberating Visions*.[3] With the exception of Louis Lomax's *To Kill a Black Man*,[4] Cone's is the first book-length study devoted exclusively to comparing the two figures.

Although the trajectory of their social acceptance has been wildly different, King and Malcolm X scaled the heights of cultural popularity only after their apocalyptic martyrdoms. Although he is now shrouded in myth and legend, King's popularity plummeted in the years prior to his death because of his opposition to the Vietnam War, the rise of Black Power, and his turn toward matters of class inequality. And when he was assassinated, Malcolm was diligently redefining his ideological identity and winning increasing popularity among an audience previously denied him because of his role in the Nation of Islam. But it has taken nearly a quarter century for his appeal to fully emerge and for his image, voice, and message to find a new place in the black cultural imagination. As Cone observes:

> Twenty-five years after his assassination, there is a resurgence of interest in him, especially among the young who were not born when he died. Malcolm's name, words, and face appear on buttons, T-shirts, and the covers of rap records. His life has become the basis of films, plays, and even operas. He is now being quoted by mainstream black leaders, who once despised him. Conferences, seminars, and parades are being held in his honor, and streets, schools, and organizations are being named after him. People are making annual pilgrimages to his birthplace and grave site.

Although research on King is voluminous and growing daily, the literary attention paid to Malcolm is only now swelling to match his renewed popularity. Bruce Perry's recent biography of Malcolm X and Spike Lee's upcoming film about him will most certainly stimulate more interest in the man's legacy, as will Cone's fine comparative study.

Cone's text also deftly explores the differences between King and Malcolm X, which upon cursory glance appear conspicuous. After all, their differences from birth might be considered a study in suggestive polarities: south/north, middle-class/poor, light-skinned/dark-skinned, tall/short, educated/auto-didact, and slow-southern-cadency/rapid-fire-oratory. And Cone goes to great lengths to show how substantial their differences were. He shows us how the social, political, and economic forces that produced them, as well as the geographic regions that were the scene of their major contributions, reveal a great deal about the character and limitations of their respective contributions. King was reared in a comfortable, middle-class home in Atlanta that nurtured his sense of self-worth in the bosom of a vibrant black religious faith. Malcolm X's first memory in 1929, ironically the year of King's birth, was a nightmare, a terrifying remembrance of the burning of his family home in Lansing, Michigan, by white vigilantes.

Cone's introductory chapter shows how King and Malcolm X participated in venerable traditions of integrationist and nationalist social thought and practice, and hence were neither completely nor finally the inventions of mass media or white society. Each was fundamentally a creative and singularly gifted political and social actor within a rich and particular ideological heritage. Although Cone delineates the specific marks of each tradition on King and Malcolm X, he also concedes that the rhetoric of nationalism and integrationism were used to express complex beliefs that were sometimes combined by black leaders and intellectuals in their struggles against slavery and oppression:

> Of course, no black thinker has been a pure integrationist or a pure nationalist, but rather all black intellectuals have represented aspects of each, with emphasis moving in one direction or the other, usually at different periods of their lives. . . . When blacks have been optimistic about America—believing that they could achieve full equality through moral suasion and legal argument—they have been integrationist and have minimized their nationalist tendencies. On the other hand despair about

> America—believing that genuine equality is impossible because whites have no moral conscience or any intention to apply the laws fairly—has always been the seedbed of nationalism.

Cone's abbreviated genealogy of conflicting and sometimes converging black ideological traditions provides a helpful scheme for comprehending continuities between past advocates of resistance to racist oppression and his twin subjects, King and Malcolm X. It may also result in closer attention to the significant and suggestive dissimilarities between King and Jesse Jackson, Malcolm X and Louis Farrakhan—dissimilarities that are often overlooked in the avid search for successor messiahs in our era of racial desperation.

Cone skillfully contrasts the impact of their early lives on the development of their thought in sketching a kind of existential ecology of the origins of King's dream and Malcolm X's nightmare. King's embrace of crucial elements of a Booker T. Washington version of accommodationism and a Frederick Douglass version of integrationism, supported by his father's and grandfather's philosophies, found expression in his early leadership style. And his absorption of the ideals of Christian brotherhood and universal love preached in the black church shaped his understanding of acceptable forms of protest and resistance to racism.

Cone's point here, set against the stream of one school of King interpretation, is that the black church was the primary influence on King's life and thought, and that only later did white Protestant liberal theology, Gandhi, Niebuhr, and strands of the social gospel play a role. In intellectual biographies of King, such as Kenneth Smith's and Ira G. Zepp's *Search for the Beloved Community* and John J. Ansbro's *Martin Luther King, Jr.: The Making of a Mind*,[5] the latter influences have been accorded primacy. Other recent studies of King have acknowledged the decisive role of black church faith and culture in shaping King's thought, such as Lewis Baldwin's *There Is a Balm in Gilead* and Fred Downing's *To See the Promised Land*.[6] And in a few scattered essays, Cone has argued for the preeminence of black Christian values and practice in understanding the moral vision and social protest of King, an argument he elaborates in the course of his book:

> The *faith of the black experience* began to shape King's idea of God during childhood, and it remained central to his perspective throughout his life. This point needs emphasis because many interpreters have failed to acknowledge the *decisive* role of the black religious tradition upon King's thinking. Without denying other important influences—liberal Protestantism, Gandhi, Niebuhr, among others—we still must emphasize that no tradition or thinker influenced King's perspective as much as the faith which blacks created in their fight for dignity and justice.

Moreover, King's virtually unlimited optimism about the possibilities of interracial coalitions defeating racism developed only after he conquered his "antiwhite feeling" in college, where he encountered whites in interracial organizations. As Cone points out, King's desire to explore the merits of integrationism almost blinded him to the necessity for addressing racism in his graduate work:

> It is important to note that he did not even mention racism in most of his graduate papers that dealt with justice, love, sin, and evil. In six years at Crozer and Boston, King never identified racism as a theological or philosophical problem or mentioned whether he recognized it in the student body and faculty. . . . Like most integrationists of his time, and in contrast to Malcolm and the nationalists, Martin appeared to be glad merely to have the opportunity to prove that Negroes could make it in the white man's world.

Here, and throughout his book, Cone gives the sharpest criticism of King's psychological disposition toward white society articulated since John A. Williams's *The King God Didn't Save* and David Lewis's *King: A Biography*.[7] While avoiding the more exaggerated effects of Williams's self-conscious debunking of the King myth and supplying a more nuanced reading of the black religious roots of King's thought than found in Lewis's treatment, Cone vigorously challenges and critiques King's weaknesses.

He is just as balanced toward Malcolm X. Cone discusses Malcolm X's origins in Omaha, tracing the influence of his parent's nationalist activity on his worldview. Like King, Malcolm X's father was a Baptist preacher, although on a much more modest scale, preaching as an itinerant or "jackleg" minister. Malcolm X's father was president of the Omaha branch of Garvey's UNIA, while his mother was the group's reporter. During his childhood, Malcolm X was subject not only to white violence, but also to a vicious circle of domestic violence as his father beat his mother and they both abused their children. Malcolm lost his father early, and it is not clear whether his death was accidental or murder. What is clear, though, is that Earl Little's death had a traumatic effect on Malcolm X's family, leaving mother Louise Little to rear eight children during the depression. She eventually suffered a mental breakdown, and the children were placed in several foster homes.

After experiencing the ravages of integrated schooling, Malcolm dropped out of high school to live with his half sister in Boston. Malcolm had already begun to steal in Nebraska because of extreme hunger, and he expanded his hustling repertoire in Boston. He used cocaine and established a burglary ring to support his expensive habit. After he was caught and sent to prison, Malcolm X displayed a resentful attitude until his conversion to the teaching of Elijah Muhammad, founder of the Nation of Islam.

As Cone explains, Malcolm X was drawn to the Nation because of its definition of the white man as the devil and its strong emphasis on pride in black culture and history. Malcolm's many difficulties with whites in adolescence and his experiences in Boston's ghetto prepared him to reject nonviolence and integration and to accept a strong separatist philosophy as the basis for black survival in racist America:

> Malcolm's experience in the ghetto taught him that the black masses could be neither integrationist nor nonviolent. Integration and nonviolence assumed some measure of political order, a moral conscience in the society, and a religious and human sensitivity regarding the dignity and value of all persons. But since the masses in the ghettos saw no evidence of a political order that recognized their humanity or a moral conscience among white people, an appeal to integration and nonviolence sounded like a trick to delude and disarm poor blacks, so whites would not have to worry about a revengeful response to their brutality.

In the first section of his book, Cone gives us a good sense of how King and Malcolm X were formed and what differences their respective social origins made on the way they thought about race and American society.

Cone devotes two chapters to exploring King's and Malcolm X's understanding of America through the metaphors of dream and nightmare, metaphors that would define their different approaches to racial justice. Cone probes the social sources of King's American Dream, linking King's vision to the white public, "because he believed they had the material resources and moral capacity to create a world based on the principles that they claimed to live by." Cone also explains that King urged black people to enact their redemptive roles in American society by pursuing self-respect, high moral standards, whole-hearted work, leadership, and nonviolence. Despite severe challenges to King's faith in the plausibility of American democracy, especially after the bombing of a church in Birmingham that killed four innocent black girls, he continued to believe that the American Dream would soon be fulfilled.

From the very beginning, however, Malcolm X understood that the conditions of black Americans were a nightmare of racial injustice, urban poverty, and drug addiction, all presided over by the negligence and hypocrisy of white liberals and unprincipled racists. Here and throughout, Cone makes clear that Malcolm X's unbridled anger toward white racism provided a strong counterpoint to King's integrationist philosophy, making King's views, once deemed radical, seem acceptably moderate by comparison. Once Malcolm X left the Nation, however, he discovered that many integrationists were more radical and militant than he had formerly believed. Still, Malcolm continued to enliven the role of the angry black in order to provide a sharp enough contrast to King that white people would gladly listen to his demands.

For most of Malcolm's life, King avoided him. Of course, Malcolm had developed a side career of verbally assaulting "so-called Negro" leaders, taking special delight in tagging King with a jumble of colorful but caustic monikers, including "religious Uncle Tom, traitor, chump and the Reverend Dr. Chickenwing." For his part, King believed that Malcolm X's promulgation of black anger and his statements about the "reciprocal bleeding" of whites and blacks were irresponsible and morally wrong. King also believed that violence as a tactic of survival was suicidal in light of the fact that blacks were only 10 percent of the population and therefore grossly overmatched and underarmed.

Cone probes Malcolm's conception of divine justice, predicated upon a philosophy of an eye for an eye, and explores his advocacy of self-knowledge, self-love, self-defense, racial separatism, and most of all, racial unity, "the dominant theme of his ministry." After he examines the impact of King's and Malcolm X's faith and theology on their versions of the American dream and nightmare, Cone details the unraveling of King's faith in American justice and Malcolm X's reexamination of a strong version of separatist black nationalism after his break with Muhammad.

King's confrontation with persistent racism caused him to reject his former optimism about the capacity or willingness of whites to practice social justice. Although Cone details King's growing pessimism about the structural racism and economic inequality of American society, he doesn't tell us that this prompted King to advocate "nonviolent sabotage," which included blocking the normal functioning of the government as a sign of deep social frustration and moral outrage. Cone reveals that King also began to ponder the virtues of "temporary segregation" as a means of reconstituting the economic health of black communities, since American society had not shown serious interest in reordering social priorities and redistributing wealth.

In his mature stride, King also increased his emphasis on black pride, appealing to a theme that had been implicit in much of his work but now, because of the challenges to nonviolence posed by Black Power, required an explicit articulation. Such moves caused David Halberstam to call King a "nonviolent Malcolm X," a characterization King rejected. Nonetheless, his later thinking is detailed by Cone in a way that leaves no doubt that King's shift to progressive and radical social thought was a permanent feature of his mature civil protest.

But, as Cone shows, Malcolm X too was changing. His break with Muhammad had freed Malcolm to become publicly political, an opportunity that Malcolm X used to attempt to join forces with King and progressive elements of the traditional civil rights community. But Malcolm's reputation of advocating violent self-defense had been so deeply entrenched that even his move away from Muhammad didn't prevent the white media from viewing Malcolm as a rabid racist and destructive demagogue. As Cone notes, this troubled Malcolm X, who had a genuine desire to forsake his recent past and articulate his racial demands to a wider audience. Rebuffed and scorned, Malcolm entered into a phase of radical rabble-rousing, still specifying the absurdity of white racism, while displaying a newfound openness to limited white support of black freedom. Even after his journey to Mecca, however, Malcolm never surrendered his advocacy of black unity as a precondition to black freedom, a unity that could never result if even well-intentioned whites participated in black organizations.

X's stress on unity is a theme that resonates with Cone's own thinking and shapes his understanding of King and Malcolm X throughout his book. It also limits his understanding of the two figures. In a discussion of the impact of the faith of the black experience on King's idea of God, Cone says:

> As different as Martin's and Malcolm's religious communities were, Martin's faith, nonetheless, was much closer to Malcolm's than it was to that of white Christians, and Malcolm's faith was much closer to Martin's than it was to that of Muslims in the Middle East, Africa, or Asia; that was true because both of their faith commitments were derived from the *same* experience of suffering and struggle in the United States. Their theologies, therefore, should be interpreted as different religious and intellectual responses of African-Americans to their environment as they searched for meaning in a nation that they did not make.

But is this accurate? Is it true that the experience of black suffering and struggle is the primary basis of unity, even when the differences between black people are strong and persistent? While Cone may be right to suggest that King and Malcolm X were closer to one another than they were to white Christianity and orthodox Islamic belief, this must be proved by citing historical evidence. As Cone has so convincingly shown us, King and Malcolm X were deeply divided not only about their tactics of social protest, but about their anthropological, social, and psychological understanding of human beings.

It is, therefore, conceivable that a white person who embraced King's understanding of human community, love, interracial coalition, and the limitations of injustice of white racial practices might indeed have more in common with King than a black person who held highly divergent views about such issues, despite a shared experience of racial suffering. The case of Supreme Court Justice Clarence Thomas and other black conservatives proves that there is no necessary or automatic similarity in the interpretation of the "black experience" and that suffering due to racism is no guarantee of unanimity on the means to achieve racial justice. Thus, King would have had (and I believe he did have) more in common with say, Michael Harrington, than he would have had with George Schuyler when it came to issues of racial and economic justice.

Cone himself provides ample support for the belief that King and Malcolm X, as a result of their concrete set of historical experiences, were indeed converging on a similar, although by no means identical, view of racial justice and economic health for black people. But as Cone also makes clear, they had enormous and long-standing barriers to overcome to achieve even limited ideological parity. For instance, Malcolm's earlier views of violence, as Cone points out, "were hardly different from that of the whites he criticized." And in criticizing King and Malcolm X for their abominable views on women, Cone points out how they had more in common with white men than with black women:

> While Martin and Malcolm challenged white values regarding race, their acceptance of black male privilege prevented them from seeing the connection between racism and sexism. While both differed sharply with most white men when it came to matters involving race, they shared much of the typical *American* male's view of women. Martin's and Malcolm's views regarding women's place were not significantly different from those of men of other races.

The call for racial unity is usually premised on the assumption that the experience of black suffering will itself guarantee similarity of perspective. But the complexity and diversity of racial experiences cautions against advocating racial unity based on the presumption of homogeneity. Neither does it bode well for trying to explain the genuine and irresolvable differences between King and Malcolm X, no matter how much we appeal to their same experience of suffering and struggle. Besides, other dimensions of struggle to which King and Malcolm became more sensitive, such as class inequality, mean that the experience of suffering, although crucial and certainly central, is not the exclusive or exhaustive basis of racial unity.

Because Cone believes that both King and Malcolm X promoted self-knowledge and respect for one's history and culture as the basis for unity—without which there could be no freedom—the view of unity based on sameness of experience fails to capture other enabling forms of racial solidarity. Furthermore, it imposes a narrow view of their uses of history and culture, especially in King's case. Such a view leads Cone to stress the necessity and crucial ingredients of self-esteem in combating black disunity and the corrosive racism that destroys black culture without supplying a trenchant criticism of the social forces that help construct and define self-regard. Regarding the latter, Cone concludes:

> It is not easy to survive in a society that says that you do not count. Many do not survive. With the absence of black pride, that "I am somebody" feeling, many young African-Americans have no respect for themselves or for anybody else. . . . Malcolm X is the best medicine against genocide. He showed us by example and prophetic preaching that . . . we can take that long walk toward freedom. Freedom is first and foremost an inner recognition of self-respect, a knowledge that one was not put on this earth to be a nobody. African-Americans can do the same today. We can fight for our dignity and self-respect.

While Cone's claims are undeniable, what is needed at this point is a complex and detailed cultural criticism in light of the social vision and religious values that King and Malcolm X promoted, values that Cone has expressed in his own work. It seems odd that Cone prescribes self-respect and self-esteem without giving a sharp or substantial analysis of the social resources for such qualities and the political and economic reasons that prevent their flourishing in many urban black communities across the country. It is precisely here that we want the full analytical power of black theology and the best available insights of progressive social theory brought to bear upon the various crises that confront black Americans in tracking a path for those who take the mature King and Malcolm X seriously. Here Cone's treatment falls noticeably short.

Nevertheless, Cone's study of King and Malcolm X is admirable. Cone gives a life-sized portrait of two figures who have grown larger than life. And with the phenomenal resurgence of interest in Malcolm, Cone has not been afraid to criticize him for his often lethal sexism, his advocacy of impractical strategies of violence, and his almost exclusive focus on race, which was only decentered after his break from the Nation of Islam.

The imaginative virtue of Cone's book is that he has shown that Martin and Malcolm needed each other, that their ideas and social strategies brought them to a strange but effective symbiosis. His title, employing his subjects' first names, is a symbol of the first-name familiarity we feel with these great men and a striking emblem of their genuine humility. As we struggle to take measure of their extraordinary accomplishments, Cone's book will be indispensable in charting how two supremely human and heroic figures occupied and defined their times with empowering vision and sacrificial action.

Notes

1. James H. Cone, *Black Theology and Black Power* (New York: Seabury Press, 1969).

2. James H. Cone, *Martin & Malcolm & America. A Dream or a Nightmare* (New York: Orbis, 1991).

3. Peter Paris, *Black Leaders in Conflict*, 2nd ed. (Louisville, Ky.: Westminister Press/John Knox Press, 1991); and Robert M. Franklin, *Liberating Visions: Human Fulfillment and Social Justice in African-American Thought* (Minneapolis, Minn.: Augsburg Fortress, 1989).

4. Louis Lomax, *To Kill a Black Man* (Los Angeles: Holloway House, 1968).

5. Kenneth Smith and Ira G. Zepp, *Search for the Beloved Community: The Thinking of Martin Luther King, Jr.* (Valley Forge, Pa.: Judson Press, 1974); and John J. Ansbro, *Martin Luther King, Jr.: The Making of a Mind* (New York: Orbis, 1982).

6. Lewis Baldwin, *There Is a Balm in Gilead: The Cultural Roots of Martin Luther King, Jr.* (Minneapolis, Minn.: Augsburg Fortress, 1991); and Frederick L. Downing, *To See the Promised Land: The Faith Pilgrimage of Martin Luther King, Jr.* (Macon, Ga.: Mercer University Press, 1986).

7. John A. Williams, *The King God Didn't Save* (New York: Coward-McCann, 1970); and David Lewis, *King: A Biography,* 2nd ed. (Urbana: University of Illinois Press, 1978).

Improvisation

King: A Metaphor for the Sixties

The 1980s have witnessed a voracious historical appetite for the 1960s—that decade's contending ideologies and contradictory achievements, its noble successes and equally notorious failures. Central to the era's definition was the adventurous civil rights movement, and at the movement's heart was Martin Luther King, Jr., who, by virtually any measure, was an extraordinary person. Taylor Branch's *Parting the Waters: America in the King Years, 1954-63* (Simon and Schuster, 1988) captures the towering but imperfect genius of King and the movement that made such startling and unexpected American history. It manages to steer a judicious course between the fateful options of uncritical celebration and unsparing disapprobation. And like King himself, Branch's text benefits from eloquence in the service of truth.

Branch opens his book by bringing to light the achievements and foibles of Vernon Johns, the brilliant preacher who was King's pastoral forerunner in Montgomery, Alabama. In the process, Branch not only details Johns's cantankerous eccentricities, which elicited, in turn, opprobrium and endearment, but he also unearths the intertwining history of the Baptist churches that came to be occupied by King and Ralph Abernathy—whose own lives became immortally connected.

Branch illumines, too, the complex heritage into which King was born, touching upon the engrossing admixture of worldly ambition and religious discipline that lighted on King, Sr. Senior's tough upbringing, which taught lessons about even tougher survival, imprinted in his personality an overbearing bent that provided a colorful background for some personal conflicts between him and his son. Branch captures the tensions between King's fundamentalist background and the exciting though waning liberalism that was then in vogue at Crozer Theological Seminary, which King attended. He also recounts King's intellectual growth as King encountered the philosophy of personalism, the tenets of the social gospel, and the penetrating social criticism of Reinhold Niebuhr.

To his credit, however, Branch never forgets that the black

church experience was not only foundational but remained central to King's moral perspective, political involvement, and social activism. For better and worse, it also shaped to a large degree the agenda of the civil rights movement. Branch shows how the black church ethos, built in part on preacherly dominance and pastoral privilege, projected its great talents and lamentable shortcomings alike onto the civil rights movement. In a multitude of portraits, descriptions of church life and denominational culture, and details of bruising internecine battles, Branch makes the phrase "black church" come alive. He reveals James Lawson's mature understanding of nonviolence (in many ways, more sophisticated than King's). He describes the tactical innovation and ruthless administrative style of Wyatt Tee Walker. Branch portrays, too, the bitter contest for leadership of the National Baptist Convention, the largest body of black Christians in America. King allied with Gardner Taylor, the pastor of New York's fourteen-thousand-member Concord Baptist Church of Christ, against the convention's daunting conservative president, Joseph H. Jackson, who opposed King and in many ways the movement.

Branch documents the sexism that pushed Ella Baker out of the Southern Christian Leadership Conference (King's own organization) and indicates how it underplayed the accomplishments of women like Jo Ann Robinson, who with her female colleagues in the Women's Political Council, initially conceived the bus boycott in Montgomery. Branch talks of the steadying influence of Stanley Levison, King's closest white friend and supporter, who remains maligned behind a veil of rumors about his alleged Communist activity. We also get a better feel for the enormous contributions of Bayard Rustin, whose strategic planning and knowledge of nonviolent resistance were placed at King's disposal almost from the beginning, and who was eventually forced away from King because of homophobia (Rustin was secretly gay) and his politically radical background.

Branch takes the measure, too, of Bob Moses, at once enchanting and enigmatic, a courageous philosophy graduate student at Harvard who became a volunteer for the Student Nonviolent Coordinating Committee. As SNCC's field representative in Mississippi, he eventually, with Fannie Lou Hamer, made history of his own in the famous Freedom Summer voter registration drive of 1964. We glimpse the Kennedys, John and Robert, whose legacy as political pioneers of civil rights was gained more perfectly in death than justly in life. Branch also sketches the grim development of the technology of surveillance, as practiced by J. Edgar Hoover's FBI, which itself crushed thousands of liberties and not a few lives.

What is most striking about Branch's book is the artful manner in which it fuses rich historical detail and acute social analysis in order to illuminate the dark edges of an enormously complex time. It is not that the events themselves have never been reported before, nor is it the case that the characters are entirely new (although some are). What is fresh about Branch's book is that it allows us to gain a sense of the trauma and thrill of events that shook a nation to the roots of its own identity. Branch does so by providing a microscopic view of the civil rights movement's immediate sociohistorical and cultural environment, while faithfully pulling back for a telescopic vision of how it fit into the pattern of global events.

Branch's title alone, of course, signals a bold act of historical imagination, a monumental move to reinterpret the shifting contours of an epoch whose meaning is still expanding. By placing King and his people squarely at the defining center of the sixties, Branch has focused on a historical juggernaut whose significance we must continually work hard to understand and achieve. With such meticulously wrought scholarship, Branch has proven himself equal to the task. The thought that Branch's 1,064 pages only lead us from the Montgomery bus boycott to Kennedy's assassination in 1963 is astonishing enough, but the thought that we can look forward to another finely tuned work of masterly intricacy and convincing depth in his second volume is simply exhilarating.

18

For Jonathan's Sake: The Morality of Memory—a Sermon

Gratitude, certainly, must count as one of the central virtues of the Christian faith. The posture of appreciation for a kind and helpful word spoken or a hospitable gesture performed is consistently affirmed throughout the Bible. In one respect, this is so because the biblical conception of gratitude derives from an explicit acknowledgment that, in James's words, "all that is good, everything that is perfect . . . is given from above" (James 1:17). Thus, the origin of the many manifestations of mercy, kindness, justice, peace, and love may be traced back to God, the ultimate source of whatever form of prosperity we may enjoy.

Of course, the possibility of gratitude often depends on the ability (but most likely the willingness) to recall an act or a pattern of love and sacrifice revealed to us through the life of a person, the generosity of an institution, or the richness of a tradition. To be thankful, then, requires that we remember. The powerful and fruitful manner in which memory and gratitude are linked is seen in our present text, 2 Sam. 9:1–8.

This text, along with chapter 10 of 2 Samuel, though, is generally regarded as uninteresting and peripheral to the meaning of the larger narrative. However, I think there are powerful truths tucked away in the folds of this neglected passage, and I hope, with the proper homiletical twists and textual shakes, we will nudge them free for our inspection and inspiration.

This text opens with David's question, "Is there anyone still left of Saul's family so that I can show him kindness for Jonathan's sake?" The immediate background of this text's place in relation to the larger narrative makes it all the more remarkable and intriguing. Recorded in 1 Sam. 16:1 through 2 Sam. 5:5 are the astounding features, the broad and bold lineaments, of David's feats of greatness, which expanded his popularity to iconographical proportions. David is indeed the central figure in Israel's memory. He is one of a class of historic personalities who, as Walter Brueggemann says, "has a literary future." That is to say, David's memory is generative, is seminal, continually producing stories that testify to his towering stature.

Any perusal of the narrative indicates why David reigns as such a stellar figure in Israel's history. As a young lad shepherding his family's sheep, he entered Saul's army and immediately confronted the menacing specter that loomed large against his people in the form of a grotesque giant, Goliath. At first accepting, then rejecting, traditional armor, David instead opted for the tools of his own trade, which had served him well in protecting innocent sheep from preying wolves.

So with five smooth stones and a slingshot, David hurled the hope and honor of his people against this gargantuan threat and behemoth brutality symbolized in Goliath's presence. Goliath fell to David's calculated and precise assault, as did the entire nation of Israel to his potent charisma and his enormous chutzpah. As with Martin Luther King, Jr., centuries later in Montgomery after the bus boycott, this event catapulted David into the national spotlight, and for a long stretch, after the intervening period when he was a victim of Saul's jealousy, he passed from victory to victory.

And in the midst of this pleasant and plush atmosphere, in the midst of being thoroughly ensconced in a niche of political and national importance, in the midst of being celebrated as the hero of Israel and the apple of God's eye, if you will permit me the use of a "sanctified imagination," a thought must have crossed David's mind about his past, especially when times were lean and life was vicious. To his credit, the bright sun of his current prosperity did not totally eclipse from his view the terror of his past predicament.

Some shivering moment in the midst of his opulence called David down from the ecstatic heights of unalloyed joy and forced him to mix his thoughts with the pain and poverty of his former life. Those were not days visited with an unmitigated joie de vivre, and those were certainly not nights bathed in peaceful benediction. No, those were "harried days and haunted nights" spent in feverish flight from the pathological pursuit of an insanely jealous political chieftain, who, to make matters worse, was the father of his best friend.

We can understand David's mode of thought and empathize with his mood of being. In the center of every thundering victory, of every howling success, of every mountaintop experience, there is a still small voice that beckons us to recall our roots, to measure ourselves against the youthful idealism that started our journeys, and to see ourselves in light of what, and who, and where, we once were. For David, the image of his struggles toward maturity, of his treacherous trek to becoming the dominant presence in a nation, were conjured up and evoked by one word: Jonathan.

In a startlingly visceral manner, David understood that he hadn't made it to his present position without the love, truth, loyalty, support, belief, and faith of his late friend Jonathan. By raising his question—"Is there anyone still left of Saul's family so that I can show him kindness for Jonathan's sake?"—David provides due recognition for the central significance of Jonathan's contribution to his, and really Israel's, life.

In a real sense, we have an ethical imperative to remember those persons, ideas, institutions, and traditions that have shaped our lives in the most profound ways. There is a moral dimension to our memories, in selectively recalling who and what helped us be what we are today. The example of the Bible often warns against a pernicious amnesia, a flawed forgetfulness that preempts the proper expression of gratitude, especially in the face of some good fortune we presently enjoy.

How tragic it was, for instance, when Joseph was wrongly jailed and further wronged by an ungrateful lapse of memory. The cupbearer and chief baker of the pharaoh were also jailed with Joseph. He was kind enough to interpret their dreams, which foretold the baker's death and the cupbearer's restoration after their release from prison. Joseph asked the cupbearer upon his release to "be sure to remember me when things go well with you, and do me the kindness of reminding Pharaoh about me, to get me out of this house (Gen. 40:14). But after the cupbearer's release from prison, "the chief cupbearer did not remember Joseph; he forgot him" (Gen. 40:23).

This example has particular importance for African-Americans in late twentieth-century American culture. We must recall, and not forget, how we have arrived where we are. We must accentuate the need for memory, for being grateful for past luminaries and movements that have shaped our community from one era to another. Mary Frances Berry and John Blassingame, in their recent history of Afro-Americans, *Long Memory*, indicate that for our slave forebears, memory itself became an instrument of survival. They passed from generation to generation the great practices, rich traditions, and strong beliefs that sustained them through cruel circumstances and devastating days.

The tragedy is that so often we have forgotten "how we got over." When we survey the plight of our present African-American life, we are able to observe the consequences of forgetting. Our inner cities more closely resemble bombed war zones than inhabitable and thriving spaces of residency. Sizable portions of our communities have been seized by the subversive presence of drug pushers, who sell our black youth temporary tickets to euphoria, and often permanent passes to prison. The shift away from nonskilled labor in postindustrial American work and the growing stature of the steel collar, automated technology, are continually depleting the already weakened economic base of most black families and communities. Unemployment rates are staggering, dropout rates are demeaning, and the level of literacy is constantly declining.

These harsh and bitter circumstances for most Africans in America have tested our moral resolve, our spiritual resources, and most acutely, our communal memories. But we must remember that even under the most inhumane assaults of slavery and racism, black identity, although severely challenged, was maintained. This remembering can fuel the engines of desire to reconstruct the infrastructure of black communities and redesign coping mechanisms to fit our present circumstances.

When we recall both our collective and individual past, it reminds us that we have not gotten where we are alone. None of us is self-made or self-produced. All of us owe some Jonathan, whether a person, institution, or tradition, for contributing to our lives. All of us are the beneficiaries of others who have sacrificed for us, loved us, and worked for us.

Our parents have worked for long hours, often in conditions that defy our imaginative powers to portray their tedium and sometimes outright cruelty. Our older siblings have sacrificed their chance for a higher education so that younger ones could matriculate in college. Some wise senior citizen pushed past the cantankerous and childish temperament we displayed to see the cry for attention, feeding our need for importance. Some teacher has given us books to read, to stretch our minds and deepen our thinking, compelling us to exceed low expectations and rise to educational excellence. Some minister or pastor has rescued us from the ennui and spiritual stupor of unfocused life plans by uttering a word of advice and direction that lifted the fog of doubt and permitted the sun to rise on our hopes and dreams. Some bosom friend has heard our frustrations and fears, our angers and anxieties, and has encouraged us to do our best. All of us have benefited from such persons.

Jonathan did this for David. Jonathan introduced himself to David and apparently assumed a major responsibility for their relationship. Jonathan loved David as his own soul. Jonathan stripped off his cloak, sword, bow, and girdle and gave them to David. Jonathan interceded on David's behalf with his father Saul, who desired to destroy David. Jonathan listened to David's agonies and acted to save him.

With David, therefore, we recognize that at the deepest level of our lives we are debtors. Like David, we should remember our Jonathans, and be grateful for what they have done for us, for nothing approaches the opprobrium of ingratitude. David realized this, and for Jonathan's sake, he wanted to show kindness as a result of what Jonathan had meant to him.

A deep truth about life emerges when we consider how David sought to express his gratitude. As is the case with us at times, David was unable to return gratitude directly to Jonathan, but, for Jonathan's sake, he sought to pass it on. Thus, David sought out Mephibosheth, the son of Jonathan, to support him for Jonathan's sake. One way of expressing gratitude is to support and encourage the heir and legacy of the persons, traditions, and institutions that have benefited us.

That is why African-Americans in particular, and Americans in general, should express gratitude for the blood that was shed in the civil rights movement, for the hundreds of thousands of miles walked; for the blisters, bruises, and cuts; for the loss of jobs, limbs, and even lives through brutal assassinations. We pay homage and render gratitude by supporting the "offspring," the legacy, of the civil rights movement, by continuing to explore and extend the ideas espoused during that period in our national history. We continue to devote our intellectual, spiritual, and financial resources to the identification and eradication of racism and classism in American culture. For our Jonathan's sake, for the movement's sake, we must continue to expand our knowledge and insight about the need for social justice, economic rehabilitation, and redistribution of resources. For the movement's sake, we must continue to fight for the preciousness of life and the fundamental dignity and sacredness of all human beings.

This is why we as progressive Christians affirm that the movement for the realization of women's freedom has benefited us all. Thus, for Jonathan's sake, the women's movement's sake, we must continue to resist the patriarchal norms that constrain the social mobility, contain the vocational aspirations, and conceal the political destiny of women. For Jonathan's sake, the women's movement's sake, we must continually wrestle with the structure of our language and concede the rightful inconvenience of all demands for equality, justice, and freedom. Like David we must, for our Jonathan's sake, express gratitude by supporting the liberating traditions, which are the legacies of all those who have helped us.

David's commitment to Mephibosheth was *for* Jonathan's sake and not *because* he, Mephibosheth, was perfect. In fact, he was crippled in both feet. Like all of us, he was flawed. Hence the demand for perfect people and causes to which we can commit ourselves, even if they are the legacies of those who have aided us, is misled. Although we must strive for excellence, we must not demand perfection, because all of us are handicapped and crippled in some manner. And any institution to which we belong, any organization or tradition in which we participate, is imperfect.

The church is not perfect, because human beings constitute its membership. We are members of the church because we have been called together in common acknowledgment of our need for God's guidance. Even though we are the community of the redeemed, we remain, in varying degrees, plagued by the problems of our human nature. Robert McAfee Brown is right in observing that the church is like Noah's ark: if it wasn't for the storm on the outside, we couldn't stand the stink on the inside. We are here for God's sake, because God extended to us the life of Jesus.

This point is also instructive when we reflect on a phenomenon that has engulfed and galvanized much of the black community: the Jackson presidential campaign. The Jackson campaign has already in a fundamental way transformed the shape and contours of modern politics. And for those seeking an explanation of the way it has affected the majority of African-Americans, it is helpful to see that the Jackson campaign has generated a profound sense of renewed pride and offered hope to black people that justice may yet be done in America. It represents the most powerful coalition of blacks and other progressives since the time of the civil rights movement.

But it is not a perfect movement. And Jackson is not a perfect man. He is flawed like Mephibosheth. But like Mephibosheth he is the recipient of our attention and commitment not simply because of who he is, in the strict sense, but because of the tradition he is related to, and heir of. We are committed for Jonathan's sake, in this case, for all those African-Americans and other progressives who fought for the right to eat at any lunch counter, drink at any water fountain, to ride any bus, to go to any park, to live in any neighborhood, and to be able to vote for any person we choose.

We support Jackson's coalition for the sake of those who walked when they could have ridden, bled when they could have fought, prayed when they could have punched, and loved when they could have hated. All of their efforts in part looked forward to this unimaginable possibility. So it is not for Jesse's sake alone, but really for Martin, for Rosa, and for Malcolm; for Pauli Murray, for Medgar, and for Fannie Lou Hamer; for four little girls blown up in a Birmingham church, and for Rustin, Forman, and Angela Davis; and for James Baldwin and Harold Washington and all the unnamed saints who sacrificed their talent, energy, and, for some, even their lives.

The story of Jonathan, David, and Mephibosheth reminds us of the moral nature of memory, of remembering those persons, ideas, and traditions whose contributions to our lives have been deep and abiding. Of course, this is not at all alien to our larger experience as Christians. We know that it is not for our sakes that the love of God is spread generously and mercifully across our lives, not for our sakes alone that we receive the gifts and talents that we possess. But it is for God's sake, for the sake of Jesus, who died on Calvary, that we live, move, and have our being. May we remember, and never forget.

Improvisation

James Forbes and Riverside Church

The week of February 6, 1989, was a special period of recognition of the abilities of African-Americans. Bill White was named president of baseball's National League, the first black to head any national professional sports enterprise. Ron Brown became the first black to head a major political party when he was selected to chair the Democratic National Committee. Barbara Harris was consecrated suffragan bishop of the Diocese of Massachusetts, the first female bishop ever in the Anglican tradition.

And James Forbes, Jr., was elected, from an initial list of almost five hundred names, to fill the famed pulpit at New York's Riverside Church, following in a tradition of great preachers that began with Harry Emerson Fosdick and continued through William Sloane Coffin.

Forbes's deft blending of prophetic criticism and priestly patience makes him peculiarly suited to the Riverside ministry. He possesses a sociospiritual acumen that addresses issues like racism, sexism, classism, and homophobia, while generating authentic pastoral responses to the people who both combat and embody these ills.

As Joe R. Engle Professor of Preaching at Union Theological Seminary, Forbes has displayed a delightful zest for what many considered a dying art form. Under the discipline of a sanctified imagination, Forbes transformed the tedium of homiletics into an exciting adventure into the labyrinth of sacred speech. As a lecturer (most notably, in Yale's Beecher Lectures), conference speaker, and revival preacher, Forbes has crisscrossed America in pursuit of his vocation of making the word come alive.

It speaks well for Riverside that it chose Forbes to lead it into the next century. While white liberal Protestantism has been rich in rhetoric, it has often shortchanged action, particularly in regard to race. Riverside has worked hard to create a multiracial and diverse community of believers; about one-third of its twenty-two hundred members are black and Hispanic. This intention should be well served by Forbes, who, as search committee chair J. Richard Butler told the congregation, is committed to "plurality, inclusiveness, and justice." By naming Forbes pastor, Riverside has helped liberal Protestantism to practice what it preaches.

Forbes's ministry at Riverside also portends a more substantial recognition for the power of the African-American religious tradition, especially its great preaching heritage. Although the world sampled the richness of black preaching when it listened to Martin Luther King, Jr., and Jesse Jackson, and now Carolyn Knight and Prathia Wynn, the heart of this tradition has been largely unexplored by those outside the black community. Forbes's high visibility, then, promises a hearing for the homiletical styles, rhetorical practices, and oral nuances that characterize the best black preaching.

Forbes marched down the aisle of Riverside Church in 1962 to receive his degree from Union Theological Seminary. He told the *New York Times* after his selection that at that time, "I never would have thought that this pulpit was in the realm of possibility." For some young marginalized or minority seminarian, the possibility of serving God at whatever vocational height one's gifts can manage is now concrete.

That Riverside Church, which addresses AIDS education, South African apartheid, native American justice, and disarmament issues, has embraced this son of a black church—with his Pentecostal roots—promises a new day for liberal Protestant Christianity.

19

Rap Culture, the Church, and American Society

The fevered response that rap culture has recently evoked presents a telling contrast to the tepid indifference that greeted its obscure origins in New York's ghettos little more than a decade ago. At best, rap was first viewed as a faddish sideshow to New York's carnival of urban decay, a ritual diversion of social boredom and criminal imagination into culturally useful acts of rhetorical invention. As rap evolved, its artists ingeniously inhabited the creative constraints of living primarily by the word (rap's strict originality depends on its speech, not its music, which is usually borrowed, although often imaginatively, from other records through a process called "sampling"), and redefined the pop music convention of creating an identity through oral performance.

Although other performers have artfully, even monumentally, shaped this practice (Robert Johnson, Billie Holiday, Frank Sinatra, Hank Williams, Elvis Presley, Michael Jackson, and Madonna), rap affords a range of musical and cultural identities to be formed with remarkable immediacy and astonishing vigor. Rap artists sense that as they are inventing a musical genre that measures the pulse of black youth culture, they are also inventing themselves. From the ready resources of culture, history, tradition, and community, rap artists fashion musical personae who literally voice their hopes, fears, and fantasies: the self as cultural griot, feminist, educator, or itinerant prophet of black nationalism; but also the self as inveterate consumer, misogynist, violent criminal, or sexual athlete. It is this ever-expanding repertoire of created selves that invites us to interrogate the values and visions of rap culture, to perceive the force of its trenchant criticism of racism, historical amnesia, and classism, and to gauge its surrender to American traditions of sexism, consumerism, and violence.

The most obvious feature of rap culture is its form, which values the spoken word and prizes the central place of drum, song, and story in an oral tradition with deep roots in African-American culture. Animal fables, spirituals, blues, ghost tales, slave reminiscences, toasts, and sermons constitute a rich and complex black oral culture that has powerful precedence in African societies. Rappers imagine and implement innovative uses for black orality, juxtaposing their verbal fire and ice to the sonic wizardry of a DJ (the person in charge of music). The DJ's reputation turns on a revealed facility to sift through sonic sources; lift bites of musical, vocal, or televisual sound; and graft these onto new texts (rap lyrics), rendering obscure beats irresistible, monotonous monologue colorful, famous melodies haunting, pedestrian rhythms hypnotic, and loping bass lines crisp and sharp.

The improvised and nuanced experiment in orality by black youth culture is a ripe moment for educators, community activists, religious leaders, and parents to acknowledge and encourage the healthy, productive effects of rap culture. Rap has almost singlehandedly reignited popular and academic interest in black oral practices, spawning articles, books, journalism, conferences, and impassioned conversation across a variety of racial, sexual, ideological, and class boundaries.

Rap has also created for its participants a way of being in the world, an ontological stance as it were, that joins the best features of street society (savvy about rules of survival, ability to adapt quickly in an environment of constant flux, the development of a language of chic, hip, and cool that has influenced the larger American culture) to the best impulses of black bourgeois society (appreciation for literacy, valuing of educational achievement, valorization of broad sorts of skill and discipline).

But rap culture faces a difficult path to broader acceptance. Rap is still shunned by many radio stations (including black ones). The media invariably fasten onto rap's violent and misogynist messages while ignoring its salutary embrace of history, literacy, and community. And rap continues to be targeted by a motley force of detractors whose common trait is their truculent criticism and disdain of rap's alleged thoroughgoing decadence. The bitter fray of opposing beliefs about rap's status often obscures its important influence on critical conversations about black culture.

While rap's experimentation with rhetorical practices affirms the continuing vitality of black oral culture, its fascination with material wealth indexes the dire economic straits of rap's most desperate audience, the black ghetto poor, and reveals the degree to which rap culture is captive to the culture of consumption. Although rap has explored pop terrain with considerable commercial success (M. C. Hammer), has crossed racial boundaries and created a white rap superstar with controversial fanfare (Vanilla Ice), and has drawn its most militant voice from the suburbs (Public Enemy), its most faithful constituency remains the ghetto poor. Rap's origins in the black ghetto continue to influence most rapper's styles of delivery, rap's aesthetic sensibilities, the major themes that haunt rap lyrics, and the economic aspirations of rap's participants.

A dominant desire in both rap culture and the so-called underclass is to escape economic and material deprivation and to color the American Dream black and green. One way of achieving the dream is through criminal activity ranging from petty robbery, fencing stolen goods, and armed burglary to the now sprawling multinational entrepreneurial operations associated with drugs. The drug culture has generated its own illegitimate, underground political economy that is buttressed by the manufacturing, production, packaging, and distribution of mostly "crack" cocaine. A recent alternative to drugs as a means of escape from economic hardship is rap music, which, in any case, is more achievable for a greater variety of youth than yet another route of historic escape, sports, and considerably less lethal than involvement in the political economy of crack.

Rap's voracious materialism also feeds on an undisciplined acquisition, accumulation, and consumption of material goods that has pervaded most segments of American society. Rap videos, like so many other visual vehicles of American popular fantasy, are generously embellished by the icons of material excess, including high-priced automobiles, expensive designer or casual wear, and great amounts of ostentatious jewelry. The unquestioning pursuit of material wealth is reflected in the metaphors of abundant living that dominate the lexicon of rap culture: getting paid, living large, collecting dividends.

Examining this aspect of rap culture provokes those of us in the church to reflect upon the various subtle and conspicuous manners in which we have similarly capitulated to the culture of consumption, exhibiting an unprincipled deference to materialism that has often compromised intellectual vision, psychic energy, and moral concern for more substantive social issues. Hence, our pursuit of materialism blinds us to how the inequitable concentration of wealth in limited and identifiable segments of society helps create a ravenous desire for material goods in those areas sorely afflicted by poverty and deprivation.

Rap culture, too, is obsessed with the ornamental and orgiastic elements of sexual fulfillment. Rap lyrics and videos are permeated by the emblems of sexual addiction, and personal freedom often is envisioned through tropes of sexual release. Moreover, sexual domination and verbal abuse are often viewed as marks of manhood. Despite the increasing visibility of women rappers, rap culture remains, to sample the words of James Brown (*the* major source of rap's aural boom), "a man's world." Such machismo invariably portrays the exclusive function of female sexuality as the satisfaction of male desire. Of course, rap's sexism magnifies the sexist practices, misogynist beliefs, and patriarchal ideas that are enforced and sustained in complex and subtle ways across our society, including ecclesiastical life.

Rap's sexual excess also seems to be inversely proportional to the general repression of sex in American culture, which is especially acute in religious circles. Discussions of ideas about sexuality in rap represent a pregnant point of entry for church members into the paradox of sexual repression, which is linked to an ironic denial of the body that has scandalously, even heretically, threatened a sophisticated Christian theology of embodiment.

Such discussions can also foster reflection about the redemptive and healthy functions of sexuality, which are also represented, although far less noticeably, in rap lyrics and videos. Overall, examining and criticizing rap culture's visions of sexuality presents ample opportunity to discuss positive forms of sexual fulfillment and to criticize, for instance, the brutal objectification of female sexuality that sadly persists in our society. Dialogue about rap culture and sexuality also forces the church to be more open and direct about its ambiguous theology of embodiment, to rethink its rigid conceptions of sexual identity, and to reexamine its contradictory and hypocritical codes of sexual behavior.

At its best moments, however, rap culture offers the possibility for a renewed appreciation of the complex and well-nigh immortal achievements of a people subject to the hostile forces of enslavement, exile, diaspora, and migration in the New World. While rap's form connects it to a rich field of African-American cultural practice, its messages of historical remembrance and prophetic social criticism connect it to a powerful history of African-American cultural resistance, rebellion, and revolution. The values of memory and social criticism link us with a racial past to which we can resolutely and hopefully appeal in resisting present forms of social hopelessness, historical amnesia, and cultural nihilism. In their art of historical retrieval, rap artists help illumine figures and movements that have given insight and inspiration in hard times.

For instance, Public Enemy, a politically controversial rap group, often laces its lyrics with literate allusion to historical figures from Chesimard to Malcolm X, the central ideological icon of a revived black nationalist rhetoric that is common among many rap groups. More importantly, however, Public Enemy is a forceful, prophetic voice in young black culture that holds up standards of historic racial achievement as incentive to combat contemporary forms of racist and classist oppression. Although plagued by strands of anti-Semitic ideology (about which the church knows much, and intimately), Public Enemy represents one of the most consistently critical voices in rap culture. Public Enemy rapper Chuck D. has even dubbed rap the "CNN" of black youth culture.

Rapper KRS-One, a former homeless person who was helped off the street by his future wife, Ms. Melody (a self-confessed "born-again rapper"), engages in what he calls "edutainment," a persuasive mix of education and entertainment. KRS-One makes learned allusion to sources such as Martin Bernal's *Black Athena,* speaks throughout America's public school systems, makes rap records that counsel antiviolence activity, and gives more than passing comment upon a range of social issues from police brutality to the chemical contents injected into beef as a hidden source of addictive behavior. He is one of rap's most important influences, and his willingness to lecture about his craft and social vision opens up intellectual space for wider segments of American culture to be introduced to rap culture's redeeming strengths and challenging social messages.

Rap culture represents the voice and vision of a significant segment of young black culture. It has provided many youth a means of escape from the material seductions of the drug culture, while permitting others to express incisive social criticism about a range of issues such as racism, classism, and an empty sense of cultural pride or historical achievement. Rap also mirrors the varieties of sexism that persist in many poor black communities, themselves reflections of the patriarchal tendencies that are dispersed throughout our culture. Only by confronting the powerful social criticism that rap culture articulates can we hope to understand its appeal to millions of black and white youth. And by examining its weaknesses and blindnesses, we are encouraged to critically confront our similar shortcomings, which do not often receive the controversial media coverage given to rap culture. In so doing, we may discover that many of the values that are openly despised in rap culture are more deeply rooted and widely shared than most of us would care to admit.

Improvisation

Cornel West's Prophetic Criticism

"Afro-American intellectual activity is alive and well in the 1980's," writes Cornel West in an essay from his new book, *Prophetic Fragments* (Eerdmans and Africa World Press, 1988). This is due in no small measure to the incisive scrutiny, expansive vision, and profound depth West brings to bear upon an impressively wide range of intellectual concerns. West, the newly appointed professor of religion and director of Afro-American studies at Princeton University, has taught philosophy of religion at Yale Divinity School and more recently was professor of philosophy and Christian practice at Union Theological Seminary in

New York. This book is a collection of West's essays, articles, reviews, and even fiction. It provides a peek into the vocational workshop of a critical and constructive intellectual who is unstintingly prolific and unfailingly provocative.

West's aim in this book is to "examine and explore, delineate and demystify, counter and contest the widespread accommodation of American religion to the political and cultural status quo." This project is enacted from the perspective of the prophetic stream of the Christian tradition, adopting what West terms a "principled prophetism." This principled prophetism incorporates the best of modernity and secularity (tolerance, fallibilism, criticism) while simultaneously criticizing the idols of modernity and secularity (science, technology, wealth).

The book is divided into three sections. The first and largest section is titled "Religion and Politics." Under this rubric, West's essays skillfully explore relationships between American religion and the social, economic, and political crises haunting the national and international scene: racism, sexism, classism, imperialism, and capitalism. Thus, in essays such as "The Prophetic Tradition in Afro-America," "Contemporary Afro-American Social Thought," and "Toward a Socialist Theory of Racism," West employs a subtle and insightful analysis of the social logics, the philosophical and ideological legitimations, and the political and cultural practices under which racism persists. He deepens and extends the scope of his analysis of racism begun in his first book, *Prophesy Deliverance!* West's theory of racism is complex (that is, it is multileveled, including economic and cultural factors) and antireductionist (that is, he doesn't explain racism's cause with reference to one element, such as the intentions of white racists).

This section also finds West continuing to refine his understanding of the relationship between progressive, Marxist-informed social analysis of the crises of capitalist civilization and prophetic Christian belief and practice. In both "Religion and the Left" and his essay on Alisdair MacIntyre, West contends that a major contribution of Marxist social analysis to Christian thought is its capacity to examine and criticize the economic circumstances, political situations, and historical conditions under which victimized peoples live. Likewise, Christian thought forces Marxist thinkers to take the culture of the oppressed seriously, allying Marxism with powerful resources of revolt against structures, modes, and forms of cultural alienation and spiritual despair. West's superb essay on Martin Luther King, Jr., contains the crucial insight that King was, in Italian social theorist Antonio Gramsci's term, an organic intellectual who "linked the life of the mind to social change with such moral persuasiveness and political effectiveness."

The second and shortest section of essays is titled "Religion and Culture." Here West mainly examines the socioeconomic contexts and historical content of the cultural practices, styles, and products (especially Afro-American ones) of postmodern America. Particularly penetrating are his analyses of forms of Afro-American musical expression. In "Sex and Suicide" West criticizes the rejection of transcendent meaning in life and history in the performer Prince, who "in his music and performance style promotes and encourages an orgiastic way of life in which sex is the opiate of the people." In "On Black-Jewish Relations," West tackles a ticklish subject, charting the various stages this relation ship has endured, offering suggestions for its repair.

In the third section, "Religion and Contemporary Theology," West comments upon several significant texts, figures, and problems that, in varying ways, bear upon important theological issues. In reviews of books by Juan Luis Segundo, Sharon Welch, and Franz Hinkelammert, West explores various alternatives within current liberation theology. He thinks Segundo's philosophical anthropology is philosophically confused, because it asserts that faith is at once a set of premises that circumscribe knowledge and a king of knowledge in itself. West concludes that Welch's deep distrust of rational argumentation as a basis for fundamental convictions leads her, ironically, to fail to take seriously an important aspect of her key notion of practice: reflection. "Practice," West says, "possesses a reflective and activist component." In Hinkelammert, West discovers a refreshing voice in contemporary liberation theology that is broadly interdisciplinary, that grounds liberation theology in a more detailed social-analytical viewpoint and biblical perspective, and that "examines the implications of his views on modern Catholic thought."

"The Crisis in Theological Education" is a hard-hitting critique of the current condition in American seminaries and divinity schools. A major reason for the crisis is that seminary and divinity school faculties "teach as they do with little reflection or consultation about what they do, why they teach what they do, and whether what they teach aids their students in preparation for Christian ministry." What to do? Part of the solution, West thinks, lies in reshaping and reforming the self-image of seminary professors (from careerists to vocationally responsible persons creatively linking the life of the mind with service to the people of God). Also, there must be a concomitant loosening of the stranglehold that the eighteenth-century German "theological encyclopedia" movement has on the theological curriculum, exalting theology as the queen discipline before which biblical studies, church history, and practical matters must intellectually genuflect. Instead, Christian theology (with a "hermeneutical historical consciousness at the center" that yields powerful social analyses) must interpret the Christian faith in conversation with other disciplines such as anthropology, philosophy, and history.

Cornel West's exciting book is important on at least two counts. First, it presents a model of Afro-American intellectual activity that encompasses black life and thought in the larger American and international scene. On the one hand, West's essays show what it means to take Afro-American intellectual practices seriously. This means that West isolates and emphasizes the crucial features of these traditions, products, and practices that are central to refining black intellectual discourse, examining black cultural production, and ameliorating the black sociopolitical condition. It also means that West is critical of those elements of black religious and intellectual life, culture, and politics that merit rejection, resistance, or reform in order to achieve these goals.

West also offers a glimpse of the Afro-American intellectual examining, debating, and criticizing ideas, events, and movements outside black life. As such, he provides a helpful understanding of how the term "Afro-American" functions in the phrase "Afro-American intellectual": both as a referent to areas of intellectual enterprise that focus needed critical attention upon all aspects of black existence and as the sociocultural location that grounds one's intellectual perspective upon a wide variety of political, philosophical, and religious problems and concerns.

Second, West's book also reveals the coming of age of Afro-

American prophetic Christian thought. His essays link the insights and ethos of the black religious tradition with powerful and often persuasive forms of social analysis and criticism. West's essays also indicate the prophetic black church's enormous potential for turning the corner on liberal and left-liberal social critique to radical interrogation of existing economic arrangements, political options, and historical conditions. Of course, this does not suggest that West's writings express the conscious political radicalism and social criticism of the majority of those who constitute the black church. But his analyses and criticisms are deeply anchored in and shaped by an Afro-American religious tradition that makes it very difficult for his perspective to be ignored or denied.

20

"God Almighty Has Spoken from Washington, D.C.": American Society and Christian Faith

As usual Stanley Hauerwas (this time with Michael Baxter) has, in "The Kingship of Christ: Why Freedom of 'Belief' Is Not Enough," given us a great deal to think about in wrestling with the persistent problems growing out of the church-state debate. Arguing that there are irresolvable tensions between American society and Christian faith, the authors deliver a tough rebuke to those theologians who "posit some kind of harmony between the two by means of a so-called church-state theory."[1] The authors further maintain that most Christian theologians conspire to "privatize and subordinate Christianity," especially when they assume that "Christianity consists of a set of beliefs (mere belief) that can be abstracted from practices and actions (conduct)."[2] The danger, as the authors see it, is that Christian belief gets removed from its legitimate social context in the church and becomes conceived as a matter of individual freedom. The remedy that Hauerwas and Baxter propose is for Christians to reclaim their ecclesiastical and social identity as "the people who acknowledge the Kingship of Christ."[3]

One need not accept (and indeed I don't) the authors' arguments about the value and function of church-state debates in discussions of religious freedom to affirm that the Kingship of Christ is crucial for the health of Christian churches. Still, I remain deeply suspicious of their claims about the social form that best serves and expresses Christian belief. Their arguments about the church's role in society suffer from the same flight from social embodiment that they claim characterizes their opponents in the church-state debate. And the intellectual road Hauerwas and Baxter travel inductively from their conclusion of Christ's Kingship—leading through arguments about freedom and political practice, the insuperable conflicts introduced by church-state debates, and the relation of civil religion to authentic Christian belief—is marked by signs of confusing detours and confounding dilemmas.

In my response to Hauerwas and Baxter's position, I will show how their narrow focus on secondary, less helpful issues in the history of church-state debates obscures more compelling and primary points of concern that have a better chance of illumining these debates. Then I will show how Hauerwas and Baxter's views of religious indifferentism rest on faulty analogies between free speech and freedom of religion, reveal an inadequate theory of politics, and are plagued by insurmountable dilemmas. In the end, their worries about indifferentism pale in comparison to the specter of irrelevance posed by Hauerwas and Baxter's beliefs to the lives of everyday Christians perplexed by the right relation between religion and politics.

Finally, I will argue that their understanding of the Christian tradition implies a homogeneous idea of faith that excludes from consideration other relevant examples of the relation between church and society that might challenge or support their views. Among other helpful models, the example of the prophetic black church presents a vital vision of the relationship between faith and politics that preserves Christian identity while expanding the possibilities of democracy, an unjustifiable task for Christians from Hauerwas's point of view, but a central claim of black prophetic Christianity.[4]

Hauerwas and Baxter's misgivings about the First Amendment in their present essay derive partially from a narrow interpretation of church-state relations by columnist George Will.[5] As Hauerwas and Baxter explain, for Will the "heart of the constitutional understanding of 'religion,' " is the "distinction between 'conduct' and 'mere belief.' "[6] According to the authors, Will elaborates this distinction by saying that the Founding Fathers sought to avoid the religious controversies that plagued Europe by establishing in religion's stead the commercial republic of capitalism. Influenced by John Locke, who maintained that the truth of religion cannot be established by reason, Thomas Jefferson shaped the American doctrine of the free exercise of religions, which made religions private and subordinate to the political order. As long as religion is mere belief and private, the logic goes, it is free and unrestricted. But when it becomes a matter of conduct or behavior, religion is subject to the rule of law. For Will, this represents the Founders' genius; for Hauerwas and Baxter, it is sheer anathema, an intolerable rub.

But Will has a severely limited and self-serving view of the First Amendment. Even if we acknowledge the distinctions many Founders made between belief and behavior, we are not automatically bound to Will's interpretation of their views. Indeed Hauerwas and Baxter's worries are legitimate only if Will's argument about the Founders' beliefs turns out to be *the* crucial distinction in the constitutional view of religion. But the most important distinction is not between conduct and mere belief, but between freedom of conscience and the coercion to believe. This distinction is made clear when we carefully consider in historical context the easily misinterpreted terms of James Madison and Thomas Jefferson, the prime architects of the constitutional concept of freedom of religion.

James Madison, who contributed key phrases to the important Virginia Declaration of Rights, an exemplary document defending freedom of religion, proposed the language of the First Amendment that was eventually revised and enacted by the First Congress.[7] In proposing the First Amendment, Madison was as greatly influenced by the suffering of religious dissenters at the hands of the Church of England as by enlightenment ideals of reason's superiority and the doctrine of natural rights.[8] These ideals led Madison to declare that religion "can be directed only by reason and conviction."[9] And the brutal battles fought over religious freedom led him to conclude that "all men are equally entitled to the free exercise of religion according to the dictates of conscience."[10]

Such religious battles also convinced Madison that religious belief must not be established or imposed by the state. This was especially true for a revealed religion like Christianity, whose claims to the exclusive possession of truth also opened the possibility of religiously justified claims to political power.[11] To circumvent this possibility in the embryonic nation, Christianity had to be shorn of its potential political authority, a strategy achieved by challenging Christianity's biblical authority and asserting its status as a reason-governed discourse, a transformation that profoundly shaped Madison's views of religion, and Jefferson's as well.[12]

Indeed, Jefferson, in the strong embrace of Lockean liberalism, natural rights philosophy, and enlightenment rationality, also rejected Christianity's status as revelation.[13] With Madison and other similarly enlightened men, Jefferson declared religion to be a matter of opinion.[14] This view led him to proclaim that, should the neighbors of Americans say that there are twenty gods, or no God, such a statement would neither "break their legs or pick their pockets," precisely because it is not backed by the force of law.[15] For Jefferson and the Founders, such an opinion is distinguished from officially established and recognized beliefs. Since the government is derived from the natural rights of human beings and not divine revelation, such opinions would neither mandate punishment nor require exceptional protection for their utterance. To act otherwise, as if the religious opinion that there was no God or that there were twenty gods could cause injury to be inflicted upon its bearer, is to acknowledge that such an utterance fractured a legally sanctioned belief about God. But this would be contrary to the constitutional view of religion.

And more important for the fledgling nation, Christianity was no longer to be protected from challenge or dissent under cover of legal sanction. Thus, the interests of nonbelievers, unorthodox believers, and dissenting Christians converged around the disestablishment of religion and the establishment of religious freedom. In view of this history, the central distinction in the constitutional view of religion is indeed between freedom of conscience and the coercion to believe. Hauerwas and Baxter's acceptance of Will's distinction between mere belief and conduct as the primary constitutional religious issue causes them to overlook the bitter cultural and interpretive wars fought over the freedom of religion by citizens oppressed by the intolerant behavior of the established church. By viewing the issue of the freedom of religion in relation to the historical events I have just sketched, Hauerwas and Baxter might be led to accentuate the struggles of oppressed Christians and other citizens against the power of the church when it is officially entrenched by law in a classic Constantinian contract with the state.[16] Ironically, the Constantinian compromise of the church is a favorite theme of Hauerwas's ethical reflections, and invites vigorous exposition in the present context.[17] But Hauerwas and Baxter's pursuit of a less important constitutional distinction has diverted their attention from a suitable occasion to press one of Hauerwas's more powerful charges.

Even a cursory reading of the events precipitating the development of the First Amendment suggests that it was a brilliantly preemptive and bloodless resolution of religious conflict. By disestablishing religion and establishing religious freedom, the Founders translated an a priori denial of privilege to any one religion in particular as the principle for extending privilege to them all. The crucial distinction in the constitutional view of religion is the one between enforced religious views and the freedom to practice the religion of one's choice or community. Viewing the freedom of religion debate in this manner allows us to understand what really was at stake for citizens who endured hardship because of their opposition to the politically protected claims of official and legal Christianity.

But Hauerwas and Baxter's silence on this aspect of the church-state debate is rooted perhaps in a presumption of the homogeneity of the Christian experience, a point I will take up in greater detail later. For now, it is enough to say that the freedom-of-religion debate pointed to the vibrant religious diversity, especially within Christianity itself, that was mocked by the rigid constraints and narrow practices of the Church of England and by established religion in the colonies. Established religion defined the church in the singular, but the existence of New Light Presbyterians, Strict Congregationalists, Separate Baptists, and even Methodists demanded that it be reconceived in the plural.[18]

Conflicts created by the quest for the tolerance of religious pluralism is an inescapably key theme that must be addressed in any credible account of the events surrounding and leading to the First Amendment. Their avoidance is certain to lead to truncated and self-serving versions of events that shaped, in principle, the democratic destiny of our nation. Indeed, the religious question played a crucial role "in the beginning of free government. No question was then more important, none played so prominent a role in the thought of the pertinent theorists—Hobbes, Locke, Spinoza, Bayle, and, to a lesser but still significant extent, even Montesquieu—and even if it could be said that they solved it, or answered it, in principle, it was left to the American Founders to be the first to solve it, or to try to solve it, in practice."[19]

Of course, as Hauerwas and Baxter's discussion of *Employment Divison, Dept. of Human Resources of the State of Oregon v. Smith and Black* proves, freedom of religion has met limitations in the form of state proscription of religious beliefs that intersect the nebulous area between important aspects of law and faith. We have also seen the opposite effect in the case of the Jonestown mass suicides, where the failure of state intervention in the name of freedom of religion perhaps inadvertently aided the economic and religious exploitation and deaths of over nine hundred persons.[20] But uses of freedom of religion have largely safeguarded the religious liberties of faith communities to pursue the practice of their beliefs in a society where religious prejudice, bigotry, and intolerance were not given legal underpinning.

The glaring exception, of course, is chattel slaves, who were for most of their enslavement legally barred from free worship without white supervision. But even black Christians came to cherish the First Amendment because it protected their hard-won freedom to worship without governance, while also giving legal expression to their concern that other groups not suffer similar penalties of social and religious intolerance. The formulation of the First Amendment by the Founders presented a tenable solution to the religious suffering created by the legalization of Christianity. It may be cogently argued that with the First Amendment, a large and vital Christian purpose was served, that the ideals of Christian love and tolerance were ironically promoted through the government's refusal to cede Christianity official status. By keeping believers from maiming one another over religious dispute, the government instituted in law what Christian belief aimed for in principle but failed to practice. It would not be the last time the government intervened in the face of the failure of Christians to act on their beliefs, a topic about which I shall have more to say later.

Overall the First Amendment has been very good for Christianity. It forced Christian churches to appeal to potential adherents on the basis of persuasive preaching, sound theology, superior ways of life, and sacrificial action.[21] Once they were cut from the strings of official obligation, independent Christian churches were free to prophetically address the state and to criticize practices that were offensive to moral principles to which churches strongly adhered. The benefits of the separation of church and state are nicely summarized by John Bennett, who says that it fulfills the "need of religious institutions to be free from control by the state," that it satisfies the "need to protect citizens from interference with their religious liberty" by either state power or religious groups, and that it "is favorable to the health and vitality of churches."[22]

The alarm set off in Hauerwas and Baxter by Will's insistence that the free exercise of religion rests on religion's privatization and subordination is largely unnecesary. Perhaps we can reach a clearer understanding if we examine the two terms of Will's contention separately. To proclaim that religion will not carry the weight of law by being disestablished is not the same as saying religion will be made private.[23] It is very important not to collapse the two as Will has done, a move Hauerwas and Baxter fail to challenge. Indeed, many of the Founders promoted the advantage of the public expression of religion even as they asserted the necessity for religion's disestablishment.

Because the Founders were not orthodox Christians, the views they held about the role of religion in the republic had more to do with its preservative function in national life and its support of political institutions than its strictly redemptive role as envisioned by partisan believers.[24] Benjamin Franklin, for instance, saw the virtue of what he called "public religion," the forerunner of what we know today as civil religion.[25] Martin Marty says that by public religion Franklin "meant not the end of sects but of sectarianism, not the end of their freedoms but the increase of their duty to produce a common morality. Wherever he saw churches agreeing, he encouraged their support of the common weal, and he opposed their spats over their peculiarities. His faith . . . was in . . . the need to do good."[26] Franklin's views resonated with other Founders, who sought to fashion a public polity based on the premise that a common moral community underlay the republic. As Marty says: "Fortunately for later America, the

Founding Fathers, following the example of Franklin, put their public religion to good use. While church leaders usually forayed only briefly into the public arena and then scurried back to mind their own shops, men of the Enlightenment worked to form a social fabric that assured freedom to the several churches, yet stressed common concerns of society."[27]

George Washington, too, subscribed to a belief in the public utility of religion, asserting the link between religion and public morality as the foundation of national flourishing. In his farewell address, Washington stated:

> Of all the dispositions and habits which lead to political prosperity, religion and morality are indispensable supports. In vain would that man claim the tribute of patriotism who should labor to subvert these great pillars of human happiness, these firmest props of the duties of men and citizens. The mere politician, equally with the pious man, ought to respect and to cherish them . . . . Whatever may be conceded to the influence of refined education on minds of peculiar structure, reason and experience both forbid us to expect that national morality can prevail in exclusion of religious principle.[28]

And even Thomas Jefferson, despite his unorthodox Christian beliefs and his individualization of religious faith, demonstrated appreciation for religion's public function in the republic, especially since the proliferation of religious bodies would serve as a built-in check and balance to American religious life. According to Jefferson, the function of "several sects perform the office of a Censor morum over each other."[29] He also valued religion for lending moral support to political liberty when he queried, "And can the liberties of a nation be thought secure when we have removed their only firm basis, a conviction in the minds of the people that these liberties are the gift of God?"[30]

Of course, it is exactly the public expression of religion along these lines that disturbs Hauerwas and Baxter, who hold that national or civil religion is "counterfeit" Christianity uprooted from an account of the good. Even if one maintains this view, however, it doesn't negate the fact that there is nothing in the First Amendment that prohibits the public expression of religion, including Christianity, in the republic. Thus, as Hauerwas and Baxter present his case, Charles Taylor's arguments about religion and political life are on target: there was neither intent nor need in the separation of church and state to exclude God or religion from the republic.

Similarly, the subordination of religion to the political order is not as bad as Hauerwas and Baxter deem it to be, because it doesn't mean what they fear it to imply. I have already hinted at my response earlier by suggesting that one virtue of the separation of church and state is Christianity's enhanced potential to address the state on politically independent terms. But Will's claim is also legitimate, that religion was to be made subordinate to the political order. The tension that arises from these apparently contradictory claims can be relieved by examining the two ways in which we can read religious subordination: either functionally or morally.

First, since American society was deliberately constructed upon secular principles to avoid the fatal conflicts occasioned by established religion in the England of the Founders' recent memory, the subordination of religion to the state went hand in hand with the creation of the nation and the establishment of the freedom of religion. Saying that religion is subordinate to the political order is the positive statement of its more generally repeated negative formulation: that religion will not be established, or politically justified, in American society. What is meant is that religion will not function officially to adjudicate national disputes, will not occupy legal status to enforce civil codes, and will not be the means by which social goods are distributed. These functions are left to the political realm. Hence, in a legal sense, religion is functionally subordinate to politics.

On the other hand, if by subordinate it is meant that religion will surrender its independence to the political order to merely justify, or even sanctify, its practices; that religion will abdicate its role as critic of governmental and state practices; that religion will no longer provide moral visions and ethical principles by which advocates of justice may call society to judgment, then religion is without question *morally insubordinate* to and *politically independent* of the political realm. Its functional subordination by no means entails its moral subordination.

The difference is that functional subordination is the very premise by which American religions can claim their freedom to express faith and exercise their belief, especially in the social and public sphere. But moral insubordination is the way religions preserve their integrity and viability and perform their real worth to the republic by calling it to judgment in relation to their specific moral visions. Moreover, as I will more fully argue later, if the moral visions of religion are to have public persuasion, they must be cast in terms that transcend narrow or sectarian religious language and concern, demonstrating their relevance by their prophetic judgment of, or application to, the nation in compelling public terms.[31]

Given these distinctions, Hauerwas and Baxter's worries that religion becomes private and subordinate to the state in the First Amendment are dissolved when we bring more precision to our understanding of the terms of religion's relation to the state. If Hauerwas and Baxter's real concern is to resist the privatization and moral subordination of Christianity, their fight is not with constitutional views of religion, but with forms of Christian experience and belief that claim that the church's most perfect social expression is limited to ecclesial expressions, as Hauerwas and Baxter proclaim.

Ironically, then, it is Hauerwas and Baxter who turn out to be the real opponents of the full social embodiment of Christianity. By refusing to acknowledge the legitimate expression of Christian faith outside the perimeters of the church, Hauerwas and Baxter contribute to a fatal narrowing of religious belief, a position that has led to Hauerwas being characterized (fairly I think) as a sectarian.[32] Their sectarian belief conflicts with Hauerwas and Baxter's intent to resist the privatization, and indirectly, the subordination of Christianity.

Their views also lead them to de-emphasize the crucial features of the church-state debate that have the best chance to illumine the historical conflicts over religious tolerance, plurality, difference, and diversity, issues that also clearly affect our contemporary religious and cultural scene. More important, their position also reduces the potential impact of the gospel on the lives of Christians struggling to understand the proper role of faith in contemporary political debates.

Hauerwas and Baxter's deficiencies are further magnified in the way they make analogies between freedom of speech and freedom of religion in pressing their case. Drawing on an essay by Stanley Fish, the authors claim that just as freedom of speech has paved the way for "indifferentism" in speech, so freedom of religion has led to "religious indifferentism." According to Hauerwas and Baxter, Fish claims that speech has become a matter of indifference because it has been severed from an account of the good that assigns value to "free speech," which in reality has built-in limits against those expressions its exponents deem harmful to its flourishing.

In this view, freedom of speech is really an illusion. Furthermore, all the distinctions that Will made about religion find analogous expression in "a private sphere not only of speech and ideas, but also of 'mere speech' and 'mere ideas,' of speech and ideas understood apart from any substantive account of the good which they serve."[33] The same holds for religion. As Hauerwas and Baxter say, "Inherent in Christian convictions is a substantive account of the good," an account that is in tension with "all so-called 'political' accounts of the good."[34] Moreover, when political accounts of the good underwrite a vision of God and Christianity that are rooted in civil religion, there is conflict with genuine Christianity. Hauerwas and Baxter state that when Christianity gets separated from its embodied social form, Christian belief becomes "asocial" and degenerates into mere belief, while a "counterfeit" religion, a religion of the nation, rises to take Christianity's place.

On the face of it—judging from the passages they cite—Hauerwas and Baxter's use of Fish's work appears consonant with their project, an act of untroubled appropriation. But closer reading of Fish's essay suggests that there are irresolvable tensions between his views and Hauerwas and Baxter's, tensions that have to do primarily with theological presumptions in Fish's work that are diametrically opposed to Hauerwas and Baxter's beliefs. Such tensions place Hauerwas and Baxter in a confounding dilemma. As a result, for Hauerwas and Baxter to successfully adopt Fish's arguments, they will either have to substantially alter their positions or give up their present beliefs about the appropriate social expression of Christian faith.

The tensions between Fish's analysis and Hauerwas and Baxter's use of it are glimpsed in Fish's discussion of the possible objections to his view of free speech as articulated by its defenders. What the defenders of free speech could say, Fish hypothesizes, is that he has not appropriately anticipated future revisions to his specific account of the good for which speech stands, thus prematurely closing possible valid interpretations to future generations: "My mistake, it could be said, is to equate the something in whose service speech is with some locally espoused value (e.g. the end of racism, the empowerment of disadvantaged minorities), whereas in fact we should think of that something as a now inchoate shape . . . we cannot now know . . . and therefore we must not prematurely fix it in ways that will bind successive generations to error."[35] But Fish demurs from this position on the First Amendment, saying that it "continues in a secular form the Puritan celebration of millenarian hopes, but it imposes a requirement so severe that one would expect more justification than is usually provided."[36] Fish continues: "The requirement is that we endure whatever pain racist and hate speech inflicts for the sake of a future whose emergence we can only take on faith. In a specifically religious vision like Milton's, this makes perfect sense (it is indeed the whole of Christianity), but in the context of a politics that puts its trust in the world and not in the Holy Spirit, it raises more questions than it answers."[37]

For Fish, this alternative to his view makes "perfect sense" only if it is rooted in a Christian interpretation of events that he implies does not prevail in our culture, or at least not in the political realms where decisions about the First Amendment are debated and resolved. Such a Christian interpretation of events, which would counsel enduring the present penalties imposed by free speech, could only be supported by belief in a future guaranteed by religious faith. Moreover, such a Christian perspective is only coherent within a political framework that puts its trust in the Holy Spirit. Thus, the key features of this opposing view to Fish's position are dependent upon the premises of a religious worldview to make its claims cogent.

Also, such a religious perspective would influence the political expression of the alternative to Fish's position, and could therefore in no way be identical to his views of free speech or, by extension, free religion. As Fish has already indicated, one such crucial difference between his position and its alternative might be that free speech in the abstract must be protected, even though it means the present and concrete suffering by blacks and minorities, because of a future disclosure of truth that in retrospect will alter how we perceive present suffering. The good to be revealed in the future guaranteed by faith, we can infer, will compensate for, or at least justify, the present suffering.

The point is that Fish's view is predicated upon an explicitly secular view that would seem to severely contradict Hauerwas and Baxter's views. The sorts of evidence that count in the realm of faith will not do for the secular realm—the requirement, as Fish says, is too severe. The opposite is also true, that the sorts of evidence sufficient in the secular realm will not wash in the realm of faith. The severe requirement that Fish cannot imagine bearing derives from its linkage to a Christian worldview where evidence is supplied by faith and trust in the Holy Spirit. This latter alternative—which Fish says requires that we acknowledge "the (often grievous) consequences, but that we . . . suffer them in the name of something that cannot be named"—is the second of two unacceptable alternatives (and the one not mentioned by Hauerwas and Baxter) to his position. The first is the alternative Hauerwas and Baxter do mention, the position that makes speech inconsequential and a matter of indifference.

This second alternative to Fish's position seems ideally suited for Hauerwas and Baxter, and given their religious outlook—which emphasizes the social expression of Christianity in the church and opposition to secular liberal society as the "politics that know not God"[38]—the one that they would logically adopt. The only problem is that by adopting such a view Hauerwas and Baxter immediately face a dilemma. In accepting the religious basis of society signified by trust in the Holy Spirit and the Kingship of Christ, they are identified with a position that Fish claims is opposed to the sort of secular logic that clinches the case that he makes for speech inconsequentialism and that Hauerwas and Baxter by analogy extend to religious indifferentism. On the other hand, if Hauerwas and Baxter reject the secular logic of Fish's position, they have destroyed the basis of their argument for the indifferentism of freedom of religion and would have to forfeit their claim that it has corrupted the church-state debate, because it is rooted in the sort of reasoning they find offensive to Christian belief. Either way, Hauerwas and Baxter are caught in a damning dilemma.

There is yet another point of tension between Hauerwas and Baxter and Fish. Fish contends that both alternatives to his views—speech as inconsequential, and present suffering for the sake of a nameless something—are unpersuasive. But he admits that "many in the society seemed to have bought them."[39] Why? Because such persons avoid facing

> what they take to be the alternative. That alternative is politics, the realization (at which I have already hinted) that decisions about what is and is not protected in the realms of expression will rest not on principle or firm doctrine but on the ability of persons and groups to so operate (some would say manipulate) the political process that the speech they support is labelled 'protected' while the speech inimical to their interests is declared to be fair game.[40]

To those who respond that politics would render the First Amendment a "dead letter," or that it deprives us of norms in determining "when and what speech to protect," or that it effaces the distinction between speech and action, Fish argues for the primacy of politics.[41] Fish responds that

> the First Amendment has always been a dead letter if one understood its 'liveness' to depend on the identification and protection of a realm of 'mere' expression or discussion distinct from the real of regulatable conduct; that the distinction between speech and action has always been effaced in principle, although in practice it can take whatever form the prevailing political conditions mandate; that we have never had any normative guidance for marking off protected and unprotected speech; rather, that the guidance we have had has been fashioned (and refashioned) in the very political struggles over which it then (for a time) presides.[42]

In sum, for Fish the "name of the game has always been politics, even when (indeed, especially when) it is played by stigmatizing politics as the area to be avoided."[43]

As if Hauerwas and Baxter's arguments were not already on the ropes because of their earlier dilemma, this last argument of Fish's deals a fatal blow to their aspirations to make Christianity social but not political, especially because so much of their argument hinges on the effective correlation between Fish's views on free speech and the conclusions Hauerwas and Baxter draw from them about the perils of free religion. Fish explicitly endorses politics as the means by which claims of free speech are made intelligible and cogent, precisely because politics has been the implicit basis of understanding and applying the amendment from the very beginning. The same, presumably, should hold for the application of politics to free religion claims. But Hauerwas and Baxter are unwilling to cede the primacy of politics in making the claims of Christianity cogent or in adjudicating religious conflict, which is the obvious application of Fish's position to their own. Again, they are faced with a dilemma: if they give up politics, they give up the punch line to Fish's arguments, severely compromising the force of his contentions and, by extension, their arguments. But if they adopt politics, they abort their arguments about the primacy of a confessional God and ecclesial religion to politics. Either way, a principle they cherish is surrendered.

In some places in their essay, it appears that Hauerwas and Baxter will stick with Fish all the way through. They say that with "the indifferentism which inevitably ensues when speech is considered apart from the Good, 'freedom of speech' enjoys a protection in the United States according to arbitrary patterns of political influence and power as much as according to any consistent application of constitutional principles."[44] It seems as though they are on the verge of acknowledging that value-laden, good-dependent notions of free speech, and by analogy free religion, need to be negotiated by politics, which in this case amounts to the struggle to assign value to goods defined in the abstract.

But Hauerwas and Baxter dismiss such hopes by saying that only "within the ecclesial context, that is, only within a context in which the social landscape is imbued with the presence of Christ, can Christianity emerge as an alternative both to liberal freedom and civic freedom, and more generally, to the political project we call the United States of America."[45] For Hauerwas and Baxter, the task is to "provide an alternative vision to the political vision of America, one that is shaped by the acknowledgment that true political authority is to be found not in any republican virtues, new or ancient, nor in any set of governmental procedures, but in Jesus Christ who is our true King."[46] So much for politics!

By refusing to enter the fray, to give political justification and arguments for their beliefs about the Christian good, Hauerwas and Baxter not only repudiate their connection with the sort of social activity that Fish describes as necessary for those who refute nebulous concepts of the freedom of speech, but they also risk a more serious setback with disturbing consequences for the Christian church: they fail to offer to everyday Christians stuck in the gritty interstices of politics adequate resources and substantive recommendations for moving beyond paralysis, confusion, or wrong practice. Just when Christians caught in the punishing political dilemmas of contemporary society need a note of reveille, retreat is sounded. Thus, the most harmful effect of Hauerwas and Baxter's views of free speech and free religion may not be the indifferentism they worry over, but the sheer irrelevance of their views to the church to which they are committed.

This irrelevance is pegged on the peculiar social but apolitical vision Hauerwas and Baxter have of Christian faith. By failing to take politics seriously, they can do little more than lament, for instance, the loss of rights by Smith and Black in the Supreme Court case they cite. At best, they can make intellectual moves to reject the distinctions that have made religion a matter of indifference. Because they refuse to engage a public beyond the church, Hauerwas and Baxter have little chance to affect the manner in which discussion is formed around these issues in the public sphere. More poignantly, Hauerwas and Baxter's modus operandi cannot affect future legal and political decisions that similarly impact other citizen's lives and their freedom of religious beliefs.

Hauerwas and Baxter's problems are also rooted in yet a third dimension of their discussion of religious indifferentism that they themselves seem not to take seriously: a substantive account of the good that is the background to their notion of Christian faith. Not only should speech have an account of the good, as Hauerwas and Baxter contend, but by extension of their analogy between free speech and free religion, so should Christian faith. The point here is not to highlight an account of the good to which Christian faith can be said to generally refer—Christian love, peace, or justice, for instance—but to elaborate the specific cultural contexts and social visions that have decisively shaped and made possible specific faith communities. I suspect this is not high on Hauerwas and Baxter's agenda because their procedures and assumptions imply a homogeneity about the Christian faith that masks the social roots and cultural contexts of the ecclesial embodiment of religious belief.

Hauerwas and Baxter's approach mutes the radical diversity and complex pluralism within the Christian faith, a situation that long ago made it untenable in certain sociological and theological senses to speak primarily of The Church.[47] Because of their procedures, Hauerwas and Baxter have failed to take into consideration, or even argue against, an expression of Christian faith that has creatively confronted many of the problems discussed by the authors: the black church.[48] By turning now to this example, I intend to illumine the relation between religion and politics in one of the most helpful but neglected models available.

Black Christian churches have had quite a different approach to the First Amendment than the position argued by Hauerwas or Baxter, largely because of the prominence of legal issues in determining the status, fate, and humanity of African-Americans for much of our history. And with the central importance of religion to African-American culture, the strong and vital connections between civil and religious concerns has been well established. Not only has religion helped sustain black survival in times of racial and national crisis, but it has furnished principles and persons to justify black claims to equal humanity and social justice in government, church, and school.[49]

Although it is by now common to cite the black Christian experience in debates about the relationship between religion and politics, the black church is rarely viewed as a genuine source of information about these matters in ways that count. As Cornel West has stated:

> Ironically, the black church experience is often invoked as an example of the religion/politics fusion, but rarely as a source to listen to or learn from. Instead, it is simply viewed as an instance that confirms the particular claims put forward by the respective sides. The black experience may no longer be invisible, but it remains unheard—not allowed to speak for itself, to be taken seriously as having something valuable to say.[50]

The black church view of the relationship between religion and politics has roots in the denominational affiliations that shaped it, the ongoing experiences of oppression in national life that black religion ceaselessly addresses, and broad experiments in American civil religion.

Black Christians are overwhelmingly Baptist and Methodist, a legacy that extends back to slave culture.[51] Because it was illegal to baptize and preach to slaves during much of slavery, the process of exposing slaves to Christianity was gradual. As slaves were eventually incorporated into Christianity on limited terms in the mid-1700s, they were deeply affected by Methodists and especially by Separate Baptists. The Separate Baptists were viewed with suspicion by both the established church and society at large during their initial stages of growth in the early 1700s.[52] Deeply disinherited, poor, without formal training, and broadly suspicious of external authority, the Separate Baptists naturally appealed to slaves who were even more ostracized from American culture than the Baptists because of their legal status as personal property.

But as they grew, Separate Baptists continued to exhibit two traits that marked their early years: their opposition to slavery and their enthusiastic leadership of the fight against established religion.[53] Thus, at the base of the denomination to which slaves were overwhelmingly drawn, and in which they eventually established independent churches in the mid-1800s, was an emphasis on the strong relation between political and civil issues and personal and communal religious belief. The arguments that radical religious dissenters made for freedom from slavery and freedom of religion prefigured the legal and social arguments advanced by black intellectuals, organizers, and leaders in the fight against institutional racism in two important ways.[54]

First, the religious dissenters' arguments expressed religious themes of social justice linked to belief in God. The arguments of Isaac Backus and John Allen against slavery and religious intolerance pictured these injustices as offenses not only to civil society, but to authentic Christian belief.[55] Second, although their arguments were unquestionably motivated by religious concern, dissenters cast their arguments in the language of civic piety and civil responsibility in making moral claims on the state to act justly.

These two narrative strategies were adopted and ingeniously expanded by black Christians, especially the prophetic wing of the black church. This vital branch of black Christianity has relentlessly explained and justified the moral and religious claims of black Christian belief in the language of civic piety, whose vocabulary includes legal redress, moral suasion, civil rights, and political proclamation.

This last point reveals as well African-Americans' participation in and expansion of traditions of American civil religion. Although for Hauerwas and Baxter it is "counterfeit" religion, a progressive, largely liberal version of civil religion is critically celebrated within African-American prophetic Christianity.[56] As Charles Long says, "The distinction between civil religion and church religion is not one that looms large for us."[57] He continues:

> In the first place, it is the overwhelming reality of the white presence in any of its various forms that becomes the crucial issue. Whether this presence was legitimated by power executed illegally, or whether in institution or custom, its reality, as far as blacks were concerned through most of their history, carried the force of legal sanction enforced by power. The black response to this cultural reality is part of the civil rights struggles in the history of American blacks.[58]

Long further argues that it is not incidental that black churches have been the locus of civil rights struggle because it "represented the black confrontation with an American myth that dehumanized the black person's being."[59] Furthermore, the "location of this struggle in the church enabled the civil rights movement to take on the resources of black cultural life," such as organization, music, artistic expression, and proficiency in collecting limited economic resources.[60]

In appropriating and improvising upon a vocabulary of civic piety, black Christians have appealed to the sacred symbols of national life and its democratic principles, which find literate expression in the Constitution and the Declaration of Independence. Perhaps the most famous example of this long-standing black church tradition is symbolized in the brilliant career of Martin Luther King, Jr. Like his Separate Baptist predecessors and his

Black Baptist ancestors, King employed the language of civic piety (particularly civil rights) in articulating at once the goals of African-American religion and a version of liberal democracy.[61] Although he remained rooted in his religious base, King transcended the narrow focus of sectarian and myopic religious concerns to embrace a universal moral perspective in addressing, first, the specific suffering of black Americans and, eventually, the economic exploitation and racial oppression of other "minorities."

But King's genius lay in his ability to show how increased democracy for African-Americans served the common good by making democracy hew closer to its ideals than its performance in the distant and recent past suggested. King spoke a language of civic piety (especially civil rights) that resonated with crucial aspects of American moral self-understanding, particularly since such self-understanding was closely linked to ideals of justice, freedom, and equality. King and his colleagues creatively reinterpreted documents of ultimate importance in national life—particularly the Declaration of Independence and the Constitution—in extending the goods at which they aimed (including democracy, justice, and equality) to blacks and others excluded from their original intent.[62]

Shaped profoundly by the black Christian church and rooted in black theological perspectives on love, justice, equality, and freedom articulated in the rich history of black resistance to racism, King and his cohorts forged empowering connections between their religious beliefs and the social, civic, and legal goals to which they believed their faith committed them. Indeed, they translated their religious efforts into the language with the best chance to express their goals in the national arena. For the black church, justice is what love sounds like when it speaks in public, civic piety is love's public language, equality its tone of voice, and freedom its constant pitch. For Hauerwas and Baxter, such translation may prove problematic, but for black Christians it has meant survival.

Such acts of translation also rest on the black Christian belief that the entire world belongs to God, that religious truth is not bound to the sanctuary, and that God often employs apparently disinterested or even hostile persons, forces, and institutions to achieve the divine prerogative. This truth can be partially glimpsed in the popularity of the scripture "You meant evil against me; but God meant it for good."[63] This often-quoted passage forms one of the most visible hermeneutic strategies employed in the black church, one that reflects a strong doctrine of providence and a serviceable theodicy geared toward black survival and a momentous confrontation with suffering and evil.

For prophetic black Christians, not only is speaking the language of civil society not taboo, but the messages of God are likewise not limited to homiletical proclamation, theological discourse, or other ecclesial expressions of God-talk. Since the world belongs to God, and the powers that exist, even if evil intentioned, may have good consequences in the eyes of faith, God can use whatever forum necessary to deliver divine gift or judgment. This whole theological approach is implicit in the statement by a jubilant black person who, upon hearing of the 1956 Supreme Court decision declaring segregated transportation in Montgomery, Alabama, unconstitutional, exclaimed, "God Almighty has spoken from Washington, D.C."[64] For black Christians, God is the original and ultimate polyglot. The language of civic piety (especially civil rights) serves God's purposes, as does the language of theological study and religious devotion. Thus, the civil rights movement helped foster a progressive understanding of the relation between religion and politics that rested on precedents of such interaction in American civil religion.

I have given this severely abbreviated genealogy and justification of the positive relation of religion to politics in African-American Christianity to suggest the rich resources it contains for critical thinking about the relation between church and society. The progressive and prophetic black church, as I have sketched it here, rejects the premises of Hauerwas and Baxter's arguments about the relation of faith and politics. Faith has a large part to play in the public arena, but only if it will redescribe its goals in languages that are publicly effective, accompanied by the politics with the best chance to make those goals concrete and relevant. Black Christianity avoids attempts to impose Christianity on the world, a strategy as old as religious establishment and as new as national attempts to manipulate God for political favor.[65] Rather, it retains the strengths and insights of religious belief while making arguments for the common good and public interest that are subject to criticism and open to revision because they are neither final nor infallible.

Its history prevents black Christianity from endorsing Hauerwas and Baxter's pessimistic views about the ability of Christian faith to mix with politics without losing its soul, without surrendering its capacity to criticize liberal democracy. Hauerwas and Baxter are right to remind us that Christian faith is in perennial tension with all political accounts of the good. Indeed, the history of African-American prophetic Christianity is the story of the relentless criticism of failed American social practices, the constant drawing attention to conflicts between political ideals and realities, and the ageless renewal of a commitment to broaden the bounds of liberty so that democracy is both noun and adjective, both achievement and process. But some political accounts of the good are better than others, and only those Christian communities willing to risk the erosion and expansion of certain aspects of their Christian identity in secular affairs have the opportunity to affect the public interest for the better.

This, of course, is why Hauerwas and Baxter's views of the various problems associated with the freedom of religion are viewed suspiciously by the prophetic black Christian church. By avoiding the nasty and brutal sphere of politics, Hauerwas and Baxter cannot adequately account for the black struggle and suffering endured to receive the freedoms the First Amendment guarantees. Black Christians have always understood that the batteries are not included, that American ideals, principles, and promises are never given, but must be secured through political struggle in the public realm. With Fish, they recognize that the "game has always been politics."[66] Hauerwas and Baxter's account not only masks the social and political roots of their own faith, but it effectively discounts the experience of black Christians who provide precisely the sort of example of the relation between church and politics that might have a chance of bringing greater clarity to this complex debate.

Finally, black prophetic Christians are wary of theological discussions that reduce the social embodiment of Christianity to the church and that portray the state as the enemy of Christian freedom. If theological justifications of slavery had not done so before, white Christian opposition to the civil rights movement chastened black Christian expectation of white Christians' moral and religious support of the goal of African-American liberation.[67] While arguing that the role of the church was to attend to the spiritual aspects of life in the church while avoiding the acrimonious and schismatic business of politics at all costs, many white Christian churches ironically furnished ideological and theological support to the forces that impeded the progress of the civil rights movement.[68]

The greater and more tragic irony, however, is that often white Christians actively opposed black progress by participating in White Citizens' Councils, the Ku Klux Klan, or other hate groups that harassed and even murdered black Christians. Even if they didn't actively participate in such heinous crimes, many white Christians "retreated into the womb of an ahistorical piety."[69] By adopting positions similar to those that Hauerwas and Baxter suggest, these white Christians were rendered impotent to affect the lives of their black Christian colleagues because their theological stance was deeply apolitical and hence unable to make claims on the public good in ways that were immediately helpful to black Christians.

Moreover, it was not the white Church-qua-Church that called for the end of such barbaric and evil practices or that actively intervened to prevent the murder and maiming of black life. It was the sustained social and political struggle of a tiny band of black prophetic Christians and their allies who, by sacrificial action, civil disobedience, and appeals to the American conscience by means of the language of civic piety, forced the *state* to intervene through legal and political measures. As in the religious situation of colonial America during Revolutionary times, the state intervened to prevent one group of Christians from killing others.

Once again, civil protest and political power had put into law what Christian belief had professed but failed to practice. And black Christians interpreted such intervention as an extension of the providence of God over even secular political structures, as black Christians heard God Almighty speaking from Washington, D.C. This does not mean that the state is uncritically praised as the unwavering instrument of divine deliverance. It is, however, one of the legitimate means available to black Christians seeking to secure and protect their freedom, so long denied by law and Christian practice.

The poverty of Hauerwas and Baxter's vision of the social embodiment of Christianity becomes even more evident when they return to one of the bleakest epochs in modern Catholic Christendom, the papacy of Pope Pius XI, to draw examples of Christ's Kingship. Pope Pius XI, according to Hauerwas and Baxter, "boldly and bluntly asserts the importance of publicly recognizing and celebrating the Kingship of Christ in reconstituting the entire social order."[70] The whole point behind the feast celebrating Christ's Kingship was to emphasize that "the common good is to be defined by Christ."[71] Furthermore, Hauerwas and Baxter claim that, in opposition to Will's celebration of the secularism that led to the subordination of religion to politics, "Pope Pius XI sees such a subordination as the undoing of any true politics."[72] Finally, Pope Pius XI, according to Hauerwas and Baxter, "resists the temptation to conceive of politics in anything less than soteriological terms."[73]

But Pope Pius XI is precisely the sort of figure who is an example of Hauerwas and Baxter's worst fears: he promoted the moral subordination of Christianity to the political order. By signing a concordat with Mussolini in 1929, Pope Pius XI made Mussolini's regime the first government in modern Catholic history to receive official recognition by the Vatican, thus supplying theological justification to the dictator's murderous Fascist maneuvers.[74] Pius XI "deliberately sabotaged democracy, the strongest opponent of Communism, for the politically and morally ruinous experiment of Fascism."[75] Pius XI was also a particularly cruel foe of religious tolerance and diversity.

Pius XI facilitated the "marriage of convenience" between Catholicism and Fascism that helped to destroy the Popolari (the Christian Democratic party), the People's party, which was the second legitimate party in parliament and the only real alternative to the Fascists.[76] More viciously, he requested the resignation of priest Don Sturzo as general secretary of the Popolari, banishing him from Rome at the height of the Popolari's fight against Mussolini. After his departure, the Fascists moved to expand their efforts to "wipe out the 'white' trade-unions, co-operatives, and youth organizations."[77] Pius XI also used his proximity to Mussolini to repress the freedom of religious minorities, urging Mussolini to restrict Protestant missions in Italy and to outlaw Freemasons. Pius XI was also pleased when Mussolini prevented the building of a Muslim mosque in Rome and when the dictator persecuted Waldensians, Pentecostalists, the Salvation Army, and eventually Jews.[78] After the Concordat of 1929, Mussolini exempted priests from taxation and employed public funds to prevent the financial collapse of Catholic banks.[79]

Most appallingly, the official pact between Mussolini and Pius XI led to the Vatican's declaration that the dictator was a man "sent by providence."[80] Pius XI compromised the politically independent, socially prophetic, and morally insubordinate voice of the church by officially colluding with Mussolini's Fascist party to stamp out democracy, restrict the religious freedom of other denominations and religions, and betray some of the church's own priests and members in an effort to placate Mussolini. As Denis Mack Smith says, Mussolini claimed that "the Church, as a result of their treaty, was no longer free but subordinate to the State."[81] During Mussolini's dictatorship, and because of Pope Pius XI's fatal compromise, this was tragically true.

The concordat with Mussolini is the infamous political legacy of Pius XI's reign. He is hardly the figure to whom we should turn in thinking about Christ's Kingship. Even Hauerwas and Baxter's statements about Pius XI's insistence on the link between soteriology and politics seems more appropriately elaborated, and less severely compromised, by contemporary exponents of that belief, especially liberation theologians.[82] And although most liberation theologians are completely committed to the radical transformation of society in light of Christ's Kingship—and are equipped with penetrating social analysis, progressive political activity, and broad historical investigation—few are willing to exclusively identify the Kingdom of Christ with the kingdom of this world. Pius XI failed to remember Hauerwas and Baxter's lesson: that Christianity is in extreme tension with all accounts of the political good.

Given Hauerwas's belief in the unity of the virtues, the choice of Pius XI—a pope who was antidemocratic, unfaithful in fateful ways to the church and its Lord, and intolerant of religious and political freedom—as the best exponent of the Kingship of Christ is not only unfortunate, it is no less than tragic.[83] But then, given the dilemmas I have shown Hauerwas and Baxter to be trapped by and their refusal to engage the nitty-gritty world of real politics, their misled—and misleading—choice is sadly predictable.

Hauerwas and Baxter have largely missed the major areas of concern in the struggles to relate church and state, and religion and politics, because they have not viewed these matters from the perspective of those who suffered for the freedom to worship and practice their beliefs. The political struggle to implement democratic ideals in our society is the real story behind the First Amendment. It is about much more than the wall that separates church and state. If the truth be told, however, the real wall of separation most grievous to American Christianity and the Church of Christ is not between church and state; it remains the wall between black and white. About that, Hauerwas and Baxter have nothing to say.

Notes

1. Stanley Hauerwas and Michael Baxter, "The Kingship of Christ: Why Freedom of 'Belief' Is Not Enough," *DePaul Law Review* 42 (1992).

2. Ibid.

3. Ibid.

4. For a sampling of Hauerwas's criticism of Christian ethical defenses of democracy, see his essay "A Christian Critique of Christian America," in *Community in America: The Challenge of Habits of the Heart*, ed. Charles H. Reynolds and Ralph V. Norman (Berkeley: University of California Press, 1988), pp. 250–65. See also *The Peaceable Kingdom: A Primer in Christian Ethics* (Notre Dame, Ind.: University of Notre Dame Press, 1983), pp. 12–13, 111. For claims about prophetic black Christianity's contention that democracy is a fundamental norm of prophetic black Christianity, see Cornel West, *Prophesy Deliverance! An Afro-American Revolutionary Christianity* (Philadelphia: Westminster Press, 1982), pp. 18–19.

5. George Will, "Scalia Missed Point but Made Right Argument on Separation of Religion," *Durham Morning Herald,* Apr. 22, 1990, p. 5. I am not suggesting that Hauerwas's treatment of the First Amendment is limited to this essay, or that the tension between church and state, and religion and politics, is a new subject for him, or one exclusively pursued in this essay. Anyone familiar with Hauerwas's work will know of his long-standing views on such matters. See in particular Hauerwas's books, *A Community of Character: Toward a Constructive Christian Ethic* (Notre Dame, Ind.: University of Notre Dame Press, 1981), *The Peaceable Kingdom: A Primer in Christian Ethics* (Notre Dame, Ind.: University of Notre

Dame Press, 1983), *Against the Nations: War and Survival in a Liberal Society* (Minneapolis, Minn.: Winston-Seabury Press, 1985), and *Christian Existence Today: Essays on Church, World and Living In-Between* (Durham, N.C.: Lambrinth Press, 1987). I am treating, however, the specific context of Hauerwas's (and Baxter's) remarks as they relate to points they make about Will's interpretation of the First Amendment.

6. Hauerwas and Baxter, "The Kingship of Christ."

7. See Walter Berns, "Religion and the Founding Principle," in *The Moral Foundations of the American Republic*, ed. Robert H. Horwitz (Charlottesville: University Press of Virginia, 1986), p. 208.

8. See Bernard Bailyn, *The Ideological Origins of the American Revolution* (Cambridge: Belknap Press of Harvard University, 1967), p. 260. Also see Martin Marty, *Pilgrims in Their Own Land: 500 Years of Religion in America* (New York: Penguin Books, 1984), p. 162–63.

9. James Madison, quoted in Bailyn, *The Ideological Origins of the American Revolution*, p. 260.

10. Ibid.

11. See Berns, "Religion and the Founding Principle," p. 220.

12. Ibid.

13. Berns, "Religion and the Founding Principle," pp. 219–25. For an exposition on Locke's views of Christianity, see Michael P. Zuckert, "Locke and the Problem of Civil Religion," in *The Moral Foundations of the American Republic* (Charlottesville: University Press of Virginia, 1986), pp. 181–203.

14. For Madison on religion as opinion, see Marty, *Pilgrims in Their Own Land*, p. 163.

15. Thomas Jefferson, quoted in Hauerwas and Baxter, "The Kingship of Christ," p. 4.

16. As Robert Bellah defines it in "The Idea of Practices in *Habits:* A Response," in *Community in America*, ed. Reynolds and Norman, Constantinianism is the danger that "Christianity will be used instrumentally for the sake of creating political community but to the detriment of its own authenticity" (p. 277). As Hauerwas understands the term (building on the work of John Howard Yoder), which is drawn from Constantine's conversion to Christianity, it is the assumption that "Christians should or do have social and political power so they can determine the ethos of society . . . . Constantine is the symbol of the decisive shift in the logic of moral argument when Christians ceased being a minority and accepted Caesar as a member of the church." See Hauerwas, "A Christian Critique of Christian America," in *Community in America*, ed. Reynolds and Norman, p. 260.

17. See Hauerwas's works cited in note 16.

18. For the pressure these groups brought to bear upon the colonies for freedom of religion, see Bailyn, *The Ideological Origins of the American Revolution*, pp. 257–58.

19. Berns, "Religion and the Founding Principle," p. 206.

20. Interestingly, Hauerwas raises the possibility of challenging the ideals that underlay the Jonestown community, but only through intellectual or religious debate or criticism of the community; even in light of the atrocities committed there, he doesn't entertain the possibility of state intervention, or active Christian intervention, to protect the exploited victims of Jim Jones's practices. He says in "On

Taking Religion Seriously: The Challenge of Jonestown," in *Against the Nations: War and Survival in a Liberal Society* (San Francisco: Harper & Row, 1985), p. 103: "Our tragedy is that there was no one internal or external to that community able to challenge the false presuppositions of Jones's false ideals. Our continuing tragedy is that our reactions to and our interpretations of the deaths of Jonestown reveal accurately how we lack the convictions to counter the powers that reigned there." On the other hand, John Bennett sees Jonestown as an indication that freedom of religion is not absolute and as an example of the difficulty of determining when and if state intervention into religious practices should occur. Unlike Hauerwas, however, he concedes the possibility that state intervention is a plausible course of action under admittedly difficult-to-define circumstances. In "Church and State in the United States," in *Reformed Faith and Politics*, ed. Ronald H. Stone (Washington, D.C.: University Press of America, 1983), p. 122, Bennett says: "That . . . religious freedom from any limitation by the state is not absolute is well illustrated by the terrible events in Jonestown. After those events it is easy to see there should have been protection of people against such exploitation and even lethal abuse by a religious leader, but it is not easy to say exactly at what point and by what method the state should have entered the picture."

21. This view among the Founders is characterized in Martin Marty's summary of Benjamin Franklin's views on established religion in Marty, *Pilgrims in Their Own Land*, p. 158: "Yet [Franklin] attacked churchly establishment: when a religion was good, it would support itself. If a religion could not support itself and God did not care to come to its aid, it was a bad sign if then the members had to call on government for help."

22. Bennett, "Church and State in the United States," pp. 121–22.

23. It must be admitted that religion under the First Amendment becomes a matter of private choice versus public coercion, but that meaning of privacy is not in question here. Rather, it is whether religion under the First Amendment is rendered necessarily and exclusively private without the possibility of its public expression.

24. Of course, Hauerwas and Baxter might argue that the Founders viewed religion primarily as an aid, and not a critic, of the government. That may be the case, but as they point out in regard to the freedom of religion in their discussion of Will earlier in their essay, the intent of the Founders is not as important as what has occurred in practice. Similarly, what has occurred in practice is that persons and groups have appealed to their religious beliefs to challenge American government, ranging from the civil rights movement to antinuclear activists.

25. Marty, *Pilgrims in Their Own Land*, pp. 155–56.

26. Ibid., p. 157.

27. Ibid., p. 158.

28. George Washington, quoted in Berns, "Religion and the Founding Principle," p. 213.

29. Jefferson, quoted in Berns, "Religion and the Founding Principle," pp. 217–18.

30. Ibid., p. 213.

31. Admittedly this distinction between functional and moral subordination doesn't completely resolve the tensions created by conflicts of conscience over

legally established political practices. In such cases, of course, it is clear that moral insubordination takes precedence; but the violation of the law in the name of conscience results in the Christian acknowledging the conflict created by her religious beliefs by accepting the penalty of breaking the law until the law is changed, either as a result of civil disobedience or through shifted public consensus, or reconstructed public practice, later reflected in law. The examples of Christian participation in the civil rights movement, feminist movements, and antinuclear war movements stand out.

32. For instance, Ronald Thiemann has argued that Hauerwas represents one of two unacceptable options in developing an effective public Christian response to the crises of North American civilization. In characterizing the first option, represented in the thinking of theologian Paul Lehmann, Thiemann, in *Constructing a Public Theology: The Church in a Pluralistic Culture* (Louisville, Ky.: Westminster/John Knox Press, 1991), summarizes Lehmann's position, expressed by Lehmann in an essay entitled "Praying and Doing Justice": "Arguing out of the Reformed tradition's close association of faith with obedience, Lehmann asserts that proper worship always has as its goal the accomplishment of justice in the world. The righteousness of faith must result in transformative justice within the public realm. Thus Christian worship is essentially political, and the *lietourgia* of the church extends naturally and directly into political action" (p. 114). The second option is represented by Hauerwas in his book, *A Community of Character*. According to Thiemann, Hauerwas contends that "by being faithful to the narratives that shape Christian character, the church will witness to a way of life that stands apart from and in criticism of our liberal secular culture. Christian worship, then, must be an end in itself directed solely toward the cultivation of those peculiar theological virtues that mark the church as a distinctive community" (p. 114). But Thiemann concludes that neither of these options "provides us with the theological resources we need to face the distinctive challenge presented to North American Christians" (p. 114). He continues: "Neither the politicization of worship nor its sectarian separation from public life will suffice in our current situation . . . . We must find a middle way between the reduction of the Christian gospel to a program of political action and the isolation of that gospel from all political engagement" (p. 114). And in an essay, "Justice as Participation: Public Moral Discourse and the U.S. Economy," in *Community in America*, in which he clarifies the position of the National Conference of Catholic Bishops in their pastoral letter on the economy, David Hollenbach juxtaposes their belief that "the church has a responsibility to help shape the life of society as a whole" to Hauerwas's position on such matters (p. 220). Hollenbach says: "Hauerwas concludes that the church should cease and desist from the attempt to articulate universal moral norms persuasive to all members of a pluralistic society . . . . [The letter's] disagreement with Hauerwas is with his *exclusive* concern with the quality of the witness of the Christian community's own life. In the traditional categories of Ernest Troeltsch, the bishops refuse to take the 'sectarian' option of exclusive reliance on the witness of the Christian community that Hauerwas recommends" (p. 220).

33. Hauerwas and Baxter, "The Kingship of Christ," p. 11.

34. Ibid., p. 14.

35. Fish, "There's No Such Thing as Free Speech, and It's a Good Thing, Too," in *Debating P.C.,* ed. Paul Berman (New York: Dell, 1992), p. 241.

36. Ibid.
37. Ibid., pp. 241–42.
38. Quoted in Thiemann, *Constructing a Public Theology*, p. 24.
39. Fish, "There's No Such Thing as Free Speech, and It's a Good Thing, Too," p. 242.
40. Ibid.
41. Ibid.
42. Ibid, p. 243.
43. Ibid.
44. Hauerwas and Baxter, "The Kingship of Christ," p. 10.
45. Ibid., p. 17.
46. Ibid., pp. 17–18.
47. This is not to deny universal dimensions of Christian faith. It is to challenge essentialist notions of Christian identity fostered by references to Church without spelling out the church's social location, who its members are, under what conditions they practice their belief, what historical factors have shaped their faith, and so on.
48. I understand "black church" as shorthand to symbolize the views of black Christianity. The black church is certainly not homogeneous, and I shall be focusing on the prophetic dimensions of black religious faith. Hauerwas and Baxter's failure to take the black church seriously is part of a larger pattern that has rendered the black church invisible for most of its history. Even investigations of American religion have usually, until quite recently, excluded black religion as a central force in American life. As C. Eric Lincoln, in *Race, Religion and the Continuing American Dilemma* (New York: Hill and Wang, 1984), says, the "religious situation is structured in such a way that any investigation of religion in America has usually meant the religion of white Americans, unless 'Negro,' 'folk,' or 'black' religion was specifically mentioned" (p. 123). And as Charles Long says in *Significations: Signs, Symbols, and Images in the Interpretation of Religion* (Philadelphia: Fortress Press, 1986): "In short, a great many of the writings and discussions on the topic of American religion have been consciously or unconsciously ideological, serving to enhance, justify, and render sacred the history of European immigrants in this land. Indeed this approach to American religion has rendered the religious reality of non-Europeans to a state of invisibility, and thus the invisibility of the non-European in America arises as a fundamental issue of American history at this juncture" (p. 149).
49. I have in mind here the large number of black ministers among current members of congress, continuing a tradition in this century established by leaders such as Adam Clayton Powell; the activity of black church leaders in the civil rights movement and the political movements it gave rise to, especially the presidential campaigns of Jesse Jackson; and the large number of black churchpersons affiliated with historically black institutions of higher education. In each area, the black church has supplied many of these persons the principles they have appealed to in making the claims of black equality, justice, and freedom to the larger American public. For two examples, see Charles Hamilton's biography of Adam Clayton Powell, *Adam Clayton Powell, Jr.: The Political Biography of an American Dilemma* (New York: Atheneum, 1991), and Roger Hatch, *Beyond Opportunity: Jesse Jackson's Vision for America* (Philadelphia: Fortress Press, 1988).

50. Cornel West, *Prophetic Fragments* (Grand Rapids, Mich.: Eerdmans, 1988), pp. 22–23.

51. See Mechal Sobel, *Trabelin' On: The Slave Journey to an Afro-Baptist Faith* (Princeton, N.J.: Princeton University Press, 1988; original ed., 1979), and James Washington, *Frustrated Fellowship: The Black Baptist Quest for Social Power* (Macon, Ga.: Mercer University Press, 1986).

52. Sobel, *Trabelin' On*, p. 85.

53. Sobel, *Trabelin' On*, p. 85; and Bailyn, *The Ideological Origins of the American Revolution*, pp. 261–62.

54. I do not mean by any measure to romanticize the religious dissenters. Although they fought against slavery, they fought more effectively, desperately, and consistently for their own religious freedom, largely out of self-interest.

55. For instance, John Allen pointed out the hypocrisy of his fellow countrymen making claims to colonial freedom while simultaneously denying liberty to slaves, employing religious terms like "sacred," "praying," and "fasting" to drive home his point. He said: "Blush ye pretended votaries for freedom! ye trifling patriots! who are making a vain parade of being advocates for the liberties of mankind, who are thus making a mockery of your profession by trampling on the sacred natural rights and privilege of Africans; for while you are fasting, praying, nonimporting, nonexporting, remonstrating, resolving, and pleading for a restoration of your charter rights, you at the same time are continuing this lawless, cruel, inhuman, and abominable practice of enslaving your fellow creatures" (quoted in Bailyn, *The Ideological Origins of the American Revolution*, p. 240). And Isaac Backus pressed arguments for the religious dissenters to be released from the bondage of the Church of England, asserting that civil and religious liberty were one. Backus tirelessly proclaimed that the church of Massachusetts "has declared the Baptists to be irregular, therefore the secular power still *force* them to support the worship which they conscientiously dissent from," and that "many who are filling the nation with cry of LIBERTY and against *oppressors* are at the same time themselves violating that dearest of all rights, LIBERTY OF CONSCIENCE" (quoted in Bailyn, *The Ideological Origins of the American Revolution*, p. 263).

56. Robert Wuthnow makes helpful distinctions between conservative and liberal versions of civil religion in *The Restructuring of American Religion* (Princeton, N.J.: Princeton University Press, 1988). About conservative civil religion, Wuthnow says: "On the conservative side, America's legitimacy seems to depend heavily on a distinct "myth of origin" that relates the nation's founding to divine purposes. According to this interpretation of American history, the American form of government enjoys lasting legitimacy because it was created by Founding Fathers who were deeply influenced by Judeo-Christian values" (pp. 244–45). Wuthnow also states that conservative civil religion "generally grants America a special place in the divine order" and that the idea of "evangelizing the world is in fact a much-emphasized theme in conservative civil religion" (p. 247). He contends that despite "formal separation between the kingdom of God and the kingdom of man, the 'two kingdoms' doctrine in conservative civil religion also confers a strong degree of divine authority on the existing mode of government" (p. 248). Conservative civil religion also grants "capitalism a high degree of legitimacy by drawing certain parallels between capitalist economic principles and biblical teachings" (p. 248).

Liberal civil religion, however, makes little "reference to the religious views of the Founding Fathers" and doesn't "suggest that America is God's chosen nation" (p. 250). Liberal civil religion "focuses less on the nation as such, and more on humanity in general" (p. 250). Wuthnow says that rather than "drawing specific attention to the distinctiveness of the Judeo-Christian tradition, liberal civil religion is much more likely to include arguments about basic human rights and common human problems" (p. 250). Liberal civil religionists also "appeal to broader values that transcend American culture and, indeed, challenge some of the nationalistic assumptions it incorporates" (p. 253). The liberal "version of American civil religion taps into a relatively deep reservoir of sentiment in the popular culture about the desirability of peace and justice" (p. 253). As a result, Wuthnow mentions, "religious leaders who champion these causes may detract from the legitimacy of the current U.S. system rather than contribute to it" (p. 254).

It would be good for Hauerwas and Baxter to keep the distinctions between the two versions of civil religion in mind when making claims about its "counterfeit" religious status. Although it probably wouldn't persuade them to change their views, it would nonetheless help them make crucial distinctions about the varying functions of civil religion as it is employed and exercised by different spheres of the citizenry, and even by different branches of Christianity.

57. Long, *Significations*, p. 152.

58. Ibid.

59. Ibid.

60. Ibid., pp. 152–53.

61. Of course, King's later beliefs about the necessity for radical social, economic, and moral transformation of American democracy presented a serious challenge to extant political arrangements. See James Cone, *Martin & Malcolm & America: A Dream or a Nightmare* (Maryknoll, N.Y.: Orbis Books, 1991), especially pp. 213–43.

62. Michael Eric Dyson, "Martin Luther King, Jr., The Evil of Racism, and the Recovery of Moral Vision," in *Union Seminary Quarterly Review* 44 (1990): 88–91, esp.

63. Gen. 50:20 (Revised Standard Version).

64. Quoted in Martin Luther King, Jr., *Stride toward Freedom* (New York: Harper & Brothers, 1958), p. 160.

65. See William Safire's comments on the attempts by both Democrats and Republicans to use God's name "as a symbol for the other side's immorality, much as the American flag was used in previous campaigns as a symbol for the other side's lack of patriotism," in "God Bless Us," *New York Times*, Aug. 27, 1992, sec. A, p. 23.

66. Fish, "There's No Such Thing as Free Speech, and It's a Good Thing, Too," p. 243.

67. See, for instance, Martin Luther King's discussion of his disappointment with the white church in *A Testament of Hope: The Essential Writings of Martin Luther King, Jr.*, ed. James M. Washington (San Francisco: Harper & Row, 1986), pp. 345–46.

68. See King's response to white clergymen who deemed his actions in Birmingham, Alabama, as "unwise and untimely," in his famous "Letter from Birmingham

City Jail," in *A Testament of Hope: The Essential Writings of Martin Luther King, Jr.* (San Francisco: Harper & Row, 1986), pp. 289–302.

69. Ernest T. Campbell, *Locked in a Room with Open Doors.*

70. Hauerwas and Baxter, "The Kingship of Christ," p. 18.

71. Ibid., p. 19.

72. Ibid., p. 21.

73. Ibid., p. 22.

74. Denis Mack Smith, *Mussolini: A Biography* (New York: Vintage Books, 1982), p. 161.

75. James Hastings Nichols, *Democracy and the Churches* (Philadelphia: Westminster Press, 1951), p. 186.

76. Nichols, *Democracy and the Churches*, p. 182; and Smith, *Mussolini*, p. 65.

77. Nichols, *Democracy and the Churches*, p. 183.

78. Smith, *Mussolini*, pp. 159, 163.

79. Ibid., pp. 159–61.

80. Smith, *Mussolini*, p. 163; and Nichols, *Democracy and the Churches*, p. 189.

81. Smith, *Democracy and the Churches*, p. 162.

82. I have in mind here liberation theologians who link notions of Christian salvation with sharp forms of social analysis that get at the economic, political, and social forces that mask liberation in concrete form. For just one recent example, see the important work by Franz J. Hinkelammert, *The Ideological Weapons of Death: A Theological Critique of Capitalism*, translated from the Spanish by Phillip Berryman (Maryknoll, N.Y.: Orbis Books, 1986).

Also, it seems that Hauerwas's desires to make the church more socially relevant is better served by citing the work of black, feminist, and liberation theologians. Especially in regard to liberation theology, Paul Lauritzen argues that Hauerwas has a great deal in common with Latin American theologian Johannes Metz, particularly regarding each author's use of narrative in their work. In "Is 'Narrative' Really a Panacea? The Use of 'Narrative' in the Work of Metz and Hauerwas," in *Journal of Religion* 1987: 322–39, Lauritzen writes: "Although these writers represent different religious traditions, both rely in significant ways on the category of narrative in their work . . . . Both Metz and Hauerwas are concerned to revitalize Christian faith, both want to make it once again socially relevant, and both are adamant that it retain its distinctiveness. That both should also place such a heavy emphasis on the concept of narrative . . . is not coincidental" (p. 323).

83. I am not suggesting that all of Pius XI's views about the social order are captured in the "Kingship of Christ." His encyclical *Quadragesimo Anno*, issued in 1931, remains one of Catholicism's most impressive statements containing the social teachings of the church, including government's role in society and in the economy, the belief in a just wage, laborers' right to organize, and strong Christian criticism of both capitalism and socialism. But this document must be juxtaposed to Pius XI's antidemocratic actions and statements during the reign of Mussolini. Neither am I suggesting personal perfection as a criterion to determine the acceptability of an intellectual position; in that case, my example of King would be immediately nullified. I am suggesting, however, that these characteristics of Pope Pius XI that I have sketched have direct bearing on the principles and proposals under discussion; there is an organic link, I would argue, between Pope Pius XI's views and practices regarding democracy, Fascism, and the morally subordinate

status of the Catholic Church and his recommendations about the Kingship of Christ. His views are suspect precisely because they have to do with his moral and theological failures in his office as pope, the official head of the Catholic church.

Improvisation

Political Correctness and the Seminary

The brief but complex struggle over "political correctness" appears to be the continuation of an older cultural war. At the heart of the debate is the tension between two values that ground American society: freedom and equality. As Martin Bernal perceptively observes, these values must be artfully balanced in a multicultural society. But the discussions about PC have lacked the sense of proportion and justice that must prevail if we are successfully to address this issue that has gained prominent if faddish coinage lately.

On seminary campuses, complaints against PC have necessarily evolved their own character of expression. In some cases, resistance to PC represents genuine attempts by progressives—blacks, feminists, womanists, gays, and lesbians—to be self-critical while pursuing a complex and nuanced understanding of equality. At some levels the struggle involves progressives' attempts to skewer the fabled pieties, ideological excesses, and romantic truisms that attend their efforts to achieve justice, freedom, and equality. Even biblically justified, theologically grounded, and historically connected quests for such ends sometimes turn on hubris and intolerance—traits not uncommon in seminaries and churches.

But these infractions are tiny when compared with the bulwark of the old guard at seminaries who do business as usual. The real problem is not PC, but SOS—the same old stuff. While the old guard may grouse about the power surrendered to blacks, feminists, gays, and liberation theologians, the power of these groups is relatively limited. The hidden and potentially unlimited power remains in the hands of narrow traditionalists. A measure of that power is that group's description of weak assaults, halting gestures of resistance, and fragile gains as an ominous threat to freedom of expression. More troubling, though, is the traditionalists' tendency to view any challenge as ridiculous. Even a cursory glance at seminary education reveals that, contrary to the fears of some and hopes of others, traditional approaches remain intact. Despite debates about the canon, multicultural education, and cultural literacy, our seminaries' libraries and syllabuses predominantly contain works by white men.

Then why all the fuss? Because what is being challenged is the sanctification of particular religious and intellectual traditions as natural, logical, and necessary. Such false universalisms mask these traditions' historical roots and cultural situations. By questioning the content and method of theological education and by challenging both its implicit universalist assumptions and the liberal democratic institutions and values to which theological education is intimately wedded, scholars who are people of color, feminists, Marxists, and others have incurred the wrath of scorn of the narrow traditionalists.

The seminary is peculiarly susceptible to such questions because of its shifting demographics. As the seminary population becomes older and more racially diverse, and as the number of women enrolled increases, fact and experience begin to contradict theory. Questions about relevant curriculum, appropriate pedagogy, and egalitarian social behavior become increasingly unavoidable. The presence of previously excluded minorities in seminaries strikes at the heart of the social practices and philosophical and theological explanations that justify and sustain racial, class, gender, and sexual domination at every level of our society. It is the sheer physical presence of what appears to be an unwieldy gaggle of "others" that disconcerts narrow traditionalists.

Some complaints about PC in academia stem from anxiety over the loss of "safe" victims. As the ground shifts beneath them, conservatives and progressives have had to renegotiate their relations with excluded minorities. In the past, victims were those institutionally voiceless individuals and groups who encountered the resistance and derision of conservatives and the sympathy and support of progressives—who together articulated by proxy the claims of the excluded groups as "safe" because they seemed fixed and identifiable. The diversity within these groups was not acknowledged; to do so would complicate the simple progressive-versus-conservative conflict.

But as blacks, women, gays, and lesbians entered seminaries and especially as they gained rough parity, a relatively secure voice, and some sense of control over their destinies, narrow traditionalists felt invaded and retreated to regroup and eventually respond in reactionary ways. Liberals, on the other hand, felt confusion and a sense of grief over the lapse of gratitude and deference from formerly excluded minorities. The struggle against PC is both backlash and sideswipe: conservative reaction and liberal resentment.

The changed demography of the seminary community offers a real opportunity to prefigure a free community of equals, one not tyrannized by narrow visions of personal or group identity on the left or by the more lethal and false visions of universal human and intellectual community on the right. Multicultural education, whether in the seminary or the wider academic community, does not require a wholesale repudiation of European culture or traditional values, but it does entail a rigorous and honest examination of the ways in which the worst aspects of Eurocentrism and narrow traditionalism have trashed cultures, traditions, and peoples not of European heritage.

The seminary has not been balkanized by womanists, blacks, feminists, gays, lesbians, Marxists, or liberation theologians; it has been intellectually and socially stretched. Barth, Tillich, and Niebuhr remain as theological icons and resources. But Cone, Ruether, Cannon, Gutierrez, and a host of others have been added to the list, and further questions about who makes the list are now entertained. Narrow traditionalists have not been forced to abdicate their rule, standards have not been surrendered, fair and just speech has not been denied in seminary communities. What has transpired is that seminaries have made the difficult attempt to share resources, divide power, and assign influence more equitably. Much of the fanfare over PC is sound and fury, or as one more central to theological education put it, straining at gnats and swallowing camels.

21

The Promise and Perils of Contemporary Gospel Music

Traditional gospel is the music of mass choirs, ecstatic solos, and pounding, clapping rhythms. "Real gospel music is an intelligible sermon in song," says Harold Bailey, who led the Harold Bailey singers in the 1960s and 1970s. Throughout its history, this church music has influenced, and been influenced by, the popular music of its time.

Today's acts—like BeBe and CeCe Winans, Sounds of Blackness, Take Six, Commissioned, Tramaine Hawkins, and the Winans brothers—have added high-priced producers, up-tempo arrangements, and pop instrumentations to traditional gospel. Thus armed they are gaining airplay on so-called contemporary urban radio, home otherwise to acts like Michael Jackson, Luther Vandross, Anita Baker, and C&C Music Factory. As gospel music gains new acceptance, it is once again moving away from its roots.

Nash Shaffer, host of a traditional gospel program on Chicago radio station WNDZ, is one of a number of gospel devotees who object to the recent popularization of the music. "The reason young people like contemporary gospel music is because of the rhythm and its secular appeal," says Shaffer, who is also the minister of music for the Vernon Park Church of God in Chicago. "The horns and the synthesizers override the message, and because of the instrumentation the message is vague and void. It gets lost in the beat and you end up having a shindig on Sunday morning."

One group Shaffer is concerned about is BeBe and CeCe Winans, whose phenomenal success started with a Grammy Award–winning debut album on Word Records. In 1988 they signed with a mainstream label, and their first album on the Capitol/Sparrow label, *Heaven,* was the second gospel record in history to go gold, after Aretha Franklin's success in 1972 with *Amazing Grace.* The current Winans album, *Different Lifestyles,* reached number one on the *Billboard* rhythm-and-blues charts, a first for gospel.

The new album is a curriculum of musical diversity—from rap and up-tempo rhythm-and-blues to a sample of a gospel shout. But it doesn't contain any purely traditional gospel. The single "I'll Take You There," which is at number seven on the rhythm-and-blues chart, is a remake of the Staple Singers classic that allows the Winans to pay tribute to a seductive blend of 1970s gospel and pop. The album's first single, "Addictive Love," which went to number one on *Billboard*'s rhythm-and-blues chart, makes codependency with the divine a palatable proposition. "We were blessed with a record company that put dollars into our budget," says CeCe Winans, "so that we could come off sounding the way we feel gospel music should have sounded a long time ago."

The Winans help make visible the implicit sensuality of gospel music, a sometimes embarrassing gift that draws forth the repressed relationship between body and soul. The suggestive ambiguity of their art is expressed in their songs, many of which can be read as signs of romantic love and sensuous delight or as expressions of deep spiritual yearning and fulfillment. In "Depend on You," the Winans sing, "I never thought that I could ever need someone / The way that I have come to need you / Never dreamed I'd love someone / The way I've fallen in love with you."

Such lyrics are exactly the problem, according to the traditionalists. "Whereas traditional gospel music talks about the love *of* God, says Shaffer, "contemporary gospel music wants to make love *to* God." Lisa Collins, who writes about gospel music for *Billboard* magazine, says she receives calls from unhappy listeners when she plays a new hit by BeBe and CeCe Winans on "Inside Gospel," her syndicated radio show. "We get numerous calls from listeners who think that there's not enough reference to Jesus," she says, "that their music has strayed too far from the church, that they water down the lyrics or that their music is playing to a secular crowd. But," she adds, "if you go to their concerts, there is no doubt that it is a ministry."

Ironically, traditional gospel music initially faced its own barriers within the church. It was an offspring of blues, jazz, and ragtime music born in the black Pentecostal churches at the end of the nineteenth century; early religious music consisted of barbershop quartet harmonies sung a capella by mostly male groups. A Chicago blues pianist named Thomas A. Dorsey forever changed black religious music in the 1920s by featuring women (and later men) singing in a choir tradition backed by piano accompaniments dipped in a blues base and sweetened by jazz riffs. Before the belated embrace of gospel music by mainline black churches in the 1940s, gospel thrived in mostly lower-class storefront Pentecostal churches, stigmatized as a sacrilegious mix of secular rhythms and spiritual lyrics.

Traditional gospel greats, including the late Clara Ward, Marion Williams, Roberta Martin, and Inez Andrews, took the exploration of jazz and blues further. These artists harnessed the seductive beats of jazz to gospel's vibrant harmonies and percolating rhythms, and transformed the anguished wails of the blues into holy shouts brimming with deferred joy. Performers as varied as Ray Charles, Aretha Franklin, and James Brown started out singing gospel, and the music can be said to have spawned rhythm and blues, soul, and funk. Gospel music gained wide popular acceptance with Clara Ward's appearance at the Newport Jazz Festival in 1957 and with the incomparable Mahalia Jackson's numerous concerts at Carnegie Hall in the late 1950s and early 1960s. (Clara Ward, in fact, was criticized in the 1960s for singing gospel music in Las Vegas.)

But gospel music's real transformation into a popular and contemporary musical art form was quietly affected by Edwin Hawkins's 1969 rhythm-and-blues-influenced arrangement of the traditional Baptist hymn, "Oh, Happy Day." The groundbreaking song was captured on a two-track recorder in the basement of a California Pentecostal church and was performed by the North California State Youth Choir, eventually selling more than two million copies. Edwin Hawkins's feat prepared the way for two divergent but occasionally connected developments in contemporary gospel music.

On the one hand, artists like Andrae Crouch and Hawkins's younger brother Walter experimented with gospel within the boundaries of the religious world. Their work was performed in church concerts and secular music halls to a largely religious audience. Their appeal was primarily defined by young black Christians seeking to maintain their religious identity. On the other hand, Edwin Hawkins's success also broke ground for groups like the Staple Singers, who performed primarily in secular musical arenas and whose themes and sound were adapted to popular culture sensibilities and recast as "message music." Thus, instead of the traditional gospel themes of God's love, grace, and mercy, the Staple Singers sang about redemptive community and self-respect.

On their 1971 reggae-influenced number one soul and pop song, "I'll Take You There," they claimed: "I know a place / Ain't nobody cryin' / Ain't nobody worried / Ain't no smilin' faces / Lyin' to the races / I'll take you there." And on their number two song, "Respect Yourself," from the same album, *Be Altitude: Respect Yourself,* they sang: "If you disrespect everybody that you run into / How in the world do you think anybody 'sposed to respect you? / Respect yourself." Their recordings from the 1970s showcase three crucial features of contemporary gospel: significant radio play on nonreligious formats, the broad use of pop music conventions to explore their musical ideas, and, at best, oblique references to divinity or God.

In the last few years, black gospel music also inspired a group of white religiously oriented singers like Amy Grant and Michael W. Smith, who are considered contemporary Christian musicians. (The dividing line between black gospel and contemporary Christian music is primarily racial, although black artists like BeBe and CeCe Winans, Take Six, and Larnelle Harris also show up on the contemporary Christian charts.) Traditional gospel music has never been completely comfortable with its parentage of black secular music. In the early parts of this century, attending nightclubs, blues bars, and dance halls was considered un-Christian and was forbidden. And there are still those who feel that the secular world should be kept out of the church. Harold Bailey, who is now the director of Probation Challenge, an organization that works with former prisoners in Chicago, says, "When we speak in terms of contemporary we are speaking of something temporary, of the moment, which is contrary to scripture. Those who want to rock will inevitably roll into hell."

The sound of contemporary gospel, many devotees of traditional gospel say, is indistinguishable from new jack swing or technofunk, and it thrives on postmodern instrumentation, contemporary pop grooves, and religiously ambiguous lyrics. Some contemporary gospel, in fact, is called new jack gospel: Teddy Riley, who most recently produced Michael Jackson's *Dangerous,* also helped produce the Winans brothers' album, *The Return*; and among contemporary gospel artists are rappers like Mike E.

But a gnawing skepticism about the church's ability to address contemporary cultural issues, coupled with a steep decline in church membership, may modify the hard line taken by traditional religionists. Contemporary gospel music is helping the uninitiated to discover, and the committed to remember, the church. One contemporary gospel artist, Tramaine Hawkins, who was heavily criticized when her single "Fall Down" was played in discos, says that the song "opened up some real avenues of ministry" and brought listeners to more traditional gospel artists like Shirley Caesar. "I tried contemporary gospel," confesses Caesar, "but it didn't work for me." She believes that she is part of a venerable tradition to which all gospel artists must return. "I'm part of the 'be' crowd," she explains. "I'll *be* here when they leave, and I'll *be* here when they come back."

CeCe Winans says that contemporary gospel brings a wider audience to the gospel message through high production values. "Being able to be played on mainstream radio without having any less quality than mainstream artists is important," she says. Without serious record company support, she says, great gospel singers of the past were deprived of a wide audience. For all its controversy, contemporary gospel music continues to evolve and inspire. Groups like Take Six, which mixes a capella jazz with gospel themes, and the Sounds of Blackness—produced by Jam and Lewis and presently touring with Luther Vandross—prove that contemporary gospel is an art form as malleable as it is durable and innovative. And as contemporary gospel music continues to provide inspiration to its religious adherents and musical delight to all appreciative listeners, it preserves and extends the classic functions of traditional gospel music.

Improvisation

A Skeptic's View of Southern Baptists

With the development of postliberal theology well under way and the fate of fundamentalists like Jim Bakker and Jimmy Swaggart so publicly and embarrassingly resolved, it would appear that evangelical Protestantism has been dealt a mortal blow. Yet more than 50 million Americans continue to find spiritual succor and moral insight in the embrace of fundamentalist Christianity. What, then, is evangelical Christianity like for these believers?

Looking for an answer to that question, Alan Peshkin became a participant-observer in an evangelical secondary school and created a sociological portrait of its religious behavior, social values, and institutional practices in a brilliant study, *God's Choice* (University of Chicago Press, 1986).

Now Mike Bryan has sought the answer as a literate amateur, becoming immersed in the daily routines, spiritual regimens, and academic teachings of a conservative evangelical religious college. His results in *Chapter and Verse: A Skeptic Revisits Christianity* (Random House, 1991) are fascinating and revealing. Bryan, once a Methodist and now a nonbeliever, enrolled for a semester at a Southern Baptist institution, Criswell College in Dallas. Next to the Roman Catholic Church, which they see as their religious archenemy, the Southern Baptists, 14 million strong, make up the largest body of organized Christians in the United States.

To his credit, Bryan does not simply report large theological battles. He skillfully weaves anecdote, narrative, class notes, and denominational history to create a balanced story of conservative Southern Baptist life. He also stocks his narrative with nifty capsules of biblical criticism, moral debates, and philosophical arguments that allow the general reader to eavesdrop on the kinds of important conversations that are taking place in most theological seminaries across America.

He details the debates in many Christian denominations over

the Jesus of history versus the Christ of faith, the ethical problems raised for Christians by contemporary culture, debates over whether to demythologize the Bible or interpret it literally, and the intellectual conundrum posed by matching a good God with an often evil world, known in theological terms as theodicy.

But Bryan only gently explores the Southern Baptist resistance to feminism. He introduces several Southern Baptist women who affirm the biblical mandate to be submissive to male authority while maintaining belief in their independence. But Southern Baptists do not often ordain women to ministry. Neither do they often engage in extensive theoretical discussions about sexist theological language, misogynist religious symbols, or patriarchal interpretations of biblical texts.

Even less does Bryan explore the thorny issue of Southern Baptists' checkered racial history. He acknowledges that the Southern Baptist denomination formed after splitting from the American Baptists in 1845 over the issue of slavery, which Southern Baptists supported. But he does not probe Southern Baptists' opposition to much of the civil rights movement of modern times or its irritating attempts at proselytizing in existing black church communities. We are left with the impression that evangelical faith leads ineluctably to social and political conservatism when in fact there are churches, like the black Progressive Baptists, that wed progressive political and social perspectives with evangelical belief.

Bryan does deftly explore the ways in which modern secular society preserves, in distorted versions or mere superstitions, remnants of religious belief even while it slights or dismisses evangelical religion. And, to paraphrase C. S. Lewis, one of evangelical Christianity's most able apologists, Bryan is constantly surprised by the joy of Southern Baptists, which he describes as "the subtle conviction of a happiness that moves beyond its own private sphere: joy to the world."

Throughout the book, Bryan manages to remain evenhanded without feigning neutrality, always up front about his agnosticism while deliberately exposing his skepticism to the evangelical zeal to convert him. In so doing, he shows he has thoroughly absorbed a critical lesson taught by William James, one of his intellectual heroes: in order to believe, one must be at the disposal of circumstances that lead to belief.

And although Bryan is subjected throughout his brief period among the Southern Baptists to repeated attempts to save his soul, in the end he maintains his secular but sympathetic nonbelief. Although the Southern Baptists failed to convert him, his enlightening and eminently fair narrative might win wider appreciation for their faith and their sincerity. A true believer could hardly do better.

Index

Compiled by Eileen Quam and Theresa Wolner

Index

Index

Index

The University of Minnesota Press and the author gratefully acknowledge permission to reprint from the following sources: Chapter 1 was originally published in *Z Magazine*, June 1989. Chapter 2 was originally published in *Artvu*, Spring 1991. Chapter 3 was previously published in *Tikkun,* Institute for Labor and Mental Health, September/October 1989. Republished from *Tikkun,* a bimonthly Jewish critique of politics, culture, and society. Subscriptions $31.00 from Tikkun, 5100 Leona Street, Oakland, CA 94619. Chapter 3 Improvisation was originally published in Chicago *Tribune Books,* January 21, 1990. Chapter 4 was originally published in *Black Sacred Music*, vol. 3, no. 2, Fall 1989. Copyright Duke University Press, reprinted with permission of the publishers. Chapter 4 Improvisation was originally published in the *Hartford Advocate*, January 16, 1989. Chapter 5 was originally published in *Cultural Studies*, 1993. Published by Routledge. Chapter 5 Improvisation was originally published in *Christianity and Crisis*, November 18, 1991. Chapter 6 was originally published in *Z Magazine*, September 1989. Chapter 6 Improvisation was originally published in the *New York Times Book Review*, December 9, 1990. Copyright 1990 by the New York Times Company, reprinted by permission. Chapter 7 was originally published in *Cultural Critique*, Spring 1992. Chapter 7 Improvisation was originally published in *Rolling Stone*, August 20, 1992. By Straight Arrow Publishers, Inc., 1992, all rights reserved, reprinted by permission. Chapter 8 was originally published in the *New York Times Book Review*, November 29, 1992. Copyright 1992 by the New York Times Company, reprinted by permission. Chapter 8 Improvisation was originally published in *Tikkun,* Institute for Labor and Mental Health, January/February 1991. Republished from *Tikkun*, a bimonthly Jewish critique of politics, culture, and society. Subscriptions $31.00 from Tikkun, 5100 Leona Street, Oakland, CA 94619. Chapter 9 was originally published in *Z Magazine*, March 1989. Chapter 9 Improvisation was originally published in *The Nation,* September 25, 1989. The Nation Company, Inc., copyright 1989. Chapter 10 was originally published in *Z Magazine*, April 1991, and in Democratic Socialists of America, *Democratic Left*, March/April 1991. Chapter 10 Improvisation was originally published in *The Nation,* July 3, 1989. The Nation Company, Inc., copyright 1989. Chapter 11 was originally published in *Emerge Magazine,* February 1992. Reprinted by permission. Chapter 11 Improvisation was originally published in *New World Outlook*, the Mission Magazine of the United Methodist Church, September/October 1991, by permission of the editors. Chapter 12 was originally published in *Z Magazine*, July/August 1989 and January 1991.

Chapter 12 Improvisation was originally published in Chicago *Tribune Books*, May 1992. Chapter 13 was originally published in *Z Magazine*, February 1989. Chapter 13 Improvisation was originally published in Chicago *Tribune Books*, August 10, 1991. Chapter 14 was originally published in *Emerge Magazine,* May 1992. Reprinted by permission. Chapter 14 Improvisation was originally published in Chicago *Tribune Books*, August 30, 1992. Chapter 15 was originally published in *Social Text*, Spring 1989. Chapter 15 Improvisation was originally published in Chicago *Tribune Books,* May 1990. Chapter 16 was originally published in the *Union Seminary Quarterly Review,* 1990, and the *Chicago Theological Seminary Register*, 1993. Chapter 16 Improvisation was originally published in *Theology Today*, April 1988. Chapter 17 was originally published in *Transition*, volume 56, 1992. Chapter 17 Improvisation was originally published in *Princeton Alumni Weekly*, July 12, 1989, copyright 1989 Princeton Alumni Publications, Inc., reprinted by permission. Chapter 18 was originally published in *Princeton Seminary Bulletin*, 1989. Chapter 18 Improvisation was originally published in *Christianity and Crisis*, March 6, 1989. Chapter 19 was originally published in *Black Sacred Music*, vol. 6, no. 1, Spring 1992. Copyright Duke University Press, reprinted with permission of the publishers. Chapter 19 Improvisation was originally published in *Theology Today*, January 1989. Chapter 20 was originally published in *DePaul Law Review*, volume 42, 1992. Chapter 20 Improvisation was originally published in *Christian Century*, copyright 1992 Christian Century Foundation, reprinted by permission from the February 5–12 issue of *Christian Century.* Chapter 21 was originally published in the *New York Times,* December 22, 1991. Copyright 1991 by the New York Times Company, reprinted by permission. Chapter 21 Improvisation was originally published in the *New York Times Book Review*, August 18, 1991. Copyright 1991 by the New York Times Company, reprinted by permission.

Michael Eric Dyson, who won the 1992 Magazine Award from the National Association of Black Journalists, is Professor of American Civilization and Afro-American Studies at Brown University. He earned his M.A. and Ph.D. degrees from Princeton University.